JAMES JOYCE

DUBLINERS, A PORTRAIT OF THE ARTIST AS A YOUNG MAN, AND EXILES

SUNIL KUMAR SARKER

ATLANTIC
PUBLISHERS & DISTRIBUTORS (P) LTD

ATLANTIC
PUBLISHERS & DISTRIBUTORS (P) LTD

7/22, Ansari Road, Darya Ganj, New Delhi
Tel.: +91-11-4077 5252, 2327 3880
E-mail: orders@atlanticbooks.com
Web: www.atlanticbooks.com

Published by Atlantic Publishers & Distributors (P) Ltd 2024

Disclaimer

- The author and the publisher have taken every effort to the maximum of their skill, expertise and knowledge to provide correct material in the book. Even then if some mistakes persist in the content of the book, the publisher does not take responsibility for the same. The publisher shall have no liability to any person or entity with respect to any loss or damage caused, or alleged to have been caused directly or indirectly, by the information contained in this book.
- The author has fully tried to follow the copyright law. However, if any work is found to be similar, it is unintentional and the same should not be used as defamatory or to file legal suit against the author.
- If the readers find any mistakes, we shall be grateful to them for pointing out those to us so that these can be corrected in the next edition.
- All disputes are subject to the jurisdiction of Delhi courts only.

Printed & bound in India by Atlantic Print Services

Dedication

I dedicate this book to my two daughters-in-law

Dr. Anuranjita Sarker

(Ophthalmologist)

and

Dr. Arunima Sarker

(Anaesthetist)

Preface

Today James Joyce stands like a tower in the middle of world literature; to miss him is to lose much of the wonders of literary themes, forms, styles and techniques. Once he was refused recognition, now his name is a buzz word the world over. His works now are being translated into many languages and being adapted for films and the stage. His short stories—unique and interesting—are oftentimes being anthologised as his novels are now chosen fields for scholarly researches.

Joyce's fictions are hard reads, no doubt, but yet they are not caviare to the common reader, if only they put their intelligence and diligence together to follow them. They are a wonderful cocktail of myth, poetry, music, stylistic innovations, varieties of experiences of life, paronomasia or word-play and satire galore that gives readers occasions to guffaw.

In this book, I have meant to help students and common readers enjoy Joyce's *Dubliners, A Portrait of the Artist as a Young Man* and *Exiles*. I have discussed *Dubliners,* somewhat in detail. As to *A Portrait of the Artist as a Young Man* and *Exiles*, I have given an abridged and elucidated version (about one third of the original) of the novel and the play, along with discussions, appreciations and criticisms about them. Although Joyce's *Chamber Music*, *Stephen Hero*, *Pomes Penyeach* and *Giacomo Joyce* are not included in the purview of this book, yet I have briefly discussed about these four works at appropriate places. Scholarly books on Joyce are not so rare but appropriate books on Joyce for those who are not scholars are very few. Frankly, this prompted me to have a try. I have designed this book to be simple and easy to read but able to lead one to the complexity of Joyce, and overcome it.

Atlantic Publishers, for about thirty years, have been very friendly to me and have published my 17 books (20 volumes), and this time they are publishing this book. I express my gratitude to the proprietors and personnel of the organization, especially to Shri Harjeet Singh Ji. My wife, Manju, has typed the entire manuscript of this book as she did those of my previous ones. My love is to her.

Sunil Kumar Sarker

Contents

1
Introducing James Joyce

Any new comer to the fictional gallery of James Joyce should, of necessity, ask: why Joyce? Joyce, because he is in the cusp of our modern and postmodern era and so in his works we will best see the form and colour of our age; because in his books we will see a variety of fictional techniques newly introduced; because in his works we will enjoy logodaedalic tricks and jugglery of words; because in his creations we will understand a new meaning of the novel; because in his narratives we will be able to see how mean things may be subjects of enormous and majestic meanings; because in his novels we will see the limit of fiction writing, the *ne plus ultra* of the novel; and because Joyce is the fictionist par excellence as Shakespeare is the dramatist nonpareil. Once denied admittance into the literary society, Joyce soon rose to dominate the same and like Shakespeare. Joyce's importance in and impact on that society now is enormous, which may be guessed from a single clause of his compatriot and admiring novelist and playwright Kate O'Brien about him: "the greatest Artist—there will never be another."

James Joyce, or, to be precise, James Augustine Aloysius Joyce, was born on 2 February 1882 to a middle-class Catholic family of Dublin, Ireland, and died in Zurich, Switzerland, in 1941 (Virginia Woolf also was born in 1882 and died in 1941). The 2nd day of February, on which day he was born, was perhaps dear to Joyce, for he gave this day to the first publication of his most famous novel *Ulysses*, when he reached the age of 40 years.

Joyce first entered the Jesuit Clongowes Wood College (in fact a school) in 1888 and in 1902 graduated with modern languages from the University College of Dublin. An exceptionally brilliant student, he was never comfortable in either of the two educational institutions for their heavily strict Catholic environment, as he was not in a pleasing milieu in his own home for his mother being an orthodox Catholic.

Joyce, even in his pre-adolescence, could quite realise his own growing creative verve in literature but all at the same time he also understood that his creativity would not find a fertile ground in the stuffy Catholic orthodoxy of his own country.

A youth of strong sense of personal independence and love of motherland, Joyce could not digest his compatriots' slavish bearing of the British yoke. His iconic leader of Ireland's struggle for independence was the legendary Charles Stewart Parnell who was unjustly pulled down from his political height on a flimsy reason of marrying a married woman. When Parnell died in 1891, Ireland still under the British domination, the nine-year-old boy, Joyce, aggrievedly composed the poem "Et Tu, Healy" in paying homage to Parnell, and denouncing Timothy Healy, whose machination caused Parnell's downfall. This beautiful poem, a broadsheet in which he wishes Parnell's soul a peaceful existence, contained the following lines:

> His quaint-perched aerie on the crags of Time
> Where the rude din of this...century
> Can trouble him no more.

At home, beside the stuffy Catholic orthodoxy there, his father, John Stanislaus Joyce was rude to him and his mother was insouciant about that.

These three depressing situations—the vexatious servile attitude of his countrymen to the British overlords (Joyce once demurred that he had to write in the language of Shakespeare), the distressing Catholic codes at home, and his father's lack of filial love for him—Joyce took to be his betrayals. Lugubriously, he was fancying, like Little Chandler in "A Little Cloud" (*Dubliners*), flying far away like the mythic Icarus from the "prison" of Ireland to somewhere in Europe where the air was not stuffy but clear.

In 1903, Joyce's mother died. The little love that Joyce enjoyed from her was lost for ever. He felt dejected, despondent. At this time he had had a chance serendipity—he met a 19-year-old charming girl from Galway, which was diametrically opposite of and far from, Dublin—and fell in love with her at first sight. It was Nora Barnacle. The day was 10 June 1904. Six days afterwards, on 16th June, Joyce and Nora for the first time openly walked thorough road in the warm weather of June. It was a red letter day for Joyce never to be forgetful of. Significantly, in his masterpiece, *Ulysses*, he narrates the hero Leopold Bloom's itinerary of just one day, the 16th June. The day is now celebrated all over the world as Bloom's Day.

As wished for earlier, after tying himself with Nora for life, Joyce was preparing to escape Ireland. And in October 1904, i.e., about three months since he met Nora, Joyce set sail for the free air of Europe, hand in hand with his life-partner. They first went to Zurich, Switzerland, via London and Paris, where he was told he might get a job but when he reached there he was frustrated. From Zurich they went to Trieste in the expectation of a job but again Joyce found no job there. Next they moved to Pola, at that time Austro-Hungary's major naval base. Here Joyce found the job of an English teacher for naval officers. Pola Joyce detested and so they went back to Trieste in March 1905 and there began teaching English at the Berlitz School. Both Joyce and Nora liked Trieste and they continued to live there until 1920. To Joyce, Trieste was second Dublin.

In Trieste, Joyce was not stationary but frequented Rome, the city that is connected with most part of his writing career. He wrote his most popular short story "The Dead" here; here he first conceived of his *Ulysses* and even wrote the now lost short story "Ulysses" here; and it was here in Rome that he got the inspiration of writing *Exiles*. However, after a stay of some seven months in Rome, Joyce went back to Trieste in March 1907. In Trieste, Italo Svevo (real name Ettore Schmitz), the famous novelist, took English lessons from Joyce on payment and in course of time became Joyce's friend. Svevo was a Jew, but converted to Catholicism. He was a partial model of Leopold Bloom of *Ulysses*. Roberto Prezioso, the editor of the Italian newspaper *Piccolo Della Sera*, was also Joyce's student for lessons in English at this time. These two students much helped Joyce financially as well as in publishing his works.

During this period, Joyce was engaged with working on *Dubliners, A Portrait of the Artist as a Young Man* and *Ulysses*, all at the same time (an enormous task, indeed!), and yet he found time to give a series of lectures on "Ireland and the Arts" at Trieste's Universita Popolare, sometime around 1907, and again in 1912 he lectured at the same university on various topics of English literature. From Trieste, Joyce applied for a teaching position in Italian at his own *alma mater* which had by then become University College Dublin but did not receive any positive response. Next, he applied for a teaching diploma in English at the University of Podua in Italy but the university did not recognize his graduate degree of Ireland.

By this time, the Joyce family grew in size: in 1905 George Joyce was born and in 1907 Lucia. In 1909, Joyce along with his family, visited Dublin and remained there to help open the Yolta Cinematography, Ireland's ever first cinema, in January 1910. Joyce was living with Nora now for about 27 years, begetting one son (George) and one daughter (Lucia) without formally marrying her, because he did not believe in the institution of marriage. But he changed his mind and in 1931 went to London and there formally registered the wedlock between Nora and himself.

As the Second World War (1939-45) was raging high, for safety the Joyce arrived Zurich from Trieste on 17th December 1940. On 10th January 1941, Joyce was admitted into a hospital for duodenal pain, due to ulceration. Next day, Joyce was operated on but, three days after his admission, on the morning of 13th January Joyce left his "mortal coil" for ever. On 15th January, Joyce's body was interned temporarily in the Fluntern cemetery in Zurich. Nora died in 1951 also in Zurich and her body was interned there as well in a temporary cemetery. Long afterwards, in 1966, both bodies were exhumed and reinterned in the permanent cemetery in the Great Hall of the University of Zurich. Many biographies of Joyce are now available, but that written by Richard Ellmann, who personally followed Joyce in his life time, is the most detailed and authentic. A fictionalized biography of Joyce may be found in Frank McGuinness's novel *The Woodcutter and His Family*.

To add here a few encomiums of Joyce would be redundant for there is no dearth of eulogy of Joyce but not the famous Argentine novelist Jorge Luis Borges's poetic homage to Joyce, "Invocation to Joyce", that concludes thus...

> what does sadness matter if there was in
> time
> somebody who called himself happy,
> what does my lost generation matter
> that vague mirror, if your books justify it.
> I am the others. I am all those
> whom your obstinate rigor has redeemed.
> I am those you do not know and those you
> continue to save.
>
> —Translated by Charles Tomlinson

Nora once dubbed Joyce as "the greatest writer in the world" (Ellmann, 743) and we will echo her words only with slight modification—Joyce is the greatest novelist the world has yet known.

Quixotic it is that this great writer was not awarded the Nobel Prize. But it is not so big a matter to deplore for Tolstoy and Henry James—literary stalwarts—were also denied the honour. Howbeit, Joyce has been immensely rewarded, not by judges of literature, though, but by eminent scientists. In 1963, when the elementary particle of matter, which is smaller than a proton or neutron, the American physicist Murray Gell-Mann, who was interested in linguistics, named it "quark." Gell-Mann got the new-fangled queer word in Joyce's *Finnegans Wake* (at the beginning of Chapter XII):

> .... Three quarks for Muster Mark!
> Sure he hasn't got much of a bark
> And sure any he has it's all beside the mark....

So far about Joyce's biography, for in this book we are not much interested in that but in his three works: *Dubliners*, *A Portrait of the Artist as a Young Man*, and *Exiles*. We will, therefore, quickly look at a few facts of his life that may have some proximate or distant, direct or tangential influence on his writing.

Firstly, Joyce's eye-trouble was miserable. It began in 1917 and was due to glaucoma. In spite of eleven operations, he never regained normal vision and had to use eye-pad for his right eye and read with magnifying glasses. This misery accompanied him till his death.

Secondly, Joyce's troubles in publishing his creative works is daunting; every work of his from *Dubliners* to *Finnegans Wake* faced rejections after rejections from publishers for reasons of morality and obscenity and obscurity because they could not see that in the modern and postmodern literary climate the *avant garde* discount these three reasons as flimsy and unacceptable; they rather welcome free moral atmosphere, free expressions about human behaviour, and intellectual complexity. To the publishers Joyce's advent was perhaps a little too early.

For the point of 'intellectual complexity', these publishers should have gone through the American writer and critic Eugene Jolas's (1894-1952) *The Revolution of the Word: Modernist Manifesto* (Ellmann, 588). It was signed by famous writers, artists and critics, including the Joyce scholar Stuart Gilbert and, of course by Eugene Jolas himself. For brevity's sake, we are not giving below all the 12 points of the Manifesto but only seven...

"1. The revolution in the English language is an accomplished fact.

4. Narrative is not mere anecdote, but the projection of a metamorphosis of reality.

   (English ! Or Too Much! . . . Blake)

5. The expression of these concepts can be achieved only through the rhythmic 'hallucination of the word.' (Rimbaud)

6. The literary creator has the right to disintegrate the primal matter of words imposed on him by textbooks and dictionaries.

   (The road of excess leads to the palace of Wisdom... Blake)

7. He has the right to use words of his own fashioning and to disregard existing grammatical and syntactical laws.

   (The tigers of wrath are wiser than the horses of instruction...Blake)

11. The writer expresses. He does not communicate.

12. The plain reader be damned.

   (Damn braces! Bless relaxes! . . . Blake)"

These aphoristic pronouncements will be fully relevant in the cases of *Ulysses* and *Finnegans Wake* but on our way through *Dubliners, A Portrait* and *Exiles* we will come across passages to which the above dicta of the manifesto will be apposite.

Thirdly, Joyce long suffered from a sense of being a cuckold. After their living together, Joyce came to know from Nora Barnacle that while she was a young girl in Galway she was "very fond of" a boy, slightly older than herself, named Michael (Sonny) Bodkin. The boy also loved her and "gave her a bracelet" (cf. "Araby" in *Dubliners*). After Nora left Galway to work in Dublin, Michael died and Nora believed that he died because she came away from Galway. The boy was "her buried life, her past" (Ellmann, 158). This knowledge haunted Joyce most of his married life; a shade of this knowledge may be discerned in "The Dead" (*Dubliners*), in *Exiles* and also in *Ulysses*. His sense of cuckoldry was later on accentuated viciously by his rival St. John Oliver Gogarty who was drawn to the lush beauty of Nora. Also once Gogarty, being jealous of Joyce secretly spread the canard that he had had a close relation with Nora. Whether as a result of all this Joyce unconsciously developed a little jealousy towards Nora we do not know, but we know that while in Rome Joyce fell into sort of Platonic love of his much younger student Amelia Popper which may be an act of retaliation.

Fourthly, Joyce could never clear his mind of worries. Economically, he suffered for long. When he self-exiled with Nora, he was so hard of money that in a letter to his mother Joyce asked her not to be anxious about them because they took two full meals each on the previous 40 hours. Another pathetic worry was the neurosis of his daughter Lucia. He took her to psychiatrist Carl Gustav Jung but to no avail. In the beginning part of his self-exile, he had to move from pillar to post for seeking some sort of service (for so great a genius!). But all these misfortunes and distresses he had the courage to face with stoic placidity because his life's lodestar was creation of superlative art.

And lastly, since his boyhood, one conspicuous trait of his personality was love of independence and love of fame. He was never a blind imitator of anything of anybody. And he had the zeal for outdoing others along with never sagging elan.

Now, how all these may have influenced Joyce's creative writing? Joyce was a quality tenor singer. Do we not, therefore, see an abundance of songs in all his works? And, in *Exiles*, do we not see the young Archie taking piano lessons from Beatrice? And have we not Joyce's book of songs *Chamber Music*? And, in *Ulysses* do we not learn that Molly was a soprano singer? Not only this far, according to scholars, the *avant-garde* prose of *Ulysses* is a sort of sonic art (music), especially in the Sirens episode of it.

Joyce's literary output in terms of volume is not so amazing but as regards technical innovations, intellectual caliber, and artistic finery astounding. Below we give a list of Joyce's creative works.

1. *Chamber Music* (1907). It is a collection of love poems. The title was chosen by Stanislaus Joyce. The poems were written for Mary Sheehy (Mrs. Thomas Kettle), one of Joyce's friends. When the collection was first published by Elkin Mathews in 1907, it contained 34 lyrics but later on two more poems were added. *Chamber Music* was praised by W.B. Yeats and Ezra Pound found in it 'the real man' in Joyce (Ellmann, 824). According to A. Nicholas Fargnoli and Michael Patrick

Gillespie, the poems, or rather the songs of *Chamber Music* express "the sentiments and moods of the youthful poet [Joyce] who experiences the rise and fall of an idealized love" (Fargnoli and Gillespie, 21). However, let us select at random some poems from *Chamber Music* for a first-hand idea about their quality.

Poem No. VII

My love is in a light attire
Among the apple-trees,
Where the gay winds do most desire
To run in companies.

There, where the gay winds stay to woo
The young leaves as they pass,
My love goes slowly, bending to
Her shadow on the grass;
And where the sky's pale blue cup
Over the laughing land,
My love goes lightly, holding up
Her dress with dainty hand.

Poem No. XIV

My dove, my beautiful one
Arise, arise!
The night-dew lies
Upon my lips and eyes.
The odorus winds are weaving
A music of sighs;
Arise, arise,
My dove, my beautiful one!
I wait by the ceder tree,
My sister,* my love,
White breast of the dove,
My breast shall be your bed.
The pale dew lies
Like a veil on my head.
My fair one, my fair dove,
Arise, arise!

*"sister" is "a female fellow."

Poem No. XX

In the dark pine-wood
 I would we lay,
I deep cool shadow
 At noon of day.

How sweet to lie there,
 Sweet to kiss,
Where the great pine-forest
 Enaisled is!
Thy kiss descending
 Sweeter were
With a soft tumult
 Of thy hair.
O, unto the pine-wood
 At noon of day
Come with me now,
 Sweet love, away.

Poem No. XXII

Of that so sweet imprisonment
 My soul, dearest, is fain....
Soft arms that woo me to relent
 And woo me to detain.
Ah, could they ever hold me there
 Gladly were I a prisoner!
Dearest, through interwoven arms
 By love made tremulous,
That night allures me where alarms
 Nowise may trouble us;
But sleep to dreamier sleep be wed
 Where soul with soul lies prisoned.

Poem No. XXV

Lightly come or lightly go:
 Though thy heart presage thee woe,
Vales and many a wasted sun,
 Oread* let thy laughter run
Till the irreverent mountain air
Ripple all thy flying hair.

Lightly, lightly...ever so:
    Clouds that rap the vales below
At the hour of evenstar
    Lowliest attendants are;
Love and laughter song-confessed
When the heart is heaviest.
    *Oread is a mountain nymph.

Poem No. XXXV

All day I hear the noise of waters
    Making moan,
Sad as the sea-bird is, when going
    Forth alone,
He hears the winds cry to the water's
    Monotone.
The grey winds, the cold winds are blowing
    Where I go.
I hear the noise of many waters
    Far below.
All day, all night, I hear them flowing
    To and fro.

Poem No. XXXVI

I hear an army charging upon the land,
And the thunder of horses plunging, foam about their knees:
Arrogant, in black armour, behind them stand,
Disdaining the reins, with fluttering whips, the charioteers.
They cry unto the night their battle-name:
I moan in sleep when I hear after their whirling laughter.
They cleave the gloom of dream, a blinding flame,
Clanging, clanging upon the heart as upon an anvil.
They come shaking in triumph their long green hair:
They come out of the sea and run shouting by the shore.
My heart, have you no wisdom thus to despair?
My love, my love, my love, why have you left me alone?

The poems from I to XXXIV are simple and replete with the poet's (Joyce's) intense love of his beloved. The diction and rhythm in them are appropriately sweet. They are fine love poems, pure and simple, of the young Joyce. But the two poems that were added to the collection (of 34 poems) at a later date—poems XXXV and XXXVI—are a little at variance with the earlier ones. Poem XXXV does not directly suggest the passion of love; maybe, the poet in his loveless loneliness moans like the "sea-bird" (see "sea-bird" in the third section of the third chapter of *A Portrait of the Artist as a Young Man*). The last poem of *Chamber Music* (XXXVI) is rather complex. Here the poet suggests certain war (WWI?) rushing upon Ireland or where the poet is: "I hear an army charging upon the land". The poem was composed in 1904 when the whole world was apprehensive of an imminent holocaust from world-wide bellicosity. In this fearful time, the poet accuses his beloved of keeping afar from him: "My love, my love, my love, why have you left me alone?" However, *Chamber Music* is not within the purview of this book and so we are not elaborating on this any further.

2. ***Dubliners*** (1914): Detailed discussion of *Dubliners* is given inside this book (Chap. 2).

3. ***A Portrait of the Artist as a Young Man*** (1916): An abridged and elucidated version of the novel and its evaluation is to be found in this book (Chap. 3). There is an earlier version of the novel, titled *Stephen Hero* (*infra*).

4. ***Exiles*** (1918): An abridged and elucidated version of this drama and its evaluation is given in this book (Chap. 4).

5. ***Ulysses*** (1922): It is Joyce's most famous, and daunting novel. Based on Homer's *Odyssey*, this 800-page novel (Prakash Books, India, 2020), according to scholars, is the limit of novel writing. Daclan Kiberd, the Irish writer and scholar, made this comment about *Ulysses*: "Before Joyce, no writer of fiction had so foregrounded the process of thinking." And Joyce himself said about this redoubtable fictional tone: "I've put so many enigmas and puzzles [in *Ulysses*] that it will keep the professors busy for centuries arguing over what I meant, and that's the only way of insuring one's immortality" (Gifford and Seidman, vii). But however difficult a reading the novel is its subject or plot is very simple and works with only four characters: Leopold Bloom, a Jewish advertisement canvasser (the protagonist),

his unfaithful wife Molly Bloom (Marion Tweedy), Stephen Dedalus (a poet) and Blazes Boylan, an advertising man and a fellow singer of Molly. *Ulysses* narrates the itinerary of Leopold Bloom of a single calendar day—16 June 1904—in Dublin. The parallelism between *Odyssey* and *Ulysses* is apparent in the equations between the principal characters of *Odyssey* (in parentheses) and those of *Ulysses*: Leopold Bloom (Odysseus), Stephen Dedalus (Telemachus) and Molly Bloom (Penelope).

Like Odysseus's journey of 20 years, Leopold Bloom and Stephen Dedalus early on 16th June, begin visiting various noted places, good and bad, of Dublin and at the end of the day return to their starting point (cf. Giambatista Vico's theory of *recorso*). What is their experiences of the day or of life? "At the end of the novel Bloom and Stephen return to their starting point, and neither has apparently found any answer to the bewildering sense of futility, frustrations and loneliness within them" (Ousby, 952). Only Molly had her imaginary sexual gratification. However, we will not any more elaborate on *Ulysses* because it is not within the content of this book.

6. ***Pomes Penyeach*** (1927): This is a peculiar collection of 13 poems, written occasionally over about 20 years, from 1904 to 1924, when Joyce was mostly busy with very strenuous creative writings: *Dubliners, A Portrait, Exiles,* and *Ulysses.* Nine of the poems were composed in Trieste, two in Zurich, one in Paris, and one in Dublin, as shown below with the titles of the poems and the places and years of their compositions:

1. "Tilly" (original title "Cabra") (Dublin, 1904)
2. "Watching the Needleboats at San Sabba" (Trieste, 1912)
3. "A Flower Given to My Daughter" (Trieste, 1913)
4. "She Weeps over Rahoon" (Trieste, 1913)
5. "Tutto e sciolto" (Trieste, 1914)
6. "On the Beach at Fontana" (Trieste, 1914)
7. "Simples" (Trieste, 1914)
8. "Flood" (Trieste, 1915)
9. "Nightpiece" (Trieste, 1915)

10. "Alone" (Zurich, 1916)
11. "A Memory of the Players in a Mirror at Midnight" (Zurich, 1917)
12. "Bahnhofstrasse" (Zurich, 1918)
13. "A Prayer" (Paris, 1924)

The title of the collection seems rather queer, but it is not meaningless. In French, *pomes* means 'apples'. "Pomes," therefore, gives the poems "the sense of windfalls brought at a wayside stall" (Fargnoli and Gillespie, 129). Initial reception of *Pomes Penyeach* was not encouraging. Ezra Pound rejected it. But, astonishingly, the book has endured and at least four of the poems have found places in anthologies: "Tilly," "A Flower Given to My Daughter," "On the Beach of Fontana" and "Bahnhofstrasse." One reason of some of the poems' endurability is their musicality: "The poems [of *Pomes Penyeach*] were also easily adaptable to music—as were those in *Chamber Music*" (Fargnoli and Gillespie, 129).

The four most anthologized poems of *Pomes Penyeach* are cited below for a first-hand experience of the collection.

Tilly

He travels after a winter sun,
Urging the cattle along a cold red road,
Calling to them, a voice they know,
He drives his beasts above Cabra.
The voice tells them home is warm.
They moo and make brute music with their hoofs.
He drives them with a flowering branch before him,
Smoke pluming their foreheads
Boor, bond of the herd,
Tonight stretch full by the fire!
I bleed by the black stream
For my torn bough!

*"Tilly" is an Irish term meaning "extra serving"

A Flower Given to My Daughter

Frail the white rose and frail are
Her hands that gave

Whose soul is sere and paler
Than time's wan wave.
Rosefrail and fair...yet frailest
A wonder wild
In gentle eyes thou veilest,
My blueveined child.

On the Beach at Fontana

Wind whines and whines the shingle,
The crazy pierstakes groan;
A senile sea numbers each single
Slimesilvered stone.
From whining wind and colder
Grey sea I wrap him warm
And touch his trembling fineboned shoulder
And boyish arm.
Around us fear, descending
Darkness of fear above
And in my heart how deep unending
Ace of love!

Banhofstrasse

The yes that mock me sign the way
Whereto I pass at eve of day.
Grey way whose violet signals are
The trysting and the twining star.
Ah star of evil! Star of pain!
Highhearted youth comes not again
Nor old heart's wisdom yet to know
The signs that mock me as I go.

Joyce's powerful prose fictions have almost totally overshadowed his meagre poetic productions, barring these two thin volumes: *Chamber Music* and *Pomes Penyeach*. Joyce is of course not an outstanding poet but he is also not a poet to be treated as trashy. The musicality, imagination, and emotion that his poems generally contain certainly qualify him to be a poet of some worth. Early in his life, Joyce betrayed his *métier* as a writer of prose fictions and so his poetic faculty was not cultivated. The poem that he composed at the young age of nine years—"Et Tu Healy" speaks enough in favour of his native poetic talent.

Beside his two collections of poems, *Chamber Music* and *Pomes Penyeach*, Joyce had two other collections of verses: his ever first collection of poems, titled *Moods*, and another collection of poems, titled *Shine and Dark*. Unfortunately, both are lost to us, like the young Joyce's verse play *Dream Stuff*. Of *Moods*, only the first stanza survives:

> In the soft nightfall
> Hear thy lover call,
> Hearken the guiter!
> Lady, lady fair
> Snatch a cloak in haste,
> Let thy lover taste
> The sweetness of thy hair....

Of *Shine and Dark* some eight poems or fragments of poems survive. Just one fragment of a poem that presents the same mood that is there in the 'Villanelle of the Temptress' ("Are you not weary of ardent ways,/ Lure of the fallen seraphim?"...) in *A Portrait of the Artist as a Young Man*:

> Wind thine arms round me, woman of sorcery,
> While the lascivious music murmurs afar:
> I will close mine eyes, and dream as I dance with thee,
> And pass away from the world where my sorrows are.
> Faster and faster! Strike the harps in the hall!
> Woman, I fear that this dance is the dance of death!
> Faster!...ah, I am faint...and, ah, I fall.
> The distant music mournfully murmureth...

However, here we will leave *Pomes Penyeach* or any further discussion on Joyce's poetry because these are not within the scope of this book.

7. ***Finnegans Wake*** (1939): Like *Ulysses,* this is another extremely difficult fiction of Joyce, and, again like *Ulysses*, it is most famous. Interestingly, while *Ulysses* took eight years to compose, *Finnegans* took 17 years. As *Ulysses* tells the story of one calendar day's edifying itinerary of Leopold Bloom, *Finnegans Wake* narrates an unknown dreamer's dream of one single night. *Finnegans Wake* is most complex, highly experimental, allegorical, plotless oneiric fiction that defines

the limit of the novel; it is the *ne plus ultra* of the fictionist. Its language is idiosyncratic, quzzical; it is full of neologisms and portmanteau words; its narrative is but a bunch of fables which are most fantastic. Its fundamental structure, like that of *Ulysses*, is built on the philosopher Giambatista Vico's (1668-1744) theory of *recorso* (return to the beginning). So the novel begins with the broken last part of a sentence ("riverrun, past Eve and Adam's, from swerve of shore to bend of bay, brings us by a comodius vicus [i.e., Vico] of recirculation [*recorso*] back to Howth Castle and Environs") and the novel concludes with the first part of that broken sentence ("A way a lone a last a loved a long the").

"On a literal level, the novel presents the dreams and nightmares of Humphrey Chimpden Earwicker (a Dublin tavern-keeper) and his family (wife Anna, their sons Shem and Shaun and daughter Isabel) as they lie asleep throughout one night" (Ousby, 330). On this thin freakish structure, Joyce has built a huge edifice of 628 pages (The Viking Press, New York, 1966) for preserving the long human history and culture of un-ending ages. However, now, we will relent here about *Finnegans Wake* for this novel is not a subject of discussion in this book.

8. ***Stephen Hero*** (1944): *Stephen Hero* may be called the *ur-A Portrait of the Artist as a Young Man*, in so far as *A Portrait* is a re-writing of *Stephen Hero*, though in the course of the re-writing *Stephen Hero* lost its crude chronology of the hero, Stephen Dedalus, and gained the hero's rising layers of emotional colouring (Joyce called *A Portrait* "a curve of emotion") and his consciousness of his blooming artistic *métier*.

When the manuscript of *Stephen Hero* was done, we do not know for certain; Sylvia Beach, however, gave the year 1903 to the manuscript of it. Like *Dubliners*, *Stephen Hero* faced series of rejections by publishers. "When the manuscript came back to its author, after the twentieth publisher had rejected it, he threw it in the fire, from which Mrs. Joyce, at the risk of burning her hands, rescued these pages [pp. 519-902 of the manuscript of *Stephen Hero*]" (Spencer, 7). The original tome of the manuscript is estimated to be around 1,000 pages. Today we have only 11 chapters of *Stephen Hero*, chapters XVI to XXVI, out of a total of over 50, and some loose pages of the manuscript. However, A. Nicholas Fargnoli and Michael Gillespie are very right when they write that "In spite of the limitations of the work, *Stephen Hero* is of importance to the understanding of Joyce's growth as a writer" (Fargnoli and Gillespie, 155). *Stephen Hero* may best be treated as a composition volume of *A Portrait*. And *Stephen Hero* is Joyce's first posthumous publication (For more of *Stephen Hero*, see pages 296-99).

9. ***Giacomo Joyce*** (1968): *Giacomo Joyce* is Joyce's second posthumous publication. It is a small collection of erotic sketches about one of his female students in Trieste, who may have been Amelia Popper (1891-1967), daughter of Leopoldo Popper, a Jewish businessman (who was a partial model of Leopold Bloom in *Ulysses*). Joyce taught her English for some time since around 1908, and he apparently put down an account of his affairs with this "mysterious girl" (Ellmann) in July or August 1914. The title of the collection is erotic because Joyce did never use the Latin equivalent of "James"—"Giacomo."

The collection *Giacomo Joyce* (The Viking Press) contains only 19 very short sketches from which we are citing but five below for an idea of the collection (we are following the sequence in *Giacomo Joyce*):

1. "Who? A Pale face surrounded by heavy odorous furs. Her movements are shy and nervous. She uses quizzing-glasses.

   "*Yes*: a brief syllable. A brief laugh. A brief beat of the eyelids."
2. "Cobweb handwriting, traced long and fine with quiet disdain and resignation: a young person of quality."
8. "A flower given by her to my daughter. Frail gift, frail giver, frail blue-veined child."
15. "She walks before me along the corridor and as she walks a dark coil of her hair slowly uncoils and falls. Slowly uncoiling, falling hair. She does not know what walks before me, simple and proud...."

18. "Whirling wreaths of grey vapour upon the heath. Her face, how grey and grave! Dank matted hair. Her lips press softly, her sighing breath comes through Kisses."

Joyce's fascination for Amelia is obvious from the above five quotes from *Giacomo Joyce*. The sketches of the collection Joyce appropriated in his other works. "After completing this work, Joyce apparently returned to it for material to use in subsequent writings. One can, in fact, find specific examples of ideas and images found in these sketches assimilated into *A Portrait of the Artist as a Young Man*, *Exiles* and *Ulysses*" (Fargnoli and Gillespie, 233). However, *Giacomo Joyce* is not within the compass of this book and so we are not elaborating any more on this booklet.

Now let us turn to our main discussion of Joyce's three principal works done up to 1918: *Dubliners, A Portrait of the Artist as a Young Man* and *Exiles*.

2

Dubliners
James Joyce

INTRODUCTION

Laura Pelaschiar, in her article "An Old Thing 'Twas, But It Expressd Her Fortune: Joyce's 'Eveline' and Shakespeare's *Othello*", has written about Shakespeare and James Joyce: "Even one single work of their output would be enough for a lifetime of scholarly research" (McCourt, 57). This is no exaggeration on the part of Pelaschiar, for Joyce secretly aspired to measure up to Shakespeare, the insuperable genius. And Joyce once asservated to Max Eastman that his reader should devote his whole life to his works. Richard Ellmann writes about Joyce in this regard: "The demand that I make of my reader," he said with a disarming smile to Max Eastman, "is that he should devote his whole life to reading my works" (Ellmann, 703). For critics his time span is more than three times that. He said he did his works "To keep the critics busy for three hundred years" (*ibid.*). And the English novelist Kathleen Mary Louise O'Brien considered Joyce "the greatest Artist—there will never be another" (Vicente, 8).

Dubliners, a rather small book, is Joyce's first prose work, published in 1914, when he was 32 years old. It is a pack of 15 short stories, some of which are as short as around six or seven pages and two are as long as about 30 and 57 pages (Penguin Classics, 1996). *Dubliners* was his starting line and *Finnegans Wake* his finishing line, no break in between. The long chain of his prose works published over 25 years are: *Dubliners* (1914), *A Portrait of the Artist as a Young Man* (1916), *Exiles* (1918), *Ulysses* (1922) and *Finnegans Wake* (1937). *Dubliners* has a very unusual and painful history of publication, as shown below:

1904. Joyce sends three stories (later on included in *Dubliners*) to *Irish Homestead*, which were published on different dates of the same year: "The Sisters", "Eveline" and "After the Race."

1905. Three new stories were sent to *Irish Homestead* but were rejected ("Clay", "The Boarding House" and "Counterparts"). In the same year (in 3rd December) Joyce sent 12 *Dubliners* stories to Grant Richards, a London publisher.

1906. Grant Richards agreed to publish the 12 stories but his printer refused to print them, objecting to the word "bloody" in the story "Two Gallants", and consequently Richards refused to publish them.

1907. By this year, over a dozen publishers, including Elkin Mathews, declined to publish *Dubliners*. (By this time Joyce completed "The Dead", the last story of *Dubliners*.)

1909. Joyce signed a contract with Joseph Hone, proprietor of the publishing company, Messrs Maunsel, for the publication of *Dubliners*.

1910. Publisher Roberts of Messrs Maunsel Publishing Company asked Joyce to make certain changes in the manuscript of *Dubliners* and Joyce agreed.

1911. Just the next year, publisher Roberts of Messrs Maunsel objects to "Ivy Day in the Committee Room" (the 12th story of *Dubliners*) pointing out that the story was an insult to George IV, King of England. Joyce was so infuriated that he, in indignation, threw the manuscript of *A Portrait* into fire, which, however, was rescued by Eileen. Joyce was so maddened that he wrote the whole history of Messrs Maunsel's wrong dealings with him, which was duly published. Joyce did not stop there; he wrote a letter to King George V praying for his opinion about whether the story "Ivy Day in the Committee Room" might offend "the memory of his father" (Ellmann, 315). The secretary of His Majesty replied that it was not appropriate for His Majesty to "express his opinion in such cases."

1913. After six years, Elkin Mathews again declined to publish *Dubliners*.

1914. On 15th June, the London publisher Grant Richards, who in 1906 declined to publish *Dubliners*, agreed to publish the book, and subsequently kept his words.

The serialization of the publication of the 15 stories in *Dubliners* does not follow the sequence of their compositions, as given below.

	Composition	*Publication*
1.	The Sisters	1
2.	Eveline	4
3.	After the Race	5
4.	Clay	10
5.	The Boarding House	7
6.	Counterparts	9
7.	A Painful Case	11
8.	Ivy Day in the Committee Room	12
9.	Encounter	2
10.	A Mother	13
11.	Araby	3
12.	Grace	14
13.	Two Gallants	6
14.	A Little Cloud	8
15.	The Dead	15

Joyce very judiciously arranged the 15 stories of *Dubliners*, keeping in mind their themes and the ages of their protagonists, so that the collection of stories could be a sort of *buildungs-roman* or biographical novel done against the background of the corrupt, paralytic and moribund city of Dublin (in this sense,

Dubliners may be deemed to be a foreshadow of *A Portrait of the Artist as a Young Man*). However, Joyce categorised the 15 stories of *Dubliners* under four stages of a man's life: childhood; adolescence; maturity but not yet in the public life; and maturity in the public life. The break-ups of the 15 stories under these four headings are as follows:

1. Childhood: "The Sisters", "An Encounter" and "Araby".
2. Adolescence: "Eveline", "After the Race", "Two Gallants" and "The Boarding House".
3. Maturity: "A Little Cloud", "Counterparts", "Clay" and "A Painful Case".
4. Maturity and Public Life: "Ivy Day in the Committee Room", "A Mother", "Grace" and "The Dead".

Perhaps, at the beginning of writing a few early stories Joyce had no thinking about *Dubliners* and so he got them published separately, but as a good number of stories accumulated, he thought of arranging the stories and writing further ones keeping in mind the four-fold groups or categories of the stories of *Dubliners*. Howbeit, Joyce was certainly writing stories at that early creative life of his to expose the decadent spiritual and moral status of Dublin, for, he complained, Dublin which once had been the capital city of Europe and the seventh city of Christendom, nobody did ever attempt to present a picture of the city to the Europeans.

Joyce planned to add one more story to the fifteen in *Dubliners* to be called "Ulysses" but ultimately dropped the idea and his planned short story "Ulysses" later on swelled into the large novel *Ulysses* (interestingly, Joyce would pronounce "Ulysses" as "Oalissays"). Edmund Wilson writes: "Ulysses" was published in Paris in 1922. It had originally been conceived as a short story for "Dubliners," and was to have been called "*Mr. Bloom's Day in Dublin*" *or something of that sort* (*my italics*). But this idea was afterwards combined with the further history of Stephen Dedalus, the hero of the autobiographical "Portrait of the Artist as a Young Man" (Wilson, 192). The title of the planned short story that Edmund Wilson tentatively called "*Mr. Bloom's Day in Dublin*" (*supra*) actually would be called "Ulysses". Ellmann writes that the protagonist of the planned (but not executed) short story "Ulysses" would be a putative cuckolded Jewish Dubliner Alfred H. Hunter (Ellmann, 230).

Joyce was a punctilious writer, he would not leave a story before it seemed perfect. In 1905, "While he still had 39 chapters to write in Stephen Hero, he was able to bring *Dubliners* towards completion much more rapidly. He rewrote 'A Painful Case' by May 8th, wrote 'The Boarding House' by July 13th and 'Counterparts' by July 16th, 'Ivy Day in the Committee Room' by September 1st, 'An Encounter' by September 18th, 'A Mother' by the end of September, 'Araby' and 'Grace' during October" (Ellmann, 207). He wanted to put out a sequel to *Dubliners*, another book of a bunch of short stories, putatively titled "Provincials" (perhaps containing stories not relating to a city like Dublin but relating to a province or uncultivated part of Ireland), but the plan did not materialize. Of all the 15 stories of *Dubliners*, "Two Gallants" and "Ivy Day in the Committee Room" were Joyce's most favourite as he considered "After the Race" and "A Painful Case" his "weakest" stories (Ellmann, 229). Interestingly, his opinions about "The Boarding House" and "Counterparts" differed widely at different times: "The Boarding-House" and "Counterparts" left him uncommonly well pleased at first, but a week later, on July 19 [1905], he blamed their mercilessness on the Tristine heat. He wrote: "Many of the frigidities of *The Boarding-House* and *Counterparts* were written while the sweat streamed down my face on to the handkerchief which protected my collar" (Ellmann, 208).

Joyce's own appreciation of the individual stories of *Dubliners* does not agree with that of the general readers and "Two Gallants" and "Ivy Day in the Committee Room" were most likeable to him. But if anthologizing be any yardstick of general readers' appreciations, "Araby", "Eveline" and "The Dead" are the most appreciated of all the stories of *Dubliners*.

Dubliners is not simply a collection of stories, it is virtually a novel, its hero or protagonist being not a single person but the city of Dublin or the Dubliners, collectively, like the hero of

A Portrait is Stephen Dedalus or the hero of *Exiles* is Richard Rowan or the hero of *Ulysses* is Leopold Bloom. If *A Portrait* is a *bildungsroman*, *Dubliners* may also be counted a virtual *bildungsroman* of the people of Dublin, for its stories relate how they grow up from childhood through adolescence, to maturity and take part in the public life. If *A Portrait* is a "curve of emotion" of its hero, *Dubliners* is a pathological report of the city of Dublin or of its denizens.

Dubliners is and is not a stand-alone work in the whole of Joycean canon but is linked with three other works of Joyce that followed it: *Stephen Hero*, *A Portrait of the Artist as a Young Man* and *Ulysses*. At the deeper level these four works are at least tenuously chained together. This may be supported by the fact that there are characters *Dubliners*, *Stephen Hero* and *A Portrait of the Artist as a Young Man* who reappear in *Ulysses*, as shown below:

1. Characters in stories of *Dubliners* who reappear in *Ulysses*:

   (a) "Grace": Martin Cunningham, Long John Fanning, Nosey Flynn, Tom Kernan and Jack Power.

   (b) "Two Gallants": John Corley and T. Lenehan.

   (c) "The Boarding House": Bob Doran and Polly Mooney.

   (d) "Ivy Day in the Committee Room": Joe Hynes.

2. Characters in *Stephen Hero* who reappear in *Ulysses*: Mrs. Dedalus and Uncle John.

3. Characters in *A Portrait* who reappear in *Ulysses*: Katy Dedalus, Simon Dedalus, Stephen Dedalus, Vincent Lynch, MacCann, William Madden, "Dante" (in *Ulysses* Mrs. Riordan) and Rev. John Conmee. The "sea bird" of *A Portrait* reappears in the "Nausikaa" episode, in Chapter 13 of *Ulysses*: "Those girls, those girls, those lovely seaside girls."

Dubliners's connection with *Ulysses* is particularly important because, as told earlier, *Ulysses* actually grew out of a discarded short story that Joyce wanted to incorporate into *Dubliners*. That discarded and unfinished story was to be built up around a real person of Dublin, Alfred H. Hunter by name. The protagonist of *Ulysses*, Leopold Bloom, Joyce modelled on this Hunter, a reputed cuckold. The last story of *Dubliners*, "The Dead", has also some affinity with *Ulysses*, in that the protagonists of both the short story and the novel (and both might have been built under the influence of Bret Harte's *Gabriel Conroy*) are betrayed by their wives.

Some critics take *Dubliners* to be the linchpin of the whole creative oeuvre of Joyce, especially of *Ulysses*. This is no great exaggeration. Let us consider certain points to weigh the opinion.

1. *Ulysses* is a circular wandering of one day. Circularity is a "sigla" or sign of *Ulysses*. And we find this circularity in many, if not all, the stories of *Dubliners*. In "Two Gallants", Corley and Lenehan cross and recross streets aimlessly. Circularity as a motif is indicated in the very beginning line of the story: "The grey warm evening of August had descended upon the city, and a mild warm air, a memory of summer, *circulated* in the streets" (*italics mine*). In "An Encounter", the truant boys started wandering from home early in the day and "had to be home before four o'clock, lest our adventure should be discovered." In "Araby", North Richmond Street is "blind", such that if one proceeds through the street, he has to come back; he is to proceed in a circular way. In "Eveline", Eveline wished to escape into the romantic Gibralter but she was pulled back by herself and returned home. In "A Painful Case", Mr. James Duffy lived a lonely life in the suburb of Chapelizod but everyday came to the city for meals and returned home. There are also symbolic circularity in the stories. In "After the Race", Jimmy, at the end of the story, realised that his rubbing shoulder with the rich Europeans was a folly and he returned to his earlier self. In "Grace", a story built on the pattern of Dante's *Divine Comedy*, Kernan fell from grace, moved through "purgation" and returned to grace.

2. *Ulysses* is a wandering adventure of a day of Leopold Bloom from 8:00 am of 16th June to 2:40 am next day during which time he meets dozens of persons, from various walks of life, of divers manners and attitudes. The novel is a gallery of portraits and a chain of tableaux—all forming a façade of life of

man in general. Likewise *Dubliners* is a gallery of characters of all ages and of different traits—all belonging to the same city of Dublin. In the novel, it is human life in space, in the collection of short stories it is human life in time.

3. Some of the themes of *Ulysses* may be found in *Dubliners*. For instance, one theme—and the most important one—common between *Ulysses* and *Dubliners* is bad marriage. This theme is present in "The Boarding House", "A Little Cloud", "A Painful Case" and, very much, in "The Dead."

4. Uniquely, *Ulysses* is heavily mapped with street names and place names of real Dublin, and so also we find all the stories of *Dubliners*, without a single exception, strewn with names of streets and places of Dublin. Joyce thus, we may say, tied together the novel and the story collection with the names of streets and places where characters of both move to and fro from time to time chonotopically.

5. Joyce's unbridled frankness about sexuality is obvious in *Ulysses* and also in *Dubliners*. In fact, it was one potential reason behind both the books being rejected by so many publishers. Briefly, *Ulysses* has a good number of sexually hot or pornographic scenes. For just an instance, let us take a slice of the pornographic scene on the middle of the "Nausikaa" episode (Ch. 13). In the Sandymount near Howth, the lame young girl Gerty MacDowell exhibited her body parts lustily to Leopold Bloom, when a long Roman candle went up high: "she let him see and she saw that he saw...and she was trembling in every limb from being bent so far back that he had a full view high up above her knee where no one ever not even on the swung or wading had and she wasn't ashamed and was not either to look in that immodest way like that because he could resist the sight of the wondrous revealment.... She would fain have cried to him chockingly, held out her snowy slender arms to him to come, to feel his lips laid on her white brow, the cry of a young girl's love, a little strangled cry, wring from her, that cry that has rung through the ages." Leopold Bloom's (he is 38 years old) sexuality, though, is not so nakedly drawn, but is expressed through two or three stochastic hints:

"O, he did. Into her. She did. Done.
Ah!

Mr. Bloom with careful hand recomposed his wet shirt. O Lord, that little limping devil. Begins to feel cold and clammy. After effect not pleasant. Still you have to get rid of it someway."

Now let us take at least one very indescent expression from one story of *Dubliners*—from "A Painful Case." The narrator tells us about Mr. Duffy: "He wrote seldom in the sheaf of papers which lay in his desk. One of the sentences, written two months after his interview with Mrs. Sinico, reads: "Love between man and man is impossible because there must not be sexual intercourse, friendship between man and woman is impossible because there must be sexual intercourse." There are many more conspicuous and hidden sexual scenes in both *Dubliners* and *Ulysses* but let us take only two more instance for the nonce—one from "The Boarding House" and the other from the *ne plus ultra* of *Ulysses*. In "The Boarding House", Polly had carnal encounter with Bob Doran (and was perhaps carrying a calf) and was direly dreaming for a marriage knot with him. When her mother went to trap Doran into marriage with Polly, "She regarded the pillows for a long time, and the sight of them awakened in her mind secret, amiable memories." And the last part of the valedictory sentence of *Ulysses* reveals to us Molly's sweet memory of Leopold Bloom's sexual encounter with her: "how he kissed me under the Moorish wall and I thought well as well as him as another and then I asked him with my eyes to ask again yes and then he asked me would I yes to say yes my mountain flower and first I put my arms around him yes and drew him down to me so he could feel my breasts all perfume yes and his heart was going like mad and yes I said yes I will yes."

Joyce has very consciously tethered together and arranged the 15 stories, composed at different times, to be a sort of novella on the city of Dublin or on the paralytic life of the people of Dublin—in their childhood, adolescence, maturity, and their public life. To Joyce the city of Dublin perhaps looked like "a patient etherized upon a table" ("The Love Song of Alfred J. Prufrock"...Eliot). Such a paralytic condition of

Dublin or Dubliners is spread over the whole of *Dubliners*. This paralytic condition of the people of Dublin is of a wide spectrum—physical, emotional, volitional, domestic, social, religious, cultural and political. It was a total and chronic paralysis, unresponsive to any stimulus whatever.

Since the dawning of his consciousness, Joyce became aware of this deplorable state of Dublin and privately grieved. He knew that the cause of it all was the Dubliners' witlessness, merely. The long subjugation of Dublin (and Ireland) by the British overlords was the cause of this paralysis. Joyce worshipped Charles Parnell who, with all his might, volunteered to break the British yoke, but the ungrateful Dubliners dumped him down. Joyce complained that he was Irish but he had to speak (and write) in the language of Shakespeare, and that none—no Irishman—ever did present this sorry state of Dublin to the Europeans, the Dublin that had once in the past stood as the seventh capital of Christendom for long seven hundred years. Joyce's bitterest observation on Dublin (or Ireland) is recorded in chapter five of *A Portrait of the Artist as a Young Man*: "Ireland is the old sow that eats its farrow." And his other observation on Dublin was given in his letter of August 1904 to Constantine Curran where he said that the motive behind his writing the stories in *Dubliners* was to reveal the hemiplegic or paralytic soul of Dublin: "I call the series [the 15 stories of] *Dubliners* to betray the soul of that hemiplegia or paralysis which many consider a city."

In naming the collection of the 15 stories Dubliners, Joyce found some symbolic justification. The Irish word "dub" or "dubh" means "black" or "dark" and the Irish word "linn" means "pool" or "pond" or "period" (time). So the word "Dublin" means "black or dark pool or time." And this explanation of the meaning of the word "Dublin" resonates with Joyce's perception of Dublin as a hemiplegic or paralytic city. Joyce wrote *Dubliners*, as he said, for the Dubliners so that they could see their own sorry state in the "nicely polished looking-glass" that the book was. In his letter of 5 May 1906, to publisher Grant Richards, Joyce wrote similarly about his reason of writing the stories: "My intention was to write a chapter of the moral history of my country and I chose Dublin for the scene because that city seemed to me the centre of paralysis. I have tried to present it to the indifferent public under four of its aspects: childhood, adolescence, maturity and public life."

True, in 1904 Joyce went into self-exile in Italy taking Nara with him and since then the good part of his life he spent away from Dublin, and yet he never ever in his life forget the city of his birth, Dublin. This is conspicuous from the fact that all his major literary productions, from *Dubliners* through *Stephen Hero*, *A Portrait of the Artist as a Young Man* and *Exiles* to *Ulysses* and *Finnegans Wake* are overtly or covertly connected with Dublin. Joyce was out and out an Irish man; he left Ireland only because he could not bear with her Catholicism (its orthodoxy), culture (its age old hang-over) and politics (its acceptance of British overlordship). He wrote in English but vied with Shakespeare perhaps for the reason that he loved Ireland against Britain. But he denounced the Britishers less and denigrated the Irishers all the more for the cause of his beloved Eire (the name of the ancient Ireland). And so he wrote *Dubliners* with a vengeance.

However, *Dubliners* is now a portal to the most complex and difficult but all-important literary world of Joyce. Joyceana has now only began to reveal itself. Musicals, plays and films have begun to come out on the great works of Joyce. But below we are attaching a short list of musicals, operas, musics, and films created on the stories of Dubliners (Fargnoli and Gellespie, 389-90):

1. "The Dead": one-act opera: Murry Boren and Glen Nelson: first staged in New York in 1993.
2. "The Dead": film: Directed by John Huston: 1987.
3. "The Dead": musical: Playwrights Horizons: 1999.
4. "Araby": film: Films for the Humanities and Sciences, Princeton, N.J.: 1999.
5. "A Painful Case": film: Films for the Humanities and Sciences, Princeton, N.J.: dale NA.

To the above information given by Fargnoli and Gillespie, we add that "The Dead" was adapted in a Bengali film, *Basu Paribar* (the Basu Family), in 2019, starring Aparna Sen and Saumitra Chatterjee (Wikipedia). The fame of Joyce has also been stamped in modern physics, where a type of elementary particle and fundamental constituent of matter has been named "quark", a word coined by Joyce and used in his *Finnegans Wake*, and a newly discovered distant star has been named after him.

Joyce (1882-1941) is a modernist writer, showing postmodernist leanings. Modernism is a nebulous word, difficult to define. However, J.A. Cuddon writes that "As far as literature is concerned modernism reveals a break away from established rules, traditions and conventions, fresh way of looking at man's position and function in the universe and many (in some cases remarkable) experiments in form and style. It is particularly concerned with language and how to use it (representationally or otherwise) and with *writing itself*" (Cuddon, 515-16). Modernism is "A general, non-specific, and comprehensive term for a movement (or tendency) in literary productions prevalent roughly between the two World Wars (1914-1918 and 1939-1945), featuring radical break with the traditional modes, style, concepts and subject matters; a credo for experimentation in all the literary elements and forms; a doubt about the legitimacy of religion, morality and the prevailing social organization; a craze for *avant-garde*-ism and the motto of 'make it new' (Ezra Pound: b. 1885); introduction into literary *oeuvres* the effects of drugs, dreams and automatic writing; inclusion of previously forbidden subject-matters; a sense of 'alienation'; and an unexampled rapidity of change" (Sarker, 108). Joyce's later and most momentous two literary productions—*Ulysses* and *Finnegans Wake*—have gone beyond modernism, and perhaps beyond postmodernism, in terms of experimentations in novelistic forms, linguistic mastery, and narrative innovations. Hints of some of these may be found in the stories of *Dubliners*.

Of Joyce's narrative innovations, two stand out as momentous: the technique of gnomon and the technique of epiphany. As these two will take longer spaces to be explained, so these will be taken up in the next chapter.

THEME, PLOT, TECHNIQUE and STYLE

THEME

Joyce planned the 15 stories of *Dubliners* very consciously as sequential parts or units of a novella, which is *Dubliners*, and so naturally the central common theme of all the stories, or of the novella *Dubliners*, is the singular theme: paralysis. It is not strange, therefore, that in the very first paragraph of the lead story "The Sisters" we come across for the first and last time in the whole book the term 'paralysis' (twice), for it is axiomatic in the book. This paralysis manifested, according to Joyce, in all walks of the Dubliners' life: physical, familial, religious, social, political and traditional. The paralysis sustained due to the mental inertia or hemiplegia (paralysis of one side of cerebrum) of the people of Dublin. It is interesting to note that the ubiquitous theme of paralysis in *Dubliners* does appear conspicuously in the very first story through the use of the word 'paralysis', twice, and the word 'paralytic', once, and nowhere ever in the whole book. But the paralytic state of the Dubliners is obvious in each of the rest 14 stories in various ways. For instance, in the ultimate story (or the coda), "The Dead", Gabriel's "soul swooned slowly as he heard the snow faintly falling through the universe." The paralysis, Joyce thought, must be predicated to the Dubliners' lack or absence of *conscience* and their atavistic subservience to the tradition of servility to the British.

Disgusted with this state of affairs, Joyce keenly felt the spar of his wish to escape this paralytic city of Dublin (or Ireland). This manifest escape motif or the theme of escape is an adjunct theme in most of the stories. This escape motif is also covertly present in some of the stories, such as in "Eveline", the 19-year-old girl, trapped in the vacuity of her life in family wants to marry Frank and depart to Buenos Ayres, or in "A Little Cloud", Little Chandler wants to leave behind his family and all and go to England to flourish there like Gallahar. This theme of escape rolls over Joyce's next literary production *A Portrait of the Artist as a Young Man* whose penultimate sentence in the fourth part of the fifth chapter is an assertation of the hero's escape motive and his quest for a remedy to Dublin's paralysis: "O life! I go to encounter for the millionth time the reality of experience and to forge in the smithy of my soul the uncreated conscience of my race." And Joyce himself escaped into Trieste, Italy, like the young hero of his fiction. It is here in the escape motive in *Dubliners* that there is an autobiographical element in it. Joyce's early escape motive or motive of self exile was born at a tender age. His will of fleeing from Ireland to Europe at that tender age we know about from the fact that when he was around 20 years of age he wrote to Lady Gregory expressing his wish to escape Ireland due to the fact that he could not adjust himself with the life in Dublin.

PLOT

In the stories in *Dubliners*, Joyce is not so much interested in plots as he is after painting the moods of the principal characters and the situations in which the moods grow. He first builds a gripping situation in which he puts the protagonist and observes the protagonist's epiphanic experiences. This is the reason why he has eschewed the requirement of a plot in his short stories. Joyce's story either lacks plot or contains a semblance of a plot. He needed no plot also because he was an impressionistic artist like Virginia Woolf, Dorothy Richardson and Marcel Proust. Joyce strived to concentrate on the inner life of a character rather than describe his outer reality.

As a modern writer (or a post-modern writer), Joyce said goodbye to the Aristotelian concept of plot as an essential component of story. The plot, Aristotle said, was an arrangement of events in their temporal sequence, but Joyce thought that concentrating on the description of the mental horizon sometimes required rupturing the temporal sequence of events, because the mind or consciousness could move forward and backward in the flow of time, as in the narrative technique of interior monologue. Further, plot has a beginning, a middle and an end but Joyce's stories begin abruptly in *media res* and closes abruptly with no definable conclusion. This inconclusivity is a hallmark of Joycean short stories. So we say that Joyce threw the requirement of a plot in a story to the winds as did Kafka, Arnold Bennet, Graham Green, Robbe-Grillet, Nabokov, Saul Bellow, Ivo Andric and V.S. Naipaul.

TECHNIQUE

1. REALISM. Joyce writes realistically and not idealistically. He presents things and events as they are there in the outer, objective world. C.A. Cuddon writes that "realism is the portrayal of life with fidelity. It is thus not concerned with idealization, with rendering things as beautiful when they are not, or in any way presenting them in any guise as they are not; nor, as a rule, is realism concerned with presenting the supranormal or transcendental.... More crudely, it suggests jackets off, sleeves rolled up, a 'no nonsense' approach" (Cuddon, 729). Two short specimens of his unembellished and stark narrative realism are given below:

(i) The beginning story of *Dubliners*, "The Sisters", begins thus: "There is no hope for him this time: it was the third stroke. Night after night I had passed the house (it was vacation time) and studied the lighted square of window: and night after night I had found it lighted in the same way, faintly and evenly." This is a faithful presentation without any hint of subjective interference.

(ii) In a very significant and consequential situation in "The Dead", where Bartell D'Arcy sang upstairs "O, the rain falls on my heavy locks/ And the dew wets my skin,/ My babe lies cold....." (from the lyric "Lass of Aughim"), Joyce coolly describes Gabriel: "He stood still in the gloom of the hall, trying to catch the air that the voice was singing and gazing up at his wife. There was grace and mystery in her attitude as if she were symbol of something. He asked himself what is a woman standing on the stairs in the shadow, listening to distant music a symbol of. If he was a painter he would paint her in that attitude. Her blue felt hat would show off the bronze of her hair against the

> darkness and the dark panels of her skirt would show off the light ones. *Distant Music* he would call the picture if he was a painter."

Though surrealism, that wanted to release the creative potential of the unconscious mind from the trammel of rationalism, and Dadaism, which declared that arrangement of unrelated materials in a certain way may give rise to aesthetic beauty, were in vogue during the early period of his literary output, Joyce consciously shied away from these two *avant-garde* literary credo and stuck to realism. Nevertheless, Joyce's realism is not absolute because his narratives are dotted with descriptions of epiphanic experiences of his characters. Joyce used the word epiphany (and epiphanic) not in any religious sense but in a secular or literary sense (see *infra*). He said that epiphany is a "*sudden spiritual manifestation*" of a hidden or previously inexperienced feature or quality of a thing, person, or situation that is of some momentous consequence to the person having the experience of the epiphany. The epiphany itself is in no sense a 'thing' gathered out in the objective world (or real world), it is just a unique segment of the consciousness of the person having the epiphany. It is in this sense that Joyce was not an absolute realist in his works.

2. SYMBOLISM. The term 'symbol' originates from Greek *symbolon* which is a combination of Greek *syn*, meaning 'together' and Greek *ballein*, meaning 'to throw.' So, in a symbol there are two things: one, a token; and two, a thing to which the token refers or points. The connection between the token and the thing the token stands for must be established by custom or convention or, in creative works, by the force of imagination. "A literary symbol combines an image with a concept (words themselves are a kind of symbol). It may be public or private, universal or local.... In literature an example of a public or universal symbol is a journey into the underworld (as in the work of Virgil, Dante and James Joyce) and a return from it. Such a journey may be an interpretation of a spiritual experience, a dark night of the soul and a kind of redemptive odyssey. Examples of private symbols are those that recur in the works of W.B. Yeats: the sun and moon, a tower, a mask, a tree, a winding stair and a hawk" (Cuddon, 885). Symbol must be differentiated from sign. A sign is explicitly tied to a signified, but a symbol and the thing symbolized are mysteriously and indeterminately connected.

The stories of *Dubliners* are heavily dotted with symbols, so much so that one may think that Joyce writes not only with words but also with symbols. His symbols in *Dubliners* are of two kinds: one kind of symbol is pervasive throughout the 15 stories and the other kind of symbol is specific to a story or stories. The first kind of symbol is not presented through a specific object or sign but is implied through narrative structure, like Dante's *Divine Comedy* which is structurally symbolic. Circularity and immobility are two common, basic and structural symbols of the 15 stories of *Dubliners*. Each story moves on and on from a point but at the end of it returns to the starting point. Two easy examples are: "Araby" and "Eveline." In "Araby", the boy starts from home at North Richmond Street with a romantic mission for Mangan's sister but returns home saddened. And in "Eveline", the nineteen-year-old girl left her depressive home to escape into the romantically coloured home of Frank in Buenos Ayres but her obligation to her mother's moral injunction tethered her back to that depressive home. This concept of circularity is present not only in *Dubliners* but, suggestively, in all works of Joyce. And this circularity may remind one of the pre-historic Egyptian concepts of uroboros (or ouroboros).

The other kind of symbol, where a thing stands specifically and overtly for a concept—for instance the Cross signifies Christianity or *Swastika* is emblematic of the sun or of good luck—is abundant in Joyce's works. Listing of the symbols in *Dubliners* may not be necessary; we are just citing some symbols from a few stories below.

1. "The Sisters": "faints and worms" (paralysis and corruption), "grey face" ("grey"=dull), "black snuff-box" ("black"=signifies mourning), "discoloured teeth" (discoloured" or yellowish=abominable), "vested as for the alter...retaining a chalice" (as if doing religious confession), "chalice he broke" (violated Christian

injunction) and "idle chalice on his breast" (wished to die as a right Christian).

2. "Araby": "North Richmond Street, being blind" ("blind"=trapped, unescapeable), "rusty bicycle-pump" (paralysis), song "The Arab's Farewell to his Stead" (illusory romance), "the great jars" (romantic eastern grandeur), "the dark entrance to the stall" (paralysis), the "curled and damp" and yellow leaves of "The Abbot, by Walter Scott, *The Devout Communicant* and *The Memoirs of Vidocq*" (books of romantic, devotional and detective stories—the first and the third books are unbecoming with the profession of the priest, the former tenant of the narrator boy's house, and they hint to the simony of the priest), and the title of the story, "Araby", is a symbol of the "Eastern enchantment."
3. "Eveline": "odour of dusty cretonne" (homesickness), "Home!" (homesickness; the word tolls Eveline Hill back to her home from her romantic imagination of escape, like the word "Forlorn"), "Buenos Ayres" (the romantic Shangri-La, for Eveline), "*The Bohemian Girl*" (a romantic opera by Michael William Balfe, earlier filmed), "the black mass of the boat" ("black"=mourning), and "helpless animal" (condition of Eveline—like a speechless animal in pain). The proper name "Eveline" itself may be interpreted as symbolic. "Eve" is "evening" and "line" is that which divides, and so evening may be thought of as a faint and shifting line between day (hope) and night (gloom). Eveline stands on the evening line, on the line of uncertainty or ambiguity.
4. "Clay": "Maria was a very, very small person" (she was an ordinary person), "*A Present from Belfast*" (Maria's nagging memory of Joe's affection for her is borne by this purse. The old and unwedded Maria felt nostalgia from it), "Maria was sure to get the ring" ("ring" is here a token of avowal of marriage), "rain"

(mentioned three times: inauspicious luck), "I dreamt that I dwelt" (song sung by Maria: old romantic wish), the tray of "clay" (death) and "prayer book" (religious life).

5. "The Dead": "Lily" (name of the caretaker's daughter, mentioned 10 times in eight pages: white flower: purity); "snow" (mentioned nine times: death); "cold" (mentioned four times: lack of affection between Gabriel and Gretta); Glue-bioler Patrick Morkan's horse, Johnny, walking round and round the stone horse on which the statue of King Billy sat (prefiguration of Gretta's moving round dead Furey or Gabriel's doing beats around Gretta's cold or unresponsive love, like the horse, Johnny, walking around in the "starch mill"); "Distant Music": title of the wished for painting of Gretta by Gabriel ["a symbol of" Gretta's old (distant) love of dead (distant Michael Furey)]; "bird" and "birds" (bird is always a symbol of beauty and happiness); and "*The Lass of Aughrim*" (a song of central importance in "The Dead", reflects Gretta's old and nagging love of Michael Furey).

Symbolism is a literary device not only of the transcendentalists and mystics, like Maeterlinck, but also of realists, like Joyce. In *Dubliners*, Joyce has employed symbols generously, as we have seen above in the five stories: "The Sisters", "Araby", "Eveline", "Clay", and "The Dead." Here a problem arises: some critics believe that some of the stories of *Dubliners* are not realistic but are naturalistic. For instance, "Edmund Wilson, long ago in *Axel's Castle*, found *Dubliners* 'a straight work of Naturalistic fiction,' different in every way from symbolist *Ulysses*" (Tindall, 8). William York Tindall agrees with Edmund Wilson on the point that at least some of the stories of *Dubliners* are straightforward naturalistic: "Filled as they are with external detail, the stories of *Dubliners* or several at least look straightforward and, if not scientific, objective. Consider 'Two Gallants,' 'Counterparts,' and 'The Boarding House'" (Tindall, 9). And if so, if not all but some of the stories are straightforwardly naturalistic can there be in them symbolism?

Yes, even then Joyce may be called a symbolist, in so far as a stark naturalist Emile Zola is a reputed symbolist. Zola said that literature should be a vehicle of experiments in the psychology of human beings like Claude Bernard experimented in human physiology. In his novel, *Germinal*, Zola has very objectively shown how the hero, Etienne Lantier, was influenced by his heredity and social environment in the matters of his emotion. Nevertheless we find, for instance, the symbol of coal mine in *Germinal* and *L'Assommoir*, the mine presenting itself as a surrogate human community. Like Zola, Joyce, though he is a naturalist, not infrequently resorts to symbolism.

3. **GNOMON.** "Gnomon" is a unique and important narrative technique, invented by Joyce and first employed by him in *Dubliners*. In his *The Concise Dictionary of English Etymology*, Walter W. Skeats writes that the Latin term 'gnomon' means "index of a dial" or "an interpreter (one who knows), the index of a dial" (Skeats, 178). Gnomon denotes two things: firstly, it refers to the perpendicular projecting piece on a sundial that throws an elongated shadow across the base when the sundial is kept in the sun and from the position of the shadow one can guess the time of the day, etc. It is to be noted here that one guess the time not from the position of the projection piece but from its shadow (or absence). In the olden days, the Chinese used to determine geographical latitudes, changes of season and, of course, the time of the day from this gnomon. Secondly, in ancient Greece the word "gnomon" meant a carpenter's square, which was an L-shaped tool with its two sides at right angles. Joyce took the term "gnomon" from Euclid's definition of "gnomon" in his *Elements* (Book II). There Euclid defined "gnomon" as "an L-shaped figure made by removing a parallelogram from a larger similar parallelogram".

In the carpenter's gnomon, a smaller parallelogram is taken away (absent or missing) from the whole parallelogram so that the larger part of the whole parallelogram remains (present) and this larger part is called gnomon. The absent smaller parallelogram may be determined or guessed from the present larger parallelogram. This is the trick or device employed by Joyce in the stories of *Dubliners*.

In the narratives of the stories of *Dubliners*, the gnomons are missing or incomplete parts or gaps or spaces of silence—all that require straining attention and vigorous meditation on the part of the reader to guess about the missing or incomplete parts or fill in the gap or silent parts. This strategy Joyce deliberately resorted to in order to make the stories intellectual, and thus modern. We say this because he intentionally—and he himself admitted this—planned the stories to leave them ambiguous, dubious, vague. A few instances of gnomons from "The Sisters" are given below in order to illustrate the concept of gnomon.

(a) The narrating boy tells us that Old Cotter resumed his talk about the paralytic Father Flynn thus: "'No, I would not say he was exactly...but there something queer...there was something uncanny about him. I'll tell you my opinion....'"

(b) The narrator further tells us that Old Cotter again says about Father Flynn: "'I have my own theory about it,' he said. 'I think it was one of those...peculiar cases.... But it's hard to say....'"

(c) Old Cotter once more: "'What I mean is,' said Old Cotter, 'it's bad for children. My idea is: let a young lad run about and play with young lads of his own age and not be.... Am I right, Jack?'"

(d) Eliza: "'It was that chalice he broke.... That was the beginning of it. Of course, it was all right, that it contained nothing, I mean. But still.... They say it was the boy's fault. But poor James was so nervous, God be merciful to him!'" The narrator: "'And was that it?' said my aunt. 'I heard something....'"

(e) Eliza once again again: "'Wide-awake and laughing-like to himself.... So then, of course, when they saw that, that made them think that there was something gone wrong with him....'"

The above gaps or silences in the story, "The Sisters", are easily filled up by the intelligent reader if only he wills to understand it. However, he term "gnomon" appears only in "The Sisters" and in no other stories of *Dubliners*, and there only once, but the story contains the greatest number of gnomons, in the whole of *Dubliners*. Interestingly, in most cases, gnomons lead to epiphanies.

4. EPIPHANY. Epiphany, like gnomon, is a very important narrative device in Joyce's fictions: *Dubliners*, *A Portrait*, *Ulysses* and *Finnegans Wake*, particularly in *Dubliners*. The word 'epiphany' derived from Greek '*epiphaneia*' which means the manifestation or appearance or revelation of Christ to the Magi (wise men) of the East. Here the term bears a religious connotation. But Joyce has used it in a different sense—in a secular sense—in his works. He means by the term "epiphany" a sudden, ephemeral, spiritually (not in the religious sense) jolting experience that brings in a change in a person's consciousness or behaviour. Joyce is not the only person who has spoken of epiphany in non-religious sense but there are others. Poets, such as Wordsworth, Henry Vaughn, George Herbert, Gerard Manley Hopkins and P.B. Shelley, and prose writers, such as De Quincey and Virginia Woolf, have also written of epiphany. Shelley called epiphanies 'moments', Wordsworth 'spots of time', Virginia Woolf 'moment of moments' and De Quincey 'involutes.'

Before we try to understand Joyce's epiphany or a sudden spiritual revelation, it may be profitable to learn of one instance of Wordsworth's epiphany from his many epiphanies ('spots of time'). In Book VII of *The Prelude* (lines 636-64), Wordsworth sings of an epiphany of his:

....lost
Amid the moving pageant, I was smitten
Abruptly, with the view (a sight not rare)
Of a blind Beggar, who, with upright face,
Stood, propped against a wall, upon his chest
Wearing a written paper, to explain
His story, whence he came, and who he was.
Caught by the spectacle my mind turned round
As with the might of waters; an apt type
This label seemed of the utmost we can know,
Both of ourselves and of the universe;

And, on the shape of that unmoving man,
His steadfast face and sightless eyes, I gazed,
As if admonished from another world.

Before *Stephen Hero* (the earlier version of *A Portrait of the Artist as a Young Man*), Joyce did not explain epiphany though he had put a good number of epiphanies in the stories of *Dubliners*. In *Stephen Hero*, Joyce explains epiphany from behind the persona of Stephen: "By an epiphany he meant a sudden spiritual manifestation, whether in the vulgarity of speech or of gesture or in a memorable phase of the mind itself. He believed that it was for the man of letters to record these epiphanies with extreme care, seeing that they themselves are the most delicate and evanescent moments. He told Cranly that the clock of the Ballast Office was capable of an epiphany. Cranly questioned the inscrutable dial of the Ballast Office with his no less inscrutable countenance:

> ...Yes, said Stephen, I will pass it time after time, allude to it, refer to it, catch a glimpse of it. It is only an item in the catalogue of Dublin's street furniture. Then all at once I see it and I know at once what it is: epiphany.
>
> ...What?
>
> ...Imagine my glimpses at that clock as the gropings of a spiritual eye which seeks to adjust its vision to an exact focus. The moment the focus is reached the object is epiphanised. It is just in this epiphany that I find the third, the supreme quality of beauty."

Epiphany requires no special things: ordinary, quotidian things, at extraordinary moments, may emerge as epiphanies. Such an idea may be found in the following four lines of Wordsworth's *Prelude*, Book VII (lines 626-29):

How oft, amid those overflowing streets,
Have I gone forward with the crowd, and said
Unto myself, "The face of every one
That passes by me is a *mystery*! (*emphasis added*)

Or, again, the following two lines from Wordsworth's "Ode: Intimation of Immortality from Recollections of Early Childhood":

> To me the meanest flower that blows can give
> Thoughts that do often *lie too deep for tears*. (*emphasis added*)

Or the idea of epiphany may be grasped from the fourth section of *A Portrait of the Artist as a Young Man* where the hero, Stephen Dedalus, sees a girl alone by the sea-shore epiphanised as a seabird: "A girl stood before him in midstream, alone and still, gazing out to sea. She seemed like one whom magic had changed into the likeness of a strange and beautiful seabird."

Since early age, Joyce was fascinated by what he later called "epiphany" and the epiphanies that he came across he entered in notebooks. Of the numerous epiphanies in his notebooks only 40 are extant and of the 40 Joyce has reused 30 in *A Portrait*, *Ulysses* and *Finnegans Wake* but none in *Dubliners*. But this does not mean that *Dubliners* is empty of epiphanies, rather the opposite is true. Before we turn to that we must understand that the terms 'epiphany' and 'epicleti' entail similar connotations as both bear religious underpinning—epiphany is the revelation of Christ and epicleti is Christian transubstantiation. In August 1904, Joyce told his friend Constantine Curran, "'I am writing a series of epicleti'—or 'epiclets'—'I call the series *Dubliners* to betray the soul of that hemiplegia or paralysis which many consider a city'" (Mac Duff, 76). From this statement of Joyce, we may conclude that the 15 stories of *Dubliners*, each one of them, are stories based on epiphanies.

So, now, a few instances of epiphanies in *Dubliners* upon which the stories are built. A point to be noted here is that these epiphanies appear at the close of each story. At the end of "The Sisters", Eliza revealed the secret behind Father James Flynn's demise, which made all around aghast. Eliza said about the deceased Father Flynn in the form of a gnomon: "Wide-awake and laughing-like to himself.... So then, of course, when they saw that, that made them think that there was something gone wrong with him...." In an "Encounter", when the narrator in utter distress went up the slope for safety and called out 'Murphy!' for succor and Mahony (i.e., Murphy) ran towards him with break-neck speed, he (the narrator) realized that

Mahony really was not a person to despise: "And I was penitent; for in my heart I had always despised him a little."

In "Araby", when the little narrator failed to bring 'something' from the bazaar for Mangan's sister, he felt flummoxed by his own romantic illusion, like the Arab owner of the steed. He tells us "Gazing into the darkness I saw myself as a creature driven and derided by vanity; and my eyes burned with anguish and anger." In "Clay", when Maria ended her song, "I dreamt that I dwelt in marble halls", Joe realized that "there was no time like long ago" and "no music for him like Balfe." The memory of the past came to him epiphanised. "Grace" ends with Karnan's epiphanic realization: "Well, I have looked into my accounts. I find this wrong and this wrong. But, with God's grace, I will rectify this and this. I will set right my accounts."

And, lastly, Gabriel at the close of "The Dead" got an epiphanic realization of the phenomenon of love from Gretta's "choking woth sobs", broken down from the memory of her lover Michael Furey who died long ago in Galway. Gabriel "thought of how she who lay beside him had locked in her heart for so many years that image of her lover's eyes when he had told her that he did not wish to live." "Generous tears filled Gabriel's eyes. He had never felt like that himself towards any woman, but he [then] knew that such a feeling must be love."

It must be noted that Joyce has nowhere clearly defined, or explained, once for all, what actually he meant by the term 'epiphany'. Deborah Parsons writes: "A product of the earnest youthful aestheticism that as a mature artist he soon came to mock, Joyce first used the term 'epiphany' to describe the notebook sketches of Dublin life that he wrote in the early 1900s." To his brother Stanislaus he declared that an epiphany revealed "the significance of trivial things" (Ellman, 1982, 169), endowing the most common object with value. At other times, however, the experience of epiphany is presented as something from the direct opposite, an abstract aesthetic revelation rather than a prosaic object or instance from everyday life. This ambiguity is cleared in *Stephen Hero*, the early draft of *A Portrait of the Artist as a Young Man*, where Stephen explains: "'By an epiphany he meant a sudden spiritual manifestation, whether in *the vulgarity of speech or of gesture or in a memorable phase* of the mind itself...'" (Parsons, 38). Howbeit, keeping aside the two contradictory meanings aside, we can say the last mentioned of the two meanings of 'epiphany' well dovetails with the epiphanies in the stories of *Dubliners*: some sudden spiritual manifestation in everyday things or happenings, that endows them with enormous values. However, "As an artistic technique the epiphany nevertheless retains a significance for Joyce's own thinking on the novel; notably in its episodic nature, which forms the basic structure of *A Portrait*, *Ulysses* and *Finnegans Wake*, and also in the tension it reveals, and that would persist throughout Joyce's work, between the abstract and material origins of artistic creation" (*ibid.*).

5. CHRONOTOPE. Like gnomon and epiphany, chronotope is yet another important new narrative technique that Joyce was the forerunner to practice rather vigorously in his works. The Russian literary theorist Mikhail Bakhtin (1895-1975) coined the term "chronotope" from the two Greek words "chromos", meaning "time", and "topos", meaning "place". Chronotope "refers to the co-ordinates of time and space invoked by a given narrative; in other words to the 'setting', considered as a spacio-temporal whole" (Baldrick, 40). A chronotope of course is a "spatio-temporal whole" or "setting" within a narrative, but any "spatio-temporal whole" or "setting" is not a chronotope if within that spatial and temporal framework no serious change occurs in the consciousness or perception of somebody. The concept of chronotope may be apprehended on a micro level as well as on a macro level. In *A Portrait of the Artist as a Young Man*, Stephen sees the beautiful 'seabird' on the beach (a space) in the evening (a time), and he on a sudden clearly foresees the vista of his desired future life—the life of an artist—the vista that remained blurred to him for a long time before, though he was looking for it frantically. Here is a chronotope on the micro level because the spatio-temporal setting is confined within a narrow strip of the beach and within a short while. On the other hand, according to some critics, the whole narrative of *A Portrait of the Artist as a Young Man* may be taken to be a spatio-temporal whole and Stephen's psychological crisis and its resolution may be taken to be the event of a change in the consciousness or perception of Stephen, and in that case the novel, *A Portrait of the Artist as a Young Man*, may be called a chronotope at the macro level.

Chronotopes are spatio-temporal spheres where a character finds himself put between two psychological alternatives. Such spatio-temporal spheres are: door (which exists between inside and outside of a room), window (which has inside and outside), stairway (between upper and lower floors), corridor (which lead one from one side to other side); and square, street, tavern, etc. which are away from one's house (nearness and farness). It may be noted here that in all these regions or spheres there are sorts of "thresholds" that divide the regions or spaces into halves. Interestingly, chronotopic experiences of characters in novels of some writers, such as Virginia Woolf, Franz Kafka, William Faulkner and James Joyce, happen in such spatio-temporal regions or spheres. On the other hand, in regions or spheres that have no inside outside divisions or no thresholds, such as bedroom, dining room, hall, etc., no chronotopic experiences happen to characters in novels. In such spaces, characters can only reveal their biographical facts, such as their common or ordinary thoughts and activities.

However, let us now see some chronotopic experiences of some characters in *Dubliners*:

1. In "The Sisters", the narrator boy's aunt, in the *evening*, took him to the *dead-room* where father Flynn lay in state. Nannie, the old woman, received them and then "The old woman pointed upwards interrogatively and, on my aunt's nodding, proceeded to toil up the narrow *staircase* before us, her bowed head being scarcely above the level of the banister-rail. At the first *landing* she stopped and beckoned us forward encouragingly towards the *open door* of the *dead room*." There in the dead room, the boy saw in bewilderment the corpse of father Flynn: "There he lay, solemn and copious, vested as for the alter, his large hands loosely retaining a chalice." (*emphases added*)

2. In "Araby", the narrator boy and his close friends used to look slyly at Mangan's sister. The boy tells us: "if Mangan's sister came out on the *doorstep* to call her *brother to his tea*, we watched her from our shadow peer up and down the street.... She was waiting for us, her figure defined by the light from the *half-opened door*." And "*Every morning* I lay on the floor in the front parlour watching her *door*. The blind was pulled down to within an inch of the sash so that I could not be seen. When she came out on the *doorstep* my heart leaped." (*emphases added*)
3. Eveline, in "Eveline", was romantically imagining her escape with Frank as his wife to distant Buenos Ayres and at the same time feeling a pull backwards for her home and her duty to her family. "She sat at the *window* watching the *evening* invade the avenue. Her head was leaned against the *window* curtains, and in her nostrils was the odour of dusty cretonne. She was tired." (*emphases added*)
4. In "The Boarding House", Polly flirted with Mr. Doran with the connivance of her mother, Mrs. Mooney. The scandal was known to everyone around. To save her prestige and Polly's, Mrs. Mooney went to the boarding house to compel Mr. Doran to marry Polly. Coming back victorious she called out to Polly who, *in the upper storey*, was visualizing her past flirting with Mr. Doran and was anxiously waiting for the result of her mother's adventure, and then....

   "At last she heard her mother calling. She started to her feet and ran to the *banister*.

   'Polly! Polly!'

   'Yes, mamma?'

   '*Come down*, dear. Mr. Doran wants to speak to you.'

   Then she remembered what she had been *waiting for*." (*emphases added*)
5. There are at least four chronotopic experiences in "Counterparts":

(i) At the beginning of the story, we are told that Mr. Alleyne had asked Farrington, through Miss Parker, to see him, and Farrington "went heavily *upstairs* and he came to the *second landing*, where, a door bore a brass plate with the inscription *Mr. Alleyne*. Here he halted, puffing with labour and vexation, and knocked."

(ii) Mr. Alleyne had mercilessly pulled up Farrington on the *upper storey*, and then ordered him to *go down* and do his work. Farrington "walked heavily towards the *door* and, as he *went out of the room*, he heard Mr. Alleyne cry after him that if the contract was not copied by evening Mr. Crosbie would hear of the matter."

(iii) Snubbed and disgruntled, Farrington went to his workplace *downstairs* and sat at his table but he could not fix his attention in copying the contract papers. He left his table and started for O'Neill's shop for a drink. "As soon as he was on the *landing* the man [Farrington] pulled a shepherd's plaid cap out of his pocket, put it on his head and ran quickly down the rickety *stairs*. From the *street door* he walked on furtively on the inner side of the path towards the corner and all at once dived into a *doorway*."

(iv) When at the end of office hours, Farrington could not finish copying the contract forms, Mr. Alleyne pulled him up once again: "You impertinent ruffian!...." In utter distress, Farrington "stood in a *doorway* opposite the office, watching to see if the cashier would come out alone." He required some money for another drink. (*all the italics are mine*)

6. "Grace", a story based on Dante's *Divine Comedy*, even begins with a chronotopic event: the heavily drunk Mr. Karnan fell from high down at the foot of the *stairs* in a lavatory and became unconscious. "Two gentlemen who were in the lavatory at the time tried to lift him up: but he was quite helpless. He lay curled up at the foot of the *stairs* down which he had fallen." (*emphases added*)

7. In "the Dead", there are two important chronotopic events:

(i) The singing and dancing being over and supper being ready in the hall below (after a little less than half of the story), Miss Molly Ivors swiftly went down the *staircase* for the hall. Mrs. (Gretta) Conroy leaned down over the *banister* to hear what was going on in the hall. Gabriel understood nothing about why Miss Ivors so quickly descended down the *staircase*, but remained staring vacantly at the *staircase*. "'Beannacht libh [Irish for 'goodbye'],' cried Miss Ivors, with a laugh, as she ran down the *staircase*." (*emphases added*)

"Mary Jane gazed after her, a moody puzzled expression on her face, while Mrs. Conroy leaned over the *banisters* to listen for the *hall-door*. Gabriel asked himself what was the cause of her abrupt departure. But she did not seem to be in ill humour—she had gone away laughing. He stared blankly down the *staircase*." (*emphases added*)

(ii) When Mrs. Brown and others started out for home in a horse-drawn cab, Gabriel did not see them off but stayed back, staring all alone at the staircase. "Gabriel had not gone to the door with the others. He was in a dark part of the hall gazing up the *staircase*. A woman was standing near the top of the *first flight*, in the shadow also. He could not see her face but could see the terra-cotta and salmon-pink panel of her skirt which the shadow made appear black and white. It was his wife.... He stood still in the *gloom of the hall*, trying to catch the air that the voice was singing and gazing up at his wife. There was grace and mystery in her attitude as if she were a symbol of something." (*emphases added*)

6. PERSPECTIVE. Perspective is an important term in narratology. In general sense, perspective means a particular attitude towards, or a way of regarding, something. While reading a fiction, the reader sees and experiences the events and feelings of characters through certain point of view (POV) or aperture, which is the perspective. A perspective is, therefore, a narrative tool which serves as a lens through which a reader observes characters and their actions and behaviour. In this sense, perspective is not, in fact, different from point of view. The term 'point of view' is virtually synonymous with the terms 'account' and 'perspective' in the field of narratology, so that the first person point of view in a story may also be called the first person account or the first person perspective of the story. Likewise, the third person point of view may be called third person account or third person perspective.

Howbeit, in the first person point of view, the writer tells the story, keeping himself within the purview of the story, something like: "Once upon a time I went out boating in a river when..." "The third person point of view may be of two kinds: the omniscient point of view or account or perspective (which is the most frequently used narrative technique) and the limited third person point of view or account or perspective. In the omniscient narrative, the author knows everything of each character, and he can once pop into a certain character and next into another, easily. This narrative tool is the most flexible and so most writers prefer this narrative account or perspective or point of view. On the other hand, in the limited or "close" third person account or perspective or point of view, the writer ensconces himself within a single character and then tells the story from the vantage point of that single character, and not from his own perspective.

In the beginning three stories of *Dubliners*, Joyce has adopted the limited or "close" third person perspective or account or point of view. In "The Sisters", he tells the story ensconcing himself in the person of the little boy—the fictional narrator of the story—and narrates the story from the boy's perspective. Supposedly, the boy knows, for instance, that there was no hope of Father James Flynn's survival: "There was no hope for him this time: it was the third stroke." And at the close of the story, he, the boy (or Joyce) tells us the last words of Eliza about the mystery behind Father Flynn's death: "Eliza resumed: 'Wide-awake and laughing-like to himself.... So then, of course, when they saw that, that made them think that there was something gone wrong with him....'" In "An Encounter", Joyce is playing the role of the narrator boy, who went miching with the other boys and encountered a "queer old josser". And in "Araby", Joyce imagines himself as a little boy in love with Mangan's sister. In these three stories, therefore, Joyce *himself* does not do the narratives (as he would do in the first person narrative) but he is playing the roles of three boys who are spieling. Here Joyce is an omniscient narrator but his omniscience is limited or "closed" within the three narrating boys or personae.

The case is quite different in the rest twelve stories of *Dubliners*, in each of which there is an omniscient narrator who relates the story keeping himself absolutely outside the purview of the story. Take the case of "Eveline". Eveline is romantically stirred by Frank's offer of marrying her and taking her to Buenos Ayres (her Shangri-la) as his wife. She prepares for her escape from the cage of her home, but at the last moment of her departure she imaginatively receives a thunderbolt... "Home!"—that tethers her back homewards. Joyce here, as an universal observer, perceives everything that happens in the story and just puts them down on paper. Thus, in the twelve stories of *Dubliners*, from "Eveline" to "The Dead", the point of view of the writer is omniscient and unlimited. Nevertheless, in so far as in these twelve stories Joyce is observing (and narrating) everything from the angle of a single character of each story (the central character), the point of view of these stories may be called limited or "closed" omniscient. In "Eveline", for instance, Joyce has composed the story from the angle or perspective of Eveline; in "After the Race" from that of Jimmy Doyle; in "Clay" from that of Maria; in "A Painul Case" from that of James Duffy; and in "The Dead" from the perspective of Gabriel.

7. IMPRESSIONISM. In *Dubliners*, Joyce is an impressionist writer. Literary impressionism originated in the impressionistic movement in painting, in the vanguard of which were the paintings of Claude Monet (*Impression: Sunrise*) and Edgar Degas (*The Rehearsal on the Stage*). "The impressionist painters were not interested in precise representation of objects—static objects—rather they were eager to capture fleeting impressions of objects from subjective point of view in momentary, transitory plays of light, in order to betray the inward (not outward) essence of those objects. In literature, impressionism signifies a mode of writing that is highly personal and that describes characters and scenes as they *appear to the writer and not as they really happen to be*. In this sense, impressionism is a term quite contradictory to realism. The term impressionism is used in narratology to describe the novelist's *oeuvre* of concentrating on, and portraying, the inner life of characters rather than of their externalities" (Sarker, 87). Some of the impressionist writers are Dorothy Richardson (1873-1957), Virginia Woolf (1882-1941), Marcel Proust (1871-1922) and Joseph Conrad (1857-1924). James Joyce, though like Joseph Conrad he writes realistically, like Conrad he also presents the inner mental horizons of characters, and, in this sense, again like Conrad, he may be counted an impressionist writer. Even though Joyce wrote realistically and even though he portrayed external paraphernalia of settings and realistic details of characters, what he was really after was portraying the *moods* of (principal) characters (and not their intellections or imaginings). He concentrated on the characters' attitude, anger, angst, happiness, love, hatred and such other mental aspects or states of the characters. And so he may, better, be called a literary impressionist, and his realism a "psychological realism".

8. FOCALISATION. Joyce uses the technique of focalization, a term coined by the French literary critic and theorist Gerard Genette. Focalisation refers to filtering of the narrative through the perspective or lens of a character called the focaliser. When a writer narrates a story through a character within that story, that character is to be called the focaliser and the narrative is to be known as a focalized narrative. The narrative that is not focalized is called non-focalised or zero-focalised narrative. Again, focalization may be internal or external. External focalization betrays characters' actions and behaviour but internal focalization shows characters' moods, or their temporary state of mind or feeling. External focalization works just like the lens of a camera.

All narratives from the first person point of view are focalized and no narratives from the omniscient point of view are focalized. The first three stories of *Dubliners* Joyce wrote from the limited third person point of view—from the points of view of the three young narrators—and so the three narratives are focalized. They are, further, homodigetic (not heterodigetic) narrators because they exist in the story world they narrate.

But what about the focalization in the rest twelve stories of *Dubliners*, that are narrated by no characters in the stories but by Joyce himself? Yes, there are also focalisations because in each of these stories Joyce is relating from the perspective of a single character. For instance, in "Eveline" Eveline is focalized because here Joyce has narrated the story from the perspective of Eveline; i.e., Joyce has imagined the story world through the lens (the eyes) of Eveline. And in "The Dead" Joyce has viewed the story world from the perspective of Gabriel, whatever the other characters have to do or feel or talk of.

However, three minor narrative techniques of Joyce also deserve at least a mention. Firstly, he frequently describes a major character before the character is launched in the story world. Let us take a few simple instances. In "Two Gallants", Joyce provides us with descriptions of Lenehan and Corley before they are engaged in the course of the story. About Lenehan, Joyce writes at some length: "Most people considered Lenehan a leach, but in spite of this reputation, his adroitness and eloquence had always prevented his friends from any general policy against him. He had a manner of coming up to a party of them in a bar and of holding himself nimbly at the borders of the company until he was included in a round. He was a sporting vagrant armed with a vast stock of stories, limericks and riddles. He was insensitive to all kinds of discourtesy. No one knew how he achieved the stern task of living, but his name was vaguely associated with racing tissues." And also at some length about Corley: "The swing of his burley body made his friends execute a few light skips from the path to the roadway and back again. Corley was the son of an inspector of police, and he had inherited his father's frame and gait. He walked with his hands by his sides. He was large, globular and oily; it sweated in all weathers; and his large round hat, set upon it sideways, looked like a bulb which had grown out of another. He always stared straight before him as if he were on parade, and when he wished to gaze after someone in the street, it was necessary for him to move his body from the hips. At present he was about town." Secondly, one peculiar narrative strategy of Joyce is to dot many of his stories in *Dubliners* with immoderately large number of street and place names. In "After the Race" (eight pages), there are three street (including one road) names and three place names: Naas Rd., Dame St.; Grafton St., Inchicore, Kingstown and Westland Row. But the zem is "Two Gallants" (14 pages) where there are eleven street names and twelve place names. The stree names are: Dorset St., Dame St., Baggot St., Kildare St., Nassau St., Hume St., Merrion St., Chapel St., Grafton St., George's St., and Westmoreland St. And there are twelve place names: Rutland Square, Waterhouses's clock, South Circular, Trinity College, Stephen's Green, Shelbourne Hotel, Duke's Lawn, City Hall, City Markets, College of Surgeons, Merrion Square and Ely Place. Thirdly, the stories are constructed on a design of circularity. For instance, in "Eveline", Eveline goes out with Frank to be his wife in Buenos Ayres, but returns home, alone and frustrated, and in "Two Gallants", Lenehan and Corley roam the city circle-wise. In designing his stories on the model of circularity, Joyce was influenced by Giambatista Giovanni Vico's concept of circularity and Frederich Nietzsche's philosophy of 'eternal repetition of the same'.

9. MINIMALISM. Minimalism, or literary minimalism, is "a literary or dramatic style or principle based on the extreme restrictions of a work's contents to a bare minimum of necessary elements, normally within a short form, e.g., *haiku*, epigram, brief dramatic sketch, or monologue. Minimalism is often characterized by bareness or starkness of vocabulary or of dramatic setting, and a reticence verging on or even becoming silence" (Baldick, 157). Keeping this connotation of the term 'minimalism', we can call the stories in *Dubliners* minimalistic. Minimalism eschews expatiation, verbiage, embellishment, purple patches and lofty literary style and espouses brevity and concreteness or stiffness. Minimalist writers prefer short sentences that harbor no superfluous adjectives or adverbs. They avoid intricate plots and complex character development. Simply, their moto is "Less is more" or "Doing more with less." Some of the minimalist writers are: Ann Beattie (b. 1947), Raymond Carver (b. 1938), Tobias Wolff (b. 1945), Richard Ford (b. 1944), Amy Hempel (b. 1951), Fredrick Barthelme (b. 1943), Mary Cennamo Robinson (b. 1949) and, of course, Ernest Hemingway (b. 1898), Samuel Beckett (b. 1906) and James Joyce (b. 1882).

The stories of *Dubliners* satisfy all the above-mentioned criteria of minimalist short stories. Look at the 15 stories, barring "The Dead" and "Grace", all are comfortably nestled in the short spaces, and some, that are very popular—say, "Eveline" and "Araby"—are no longer than eight pages (Penguin, 1996). In the stories of *Dubliners*, without exception, there is no plot, no development of characters, no lofty style, no intricacy but emotional subject matters and simplistic premises straightforwardly worked out with short sentences and minimal vocabulary, the end-result to be placed at the doorstep of the reader's imagination for reworking it anew.

10. PARODY AND SATIRE. The best example of Joyce's employment of parody in *Dubliners* is "Grace". According to J.A. Cuddon, parody ("mock song") is "The imitative use of the words, style, attitude, tone and ideas of an author in such a way as to make them ridiculous" (Cuddon, 640). Joyce's "Grace" is a parody of Dante's *Divine Comedy*, but when we say this we must keep in mind that Joyce has imitated in "Grace" Dante's *Divine Comedy* only on the limited score of Dante's *idea* of man's fall from the grace of God, his sufferance and turning to God, and, ultimately his regaining God's grace. Joyce, here, is not imitating Dante's "words, style, attitude, tone", but only his ideas. Dante's influence on Joyce is a commonplace. Like as he has parodied Homer's *Odyssey* in his *Ulysses*, Joyce has parodied Dante's *Divine Comedy* in the very short space of "Grace." *Divine Comedy* is divided into three parts: Inferno, Purgatorio and Paradiso. Likewise, "Grace" has three clear parts: Mr. Kernan, under the impact of boosing, falls down from the steps of a flight in a pub, gets his tongue cut, and bleeds and suffers (part one: Inferno); he is then taken home where he is persuade for long to go for a Catholic retreat and he obeys (part two: Purgatorio); and lastly Mr. Kernan feels the bliss of the life in Paradise (part three: Paradiso). Here Joyce is imitating *Divine Comedy* but in a mocking vein and hence "Grace" is a parody of *Divine Comedy*.

Satire in literature works as a guardian of ideals, values and social codes by debunking any deviation from them. J.A. Cuddon writes that the "satirist is (thus) a kind of self appointed guardian of standards, ideals and truth; of moral as well as aesthetic values" (Cuddon, 780). In *Dubliners*, Joyce has employed satire rather generously. A few instances of satire in *Dubliners* are given below.

1. "Two Gallants": This story, as a whole, may be taken to be a satire on gallantry, and its title itself has a satiric vein. Only one instance of satire from this story may suffice to see how much satiric it is. The two niggardly "gallants", Corley and Lenehan, in a "grey warm evening of August", went out in the street. Corley pursued a young woman on the road for squeezing money out of her by womanizing, while Lenehan stayed back near Shelbourne Hotel. After a while, Lenehan followed the two "lovers." "As he walked on slowly, timing his pace to theirs, he watched Corley's head which turned at every moment towards the young woman's face like a big ball revolving on a pivot."

2. "The Boarding House":

(i) Polly adventurously flirted with Mr. Doran and herself got trapped as a result. Her father, Jack Mooney, was of a weaker sort, compared to her mother, though he had "a thick bulldog face and a pair of thick short arms." Jack Mooney understandably had left the problem of Polly to Mrs. Mooney to be fixed.

(ii) To save the face of the family, Mrs. Mooney contrived to make Mr. Doran agree to marry Polly under duress, which Polly earnestly desired. Mrs. Mooney boldly went to the boarding house to confront Mr. Doran, while Polly was romantically dreaming of a happy ending of the "swelling act": "She waited on patiently, almost cheerfully, without alarm, her memories gradually giving place to hopes and visions of the future. Her hopes and visions were so intricate that she no longer saw the white pillows on which her gaze was fixed, or remembered what she was waiting for."

3. "Grace":

(i) "Grace" is a parody indeed, for like its model or template, *Divine Comedy*, it is not seriously done but done sarcastically. Both parody and satire are well commingled in it. In the third part of the story, we see Mr. Kernan, the injured person, and Mr. Cunningham sitting in the congregation in the Jesuit Church in Gardiner Street. The gathered assembly in the church is satirically portrayed as harbouring people who seemed outré in there: "In a whisper, Mr. Cunningham drew Mr. Kernan's attention to Mr. Herford, the moneylender, who sat some distance off, and to Mr. Fanning, the registration agent and mayor maker of the city, who was sitting immediately under the pulpit beside one of the newly elected councilors of the ward. To the right sat old Michael Grimes, the owner of three pawnbroker's shops, and Dan Hogan's nephew, who was up for the job in the Town Clerk's office. Farther in front sat Mr. Hendrick, the chief reporter of *The Freeman's Journal*, and poor O' Carroll, an old friend of Mr. Kernan's, who had been at one time a considerable commercial figure."

(ii) After a while, Father Purdon recited from the scripture: "'*For the children of this world are wiser in their generation than the children of light. Wherefore make unto yourselves friends out of the mammon of inequity so that when you die they may receive you into everlasting dwelling.*'" Father Purdon said that the "text" (that he recited) was one of the most difficult ones. He said: "It was a text for business men and professional men. Jesus Christ, with His divine

> understanding of every cranny of our human nature, understood that all men were not called to the religious life, that by far the vast majority were forced to live in the world, and, to a certain extent, for the world: and in this sentence He designed to give them a word of counsel, setting before them as exemplars in the religious life of those very worshippers of Mammon who were of all men the least solicitous in matters religious."

11. "UNDECIDABILITY" OR OPEN-ENDEDNESS

Modern fictions—novels as well as short stories—tend to avoid "closure" or "ending" unlike traditional ones. The writer leaves the ending part of the fiction to the reader to decide imaginatively what might be the ending, for himself. The ending remains "undecided" or open-ended, and so unwritten. Examples of open-endedness or undecidability in short fictions are Katherine Mansfield's (1888-1923) "Fly" and "The Garden Party" and Ernest Hemingway's (1898-1961) "The Old Man at the Bridge" and "The Old Man and the Sea".

In "Fly", six years ago the "boss's" young son died and was now in a grave. Old Woodifield reported to the "boss" that the grave was "Beautifully looked after...." When the "boss" was musing on death and his son, he noticed that a fly fell into his broad inkpot and it was "trying feebly but desperately to clamber out again." In spite of the "boss's" all efforts, the fly was dead. The "boss" felt a "grinding feeling of wretchedness" after shoveling off the dead fly into the waste-paper basket with a paper-knife. And then "he fell to wondering what it was he had been thinking before. What was it? It was.... He took out his handkerchief and passed it inside his collar. For the life of him he could not remember."

In "The Garden Party", the Sheridan family arranged an elaborate summer party in their garden. When in the evening the party was in full swing, news came that a man had died a little while ago, leaving behind his wife and five little ones. Mrs. Sheridan's daughter, Laura, asked her mother to stop the hilarious party on account of the regrettable death of the poor man. But her appeal fell on deaf ears. However, after the dinner of the party was over, Mrs. Sheridan asked Laura to take the orts of the dinner to the unfortunate poor family of the dead man, in a mock show of sympathy. When Laura returned from that poor family with tearful eyes, her brother, Laurie, asked her if she was crying.

> "'No,' sobbed Laura. 'It was simply marvelous. But Laurie...' She stopped, she looked at her brother. 'Isn't life...' But what life was she couldn't explain. No matter. He quite understood.
>
> 'Isn't it, Darling'? Said Laurie."

Hemingway, in his "Old Man at the Bridge", has shown how an open-ended short story looks like. In the story, the narrator saw a 76-year-old man from San Carlos sitting beside the bridge in Ebro Delta (in Spain). He was the last man during the war to leave San Carlos. He had been "taking care of animals"—two goats, a cat and four pairs of pigeons. The old man kept the cage of pigeons unlocked and, thought he, in case of artillery fires they would fly away and the cat knew how to give the slip. He was in anguish only for the two goats that he left behind. The old man told the narrator: "'I was taking care of animals,' he said dully, 'but no longer to me. I was only taking care of the animals.'" And at the end of the story, the narrator tells us: "It was Easter Sunday and the Fascists were advancing toward the Ebro. It was a gray overcast day with a low ceiling so their planes were not up. That and the fact that cats know how to look after themselves was all the good luck that old man would ever have." Is this ending clear?

In "The Old Man and the Sea", Santiago, the old man, after so many consecutive failures at catching fishes, he ultimately hooked a big fish—a marlin. There then began a fierce tussle between Santiago and the marlin, in which a chest bone of Santiago was broken. Then came a band of sharks that began to eat the marlin to the bones. Once Santiago was physically very strong and was interested in sports but now his sinews have become weak. However, when at daybreak Santiago somehow could haul his skiff to the shore he saw that only the skeleton of the marlin he could shore up. Exhausted, very exhausted he slipped into sleep. And "The old man was dreaming about the lions [about his past physical strength, perhaps]."

In *Dubliners*, Joyce has four stories that are open-ended: "The Sisters, "Two Gallants", "Clay" and "The Dead". As we have already dealt with them at some lengths, here we will discuss them very briefly only to show how they stop open-endedly.

1. "The Sisters": Father Flynn died mysteriously and his sisters could not discover the mystery, and none other than they. Eliza, the Father's sister, was meditating on the mystery. The story closes with her soliloquy, in her dozed state, about the mystery of the death of Father Flynn: "'Wide-awake and laughing-like to himself.... So then, of course, when they saw that, that made them think that there was something gone wrong with him....'" [What was that that the reader is to guess?]
2. "Two Gallants": The euphemistically dubbed two 'gallants' of the story are Lenehan and Corley. One "gray warm evening of August", Corley, the niggardly vagabond, pursued a young woman along her path for squeezing some money out of her with a show of womanizing while Lenehan, Corley's hanger on stayed back near the Shelbourne Hotel. After some time, Lenehan followed Corley and the young woman and caught Corley on the Bagost Street. By that time the young woman entered a house and Corley went to her. She came back to Corley and reentered that house. When Corley turned to Lenehan, Lenehan asked him: "'Did you try her?'"

   "Corley halted at the first lamp and stared grimly before him. Then with a grave gesture he extended a hand towards the light and, smiling, opened it slowly to the gaze of his disciple. A small coin shone in his palm." [How did Corley mulct the young woman?]
3. "Clay": In the Hallow Eve celebration, Maria repeated singing the first stanza instead of singing the second

that contained the line: "'That you loved me still the same.'" And Joe's eyes gathered tears so much that he "had to ask his wife to tell him where the corkscrew was." [The reader is to guess the intensity of Joe's love for Maria.]

4. "The Dead": Back to the hotel from the Christmas-time party, Gabriel, with all curiosity asked Gretta the cause of her being so intensely interested in the song sung by Bartell D'Arcy. She told him that the song reminded her of Michael Furey, who loved her deeply in Galway and, she believed, he died for her coming away from Galway. She said "he did not wish to live." For the first time Gabriel knew what love really was. At that moment, snow was falling all around, as the newspaper reported. "His soul swooned slowly as he heard the snow falling faintly through the universe and faintly falling, like the descent of their last end, upon all the living and the dead." "The Dead" closes with this last sentence, and the story remains open-ended or undecided. [Why should snow cover all the universe and freeze all the living and the dead? Is it because he wants to die, like Furey, to claim Gretta's love? The reader is to *guess*.]

STYLE

Style is a very important aspect of any literary creation, especially in modern and postmodern times. Style is a very cunning and evasive thing, sometimes showing itself dazzlingly, sometimes eluding notice. The style of a writer is his very own thing, like his hand-writing or his signature, very hard to imitate. In America, for some years, till the other day, competitions had been held on imitating the style of Ernest Hemingway and prizes had been awarded (Hemingway look-alike competition is held there each year even today) but so far none have been able to achieve absolute or near absolute imitation. Style is a very much persona thing, like one's face, with all its features. J.A. Cuddon writes about style: "The characteristic manner of expression in prose and verse; how a particular writer says things. The analysis and assessment of style involves examination of a writer's choice of words, his figures of speech, the devices (rhetorical or otherwise), the shape of his sentences (whether they be loose or periodic), the shape of his paragraphs—indeed, of every conceivable aspect of his language and the way in which he uses it. Style defies complete analysis of definition (Remy de Gourmont put the matter tersely when he said that defining style was like trying to put a sack of flour in a thimble) because it is the tone and 'voice' of the writer himself; as peculiar to him as his laugh, his walk, his handwriting and the expression on his face. The style, as Buffon put it, is the man" (Cuddon, 872). And what we must say, as Bosinelli and Mosher have observed, is that Joyce's style is "so uniquely his" (Bosinelli, 80).

The full-dress Joycean style is to be found in *Ulysses* and *Finnegans Wake* but foreshadows of it are there in *Dubliners*, *Stephen Hero*, *A Portrait of the Artist as a Young Man* and *Exiles*. Here we will confine our discussion on Joycean style within the space of only *Dubliners* wherefrom his stylistic development began. In a letter to the publisher Grant Richards, Joyce frankly wrote that he composed the stories in *Dubliners* "in a style of scrupulous meanness". What does Joyce mean by the phrase "scrupulous meanness"? "Scrupulous" means "directed by scruples, doubts or objections", or directed by "cautions"; and "meanness" means "of little importance" or "of low, vulgar or ordinary quality." What should we understand by the style of "scrupulous meanness", then? We should mean that the style is cautiously judicious employment of low or ordinary—and not polished or elegant—artistic expression or language. However, let us briefly discuss some of the features of Joyce's style as we find in *Dubliners*.

1. Free Indirect Discourse or Style. J.A. Cuddon explains it as "The presentation of thoughts or speech of fictional characters which seems by various devices to combine the character's sentiments with those of a narrator. In its most primitive form, indirect discourse is signaled by the narratorial 'framing' of the thought or utterance, as in Archer tried to console himself with the thought that he was not quite such an ass as Lefferts" (the unframed direct version would be Archer thought: 'I am not quite such an ass as Lefferts')" (Cuddon, 330-31). In *Dubliners*, Joyce has employed this device rather freely. Let us take some instances, at random, from *Dubliners*:

(i) "Clay": In the fourth paragraph of the story, Maria is going to take part in the Hallow Eve or Halloween celebration in the house of Joe Donnelly. She is imagining the joyful evening there: "*What a nice evening they would have, all the children singing!*" (*italics added*)

(ii) "A Painful Case": After reading, in the eatery, about the death of Mrs. Sinico in the newspaper, Mr. Duffy "gazed out of the window on the cheerless evening landscape.... *What an end!*" (*italics added*). Three sentences down, the narrator tells us about Mr. Duffy: "He saw the squalid tract of her [Mrs. Sinico's] voice, miserable, malodorous. *His soul's companion!*" (*italics added*).

(iii) "The Dead": In the first of the three parts of "The Dead", the narrator tells us that after Aunt Julia's song "*Arrayed for the Bridal*" was over and Miss Molly Ivors abruptly went away laughing, Mrs. Gretta Conroy "leaned over the banisters to listen for the hall-door. *Gabriel asked himself was he the cause of her abrupt departure?*" (*italics added*). And at the close of the story, we come across a long free indirect discourse by the narrator: "The time had come for him [Gabriel] to set out on his journey westward. *Yes, the newspapers were right: snow was general all over Ireland. It was falling on every part of the dark central plain, on the treeless hills, falling softly upon the Bog of Allen and, farther westward, softly falling into the dark mutinous Shannon waves. It was falling, too, upon every part of the lonely churchyard on the hill where Michael Furey lay buried. It lay thickly drifted on the crooked crosses and headstones, on the spears of the little gate, on the barren thorns*. His soul swooned slowly as he heard the snow falling faintly through the universe and faintly falling, like the descent of their last end, upon the living and the dead." (*italics added*)

2. Repetition of words and phrases. Repetition is a potential stratagem in literary compositions that help emphasise a particular point or imagery. The most common form of repetition is polysyndeton or multiple conjunctions (e.g., and...and...and). A few instances from *Dubliners*:

(i) "Araby": Near the close of "Araby", the young narrator overhears a conversation among two young gentlemen and a young lady where there are repetitions ('O', 'I', 'but', 'didn't'):

'O, I never said such a thing!'
'O, but you did!'
'Didn't she say that?'
'Yes. I heard her.'
'O, there's a...fib!'

Such repetition is technically called "incremental repetition" because the repetitions are accumulated step by step.

(ii) "Clay": In the very second paragraph of the story, while describing Maria, the narrator repeats the word 'very' three times in a sentence of normal length: "Maria was a very, very small person indeed, but she had a very long nose and a very long chin." In giving us further description of Maria, the narrator repeats phrases: "the tip of her nose nearly met the tip of her chin" and "the tip of her nose nearly met the tip of her chin" and "the tip of her nose nearly met the tip of her chin".

(iii) And in "The Dead", the name of "Lily" is repeated nine times, the word "snow" is repeated six times ("snowing" occurs once) and the word "cold" is repeated three times. A cautious and finical writer that he is, Joyce cannot do such repetitions without any significance behind doing so.

3. "Hazing". We are using here the term "hazing" in the sense of "puzzling", "deceiving" or "cheating" in an amusing way, somewhat like we use the word "kenning". Like Ernest

Hemingway, Joyce sometimes camouflages or "hazes" a character by not using his or her fictional name but by using pronouns or epithets, instead. A few examples are given below.

(i) "A Little Cloud": Joyce never gives us the name of the protagonist but denotes him with an epithet—"Little Chandler." And he sometimes drops this epithet and uses pronouns instead—"him", "his", "he."

(ii) "Counterparts": In the beginning of this story, Joyce tells us the name of the protagonist—Farrington—but then for the following around six pages he refers to the protagonist by the word "man".

(iii) "A Mother": Among the *artistes* who are to perform in the Ancient Concert Rooms, there is Mr. Hendrick. Joyce in most times refers to him as "the baritone" because he has a deep-toned male voice between bass and tenor.

4. Foreign or non-English Words and Phrases. James was a polyglot, knowing around 40 languages (some say, more). Naturally, he had a leaning towards using more than one language. In *Dubliners*, he has used words and phrases of tongues outside English, such as Irish (mostly), Latin, and French. Instances are the following:

(i) "A Little Cloud": *Parole de honneur* (French: meaning "word of honour") and *deochan-doruis* (*or doch-an-doris*) (Scottish: meaning "a parting drink or stirrup cup").

(ii) "Counterparts": *smahan* (Irish: meaning "a smattering").

(iii) "Two Gallants": *Lothario* (Irish: meaning "a man who behaves selfishly and irresponsibly in his sexual relationship with women").

(iv) "Ivy Day in the Committee Room": *Shoneens* (Irish; derogatory: meaning "one who prefers English attitudes, customs or lifestyle to Irish ones").

(v) "Grace": *bostooms* (Irish: meaning "fools").

(vi) "The Dead": *Beannacht libh* (Irish: meaning "goodbye").

5. Neologism. In "Grace", Joyce has coined a new term: "peloothered". The word is supposedly Hiberno-English, born out of a humorous dialectical corruption of "blootered" and "polluted", meaning drunk or thoroughly drunk.

6. Nonsense Word and Phrase. Joyce has also used at least two nonsense words in *Dubliners*.

(i) "Eveline": In the last moments before her death, Eveline's mother constantly pronounced the nonsense phrase: "Derevaun Seraun! Derevaun Seraun!"

(ii) "A Little Cloud": At the close of the story, Little Chandler's little son began to scream at his threatening order: "Stop!" His angry wife rushed to succour the kid, snatched the kid and pappered him mumbling repeatedly the nonsense word "Lambabaun!"

Joyce's using of hazing, foreign words and phrases, neologisms, and nonsense words and phrases have made *Dubliners* somewhat writerly.

Lastly, what we must say about Joyce's style is that it is "so uniquely his" (Bosinelli, 80).

DISCUSSIONS OF THE STORIES

1. The Sisters

(1)

This is the beginning story in *Dubliners* that may be said to announce the programme of, and to set the tone of, the whole of it. The programme is to expose the morally degraded *status quo* of Dublin at the very beginning of the 20th century as manifested in three cardinal national syndromes: paralysis, corruption and death. This story may also be taken to be the starting point of Joyce's writing career. Joyce, while he sent the earlier version of this story for publication in the August 1904 issue of the *Irish Homestead*, signed it not as "James Joyce" but as "Stephen Daedalus" (*a soi-disant pseudonym of Joyce*) and this Stephen Daedalus (or Dedalus) we come across next in *A Portrait of the Artist as a Young Man* (1914) where he is the hero. Further, the character of the uncle of the unnamed narrator of this story Joyce modelled on his own father John Stanislaus Joyce. So we see that early in his creative life Joyce began intruding in his fictions and continued to be present everywhere in his works, all disguised. The order of composition of the stories and the sequences in which these stories were arranged in *Dubliners*, as told earlier, are not the same. For instance, "An Encounter" was the ninth story composed but in the collection it is the second story. But, uniquely, "The Sisters" is the first story both in the order of composition and in the order of arrangement in the collection. "The Sisters" was composed 1904 and in 1905 Joyce rewrote it end to end.

Joyce arranged the 15 stories of *Dubliners*, as said before, very cunningly and with a definite plan. Not only did he sequences the stories in four chronological groupings—"childhood", "adolescence", "maturity but not public life", and "maturity and public life"—but also in a circular design, to wit, he began with death (in "The Sisters") and closed with death (in "The Dead") or began with two sisters (in "The Sisters": Nannie Flynn and Eliza Flynn) and closed with the same number of sisters (in "The Dead": Julia Morkan and Kate Morkan). These two stories are such that their titles might be interchanged without affecting the matter of the stories. Or, we may think that "The Sisters" is the prologue of Dubliners and "The Dead" is the epilogue or coda of it.

(2)

The five characters in this story are:

1. Rev. James Flynn or Father Flynn, 65, a priest, had three strokes and was now dead. So, in the story, he is a voiceless character (voiceless characters are to be found throughout Joyce's work). Flynn is an erratic character, and, perhaps, a corrupted character (of homosexuality with the narrator boy), too. He was long suffering from spiritual paralysis. His two sisters—Nannie Flynn and Eliza Flynn—used to take care of him. We know about Father Flynn from the narrator boy, Eliza Flynn and "old Cotter" Flynn's neighbour.

2. Eliza Flynn. Eliza is one of the two sisters of Father Flynn, the other being Nannie Flynn. These two sisters are the source of the title of this story—"The Sisters". Eliza and Nannie ran a shop of umbrellas and children's booties under the vague name of Drapery. It was these two sisters who looked after Father Flynn.

3. Nannie Flynn. She is another sister of Father Flynn. In the story, she has no speech and so she is also a voiceless character.

4. Old Cotter. An old man and a neighbour of the Flynn, who knew much about Father Flynn.

5. The narrator. An unnamed boy.

6. Jack. He is the narrator boy's uncle.

The story opens with the narrator's apprehension about the survival of Rev. James Flynn: "There was no hope for him this time: it was the third stroke." Father Flynn often used to tell the narrator: "I am not long for this world" but he thought it was Father Flynn's idle talk. Nevertheless, the narrator boy thought that Father Flynn was paralytic. One day the narrator heard old Cotter saying that Father Flynn was "queer" and that was when the narrator was dining at his aunt's house. Old Cotter also said that the narrator boy and Father Flynn were great friends. He told the narrator boy's uncle that instead of keeping company with the Father, he should learn to run about and to box. The narrator boy could not understand the deep meaning of what the Father then said but at night he imagined that he "saw again the heavy grey face of the paralytic [Father Flynn]." The narrator boy then wondered why the image of the Father, then already deceased, "smiled continually and why the lips were so moist with spittle." The boy thought that the Father was absolving himself of the sin of his simony.

The next morning the boy went to the shop that bore the vague name of Drapery and saw there two women (Nannie Flynn and Eliza Flynn) who "were reading the card pinned on the crape." The boy also read the notice in the card:

July 1st, 1895

The Rev. James Flynn (formerly of S. Catherine's Church, Meath Street), aged Sixty-five years.

R.I.P.

[R.I.P. = *Requescat In Pace* (may he rest in peace)]

This notice persuaded the narrator boy to believe that Father Flynn was really dead. He recalled that Father Flynn used to take snuff frequently with his trembling hand. The boy wished to look at the Father now but he went back home, instead. Curiously, he felt a sense of independence after the death of Father Flynn (the "queer" character)—"a sense of freedom as if I had been freed from something by his death." Father Flynn used to teach him Latin and about certain institutions of the Church. The narrator boy recalled that when Father Flynn smiled "he used to uncover his big discoloured teeth" which was disgusting to him. All these were now like a dream to the boy.

In the evening, the boy's aunt took him to the house of Father Flynn where his dead body was kept up-stairs, coffined: "There he lay, solemn and copious, vested as for the alter, his large hands loosely retaining a chalice [communion cup or bowl]." The boy and his aunt crossed themselves and came down stairs where there were Nannie Flynn and Eliza Flynn. The aunt told Eliza about the Father: "Ah, well, he's gone to a better world." And Eliza said: "He had a beautiful death, God be praised." Nannie and Eliza did all they could while the Father was alive and after his death, and Father O' Rourke brought flowers and candlesticks and readied papers for the cemetery. Miss Eliza Flynn sighed twice and exclaimed: "Ah, poor James!" Then she told the aunt about Father Flynn: "Mind you, I noticed there was something queer [may be, homosexuality] coming over him latterly. Whenever I'd bring in his soup to him there, I'd find him with his breviary [a book containing the daily service of the R.C. Church] fallen to the floor, lying back in the chair and his mouth open." Eliza said Father Flynn wished to go down to Irishtown, along with his two sisters, Nannie and herself, where they were born, riding a new-fangled carriage. Eliza then dried her eyes with her handkerchief. The boy narrator's aunt said,

"He was a disappointed man. You could see that." Then Eliza fell into a deep reverie. After a pause, Eliza said that the chalice that was in the deceased Father's hand was broken, and that the Father himself broke it, though the others said it was the boy's fault. After that, Eliza said, Father Flynn lost his head and was found nowhere. At last he was found on the dark chapel sitting on the confession box, "wide-awake and laughing-like softly to himself." Eliza stopped and a silence fell there. The boy knew the Father was in his coffin "solemn and truculent in death, an idle chalice on his breast." Then Eliza resumed: "Wide-awake and laughing-like to himself.... So then, of course, when they saw that, that made them think that there was something gone wrong with him...."

(3)

As we have said, there was an earlier version of this story. This present version greatly differs from the earlier version. To illustrate some of the differences between the two, let us take only the two or three sentences from the beginning and ending of the two versions.

(1) The earlier version begins thus: "Three nights in succession I had found myself in Great Britain Street at that hour, as if by providence. Three nights I had raised my eyes to that lighted square of window and speculated. I seemed to understand that it would occur at night.... Each night the square was lighted in the same way, faintly and evenly. It was not the light of candles so far as I could see. Therefore, it [the death of Rev. James Flynn] had not occurred yet."

The present version begins thus: "There was no hope for him this time: it was the third stroke. Night after night I had passed the house (it was vacation time) and studied the lighted square of window: and night after night I had found it lighted in the same way, faintly and evenly. If he were dead, I thought, I would see the reflection of candles on the darkened blind, for I knew that two candles must be set at the head of a corpse."

(2) The difference between the two "beginnings" is not so much as that between the two "endings". The ending of the earlier version goes thus: "So they opened the chapel (it was late

at night) and brought in a light to look for him.... And there, sure enough, he was sitting in his confession-box in the dark, wide awake, and laughing-like—softly to himself. Then they knew something was wrong—. God rest his soul!"

The new version ends Thus: "...and I [Eliza] knew that the old priest was lying still in his coffin as we had seen him, solemn and truculent in death, an idle chalice on his breast."

"Eliza resumed:

"Wide-awake and laughing-like to himself.... So then, of course, when they saw that [the Dead Father Flynn "loosely retaining a chalice" and "something queer coming over him latterly"], that made them think that there was something gone wrong with him...."

There was a justifiable reason behind Joyce's revising the early version of "The Sisters". "This early version, which was conceived as a self-sufficient tale, was later radically revised when Joyce turned it into the 'program piece' for the entire collection [*Dubliners*]" (Scholes and Litz, 458). The programme in the "program piece" was to reveal the "paralysis", "corruption" and "(spiritual) death" that Joyce saw in Ireland. These three cardinal syndromes (of Ireland's spiritual decay) are present in "The Sisters." After two strokes, Father Flynn had become a paralytic patient; his corruption is obvious from the narrator's slant reference to "simony" in the very beginning paragraph of the story, in the oblique reference to his relation with the narrator boy, and his sitting on the confession-box or his holding the chalice in his hand; and his spiritual death can be understood from his abnormal ("queer") behaviour.

In the story, Father Flynn is a symbol of the Church of Ireland—an ineffectual, superfluous and retrogressive institution—and also stands for the impassive and servile people of Ireland.

The "Sisters" in title of the story are: Nannie Flynn and Eliza Flynn, the two aunts of the unnamed narrator boy of the story. The unnamed narrator of "The Sisters", a sensitive boy, relates the story of Father Flynn like the unnamed immature narrators of "An Encounter" and "Araby." All the three stories are of boyhood experiences.

"The Sisters" may be called, as we have said above, the prologue or signature of the whole collection, i.e., *Dubliners*, for the three cardinal terms that appear in the very first page of the story, paralysis, gnomon, and simony, are the hints that are implicitly present in all the other stories of *Dubliners* and they potentially inform the meanings of them. Paralysis is hemiplegia (*hemi*=half, and *plege*=blow) or loss of motion or sensation. In "The Sisters", Father Flynn, for instance, suffered from paralysis. In other stories, though paralysis is used not as a motor or sensory disfunction but, metaphorically, as spiritual immobility that, for instance, Eveline suffered at the close of the story "Eveline." "Simony" is an ecclesiastic term that means buying or selling ecclesiastic privileges, e.g., pardons or other benefices. The word simony may have a reference to the biblical character Simon, the evil father of Judas Iscariot. And Joyce got the term "gnomon", as said before, from Euclid.

David Daiches, in his *The Novel and the World*, praises the arrangement of the events in "The Sisters" and "Araby": "The arrangement of the events in "The Sisters" or "Araby" produces a good short story because the result is not merely a pattern qua pattern (such has no *necessary* value in literature), but a pattern which corresponds to something in experience" (Daiches, 67). The story's main focus is on spiritual paralysis—a theme that pervades the whole length of *Dunliners*. And Father Flynn is a model illustration of the spiritually paralytic, with his loss of faith and mental breakdown.

Joyce's writings are never as clear as broad day-light, but are foggy, cloudy, blurred, at least at places, and even this story is no exception. For one thing, the relation between Father Flynn and the boy narrator is not very clear: why does the boy enjoy independence after Father Flynn's death, for instance? Secondly, why is Father Flynn "queer", in what sense? Is he "slightly mad" or does he demonstrate traits of a pederast? Fargnoli and Gillespie write that "Even the story a little resists easy explanation" (Fargnoli, 49). These authors are absolutely right in their questions: why, for instance, is the title of the story "The

Sisters" and not, for instance "Father Flynn", the central figure of the story, or something else? Why the less important Eliza and lesser important Nannie are nestled in the title? However, in one sense, perhaps, the title "The Sisters" is justified because it is they who wove the web of the story, and not Father Flynn who is dead, immobile, speechless.

2. An Encounter

(1)

This is the ninth of the stories in *Dubliners*, in order of composition, but when Joyce used it in the collection for publication and arranged the stories, he placed it just after "The Sisters", making it the second story of *Dubliners*. "An Encounter" was composed sometime before 18 September 1905. Like "The Sisters" and "Araby", "An Encounter" is a childhood piece. Joyce's brother Stanislaus has given an account of the origin of this story: "In 'An Encounter', my brother describes a day's miching [truantcy] which he and I planned and carried out while we were living in North Richmond Street, and our encounter with an elderly pederast. For he was just a 'juggins' [(*slang*) a simpleton]. Neither of us could have any notion at the time what kind of 'juggins' he was, but sometimes funny in his speech and behaviour put us on our guard at once. We thought he might be an escaped madman. As he looked about fifty and had a military air, I nick-named him 'the captain of fifty' from a phrase I had seen somewhere in a Biblical quotation" (Scholes, 459-60).

(2)

The persons in this story are:

1. The unnamed narrator, a young school-going boy.
2. Joe Dillon: another boy, who was interested in adventures, like the Indians of the Wild West, though he was intended for priesthood.
3. Leo Dillon: Joe Dillon's fat younger brother—an idler.
4. Mahony: a dark-complexioned boy who carried a catapult and "used slang freely".

5. An unnamed man: "shabbily dressed" and "fairly old", who "at times spoke mysteriously". "He's a queer old josser [a slang for a blunderer, i.e., one who goes about with strugglingly violent motion]. He "had great gaps in his mouth between his yellow teeth" and had "a pair of bottle-green eyes". He was a man whom the narrator boy despised.

"An Encounter" is an easier story than "The Sisters". In both the stories, the narrator is a young boy and in both the stories there are encrypted suggestions of paederasty, like in Ernest Hemingway's short story "A Simple Enquiry" where a senior soldier, a Major, calls a 19-year-old orderly into his room and enquiries about his personal life with homosexual intent.

The unnamed narrator boy begins the story thus: "It was Joe Dillon who introduced the Wild West [the western-most rocky part of America] to us." Joe Dillon had some knowledge of the culture of adventure of the Indians of the Wild West from his reading of books about that part of America. Joe Dillon used to play Indian battles with his young fat brother Leo after school "in his back garden". Once the narrator planned a day's miching [truancy (from school)] along with Leo Dillon and Mahony. Mahony's "big sister" wrote an excuse for Mahony and Leo for the school. Each of the three boys saved up sixpence for the adventure.

On the next morning, the three walked along the North Strand Road and ultimately came near the river. They reached the quay and crossed the river Liffey in a ferry boat and landed on the opposite quay. The narrator was curiously looking out to see if foreign sailors had green (jealous) eyes and found only one tall man with green eyes. The team then wandered into Ringsend. They "bought a bottle of raspberry lemonade for each. Refreshed by this, Mahony chased a cat down a lane, but the cat escaped into a wild field. It was too late for them to visit the Pigeon House, which was in their adventure project, for they had to return home before four o'clock lest their adventure should be discovered. They were sitting on the bank for some time silently when the narrator "saw a man approaching from the far end of the field." The narrator boy was then chewing "green stems on which girls tell fortunes." The man "walked with one hand upon his hip and in the other hand he held a stick with which he tapped the turf lightly."

He was "shabbily dressed" and "fairly old." He sat down beside the boys and told them that "one's life was undoubtedly one's schoolboy days" and that he wished to be young again. He asked the boys if they read "the poetry of Thomas Moore [1779-1852: Irish lyric poet] or the works of Sir Walter Scott [1771-1832: Scottish poet, novelist, playwright, and exemplar of European literary romanticism] and Lord Lytton [1831-91: British politician and poet]." The narrator boy pretendingly said he did. The narrator boy "saw that he [the old man] had great gaps in his mouth between his yellow teeth." The old man asked the boys which of them had the most sweethearts. "Mahony mentioned lightly that he had three totties [three little girls]." The man then asked the narrator boy how many sweethearts he had and he said he had none. They did not believe the narrator and said he must have at least one. Then Mahony pertly questioned the man how many sweethearts he had and the man confessed that when he was their age "he had lots of sweethearts."

The narrator boy wondered why, when the old man not befittingly said that when he was young he had lots of sweethearts, "he shivered once or twice as if he feared something or felt a sudden chill." The old man began to speak to the boys about the nice soft hair and hands of girls. He said he liked nothing so much "as looking at a nice young girl." The narrator says about the old man: "At times he spoke as if he was simply alluding to some fact that everybody knew, and at times he lowered his voice and spoke mysteriously, as if he were telling us something secret which he did not wish others to overhear." At last the old man slowly walked to the end of the field. Mahony commented about the man: "He's a queer old josser [clergyman or blunderer]!" The old man then went a little distance away but, after a while, came back and sat down beside the boys. Mahony caught sight of the cat that had earlier escaped him and he once again pursued the cat but soon stopped and loitered up to the far end of the field. Now the old man began to speak to the narrator boy. He said that rough boys ought to be soundly whipped. Astounded, the narrator boy looked up at his face and saw that he had "a pair of bottle-green eyes". The man now said that if a boy talked to his sweetheart, "he would whip him and whip him" so the boy would not talk to girls. "He said that there was nothing in this world he would like so well as that." He said this in a way "as if he was unfolding some elaborate mystery."

Now the narrator boy rose, bade good day to the old man and calmly went up the slope with palpitating heart while afraid that the old man would catch him "by the ankles." When the boy reached the top of the slope, he shouted at Mahony: "Murphy!] [Mahony's other name was Murphy.] Mahony hallooed in answer and ran towards him. The boy thought Mahony was running as if to bring an aid for him. The narrator boy concludes the story saying that he was repentant because in his heart he had "always despised him [Mahony] a little."

(3)

In both "The Sisters" and "An Encounter", there is something secret, shady, mysterious: in "The Sisters" mystery (probably that of pederasty) surrounds Father Flynn and in "An Encounter" it is the "fairly old" man, with repulsive yellow teeth who is wrapped up in secrecy (including probably that of pederasty). Both Father Flynn and the "fairly old" man are described as "queer", and both are supposed to be suffering from paralysis (an important theme of Joyce with reference to Ireland)—Father Flynn's hand trembles and the "fairly old" man of "An Encounter" walks with a stick.

In "An Encounter", one thing of special interest is that Joyce here uses a number of colours: blue, grey, black, green, greenish-black (the suit of the "fairly old" man) and, especially, yellow (the repulsive colour of the "fairly old" man's teeth). The use of so many colours does not seem to be of great effect, except yellow, which is the repulsive colour of the 'fairly old' man in "An Encounter".

About the plot and themes of "An Encounter", Fargnoli and Gillespie justly write: "The plot of 'An Encounter' revolves around the escapades of two young boys who spend a day 'miching', i.e., skipping school classes to wander about the city. The opening paragraphs set the emotional tone of the story with themes of freedom, adventure, and conflict introduced through allusions to America's Wild West and the mock Indian battles the boys would arrange after school. There is also a sense of restlessness and boredom ['The mimic warfare of the evening became at last as wearisome to me as the routine of school in the morning because I wanted real adventures to happen to myself', tells us the boy narrator]" (Fargnoli, 50).

William York Tindall says that "An Encounter" is a continuation of "The Sister", though "An Encounter" is less enigmatic than "The Sister." Tindall produces arguments to prove his theory of continuation: "There are evident connections between these stories. Both are told in first person *by the same boy* (italics mine), who, a little older now, is a student at Belvedre of great Denmark Street. Both stories are archetypal. The first employs the image of the father, lost missed, but not yet sought. The second employs the more active archetype of the journey or, rather, of the quest, a journey with a goal" (Tindall, 17). The quest here, as Tindall implies, is the narrator's quest for the Pigeon (symbol of the Holy Ghost) House in the Dublin's light and power (symbol of God) station. Tindall's second argument is that the two pederasts of the two stories betray some similarities between them in appearance and behavior. Both are old, both are priests, both are physically infirm (paralytic or, at least paretic), both show ugly and yellowed teeth, both present elaborate and partly incomprehensible mystery (of undeciphered wrong done), and lastly, both are queer (Father Flynn in "the Sisters" has "something queer" and the old man in "An Encounter" is "a queer old josser"). No two stories in *Dubliners* are so similar.

An essential feature of Joyce's stories is that each story ends with a certain sudden and quick revelation, which Joyce calls epiphany. Accordingly, "An Encounter" closes with the narrator boy's experience of an epiphany, which is his altered recognition of Mahony (Murphy). At the fag end of the story, he, for fear that the mysterious hag-like old man (the pederast) may seize him "by the ankles", quickly "reached the top of the slope" with beating heart and turned round and even though he did not see Mahony around called out: “Murphy!” Mahony hallooed in answer. The narrator boy then tells us: “How my heart beat as he came running across the field to me! He ran as if to bring me aid. And I was penitent; for in my heart I had always despised him a little.” The boy's previous image of Mahony collapsed when at this split-second he saw Mahony in a quite new light and presumed him to be bringing an aid for him.

3. Araby

(1)

Of the fifteen stories of *Dubliners*, “Araby” is, perhaps, the most anthologized story of James Joyce. It is Joyce's eleventh story in order of composition, but when Joyce arranged the stories for *Dubliners*, he placed it just after “An Encounter”, making it the third story in the collection and the last one in the group of boyhood stories in it. “Araby” was written in October 1905. Interestingly, like the two foregoing stories, “Araby” is also narrated by an immature (preadolescent) boy. Secondly, in all these three stories there is a priest or a mention of priesthood. For instance, Father Flynn was a priest (“The Sisters”); Joe Dillon “had a vocation for the priesthood” (“An Encounter”); and the former tenant of the house where the unnamed narrator boy of “Araby” lived was a priest. One justifiable reason of keeping “Araby” in the third place in the group of three boyhood stories is perhaps the fact that in this story the unnamed narrator is supposedly older than the unnamed narrators of “The Sisters” and “An Encounter”, for in the narrator of “Araby” we find in the narrator a drive for love of a girl, which is quite absent in the previous two childhood stories.

(2)

The persons in the story are:

1. The unnamed school-going narrator: the principal character.
2. Mangan, a friend of the narrator, who inspired the narrator to visit the bazaar called Araby.

3. An unnamed young girl whose beauty attracted the narrator. She is sister of Mangan.
4. Mrs. Mercer was an old, garrulous woman.
5. The narrator's uncle (modeled on Joyce's father, John Stanislaus Joyce) and aunt.

The house in which the narrator lived was on the North Richmond Street, a cul-de-sac. The earlier tenant of the house was a priest, who had left behind a few dog-eared yellow-coloured books, such as Walter Scott's *The Abbot* (a prose romance) and *The Devout Communicant* (a religious book) and *The Memoirs of Vidocq* (detective Vidocq's memoirs in French). The narrator loved the memoirs the most. In the opposite house, lived Mangan and his sister. The narrator used to stealthily observe her from a shady vantage point, while his heart would palpitate. When she would come outdoors, the narrator used to walk hurriedly to follow her, holding his school books tightly. This happened morning after morning, so that her name itself was as if a summons.

On Sunday evenings, the narrator had to go to the bazaar with his aunt to carry some parcels. In the bazaar, he would hear shop-boys sing litanies and street-singers sing the song "*come-all-you*" about O'Donovan Rossa, or sing "a ballad about the troubles in our native land [Ireland]." [The song "*come-all-you*" is a Fenian ballad, i.e., a ballad of Ireland's independence from English domination, composed by O'Donovan Rossa. The ballad comprises eight stanzas, each stanza containing four verses. The beginning verse of the ballad is: "Come all ye rave United Men, who'd right your country's wrong."]

The narrator tells us that the girl's name would sometimes crop up in his prayers and often his eyes would be full of tears while he recalled her. He thought if he would ever speak to her he would not know how to express his adoration of her. He thought "my body was like a harp and her words and gestures were like fingers running upon the wires." One evening he went into the back drawing-room and, while it was drizzling, he saw a distant lamp gleaming below. Then the girl, Mangan's sister, spoke to him. She asked him if he was going to the bazaar, the *Araby*, and that she would like to go there. But she told him that she would not be able to go to the bazaar "because there would be a retreat [retirement for religious meditation for sometime] that week in her convent." In the light of the lamp, the narrator deeply enjoyed the beauty of the white curve of her neck and of her lit up hair.

> "It's well for you", she said.
>
> "If I [the narrator] go", I said, "I will bring you something."

Since that assurance of his given to Mangan's sister, the narrator was very anxiously waiting for the next Saturday to go to *Araby* (the bazaar) to buy that "something" for the girl. Even the "syllables of the word "Araby" was to him an "Eastern enchantment". He asked his aunt for permission to go to *Araby* on Saturday night. She agreed but suspected that his ecstatic enthusiasm might be due to the secret rites of Freemasonry (a secret non-religious, non-political association mostly of stone-masons, bounded together by sympathetic and ethical injunctions).

On Saturday morning, the narrator boy went to the upper part of the house, looked down and saw the "dark house where she lived" but he saw nothing but only the "curved neck" of her conjured up by his own imagination. In the evening, the boy saw Mrs. Mercer waiting for his uncle to partake of the dinner. It was after eight o'clock and yet he did not arrive. His aunt told him: "I'm afraid you may put off your bazaar for this night of Our Lord." At nine o'clock his uncle returned and sat for dinner. The narrator boy asked him for money to go to the bazaar because his uncle earlier had forgotten to give him money. His uncle first meant to dissuade him from going to the bazaar at that late hour, but then told his aunt: "Can't you give him the money and let him go? You've kept him late enough as it is." The boy's uncle said that he was sorry to forget to give him money and said that recreation was necessary for boys after study: "All work and no play makes Jack a dull boy." After this, his uncle asked him where he was going (with the money) and the boy answered truly. Then, very significantly, his uncle asked him if he knew the poem "*The Arab's Farewell to his Steed*". ["*The Arab's Farewell to his Steed*" is a ballad by the English writer and social activist Caroline Elizabeth Sarah Norton (1808-77).] The ballad consists of six stanzas, each stanza having eight lines. The first and the second stanzas of the ballad may suffice to give us an idea about what the uncle of the boy meant to say to the boy. The first stanza runs thus:

> "My beautiful! my beautiful! that standest meekly by,
> With thy proudly arched and glossy neck, and dark and fiery eye,
> Fret not to roam the desert now, with all thy winged speed;
> I am not to mount on thee again—thou'rt sold, my Arab steed!
> Fret not with that impatient hoof—snuff not the breezy wind—
> The further that thou fliest now, so far am I behind;
> The stranger hath thy bridle-rein, thy master hath his gold—
> Fleet-limbed and beautiful, farewell; thou'rt sold, my steed, thou'rt sold."

In the first stanza, the owner of the horse dreams that he has sold his steed against *gold* and repents. In the last stanza, there is the reversal—the dream of the owner vanishes and he comes to himself. He throws away the buyer's *gold* and grips first the hold of the horse in joy as the last three lines of the concluding stanza will tell us:

> "'Tis false, 'tis false, my Arab steed! I fling them back their *gold*!
> Thus, thus, I leap upon thy back, and scour the distant plains;
> Away! who overtakes us now shall claim thee for his pains!"

The gold from the buyer, though attractive to the gullible dreamy boy, was false and ephemeral. [When his senses came back to him, he realized the truth of it all.] The uncle of the boy wanted, through his reference to the above ballad, to tell the boy that he was going to the bazaar or, rather, going to love Mangan's sister, in an exotically dreamy state, and that what he was running after was but illusory, was a mirage.

However, the narrator boy took a florin (a two-shilling piece), supposedly from his aunt, and took a seat in a third-class empty train carriage, and reached the bazaar which he recognised from the "magical name"—*Araby*—displayed on a large building. He entered the bazaar through a turnstile "handing a shilling to a weary-looking man". Almost all the stalls of the bazaar were then closed, it being "ten minutes to ten", and a "silence like that which pervades a church after a service" prevailed over the bazaar.

The befuddled narrator tells us: "Remembering with difficulty why I had come, I went over to one of the stalls and examined porcelain vases and flowered tea-sets." There he saw "a young lady talking and laughing with two young gentlemen", apparently the two gentlemen were flirting with the lady. Seeing the narrator boy, the lady asked him if he wanted to buy anything, just out of her sense of duty. The boy gazed at the great porcelain jars that "stood like eastern guards" and almost inaudibly said: "No, thank you." The young lady resumed talking with the two gentlemen. The boy then walked down the middle of the bazaar. The light in most part of the bazaar went out, which signaled the closure of the bazaar. The upper part of the hall was drowned in utter darkness. The narrator boy ended his story thus: "Gazing up into the darkness I saw myself as a creature driven and derided by vanity; and my eyes burned with anguish and anger." The boy earlier felt proud ("vanity") before Mangan's sister when he told her that he would bring her "something" from the bazaar ("*Araby*") but when he found the bazaar virtually completely closed he suffered extreme mental pain ("anguish") and became angry against himself for showing her so much of pride. The boy now recognized his earlier ineffectual swelling pride in his heart full well, and this was his "epiphany".

(3)

Joyce, we repeat, very intelligently arranged the 15 stories of *Dubliners*. Let us look at the first batch of three stories. The boy narrators in "The Sisters" and "An Encounter" seem to be younger to the boy narrator of "Araby" because the earlier two do not show the instinct of love of the opposite sex as does the narrator of "Araby". The narrator of "Araby", supposedly, is in the early adolescence stage, and his love of Mangan's sister is of that stage. It may be noted that just immediately after "Araby" Joyce placed the clearly adolescence story of "Eveline" where the pull of love is much stronger than in "Araby." [Joyce named the character Mangan after the ancient famous Irish poet James Clarence Mangan 1803-49.]

The story-line of "Araby" is quite straight like that of the next story "Eveline": it begins in the narrator boy's falling into the illusive love of Mangan's sister, moves forward without carrying along any floss on the way, and ends in his disillusionment. Joyce, in this story, has very well captured the psychology of the pre-adolescent boy's precocious love of the girl and the straightened circumstance in which he strives to proffer a loving gift to her. In this sense, there are not more than two or three stories in *Dubliners* that can be compared with "Araby" in aesthetic beauty.

The two core themes of *Dubliners*—spiritual paralysis and spiritual death of Dublin—are commendably presented even in this story of Romantic love through the shattering experience of the boy. The paralysis and death are illustrated through symbols such as: the "blindness" of North Richmond Street; the death of the priest who was earlier the tenant of the house where the narrator boy now lived; an "uninhabited house of two stories" standing at the blind end of the North Richmond Street; the other houses of the Street gazing "at one another with brown imperturbable faces" like paralytic patients; the "curled and damp" pages of the books of the deceased priest; and the priest's "rusty" bicycle-pump. Thus, we see that in the two beginning paragraphs James very craftily painted a picture that speaks of spiritual paralysis and spiritual death. The story also ends with a sense of spiritual darkness and physical immobility, which symbolize paralysis and death. This happened when the light went out in the bazaar and the "upper part of the hall was now completely dark" and the disillusioned narrator boy stood flummoxed for a little while in the middle of the bazaar, immobile. However, thus through the suggestions of spiritual paralysis and physical immobility of the narrator boy, Joyce speaks of the paralysis and immobility of or Ireland.

The title of the story, "Araby", deserves attention. "Araby" is the name of the bazaar where the narrator experiences an epiphany (in the sense of Joyce) that sends him the message that his love of Mangan's sister will end in futility. The word "bazaar" originated from the Persian (Iranian) *bazaar*, meaning "market." The title of the story, therefore, suggests some connection of it with the Orient (or the western and southern part of Asia). Again, the term "Araby" is derived from the word "Arab" which also points to the East or Orient (L. *oriri* = to rise) where the sun (figuratively, "hope") rises. The suggestion of the Orient also occurs near the end of the story where we hear that when the bazaar was about to be completely closed there stood a lone stall still lighted and in that stall "great jars" "stood like *eastern* guards" (*emphasis added*). Fargnoli and Gillespie expatiate on Joyce's use of the terms "bazaar" and "Araby" and Joyce's suggestion of Orientalism in "Araby": "In Joyce's time such bazaars were fairly common in Dublin. In fact, a "Grand Oriental Fete" was actually held in May 1894 ["Araby" was written in October 1905 and in 1894 Joyce was in Dublin], which corresponds with the approximate time of the story. Postcolonial interpretive theory has given readers a sophisticated sense of Orientalism, but nonetheless one needs to avoid making an over-determined response to the setting. When Joyce wrote the story, the word *Araby* would be read as a variation of the term Arabia; applied to the bazaar, it would immediately evoke the exotic overtones of a distant and mysterious land. At the same time, the commercial banality of the fair would be apparent to all but the most determined idealistic *Dubliner*" (Fargnoli and Gillespie, 51).

Prof. Harry Stone rightly says that there are autobiographical elements in "Araby." We have already seen that in all probability when Joyce was 12 years old he visited the "Grand Oriental Fete", the supposed model of "Araby." Prof. Stone says that like the narrator boy of "Araby", the young Joyce at one time lived exactly on North Richmond Street and the Street was exactly as described in this story. But more than that, the similarity between the narrator boy and the young Joyce lies in the spiritual sphere. Prof. Stone writes: "The boy in 'Araby' like the youthful Joyce himself, must begin to free himself from the nets and trammels of society [recall his and the girl's constraints imposed on their movements by their respective families].... The boy must dream 'no more of enchanted days.' He must forgo the shimmering mirage of childhood, begin to see things as they really are. But to see things as they really are is only a prelude. For in the distance lies his appointed (but yet unimagined) task: to encounter the reality of experience and 'forge the uncreated conscience of his race.' The whole of the struggle, of course, is set forth in *A Portrait of the Artist as a Young Man*. 'Araby' is the identical struggle at an earlier stage, 'Araby' is a portrait of the as a young boy" (Scholes and Litz, 305-06). And another autobiographical element in the character is Mangan. Prof. Stone writes: "In 'Araby' as in Joyce's life, Mangan is an important name. In life Mangan was one of Joyce's favorite Romantic poets, a little-known Irish poet who pretended that many of his poems were translations from the Arabic although he was totally ignorant of that language. Joyce championed him in a paper delivered as a Pateresque twenty-year-old before the Literary and Historical Society of University College, Dublin, and championed him again five years later, in a lecture at the Universita Popolare in Trieste, as 'the most significant poet of the modern Celtic world, and one of the most inspired singers that ever used the lyric form in any country'" (Scholes and Litz, 308). However, Ezra Pound unreservedly praised Joyce's prose, economy in composition, and realism in all his works, including this story. But he is effusive, so to say, in his commendation of "Araby": "Mr. Joyce's 'Araby', (for instance), is much better than a 'story', it is a vivid writing" (Deming, 67).

4. Eveline

(1)

"Eveline" has something very exceptional: it is the story which, when Joyce sent it for publication in the September

10, 1904 issue of *Irish Homestead*, he signed not as "James Joyce" but as "Stephen Daedalus" (later on Dedalus)—his *nom de plume* and the name of the hero of *A Portrait of the Artist as a Young Man* and also the name of the protagonist of the 767-page modern epic novel *Ulysses*. "Eveline" is the fourth story of *Dubliners* and the first story in the group of four adolescence stories in the book. And, unlike the previous three boyhood stories that are written from the first person perspective, "Eveline" is the first story that is written from the third person perspective, from which perspective all the rest stories of *Dubliners* are done. "Eveline" is a story of hard pressing indecision, which may be reflected in the title of it—the line that divides day and night (Eveline = evening line)—the indecision that the protagonist Eveline Hill suffers. The indecision is between the call of duty and the magnetic pull of romantic love. "Eveline" is the shortest of all the stories of *Dubliners*.

Joyce heavily revised three of the fifteen stories of *Dubliners*: "The Sisters", "The Boarding House" and "Eveline". In "Eveline", he revised the earlier version of the story, published in the *Irish Homeland*, on two points: one, he replaced words and phrases not quite appropriate with more effective ones; and two, he added material that bears symbolic undertone. However, here we will deal with the final version of the story that is there in the 1914 publication of *Dubliners* (reprinted in 1926 by Penguin Books).

(2)

The principal characters of "Eveline" are:

1. Eveline Hill. She is the protagonist of the story—a nineteen-year-old spinster with whom Frank fell in love and urged her to elope with him. Entangled in the family's network of constraints and bound by her sense of duty, she was gasping for freedom from home. Eveline was modelled on the daughter of Ned Thornton, a tea-taster and a neighbor of Joyce in North Richmond Street.

2. Frank. He is a young man from Buenos Aires (Argentina, South America). He fell in love of Eveline and decided to elope to Buenos Aires with the willing Eveline but at the last moment of embarking the boat his fiancée, Eveline, impassively stayed behind. The focus of the story remaining almost wholly on Eveline, Frank's character being almost subdued.
3. Eveline's Father. The unnamed father of Eveline cruelly dominated over her. He is a mute character.
4. Harry and Ernest. Two brothers of Eveline, also mute.

The story "Eveline" begins with a sullen, morose and sedate picture of Eveline: "She sat at the window watching the evening invade the avenue. Her head was leaned against the window curtains, and in her nostrils was the odour of dusty cretonne. She was tired." She was thinking gravely about her past against her present, her past being brighter than her present. So much has changed, not only in her family but in the surrounding of her house. Her family now consisted of her father, her two brothers—Ernest and Harry—and herself, her mother being dead. There was a field near their "brown houses" in the past but now new "bright brick houses" had risen up in that field, where youngsters would in the past play but some of them were now either dead or had gone abroad. "Everything changed." Now she was going to go away like the others, to leave her home (*emphasis added*) to be free from the trammel of her house.

Eveline was thinking like that moodily, when the unpronounced but thought about word "Home!" struck her like lightning, like the word "Forlorn!" in Keats "Ode to a Nightingale" struck the poet. She looked back to search her passionately familiar objects in the house, for instance, the photograph of the priest, her father's friend, who was then in Melbourne, and the "coloured print of the promises made to Blessed Margaret Mary Alacoque" hung on the wall. Now she was going away leaving home behind but these and other familiar objects, emotionally attached to her, were pulling her back.

She fell in love with Frank and agreed to elope with him. She was now re-thinking about her decision: "Was that wise? She tried to weigh each side of the question." On the one hand, "she had shelter and food" here in the house. On the other hand, she had to do hard works in the house and also in the grocery ("Stores") where she served. She was thinking how her acquaintances would interpret her departure; she thought they would think her action was wrong, because in her absence her place in the grocery would be filled up by Miss Gavan, her inferior. Nevertheless, she would not be very sorry to leave the grocery because in her married life in a distant land (Buenos Ayres), people would respect her and she would be far away from her father's violence and, also, no more she would have to involve herself in altercations ("invariable squabble") with her father for money on Saturday nights. On Saturday nights, she recalled, her father would unjustly accuse her of squandering his hard earned money. Further, "She had hard work to keep the house together and to see that the two young children [Harry and Ernest] who had been left to her charge [by her dead mother] went to school regularly and got their meals regularly. It was hard work—a hard life—but now that she was about to leave it she did not find it a wholly undesirable life."

Eveline was now going to be Frank's wife and going with him by night-boat to his home in Buenos Ayres. She was fondly recalling how they fell into love with one another. Though it was a long time ago, it seemed to her to be a few weeks back. She first saw him standing at the gate of the "Stores" where she worked and he wore a peaked cap and his "hair tumbled forward over a face of bronze." After that they used to meet every evening. "He took her to see *The Bohemian Girl* and she felt elated as she sat in an unaccustomed part of the theatre with him." *The Bohemian Girl* is an opera based on a romantic plot of Cervantes that "involves kidnapping and hidden identities" of Arline and Thaddeus. "Arline, the Bohemian girl, is stolen by Gypsies at the age of six and lives with them for twelve years, tended by Thaddeus, an exiled Polish nobleman who had fallen deeply in love with her. Although Arline does not know the secret of her high birth she is vaguely aware that she is not of the Gypsy race, and she tells Thaddeus of her dreamlike memories in the famous song 'I dreamt that I dwelt in Marble Halls.' Thaddeus, not wishing to lose Arline, does not reveal her origins, but she is ultimately recognized by her father the count and restored to him. She remains true to her lover, and Thaddeus finally claims her hand by proving himself to be of noble birth" (Scholes and Litz, 465).

People understood that Frank was courting Eveline when Frank, who was a little fond of music and song, sang the love song "The lass that loves sailor." "The Lass That Loves A Sailor" is a song by Charles Dibdin (1745-1814). The song consists of three stanzas, each stanza having nine verses. The first stanza of the lyric may suffice to give us the importance and significance of the song:

> The moon on the ocean was dimmed by a ripple,
> Affording a chequered delight,
> The gay jolly tars [sailors] passed the word for the tipple
> And the toast, for it was Saturday night.
> Some sweetheart or wife, he loved as his life,
> Each drank, and wished he could hail her,
> But the standing toast that pleased the most,
> Was the wind that blows, the ship that goes,
> And the lass that loves a sailor.

Hearing Frank sing the song, Eveline would feel "pleasantly confused." Frank loved her deeply and used to call her "Poppens" for fun, and would tell her "tales of distant countries" like Othello told Desdemona tales of his furious naval battles and his mortal distresses. Frank would also tell her stories of formidable Patagonians [big-footed giants]. But her father was not happy with their relation. He had forbidden her to mix with Frank and one day even quarreled with him, after which she would meet him secretly.

That evening she was sitting at the window with her two letters on her lap—one to Harry and another to her father. The letters, supposedly, were about her departure from home. In spite of his violence on her, Eveline knew her father would miss her. She was now recalling her father's brighter side: "Not long before, when she had been laid up for a day, he had read to her a ghost story and made toast for her at the fire. Another day, when their mother was alive, they had gone for a picnic to the Hill of Howth. She remembered her father was "putting on her mother's bonnet to make the children laugh." All these memories were now pulling her backwards.

She was sitting there in the same place all that while "against the window curtain, inhaling the odour of dusty cretonne", as at the beginning of the story. She recalled her mother's last moments: her mother was hearing "a melancholy air of Italy" and her father, apprehensive of her mother's imminent death, gruffly interjected: "Damned Italians! Coming over here!" And when her mother was in her "final craziness [*rigour mortis*, in medical terminology]" her mother spewed the nonsense words: "Derevaun Seraun! Derevaun Seraun!"

Eveline's dying mother's nonsense words sounded like a terror: "Escape!". Eveline, too, thought "She must escape [from the stern constraints at home]!" Frank would save her. He would give her life, perhaps love, too. But she wanted to live. Why should she be unhappy? She had a right to happiness. Frank would take her in his arms, fold her in his arms. He would save her. She rose and straight away went to the station at the North Wall. There at the station, she found Frank among the "swaying crowd." Frank held her hand and spoke to her "something" about their journey, but due to noise she could not hear anything. She caught a glimpse of the "black mass of the boat" which would carry them to Buenos Ayres. Eveline "felt her cheek pale and cold and, out of a maze of distress, she prayed to God to direct her, to show her what was her duty." Frank's and Eveline's passage had already been booked. The whistle of the boat blew mournfully. In her pressing indecision about whether to escape her home with Frank, leaving all her duties to her father and to her two young brothers (as she was charged by her deceased mother), she questioned her inner self: "Could she still draw back after all he [Frank] had done for her?" Eveline was in distress and she was feeling a tendency to vomit ("nausea"). She began to pray fervently but silently ("moving her lips").

A bell was sounded as a signal of the departure of the boat and the sound of the bell reverberated in her heart. Frank caught hold of her hand and shouted at her in urgency: "Come!" Eveline felt that all the seas of the world were mutinous about her heart and that Frank was dragging her to drown in those tumultuous seas. To save herself, she caught the iron railing with all her might and main. Frank cried out again at her: "Come!" Eveline responded in her tenor: "No! No! No!" She now precisely realised that it was impossible for her to go with him and so she clutched the iron railing with all her might, madly. In her extreme distress she sent a "cry of anguish" across the sea. Frank called her to follow him: "Eveline! Evvy!" And rushed to embark the boat that was about to depart, still calling her to follow. But Eveline shouted at him to go on without her and, like a "helpless animal" stayed back, "passive" and pale ("white") in face. And there was no sign of love or well-wishing for Frank, or even of remembrance of him, in her face.

(3)

The presence of Shakespeare is everywhere in James Joyce's works, only it is dimly visible or invisible, because buried deeply in the thickness of the works of the bard. However, in "Eveline", Shakespeare's presence may be cognized without effort. "Eveline" is perhaps a shorthand transcription of *Othello*. Summoned by the Duke and questioned about the love that grew between him and Desdemona, Othello speaks out:

> Her father lov'd me, oft invited me;
> Still question'd me the story of my life
> From year to year—the battles, sieges, fortunes,
> That I have passed.
> I ran it through, even from my boyhood days
> To th' very moment that he bade me tell it;
> Wherein I spoke of most disastrous chances,
> Of moving accidents by flood and field;
> Of hairbreadth scapes i' th' imminent deadly breach;
> . . . . This to hear
> Would Desdemona seriously incline;

She loved me for the dangers I had pass'd;
And I lov'd her that she did pity them.

(I, iii, 128-68)

And in "Eveline", we hear that Frank took Eveline to see *The Bohemian Girl* and sang to her "the lass that loves a sailor". Frank told her: "He had tales of distant countries. He had started as a deck boy at a pound a month on a ship of the Allan Line going out to Canada.... He had sailed through the Straights of Magellan and he told her stories of the terrible Patagonians." From this we understand that this was the reason why Eveline fell in love with Frank. And then how the drama and the story end? The drama ends in the deaths of Desdemona and Othello and the story closes with pains in the hearts of Eveline and Frank. The similarity between the play and the short story may be extended on another point. On the night in which Desdemona was strangled by Othello, she recalls the "willow" song that her mother's servant, Barbary, would sing:

My mother had a maid call'd Barbary:
She was in love, and he she lov'd prov'd mad,
And did forsake her. She had a song of "willow":
An old thing 'twas, but it express'd her fortune,
And she died singing it.

(*Othello*, IV, iii, 25-29)

In "Eveline", the song that Frank sang for Eveline—"the lass that loves a sailor"—has in it a distant echo of the romantic song that Desdemona recollects.

We may proceed even further. Desdemona pleads for her "divided duty" in the Senate where her father is also present:

My noble father,
I do perceive here a divided duty:
To you I am bound for life and education;
My life and education both learn me
How to respect you, you are the lord of duty but here's my husband,
And so much duty as my mother show'd
To you, preferring you before her father,

> So much I challenge that I may profess
> Due to the Moor my lord.
>
> (*Othello*, I, iii, 180-89)

Eveline promised to keep her mother's charge, when she was in her death-bed, to "Keep home together", i.e., on the one hand to take care of her old and violent father and her two young brothers, and, on the other hand, "She consented [to Frank] to go away, [and] to leave her home." Psychomachia is present both in Desdemona and Eveline, but Desdemona overcomes it with her stronger will while with her timidity Eveline became flummoxed, immobile, paralytic—a state that reflects Joyce's view of Dublin.

The ending of "Eveline" is perspicuously ambiguous, like the endings of almost all of Joyce's works, lending it to alternative interpretations: why did Eveline stay behind? Was it because her love of Frank was shallow or was her sense of duty all the more stronger? Again, why did Frank leave her behind? Was it because he was not a Romeo, because he had no love but only lust? Or what? We are not absolute. However, "Perhaps the most striking is Hugh Kenner's speculation that Frank had never intended to take Eveline to Buenos Aires but rather meant to turn her into a prostitute in Great Britain" (Fargnoli and Gillespie, 53).

"Eveline" has another special feature: in it for the first time we find Joyce's technique of exaptation, which later on he used extensively in *Ulysses*. "Exaptation and the related term cooption describe a shift in the function of a trait during evolution. For example, a trait can evolve because it served one particular function, but subsequently it may come to serve another.... Bird feathers are a classic example: initially they may have evolved for temperature regulation, but later were adapted for flight. Note here that when feathers were *initially used to aid in flight they were doing so exaptively*; however, since they have since been shaped by natural selection to improve flight, in their current state they are now best regarded as adaptations for flight" (*emphasis added*) (Wikipedia). In "Eveline", Joyce has used *Othello* exaptively as in *Ulysses* he has exaptively used Homer's *Odyssey*. The tragic love story of Othello and Desdemona and the tragic love story between Frank and Eveline are similar (but not same) and Joyce has used the former story in "Eveline" with a twist, or exaptively, as in *Ulysses* he has used the story of *Odyssey* with a flexure, i.e., exaptively.

In the three stories previous to "Eveline", Joyce used the first person narrative technique, and in "Eveline" for the first time he has used the third person narrative technique and continued to use this technique through the last story, "The Dead." "Eveline" is also the first story where for the first time we find the escape motive conspicuous. The escape motive is there in "The Encounter" where the narrator boy travels truantly, and in "Araby" where also the narrator boy shows romantic attraction to go to the bazaar, but in both the stories the escape motive is not as conspicuous as in Eveline's romantically coloured imaginary flight to Buenos Ayres (in South America).

5. After the Race

(1)

This is the second of the stories in the group of "adolescence stories" in *Dubliners*, though in order of composition it was the third of the fifteen stories of the collection. "After the Race" was first published in *The Irish Homeland* on 17 December 1904. Joyce himself was not satisfied with this story (and justifiably) as he was not content with "A Painful Case." In August 1906, Joyce wrote to his brother Stanislaus that he "would like to 'rewrite' it" and that "After the Race" and "A Painful Case" were "the two worst stories" (Scholes and Litz, 466). But the story was not re-written and it appeared in *Dubliners* in 1914 in its original form. "After the Race" Joyce enlisted in the group of "adolescence stories" but, perhaps, it could be included in the group of "public life stories" (in Dublin or Ireland), because it is about the servile submission of the poor Irish people to the rich English and their slavish desire to rub shoulders with the rich French people. However, an earlier version of this story was published in *Irish Homeland* on 17 December 1904.

(2)

The characters in the story are:

1. Jimmy Doyle. A young man of 26. His father had amassed so huge amount of property that he was alluded to in the Dublin newspapers as a "merchant prince." He is the central character.
2. Charles Segouin. A rich French man who was to start a motor establishment in Paris. He is cousin to Andre Riviere and a member of the upper class.
3. Andre Riviere. A young neatly groomed Canadian electrician. He is cousin to Charles Segouin.
4. Villona. A "huge [greatly bulky] Hungarian." He is a poor man but a brilliant pianist.
5. Routh. A young "torpid" (one "having lost the power of motion and feeling") and rich English man.
6. Farley. He owns a yacht which is a symbol of the class of the rich.

There was to be a race of cars. Cars, made in the rich Continent, were speeding through the Neas Road—where the people were poor and paralytically inactive—towards the hill at Inchicore. Poor and oppressed people gathered there to watch the race. They would be happy if the blue cars, made in Franch, would win. The race ended. The blue French cars stood second and third, and the German car, driven by a German, was declared first.

In one trimly built car four young men were seen: Charles Segouin (the owner of that car), Andre Riviere, Villona and Jimmy Doyle. They all were hilarious because of the success of the Franch cars. Jimmy Doyle "was about twenty-six years of age, with a soft, light-brown moustache and rather innocent-looking grey eyes." His nationalist father, a merchant, as told before, amassed so much money that in Dublin newspapers he was referred to as "merchant prince." Jimmy's father first sent him to a Catholic college in England, then to Dublin University for studying law, and after that to Cambridge University, and then ultimately brought him back home (supposedly unsuccessful). In Cambridge, Jimmy came close to Segouin "who had seen so much of the world and was reputed to won some of the biggest hotels in France."

After the race (from which the title of this story), the four—Jimmy, Segouin, Villona and Routh—boarded the blue car of Segouin and Segouin drove the car speedily. The four young men were hilarious, and Jimmy being the richest of them, was the most excited because he was among a company of men from the Continent, from Europe. It was pleasant for him to return to his native place (in Ireland), where "contemptable people" lived, away from such a glamorous car races. Segouin did not count Jimmy's amount of money to be great but it was true that his friendship with Jimmy arose from his "mite of Irish money." The reason of their friendship was the fact that on his father's shrewd suggestion Jimmy was going to invest money in Segouin's motor business in Paris. They now came to the awful country roads. Their "journey laid a magical finger on the genuine pulse of life and gallantly and the machinery of human nerves strove to answer the bounding courses of the blue animal [the blue car].

The car went down Dame Street and stopped near the Bank. Jimmy and Segouin alighted and a "knot of people" looked at the car with wonder in their eyes. That evening the party of the four was earlier scheduled to dine in Segouin's hotel, so Villona and Routh went home to dress. The car with Jimmy and Segouin steered out slowly for Grafton Street. Meanwhile, in the "haze of summer evening" "the city hung its pale gloves of light."

The dinner was held in Jimmy's house. Jimmy's father was feeling proud in throwing the dinner for the foreign invitees and showed "respect for foreign accomplishments." "The dinner was excellent, exquisite." "The party was increased by a young Englishman named Routh, whom Jimmy had seen with Segouin at Cambridge." Villona talked about the beauty of the English madrigal, Riviere explained to Jimmy "the triumph of the French mechanicians" [*sic*], and Segouin introduced politics, but Routh remained "torpid." The room "grew doubly hot." "The alert host at an opportunity lifted his glass to Humanity, and when the toast had been drunk he threw open a window significantly."

In the night city, the five young men now began to stroll along Stephen's Green. "They got up on a car, squeezing themselves together amid much laughter. They drove by the crowd, blended now into soft colours, to a music of merry bells. They took the train at Westland Row and in a few seconds, as it seemed to Jimmy, they were walking out of Kingstown Station. The ticket-collector saluted Jimmy; he was an old man: 'Fine night, sir!'"

"It was a serene night; the harbor lay like a darkened mirror at their feet. They proceeded towards it with linked arms, singing Cadet Roussell in chorus, stamping their feet at every: "'*Ho! Ho! Hohe, vraiment*!'" [*Cadet Roussell* is "a French drinking song with topical (and often improvised) verses, first made popular in 1782. The refrain runs: '*Ah! Ah! mais vraiment, Cadet Roussell est bon enfant*'" (scholes and Litz, 466). And *Ho! ho! Hohe, vraiment* is "a variation on the refrain of 'Cadet Roussell'" (*ibid.*).]

The five young men boarded a rowboat and made out for Farley's yacht ("the American's yacht"). "There was to be supper, music, cards.... There was a yacht piano in the cabin. Villona played a waltz [a folk or ballroom dance, in triple time, and closed position, of a couple] for Farley and Riviere." Then there was a square dance, in which Jimmy took part, and he thought that all that "was seeing life." Then there was a light supper and a Bohemian drinking. "They drank Ireland, England, France, Hungary, the United States of America." Jimmy made a speech, to which there was clapping. After that there was playing at cards, Villona playing on the piano.

Again a drinking bout. This time "They drank the health of the Queen of Hearts and the Queen of Diamonds." Jimmy obscurely understood that he was loosing in the game of cards. It was getting late. "Some one gave the toast of the yacht, *The Belle of Newport* ["Newport, Rhode Island, was a rendezvous for fashionable yachtmen"]" (Scholes and Litz, 467). The piano stopped and there was drinking once more for luck. Routh and Segouin continued playing on the cards, enthusiastically. Jimmy, though certain to loose in the game of cards, was also excited. At the end Routh won the game. Then all stood up and began their ultimate play of "talking and gesticulating" and there was uproarious cheering that shook the cabin. Jimmy Doyle knew that in the morning he will repent for his foolishness, silliness, stupidity ("folly") in rubbing shoulders with those foreigners and getting so much excited and yet at present was glad—"glad of the dark stupor that would cover up his folly." Leaning his head between his hands, Jimmy was "counting the beats of his temples" in anguish. A "shaft of grey light" of the early morning peeped through the cabin door. Villona, the "huge Hungarian" announced that the night was over: "Daybreak, gentlemen!"

(3)

"After the Race" perspicuously stands unique in the collection of the fifteen stories of *Dubliners*, in the sense that only in this story Joyce has explicitly dealt with the middle and lower-middle classes' feeling of alienation and frustration in the Irish society *vis-à-vis the nouveaux riches*. This feeling is depicted in the feeble, infirm behaviour of the new rich Jimmy Doyle and his father. A. Nicholas Fargnoli and Michael Patrick Gillespie, in their *James Joyce: A Literary Reference to His Life and Work*, write about this point about the story: "Whatever its quality, as one begins to read 'After the Race' striking differences between it and the other stories in *Dubliners* emerge almost immediately. While most of the pieces in the volume offer detailed views of the lives of Dubliners desperately struggling to survive in a hostile economic and social environment, 'After the Race' highlights the mindless prodigality of Jimmy Doyle, a popular young man from a well-to-do Dublin family" (Fargnoli and Gillespie, 54).

In "After the Race", one of the central themes of *Dubliners*, paralysis in the Irish society, has been aptly and amply portrayed in the character of Jimmy who went to different educational institutions from which he returned home without any success, without any effective activity, i.e., he had been in those institutions as a dull or insensitive student. Secondly, after the "excellent" dinner at the house of the Doyles, three of the five young men engaged themselves in music and political conversations but Jimmy kept himself away from all that. He awoke from his indolence only when the three made the milieu vibrant. Jimmy's paralytic inertness is also cognizable at the fag end of the story where we hear of his being "glad of the *dark stupor* that would cover up his folly" and see him *leaning* his elbows on the table and resting "*his head between his hands, counting the beats of his temples*" (*emphases added*).

"After the Race" is built up on another important theme—the theme of heavy economic disparity among the people of Dublin or, by implication, of Ireland. The majority of the people belonged to the middle or lower middle classes ["at Inchicore sightseers gathered in clumps" and the racing cars sped through "*this channel of poverty*" (*emphases added*)]. And there were rich people, like Jimmy's father. Money was a great concern in Ireland and this is reflected in this story. In the fifth and the sixth paragraphs, for instance, the word "money" occurs as many as six times and everywhere across the story the mite of money is perspicuous. Geographical division of Dublin on economic status is manifest in the story. At Inchicore, the racing cars ran fast through the vacant "channel of poverty" and, on the other hand, the Dame Street was abuzz with motor cars and trams.

However, the story is bereft of a well-organized plot. It seems to be a short travelogue of a group of five divergent enthusiastic young men. The title of the story, though, is interesting: "After the Race" actually begins after the race of the competing racing cars is over. The title, therefore, is appropriate too.

6. Two Gallants

(1)

To begin with, Joyce had a great "admiration" for this story. In a letter he wrote: "It is one of the most important stories in the book [*Dubliners*]. I would rather sacrifice five of the other stories (which I could name) than this one. It is the story (after *Ivy Day in the Committee-Room*) which pleases me most" (Scholes and Litz, 328). However, in the order of composition, "Two Gallants" is the 13th story of Joyce, but in the sequence of the stories in *Dubliners*, it is the sixth, and in the group in the four adolescence stories it is the third. "Two Gallants" was completed by Joyce in February 1906.

Dubliners had a troublesome (for Joyce) history of publication, and "Two Gallants" was partly responsible for the trouble. In 1905, Joyce sent 12 *Dubliners* stories to London Publisher Grant Richards (three of which were earlier rejected by *Irish Homestead*). Grant Richards objected to the word "bloody" in "Two Gallants" (the word "bloody" in the later editions of *Dubliners* occur five times: once in "Two Gallants", once in "The Boarding House", and thrice in "Grace") in the manuscript but Joyce would not budge, and so Grant Richards declined to publish *Dubliners*. After this, the manuscript was rejected by several (some say a couple of dozens) publishers. In the end, however, in January 1914 Joyce agreed to delete the trouble-making word "bloody" from the manuscript (Scholes and Litz, 328) and Grant Richards published *Dubliners* the same year.

(2)

The principal characters of the story are:

1. Lenehan. T. Lenehan is a young man. The narrator describes him thus: "Most people considered Lenehan a leech, but in spite of this reputation, his adroitness and eloquence had always prevented his friends from forming any general policy against him. He had a brave manner of coming up to a party of them in a bar and of holding himself nimbly at the borders of the company until he was included in a round. He was a sporting vagrant armed with a vast stock of stories, limericks and riddles. He was insensitive to all kinds of discourtesy. No one knew how he achieved the stern task of living, but his name was vaguely associated with racing tissues ['agglomeration, as of lies, nonsense' about horse racing]." Lenehan is one of the two "gallants" (the word is used satirically) in "Two Gallants." He is almost 31.

2. Corley. John Corley is the other "gallant" (again, the word is used satirically) of "Two Gallants." The narrator describes him Thus: "Corley was the son of an inspector of police, and he had inherited his father's frame and gait. He walked with his hands by his sides, holding himself erect and swaying his head from side to side. His head was large, globular and oily; it sweated in all weathers; and his large round hat, set upon it sideways, looked like a bulb which had grown out of another. He always stared straight before him as if he were on parade, and when he wished to gaze after someone in the street, it

was necessary for him to move his body from the hips.... He was often seen walking with policemen in plain clothes, talking earnestly. He knew the inner side of all affairs and was fond of delivering final judgments. He spoke without listening to the speech of his companions. His conversation was mainly about himself: what he had said to such a person and what such a person had said to him, and what he had said to settle the matter. When he reported these dialogues he aspirated the first letter of his name after the manner of Florentines [e.g., he pronounced 'Corley' as 'Whorely']."

Both of those two characters are worthless and malicious. Interestingly, both these characters reappear in *Ulysses* and show there, once again, their "spiritually degraded natures." For Joyce, these two characters are symbols of man's spiritual degradation, or, at least, they symbolize the spiritual degradation of the Irish society. "Two Gallants" is a story of only two degenerates (called, as told earlier, "gallants" in the sarcastic sense): T. Lenehan, a shameless sponger and a hanger-on of John Corley. The story revolves mainly round the character of Lenehan (does he represent the pre-independence Ireland as Corley does England?) whose only capital is (a store of coarse humour, ribald gossip, and horse-racing tips" (Fargnoli and Gillespie, 58). Corley ("The other" at the beginning of the second paragraph of the story) was "squat and ruddy."

One "grey warm evening of August"—It was a Sunday—Lenehan and Corley "came down the hill of Rutland Square" and started a walking tour in the city of Dublin, Corley talking all the while ("monologue") understandably about a girl. When Corley's narrative ended, Lenehan commented that what he said was very bad ("That takes the biscuit!"). Corley said his narrative was a memory of the past ("*recherché* biscuit!" Corley here referred to Marcel Proust's novel *A la recherché du temps perdu* where the taste of a biscuit soaked in tea brings back memories of the past). Lenehan asked: "And where did you pick her up, Corley?" Lenehan was meaning the girl in the narrative of Corley. As it was his wont, "Corley ran his tongue swiftly along his upper lip" and he said that one night on Dame Street he found that beautiful prostitute or disrespectful girl ("fine tart") and walked with her, and she told him that she was a domestic servant for hard menial works ("slavey"). Corley said he "put my arm round her and squeezed her a bit that night. Then next Sunday, man, I met her by appointment. We went out to Donnybrook and brought her into a field there. She told me she used to go with a dairyman.... It was fine, man."

"Corley occasionally turned to smile at some of the passing girls, but Lenehan's gaze was fixed on the large faint moon circled with a double halo." Lenehan observed Corley's leering and told him he was a gay Lothario, a proper Lothario ("a man who behaves selfishly and irresponsibly in his sexual relationship with women"). Corley made the repartee: "There's nothing to touch a good slavey." He told that he used to go with girls and spent money on them right enough and that it was "mug's game" (a fool's or simpleton's game). And then, as his habit would have it, he moistened his upper lip "by running his tongue along it" and with Lenehan he looked at the "pale disc of the moon." Then Corley said that one night he saw that slavey girl driving down Earl Street "with two fellows with her on a car." Lenehan did not buy Corley's words; he called him a "Base betrayer!"

Lenehan and Corley "passed along the railings of Trinity College." Lenehan looked at the clock over there and announced "Twenty after" and then Corley told Lenehan that the girl—the slavey—would be there all right. "Lenehan laughed quietly." Corley said he knew all the tricks to entrap such girls, and then told Lenehan that the girl he was then going to meet soon was a good prostitute: "She's a fine decent tart." The two then walked along Nassau Street and then turned into Kildare Street where a harpist was playing heedlessly before "a little ring of listeners" the melody of "*Silent, O Moyle.*" "Silent, O Moyle" is a lyric written by Thomas Moore. It refers to sea-king Lir's daughter Fionnala, who was transformed into a swan, that had human speech and could sing, was fated to wander far and wide in a lake of Ireland (Irish mythology). The lyric is as follows:

> Silent, oh Moyle, be the roar of thy water,
> Break not, ye breezes, your chain of repose,
> While murmuring mournfully, Lir's lonely daughter

Tells to the night-star her tale of woes.
When shall the swan, her death-note singing,
Sleeps, with wings in darkness furl'd?
When will heav'n, its sweet bell ringing,
Call my spirit from this stormy world?
Sadly, O Moyle, to the winter-wave weeping,
Fate bids me languish long ages away,
Yet still in her darkness doth Erin lie sleeping,
Still doth the pure light its dawning delay.
When will that day-star, mildly springing,
Warm our isle with peace and love?
When will heav'n, its sweet bell ringing,
Call my spirit to the fields above?

Lenehan and Corley walked on and reached Stephen's Green where there was noise of trams, lights and crowd. Here Corley howled: "There she [the "tart"] is!" The girl "wore a blue dress and a white sailor hat. She stood on the kerbstone, swinging a sunshade in one hand." Corley grew lively and went to meet her, leaving Lenehan behind. Lenehan asked Corley when they would meet again and Corley said: "Half ten." Lenehan asked where they would meet and Corley told him that he and the girl would come back to the "Corner of Merrion Street" where Lenehan could meet them. Lenehan's farewell words to Corley were: "Work it all right now."

Corley went to the girl straight away and talked with her. Lenehan went another way. He was recalling the girl's appearance: "She had her Sunday finery on. Her blue serge skirt was held at the waist by a belt of black leather. The great silver buckle of her belt seemed to depress the centre of her body, catching the light stuff of her white blouse like a clip. She wore a short black jacket with mother-of-pearl buttons, and a ragged black boa. The ends of her tulle collarette [*tulle*=soft, fine silk or cotton material; *collarette*=small collar or necklace] had been carefully disordered and a big bunch of red flowers was pinned in her bossom, stems upwards. Lenehan's eyes noted approvingly her stout short muscular body. Frank rude health glowed in her face, on her fat red cheeks and in her unabashed blue eyes. Her features were blunt. She had broad nostrils, a straggling mouth which lay open in a contended leer, and two projecting front teeth."

Lenehan was waiting near Shelbourne Hotel. After a while he saw Corley and the girl coming back, unnoticed by them. He saw the two "climbing the stairs of Donnybrook tram" and then he "went back the way he had come." Lenehan now looked depressed and morose. "The problem of how he could pass the hours till he met Corley again troubled him a little." He kept walking on, and then entered the bar—*Refreshment Bar*—and asked a mechanic (a skilled worker), a "slatternly girl" who waited on him:

> "How much is a plate of peas?
> "Three halfpence, sir", said the girl.
> "Bring me a plate of peas", he said, "and a Bottle of ginger beer."

Lenehan "spoke roughly in order to belie his air of gentility." The "plate of peas" was brought in and he ate the food greedily and thought of Corley and the "tart." "In his imagination he beheld the pair of lovers walking along some dark road; he heard Corley's voice in deep energetic gallantries, and saw again the leer of the young woman's mouth. This vision made him feel keenly his own poverty of purse and spirit.... Would he never get a good job? Would he never have a home of his own? He thought how pleasant it would be to have a warm fire to sit by and a good dinner to sit down to.... Experience had embittered his heart against the world. But all hope had not left him.... He might yet be able to settle down in some snug corner and live happily if he could only come across some good simple-minded girl with a little of the ready."

Lenehan "paid two pence half penny to the slatternly girl, and went out of the shop to begin his wandering again." He went into Chapel Street, then into Dame Street, and then into George's Street, where he conversed with two friends who asked him if he had seen Corley. Lenehan told them that he had spent the day with Corley and that he had been with Mac the night before in Egan's where "Holohan had stood them drinks in Egan's."

Lenehan "left his friends at a quarter to ten and went up George's street and then walked through Grafton Street where the "Crowd of girls and young men had thinned" and many groups and couples were "bidding one another Good-night." It was then ten o'clock when Lenehan reached the corner of Merrion Street, where "he expected to see Corley and the young woman return." "He wondered had Corley managed it successfully.... He suffered all the pangs and thrills of his friend's situation as well as those of his own.... All at once the idea struck him that perhaps Corley had seen her home by another way, and given him the slip. His eyes searched the street: there was no sign of them."

"Suddenly he saw them [Corley and the young woman] coming towards him. He started with delight, and keeping close to his lamp-post tried to read the result of their walk.... They did not seem to be speaking. An intimation of the result pricked him like the point of a sharp instrument. He knew Corley would fail; he knew it was no go." Corley and the young woman now "turned down Baggot Street, and he [Leheman] followed them at once, taking the other footpath. When they stopped he stopped too. They talked for a few moments, and then the young woman went down the steps into the area of a house. Corley remained standing at the edge of the path, a little distance from the front steps. Some minutes passed. Then the hall-door was opened slowly and cautiously. A woman came running down the front steps and coughed. Corley turned and went towards her. His broad figure hid hers from view for a few seconds and then she reappeared, running up the steps. The door closed on her, and Corley began to walk swiftly towards Stephen's Green."

Lenehan was also hurried towards Stephen's Green because it was beginning to rain. He saw Corley and cried out at him: "Hallo, Corley!" Corley looked back, saw Lenehan, and continued walking with the approach of the rain in his head. Lenehan shouted: "Hallo, Corley!" and went level with him. Lenehan looked at Corley's face with curiosity, but he "could see nothing there." Lenehan then asked Corley: "Did it come off?" Corley did not answer. "His features were composed in stern calm." Lenehan was baffled. A "note of menace pierced through his voice." Lenehan for the last time sternly asked Corley: "Did you try her?" Corley did not respond. He "halted at the first lamp [post] and stared grimly before him [Lenehan]. Then with a grave posture he extended a hand towards the light and, smiling, opened it slowly to the gaze of his disciple. A small gold coin shone in the palm."

(3)

We have already said that among the fifteen stories in *Dubliners*, "Ivy Day in the Committee Room" and "Two Gallants" were Joyce's most favorite. Why? Perhaps because in addition to the stories' artistic excellence, they bear his most bitter experiences of Ireland's paralysis and his "personal betrayal (it was at the time of composing the story) at its height." "Two Gallants" is a cold-blooded assault upon the conditions of Irish society. Although in a moment of nostalgia for the attractions of Dublin life Joyce could say that "'Two Gallants'—with the Sunday crowds and the harp in Kildare Street and Lenehan—is an Irish landscape", he knew full well that he had described that landscape in the "style of scrupulous meanness" which was his special barrier against sentiment and regret. Like most of the stories which deal with Dubliners of Joyce's own generation, "The Gallants" goes beyond a dispassionate rendering of Ireland's "paralysis" and treats the theme of betrayal.... When he came to write "Two Gallants" his sense of personal betrayal was as its height; only a short time before he had given full vent to his bitterness in a letter to his brother Stanistaus (witten in prose but in the form the of the poem:

> For the love of the Lord Christ change my
> Curse-o'-God state of affairs. Give me for
> Christ's sake a pen and an ink-bottle and some
> Peace of mind and then, by the crucified
> Jaysus, if I don't sharpen that little pen and
> Dip it into fermented ink and write tiny
> Little sentences about the people who betrayed
> Me and sent me to hell. After all, there are
> Many ways of betraying people.

This is the mood in which Joyce wrote his tale of Corley, a 'base betrayer', and the 'disciple' of Lenehan, and "it is a tribute to his art that such personal rancor could be transmuted into analytic irony" (Scholes and Litz, 329).

A. Walton Litz, from whom the above quotation is sourced, writes that "though in 'Two Gallants', the themes that are conspicuous are 'paralysis' (Lenehan) and 'corruption' (Corley), other subdued themes are also present in it, such as 'political frustration' and 'economic degradation'. Lenehan is dominated by Corley—the weak former is actually not the 'disciple' of the strong latter but his slave. Again the gold coin that Corley received as a tip from the 'tart' is a symbol of Ireland's or Dublin's 'economic degradation.'" Litz goes further: "Next to 'The Dead', 'Two Gallants' is Joyce's most successful synthesis of the major themes of *Dubliners*, and—as we might expect from its place in the process of composition—it is resonant with echoes from the other stories" (Scholes and Litz, 331).

"Two Gallants" is a special story indeed because in it Joyce has drawn a geographic map of Dublin, not with lines, but with not less than twenty-two street names and locations: Rutland Square, Dorset Street, Dame Street, Baggot Street, Waterhouse's clock, Donnybrook, Trinity College, Nassau Street, Kildare Street, Merrion Street, Hume Street, Stephen's Green, Shelbourne Hotel, Merrion Square, Duke's Lawn, Grafton Street, Chapel Street, City Hall, George's Street, Westmoorland Street, College of Surgeons, Ely Place and City Markets. These streets and locations verily give to the story a sense of reality.

Circularity is a motif in the story—circularity that signifies lack of direction or repetition of the same or non-progression. This circularity we find even in the first sentence of the story: "The grey warm evening of August...a mild warm air, a memory of summer, *circulated* in the streets." Secondly, Corley tells Lenehan: "First I used to go with girls, you know", said Corley, unbosoming; "girls off the South *Circular*...." Thirdly, Corley diversed from Lenehan at Stephen's Green (a down-town place) to catch the girl ("'There she is!', said Corley.") and, at the fag end of the story they *reunited at the same place*, Stephen's

Green. Fourthly, at Kildare Street the harpist was "playing to a little *ring* of listeners." Fifthly, when Corley was narrating to Lenehan his habit of catching girls of the South *Circular*, he once "gazed at the pale *disc of the moon*." And lastly, at the close of the story, Corley shows Lenehan a *circular* gold coin (*all emphases are added*).

"Two Gallants" is not an easy read; at almost every turn of it there is an allusion that contributes to the meaning of it or emphasize its meaning. The song the harpist played on his instrument—"*Silent, O Moyle*" (Thomas Moore's) "The Song of Fionnuala"—depicts the hapless, jejune condition of Ireland: "When will that day-star, mildly springing/ Warm our isle with peace and love?" The "recherche biscuit at the beginning of the story that Corley speaks of alludes to Marcel Proust's seven-volume novel *A la recherche du temps perdu* ("In Search of Last Time") in which a madeleine, dipped in tea, when tasted, brings back memories of the past. And a distant allusion is also there in "Two Gallants". Corley's chasing the young woman—the "tart"—is a comic-satiric base imitation of Dante's pursuing Beatrice.

"Two Gallants" has yet another feature: it shows a new mile-stone in the development of Joyce's prose style. A. Walton Litz writes: "By the time Joyce came to write 'Two Gallants', 'A Little Cloud', and 'The Dead', he had developed a prose style in which every detail of description contributes both to a local effect and to some larger artistic pattern" (Scheles and Litz, 331).

7. The Boarding House

(1)

This is the last one of the four stories of *Dubliners* that are grouped under the rubric of "adolescence stories". In order of composition, "The Boarding House" is the fifth of the fifteen stories of *Dubliners* but in the book it is the seventh. Unlike some stories of *Dubliners*, it was not published anywhere before it was included in *Dubliners* in 1914. "The Boarding House" is a story of contraption and social pressure to which people sometimes have to bow. Interestingly, Joyce signed the earlier version of this story, when he intended to publish it in *The Irish Homestead*, not as "James Joyce" but as "Stephen Daedalus" as he had earlier done the earlier version of "The Sisters." The original version of "The Boarding House" was written in 1905 and it was heavily revised sometime between then and 1914, when it was published in *Dubliners*. In the revised story, Joyce wanted to make the language in the earlier version "more colloquial, more appropriate to the events being narrated than to the more lofty tone of the narrative persona, "Stephen Daedalus." Thus, "obliged to enlist himself" in the earlier draft became "had to become"; "attacked his wife" became "went for his wife"; "started a boarding house" became "set up a boarding house"; "an amateur boxer" became "handy with mits"; "she had been specific in her enquiries and Polly had been decided in her answers" became "she had been frank in her questions and Polly had been frank in her answers"; plain "Lyons" became "Bantam Lyons"; "the loss of his job" became "the loss of his sit" (colloquial for situation); "had a bit of money put by" became "had a bit of stuff put by." In other revisions, Joyce is busy at the usual phrase-sharpening, and in one case he is at some pains to make his irony less heavy-handed. The last sentence [of the story], originally reading "She remembered now what she had been waiting for: this was it" became "Then she remembered what she had been waiting for" (Scholes and Litz, 235-36). We have quoted extensively here in order to show Joyce's preference for colloquial language, not only in *Dubliners* but everywhere after it.

We know *Dubliners* was refused by a good number of publishers, for various reasons, two principal ones of them being Joyce's indiscreet handling of libidinal cases, and his use of the word "bloody": once in "Two Gallants", thrice in "Grace" and once in this story—"The Boarding House."

(2)

The principal characters of "The Boarding House" are:

1. Mrs. Mooney. She was a butcher's daughter and Mr. Mooney's wife. Polly and Jack are her daughter and son, respectively. She keeps a boarding house, after she

was divorced by her drunkard husband Mr. Mooney, to maintain her family. She is called "The Madam" by the boarders of her boarding house. She was an imposing woman.

2. Polly Mooney. Nineteen years old Polly is given to lechery, for which the narrator says that she looks like a "little perverse madonna." She is the central character of the story, because her sexual affairs with Bob Doran, a boarder of the boarding house, is the central event of the story. This malapert daughter of Mrs. Mooney actually hooks up thirty-four or thirty-five years old Bob Doran.
3. Bob Doran. He is a boarder of Mrs. Mooney's boarding house. His infatuation of Polly and his sexual affairs with her is the driving force of the story. Bob Doran later on appears in *Ulysses* (in the chapter "Cyclops").
4. Jack Mooney. He was Mrs. Mooney's only son, as Polly was her only daughter. He worked as a clerk and was a "hard case", and "was fond of using soldiers' obscenities."

The story "The Boarding House" begins with the narrative of the circumstances in which the Mooney family fell apart. Mrs. Mooney, a butcher's daughter, married Mr. Mooney who was her father's foreman. After the death of her father, Mr. Mooney fell into debt and took to frequent drinking bouts and became violent against Mrs. Mooney. In this situation, the husband and the wife were separated, Mrs. Mooney having had the guardianship of her daughter Polly and son Jack. Mr. Mooney now was obliged to take service under a sheriff and Mrs. Mooney was constrained to set up a boarding house to keep her truncated family in order. Mrs. Mooney's boarding house catered mostly to "tourists from Liverpool and the Isle of Man and, occasionally, *artistes* from the music halls. Its resident population was made up of clerks from the city." The young boarders, the *resident population* of the boarding house were "chummy with one another."

Jack Mooney, Mrs. Mooney's son, was also a clerk and, as told earlier, he was a "hard case" and was fond of "soldiers' obscenities." He "was always sure to be on to a good thing, that is to say, a likely horse or a likely *artiste*. He was also handy with the mits [information that should be kept in mind when taking a decision] and sang comic songs."

"On Sunday nights there would often be a union in Mrs. Mooney's front drawing-room. The music-hall artistes would oblige; and Sheridan [one of the artistes] played waltzes and polkas and vamped accompaniments. Polly Mooney, the Madam's daughter, would also sing.

> Once she sang:
> I'm a...naughty girl
> You need'nt sham:
> You know I am."

Mrs. Mooney first sent Polly "to be a typist in a corn-factor's office" but as there she was being teased by a disreputable man, Mrs. Mooney brought her back home. Polly was very lively and Mrs. Mooney did let her freedom enough to mix with those young men of the boarding house with the view that she might pick up her life partner from among them. Polly naturally flirted with them but Mrs. Mooney observed that the young men only went as far as their enjoyment went for the time being, and so was thinking to send her back to the typewriting. Before long, Mrs. Mooney understood that Polly and one of the young men had come close to each other. The boarders began bantering their flirting. Mrs. Mooney was watching their affairs with the wisdom of a diplomat, not to lose but to gain. At the appropriate moment, she raised the question of morality about the affair.

On a bright Sunday morning, Mrs. Mooney interviewed Polly about her relation with Mr. Doran. The mother was frank in her awkward questions. In the end, Mrs. Mooney decided that Mr. Doran had violated her daughter's honour. She recognised that Mr. Doran could not plead innocence because he was thirty-four or thirty-five years of age. She raised the question in her mind: "What reparation would he make?" And she decided that "For her only one reparation could make up for the loss of her daughter's honour: marriage."

Mrs. Mooney sent her servant, Mary, to Mr. Doran to tell him that she wished to talk to him. "She felt sure she would win. He was a serious young man, not rakish or loud-voiced like the others.... All the lodgers in the house knew something of the affair; details had been invented by some. Besides, he had been employed for thirteen years in a great Catholic wine merchant's office, and publicity would mean for him, perhaps, loss of his job. Whereas if he agreed all might be well. She knew he had a good screw [wages] for one thing, and she suspected he had a bit of stuff [wealth] put by." Mrs. Mooney fastidiously readied herself for the meeting with Mr. Doran. Mr. Doran tried to have a shaving to make him presentable but due to nervousness refrained from it. He was nervous recalling his confession last night before the priest. "The recollection of his confession of the night before was a cause of acute pain to him; the priest had drawn out every ridiculous detail of the affair, and in the end had so magnified his sin that he was almost thankful at being afforded a loophole of reparation. The harm was done. What could he do now but marry her or run away?" Mr. Doran further thought: "As a young man he had sown his wild oats [dissipated his excesses], of course; he had boasted of his free-thinking and denied the existence of God to his companions in public-houses.... He still bought a copy of Reynold's Newspaper ['a London newspaper that reported on scandalous events'] every week, but he attended to his religious duties, and for nine-tenths of the year lived a religious life."

Mr. Doran was meditating whether to marry Polly or not. He knew Polly "was a little vulgar" and so could not decide whether to like her or despise her. He knew once he married he was done for, as the adage went. While he was musing like this, Polly tapped at the door and entered. Polly told him that she had told her mother A to Z of what had gone between them and that her mother would now hear all that from him. Then "She cried and threw her arms round his neck, saying: 'O Bob! Bob! What am I to do? What am I to do at all?'" She concluded the story of her helplessness and her attempting to persuade Mr. Doran with an ominous portent: "She would put an end to herself, she said." Mr. Doran comforted her feebly and thought that all that happened was not due to his own fault only but Polly herself was responsible as well. He recalled the delight he received from Polly's first physical touch: "the first casual caresses her dress, her breath, her fingers had given him." Then once she entered into his dark room in her "bath night", wearing "a loose open combing jacket of printed flannel" and having her skin perfumed.

Since then on nights when Mr. Doran would return late, Polly would warm his dinner and he would eat it with pleasure because she would be sitting beside him. And then Mr. Doran would think that perhaps they would be happy together. They used to go upstairs with candles to kiss farewell. "He remembered well her eyes, the touch of her hand and delirium...." He then echoed Polly's delirious sentence (*supra*): "What am I to do?" Mr. Doran's natural instinct of celibacy warned him not to proceed further, but, he thought, he had already committed the sin and, to save his honour, reparation (in the act of marrying her) must be done.

"While he was sitting with her on the side of the bed Mary, Mrs. Mooney's servant, came to the door and said that the missus wanted to see him in the parlour" Mr. Doran stood up, comforted Polly who was crying saying "It would be all right, never fear" and went out. Nervously, he was coming down the stairs and was wishing he could "ascend through the roof and fly away to another country where he would never hear again of his trouble." He was fearfully imagining the faces of his employer and Mrs. Mooney. On the stairs he passed by Jack Mooney and the two saluted each other coldly. Suddenly, Mr. Doran remembered the night "when one of the music-hall artistes, a little blond Londoner, had made a rather free allusion to Polly. The reunion had been almost broken up on account of Jack's violence.... Jack kept shouting at him that if any fellow tried that sort of a game on which his sister he'd bloody well put his teeth down his throat: so he would."

Polly remained sitting on the side of the bed, crying. Then she dried her eyes, went to the looking glass, tidied herself and sat at the foot of the bed. She then gazed at the pillows for a long time, "and the sight of them awakened in her mind secret, amiable memories." She was having a reverie and there was no sign of perturbation in her face. She was patient and cheerful; she was full of hopes and visions that were intricate; and though her gaze was on the pillows she did not see them. She also did not know that she was waiting for something.

> "At last she heard her mother calling. She started to her feet and ran to the banisters.
> 'Polly! Polly!'
> 'Yes, mamma?'
> 'Come down, dear. Mr. Doran wants to speak to you.'
> Then she remembered what she had been waiting for."

(3)

The events of the story occupied a brief period: from Sunday breakfast to noon mass on the same day. The prime concern is Mrs. Mooney's responsibility as a mother was to fix the secret carnal relation between Polly and Bob Doran. Both Polly and Doran committed a sin and they were then somewhat flummoxed as to what to do—they had become somewhat paralysed (one of the core themes of *Dubliners*) Mrs. Mooney made them come out of the impasse by forcing them to tie the marriage knot as per the Christian obligation. Both Polly and Doran are seducers as well as the seduced, not consciously, though: they are rather victims of their particular circumstances. The story thus shows us the nature of free will and free action.

In "The Boarding House" and "A Mother", the central character is a mother who is the absolute guardian of her daughter, the daughter being an impassive ward of her. In these two stories and in "Clay" and "Eveline", Joyce has portrayed four female characters of different traits.

8. A Little Cloud

(1)

This is the first of the group of stories in *Dubliners* under the rubric of "maturity stories." The three other stories of this group are: "Counterparts", "Clay" and "A Painful Case." "A

Little Cloud" is the eighth story of *Dubliners*, but in the order of writing it is the fourteenth story. The title of the story Joyce took from the biblical verse in *1 Kings*: 18. 44: "And it came to pass at the seventh time, that he said, Behold, there ariseth a little cloud out of the sea, like a man's hand." This biblical passage gives "an account of the defeat of the prophets of Baal ['a god of the Phoenicians, originally probably a fusion of many local gods', or 'a false god, generally'] by God's prophet Elijah." By ending a long drought that had plagued the people of Israel, Elijah manifested to them the power of God, and brought the people of Arab back to the worship of the Lord. The line from which Joyce drew the title of this story marks the turning point in the struggle of Elijah to overcome the prophets of the Canaanite god Baal.

Joyce was much delighted with this story. In a letter to his brother Stanislous he wrote in 1906 that "a page of 'A Little Cloud' gives me more pleasure than all my verses". "A Little Cloud" is a story of would-like-to-be poet Thomas Malone Chandler (or "Little Chandler") who was entrapped in his circumstances so he could not escape it and prosper like his friend Ignatius Gallahar who eight years ago had left (Dublin or Ireland) for London and then was a very well off and reputed journalist. However, "A Little Cloud" is one of the longer short stories of *Dubliners*.

(2)

The principal characters of "A Little Cloud" are:

1. Little Chandler. The unnamed narrator of the story gives us a picture of this character at the beginning of the story thus: "He was called Little Chandler because, though he was but slightly under the average stature, he gave one the idea of being a little man. His hands were white and small, his frame was fragile, his voice was quiet and his manners were refined. He took the greatest care of his fair silken hair and moustache, and used perfume discreetly on his handkerchief. The half-moons of his nails were perfect, and when he smiled you caught a glimpse of a row of childish white teeth."

"He was not so old—thirty-two. His temperament might be said to be just at the point of maturity. There were so many different moods and impressions that he wished to express in verse. He felt them within him. He tried to weigh his soul to see if it was a poet's soul. Melancholy was the dominant note of his temperament, he thought, but it was a melancholy tempered by recurrences of faith and resignation and simple joy. If he could give expression to it in a book of poems perhaps men would listen. He would never be popular: he saw that. He could not sway the crowd, but he might appeal to a little circle of kindred minds." Little Chandler had married Annie twelve months ago and he was father of "A little boy." Ignatius Gallahar was his friend.

2. Ignatius Gallahar. "His face was heavy, pale and clean-shaven. His eyes, which were of bluish slate-colour, relieved his unhealthy pallor and shone out plainly above the vivid orange tie he wore. Between these rival features the lips appeared very long and shapeless and colourless." Gallahar, eight years ego, had left Dublin for London and now was a successful journalist on the London Press. "People used to say that Ignatius Gallahar was wild. Of course, he did mix with a rakish set of fellows at that time; drank freely and borrowed money on all sides. In the end he had got mixed up in some shady affair, some money transaction: at least, that was one version of his flight [to London]. But nobody denied him talent. There was always a certain...something in Ignatius Gallahar that impressed you in spite of yourself. Even when he was out at elbows and at his wit's end for money he kept up a bold face." Gallahar was inferior to Little Chandler in birth and education but was more hungry for life than he.

"A Little Cloud" is a story of frustration with the present life of back-tracking responsibilities and consequent daydreaming about escaping this life for a better one of success and joy.

This is the story of Little Chandler. Eight years ego, Chandler had wished God-speed to his friend Ignatius Gallahar who had been going to London and who now was a successful journalist on the London Press. Gallahar has come back to Ireland and invited his old friend Little Chandler for a meeting. Sitting at his desk in the King's Inns, Little Chandler was thinking about the striking changes that Gallahar's eight years' life in London brought to him. Gallahar "whom he had known under a shabby and necessitous guise had become a brilliant figure on the London Press." On the other hand, staying in Dublin all these eight years, Little Chandler was leading a lack-lustre life. In the late autumn evening, when the children were "screaming along the gravel Paths", Little Chandler was thinking about his life and a "gentle melancholy took possession of him. He felt how useless it was to struggle against fortune, this being the burden of wisdom which the ages had bequeathed to him." He remembered his interest in poetry and his poetry books that sometimes consoled him from melancholy. Sometimes he would read out poetry to his wife Annie.

Little Chandler left the desk in the King's Inns and "walked swiftly down Henrietta Street." "He picked his way deftly through all that minute vermin-like life and under the shadow of the gaunt spectral mansions in which the old nobility of Dublin had roistered. No memory of the past touched him, for his mind was full of a present joy." Walking he reached Corless's where rich people ate oysters and drank liqueurs and where rich ladies in gorgeous attires were seen escorted by cavaliers. Little Chandler walked timidly on. At times he heard mocking, satiric laughter and felt himself very low and trembled "like a leaf" thinking the laughter was aimed at ridiculing him. From Corless's Little Chandler turned towards Chapel Street and walked on. He was thinking about Gallahar who used to say, when he was in a hopeless, desperate condition: "Half-time now, boys," he used to say light-heartedly. "Where's my considering cap?" ["Halftime" is a slang, which means "time out" and "considering cap", another slang, means "thinking cap" or brain or thinking capability.] Gallahar meant to say, "Forget to despair and think otherwise." Recalling this inspiring attitude of Gallahar, Little Chandler, in his straightened condition felt "a slight flush of pride" in himself. Really, Little Chandler admired Gallahar.

Chandler continued to walk, feeling superior who passed by him and revolting against the "dull inelegance of Chapel Street [in fact, against his own quotidian, lack-lustre life]." He thought there was no way of changing his life in Dublin, if he wanted to change it, he had to go away. He now crossed Grattan bridge and "pitied the poor stunted houses" below. He wondered whether he could write a poem about the "panorama of sunset" in the distance, and thought Gallahar might do it. As he was thinking like that, he was imaginatively going farther and farther away from his present sordid life in Dublin and approaching London where Gallahar flourished. A ray of hope peeped through the chink of his mind. He thought he was not yet old but only thirty-two. He thought he had a penchant for poetry and so "If he could give expression to it in a book of poems perhaps men would listen." All these were, in fact, a reverie—a day-dream—of Little Chandler. He turned back without proceeding farther and approached the same Corless' in a state of indecision, and then entered Corless' bar and there found Ignatius Gallahar at the counter. Gallahar called out to Little Chandler "Hallo, Tommy, old hero, here you are!" and ordered "two halves of malt whisky" for Little Chandler and himself. Gallahar took off his hat when the thinning of his hair was visible. He explained that the thinning of his hair was the result of his heavy pressure in the Press. But he said that he was very happy with his profession: "I'm deuced glad." He said that he had been feeling bad after landing again in "dear, dirty Dublin" but now, on meeting Little Chandler, he felt "a ton better." "They clinked glasses and drank the toast." Gallahar told Little Chandler (Tommy) that Chandler did not change a little (during these eight years) and advised him to go to London or Paris to change his life for the better: "Go to London or Paris: Paris for choice. That'd do you good." Gallahar even pronounced an exclamation: "...Ah, there's no city like Paris for gaiety, movement, excitement...." Little Chandler "was beginning to feel somewhat disillusioned. Gallahar's accent and way of expressing himself did not please him. There was something vulgar in his friend [Gallahar] which he had not observed before. But perhaps it was only the result of living in London amid the bustle and competition of the Press." Gallahar told him that in Paris everything was "gay" and that the Parisians believed in "enjoying life."

Little Chandler asked Gallahar if it was true that Paris was so immoral and he generally agreed with him. Gallahar told him that there were cocottes (loose women) in Paris all right but "There's no woman like the Parisienne—for style, for go." Little Chandler quipped: "Then it is an immoral city" (compared with London or Dublin). Gallahar emphatically said that Paris was incomparably immortal—"it's a rum world. Talk of immorality!" Gallahar narrated some cases of immorality and "Little Chandler was astonished." He told Little Chandler that coming to Dublin, "where nothing is known of such [immoral] things" is a sort of relaxation.

One year ego Little Chandler had married and now he had a little boy of that marriage. Chandler was musing over the difference between Gallahar's and his fortunes, between Gallahar's "vibrant and triumphant life" and his demur, jejune life, weighed down by responsibilities—a life of discontent and frustration—a paralytic life, in short. Little Chandler was dejectedly ruminating over the fact that though "Gallahar was his inferior in birth and education", yet he was enjoying a bright and vibrant life while he utterly failed to achieve anything in life. Gallahar was not married and so Little Chandler told him like a friend: "When you come next year I may have the pleasure of wishing long life and happiness to Mr. and Mrs. Gallahar." In response, Gallahar said, "I've only to say the word and to-morrow I can have the woman and the cash."

In the last shorter section of the story we are told that "Little Chandler sat in the room off the hall, holding a child in his arms. To save money they kept no servant, but Annie's [Little Chandler's wife's] young sister Monica came for an hour or so in the morning and an hour or so in the evening to help." It was about nine in the evening. Annie had to go out to buy tea and sugar and so "She put the sleeping child deftly in his [Little Chandler's] arms and said: 'Here. Don't waken him.'"

On the nearby table, there was a little lamp, the light of which fell over a photograph of Annie. Little Chandler looked at it and recalled the day when he had brought a blouse for Annie and she kissed him. He thought that romance was no more ("Hm! ....") "He looked coldly into the eyes of the photograph and they answered coldly. Certainly they were pretty and the face itself was pretty. But he found something mean in it. Why was it so unconscious and ladylike? The composure of the eyes irritated him. They repelled him and defied him: there was no passion in them, no rapture." He asked himself: "Why had he married the eyes in the photograph?" "A dull resentment against his life woke within him. Could he not escape from this little house? Was it too late for him to try to live bravely like Gallahar? Could he go to London? There was the furniture still to be paid for. If he could only write a book and get it published, that might open the way for him." Thus, Little Chandler was on tenter-hooks; on one hand, he wished to live a buoyant life like Gallahar and, on the other, his economic distress ("furniture still to be paid for") stood on his way.

Little Chandler brought down a volume of the romantic poet Byron's poems and "opened it cautiously with his left hand lest he should waken the child and began to read the first poem in the book: 'Hushed are the winds and still the evening gloom....'" He thought if he could write poems in such superb melancholic vein! "The child awoke and began to cry. He turned from the page and tried to hush it: but it would not be hushed. He began to rock it to and fro in his arms, but its cry grew keener. He rocked it faster while his eyes began to read the second stanza: "Within this narrow cell reclines her clay...." It was useless. He couldn't read. He couldn't do anything. The wailing of the child pierced the drum of his ear. It [his hope of escaping his home and going to London] was useless, useless! He was a prisoner of life. His arms trembled with anger and suddenly bending to the child's face he shouted: "Stop!" "The child stopped for an instant, had a spasm of fright and began to scream. He jumped from his chair and walked hastily up and down the room with the child on his arms. It began to sob piteously, losing its breath for four or five seconds, and then bursting out anew. The thin walls of the room echoed the sound. He tried to soothe it, but it sobbed more convulsively. He looked at the contracted and quivering face of the child and began to be alarmed. He counted seven sobs without a break between them and caught the child to his breast in fright. If it died!...."

Annie came back after buying tea and sugar and burst into room, shouting: "What is it? What is it?" The child recognized it's mother's voice and "broke into a paroxysm of sobbing." Little Chandler asked Annie not to be frightened: "It's nothing, Annie...it's nothing.... He began to cry...." Annie looked angrily at Little Chandler, picking the child in her arms. Chandler began to stammer: "It's nothing.... He...he began to cry.... I couldn't... I didn't do anything.... What?" Annie continued to soothe the child very earnestly: "My little man! My little mannie.... Mamma's little lamb of the world!... There now!"

Little Chandler's dream of London went into oblivion and he was repentant for his rough handling of the child. In shame he stepped away from the light of the lamp and into the darkness around. "He listened while the paroxysm of the child's sobbing grew less and less; and tears of remorse started to his eyes."

(3)

The story is a beautiful exemplar of familial entrapment. Little Chandler and Ignatius Gallahar were friends, though Gallahar was inferior to Chandler in birth and education. Eight years ego, Gallahar left Dublin to seek his fortune in London but Chandler stayed behind in Dublin. Gallahar could flee from Dublin because he was adventurous and strong-willed and he had no entanglement in his family. On the contrary, Chandler was timid; and one year ego he married Annie and now was the father of a child. Within the last eight years, Gallahar had established himself as a successful journalist on a London Press, while these eight years Chandler was languishing in the retrogressive Dublin and, recently, was entangled in the shackling responsibilities of his new family.

At the beginning of the story, we see how conspicuously London had changed Gallahar and how uncouth Chandler all along remained. Chandler envied Gallahar's change and thought that his native poetic *métier* could change his fortune if only he could make himself free from his family. His family was the net in which he was ineluctably entangled. And when he was thinking like this, the brunt of his anger suddenly fell upon the little innocent child, in spite of him; and, in spite of him, he became too rude to his dear child. And consequently his self-lacerating compunction gathered tears in his eyes. Chandler is like a kestrel caught in a net. In this sense, "A Little Cloud" and "Eveline" are, as if, two preambles to Joyce's *A Portrait of an Artist as a Young Man* and *Exile*.

About the style of "A Little Cloud" Fargnoli and Gillespie write: "Stylistically, the story unfolds using the free indirect discourse technique that is by now becoming familiar to readers of the collection. As the narrator describes events in the third person, while punctuating the discourse with poignant observations drawn from Chandler's point of view, the reader has exposure to both a detached and a highly subjective sense of events. The effect of this bifurcated technique is to play off any sympathy one might feel for the main character's growing dissatisfaction against an awareness of the banal, conventional nature of his life. These divergent points of view combine to emphasize Little Chandler's frustration with his own inability as a man to develop the artistic aspirations that he felt as a youth" (Fargnoli and Gillespie, 61).

The core questions of "A Little Cloud", such as "Could Little Chandler not escape his little house?", reappears in the 17th chapter of *Ulysses* ("Ithaca"). In a parenthesis, Fargnoli and Gillespie write: "(In the Ithaca episode, chapter 17, of *Ulysses*, Leopold Bloom—contemplating his options after the adultery of his wife—will ask himself these same basic questions, and come no closer to answering them than does Chandler)" (*op. cit.*, 61). But, be it as it may, we have no difficulty in understanding that Chandler is not only in an impassive stasis but is also within "his sense of entrapment and emasculation." Chandler's impassive stasis fittingly suggests the state of Ireland before Joyce's self-exile to Europe, at least in Joyce's eyes.

9. Counterparts

(1)

"Counterparts" is the ninth story of *Dubliners* and the second in the group of stories in the collection under the rubric "maturity stories." It is the sixth story of *Dubliners* in the order of composition and Joyce finished it by July 12, 1905. "This is one of the stories that the printer for publisher Grant Richards refused to set in 1906, because of Joyce's description of the young woman in Mulligan's pub whom Farrington [the protagonist] fancied. Joyce, in fact, did modify the description, but Richards still resisted publishing the collection" (Fargnoli, and Gillespie, 63). However, ultimately, after the modification, Grant Richards published the collection, *Dubliners*, in 1914. "Counterparts" is one of the relatively longer (about 15 pages) stories in the collection.

(2)

The principal characters of "Counterparts" are:

1. Farrington. Farrington is the central character. He "was tall and of great bulk. He had a hanging face, dark wine-coloured, with fair eyebrows and moustache: his eyes bulged forward slightly and the whites of them were dirty." He was married and had five children, one of whom, a boy, was named Tom. "His wife [Ada] was a sharp-faced woman who bullied her husband when he was sober and was bullied by him when he was drunk. He was copying clerk of Crosbie & Alleyne.
2. Mr. Alleyne. Mr. Alleyne was one of the two partners of Crosbie & Alleyne. He was "a little man wearing gold-rimmed glasses on a clean-shaven face." His "head itself was so pink and hairless it seemed like a large egg."
3. Nosey Flynn (who reappears in *Ulysses*), Ada (Farrington's wife), Tom (Farrington's son), Miss

Delacour, Weathers, O'Halloran and Paddy Leonard are minor characters.

The story begins with the two "counterparts" (two parts of which one is contrary to the other) or two contrary men: Mr. Alleyne, one of the two partners of the firm Crosbie & Alleyne (the other being Mr. Crosbie), and Farrington who is an amanuensis or copying clerk under Mr. Alleyne. In a furious voice, Mr. Alleyne asked Miss Parker to convey to Farrington to comply with his order to come to him. Miss Parker conveyed that order to Farrington. Farrington showed his utter resentment and anger towards Mr. Alleyne by muttering "Blast him!" But he went to meet Mr. Alleyne with all vexation and fuming. Earlier, Mr. Alleyne had ordered Farrington to make a copy of the contract between Bodley and Kirwan by four o'clock but Farrington failed to do it. This exasperated Mr. Alleyne who gave Farrington the ultimatum: "Let me tell you that if the contract is not copied before this evening, I'll lay the matter before Crosbie."

Farrington was not unfezzed; he stood his ground and was looking at the polished and fragile skull of Mr. Alleyne. "A spasm of rage gripped his throat for a few moments and then passed, leaving after it a sharp sensation of thirst." He was thirsty of intoxicating beverage. Farrington's waiting there a while more was an opportunity for Mr. Alleyne to thrash him once more: "Upon my word, Farrington, you take things easy!" He ordered Farrington to go downstairs and do his works. Farrington went to his work, but he "felt that he must slack the thirst [for wine] in his throat." It was getting darker in the evening. He thought when they would light the gas lamps he would resume his work. So he went out and entered into the comfortable bar of O'Neill's shop and ordered for a g. p. (glass of porter). Farrington gulped the porter and came out of O'Neill's shop chewing caraway seed and wondering "whether he could finish his copy in time." As he was coming to his workplace, he smelt the salubrious perfumes of Miss Delacour, who also visited the bar, in the dark and thickly foggy way back, when "the lamps in Eustace Street had been lit." Farrington at last re-entered "the office, assuming an air of absent-mindedness."

The chief clerk sternly told him that Mr. Alleyne had been calling for him. Farrington understood that the reason was his finishing the copying of the contract between Bodley and Kirwan. Confusedly, he sat down and "realized how hopeless was the task of finishing the copy of the contract before half-past five. The dark damp night was coming and he longed to spend it in the bars, drinking with friends amid the glare of gas and the clatter of glasses." He rose up and left the copy of Delacour correspondence without copying the last two letters of it which were missing from the original itself (the responsibility, supposedly, lied on Farrington). He hoped Mr. Alleyne, his boss, would not notice the missing. He then entered Mr. Alleyne's room with "the correspondence" and placed "the correspondence" (not the copyings of the contract between between Bodley and Kirwan) on the desk of Mr. Alleyne. Miss Delacour, "a middleaged woman of Jewish appearance" was there. Placing the "correspondence" on the desk, Farrington respectfully bowed but neither Mr. Alleyne not Miss Delacour noticed it. Mr. Alleyne was said to be sweet on Miss Delacour and on her money. Mr. Alleyne just tapped "the correspondence" and then flicked it towards Farrinton as if to say "you can go."

Farrington came downstairs and sat down to finish his copying. But his mind was not there, it "wandered away to the glare and rattle of the public house", to wit of the bar. He struggled to do copying but though "the clock struck five he had still fourteen pages to write." He knew he could not finish copying in time. He cursed his work loudly—"Blast it!"—and hammered "something" violently with his fist. He was so enraged that he miscopied *Bernard Bodley* of the original as *Bernard Bernard*. However, Farrington went to Mr. Alleyne. He felt physically super strong and felt an urge to do some violence. All the clerks turned round in anticipation of some calamity. Mr. Alleyne "began a tirade of abuse, saying that two letters were missing." Farrington emphatically responded the tirade saying he had copied faithfully. Miss Delacour laughed broadly. Mr. Alleyne became red like a wild rose in anger and his mouth was twitching, and then he shook his fist in Farrington's face, and the face "seemed to vibrate like the knob of some electric machine." Mr. Alleyne also pronounced a dire consequence to Farrington: "You impertinent ruffian! You impertinent ruffian! I'll make short work of you! Wait till you see! You'll apologize to me for your impertinence or you'll quit the office instanter! You'll quite this, I'm telling you, or you'll apologize to me!"

In the second section of the story, the unnamed narrator tells us that after the episode of Mr. Alleyne's demanding apology from him Farrington felt utterly let down and dejected. He thought, "Mr. Alleyne would never give him an hour's rest; his life would be a hell to him." He recalled that the rivalry between Mr. Alleyne and himself began since when Mr. Alleyne "had heard him mimicking his [Mr. Alleyne's] North of Ireland accent to amuse Higgins and Miss Parker...." Farrington "felt his great body again aching for the comfort of the public house. By this time, the fog had begun to chill him...." He was penniless; how could he get the public house comfort? On a sudden he thought going to Terry Kelly's pawn-office might be the solution ("dart"). Farrington went to the pawn-office and joyfully came out with six shillings and went on proudly through crowded streets "full of the noises of tram-gongs and swishing trolleys" and "staring masterfully at the office-girls." And as he walked he thought of narrating his story of that day to boys, the story of how he had blatantly put up before Mr. Alleyne.

Farrington first told the story to Nosey Flynn who told him that "it was as smart a thing as ever he heard" and stood Farrington a half-one. Then he repeated the story to O'Halloran and Paddy Leonard and O'Halloran stood him tailors (specially customized) of malt. After that Farrington narrated the story to the men who wanted to hear his version of the story (not other men's version) and he narrated the story with vivacity and they laughed roaringly and feted him with whiskies: "Every one roared when he showed the way in which Mr. Alleyne shook his fist in Farrington's face."

After this, Higgins, Nosey Flynn and Farrington walked towards Ballast Office [location of the Dublin Port; in "The Dead" Gabriel Conroy's father worked there] through drizzling rain and cold. The three men entered the bar of the Scotch-

House which was full of men and was "loud with the noise of tongues and glasses." Leonard introduced the three men to Weathers "who was performing at the Tivoli as an acrobat and knockabout *artiste.*" After a bout of drinking in the Scotch-House, they went to Mulligan's, because the Scotch-House was closed. There in the Mulligan's, they drank once more. "Presently two young women with big hats and a young man in a check suit came in and sat at a table close by. Weathers saluted them and told the company that they were out of the Tivoli. Farrington's eyes wandered at every moment in the direction of one of the young women. There was something striking in her appearance.... Farrington gazed admiringly at the plump arm which she moved very often and with much grace; and when, after a little time, she answered his gaze he admired still more her dark brown eyes. The oblique staring expression in them fascinated him. She glanced at him once or twice and, when the party was leaving the room, she brushed against his chair and said '*O, pardon!*' in a London accent. He watched her leave the room in the hope that she would look back at him, but he was disappointed." Farrington thought she neglected him for his want of money. He became very iracund, irate.

Paddy Leonard and others were talking of physical strength while Farrington was distracted by the curious behaviour of the young woman. Paddy Leonard now called Farrington with the objective of engaging him in the contest of physical strength with Weathers who was showing his biceps. Weathers used to show acrobatics in Tivoli (Tivoli or Tivoli Gardens of Copenhagen, Denmark was famous for fun and amusement, such as acrobatics) and he was not an Irish. To defeat Weathers and save the national honour of Ireland, Paddy Leonard engaged Farrington against Weathers in the contest of physical strength. The biceps of the two contestants were examined and then Paddy Leonard cried: "*Go!*" "Weathers brought his opponent's hand slowly down on the table." Farrington's dark wine-coloured face flushed darker still with anger and humiliation at having been defeated by such a strapling. Paddy Leonard declared that there would be three trials and two of the three times winner would be declared final winner. Weathers again brought down Farrington's hand. Farrington showed a fiercely violent expression. To quell the situation O'Halloran said that now there would be a little "smahan" (talking) among them and then they would disperse.

In the third or last section of the story, we see Farrington ("A very sullen-faced man") standing "at the corner of O'Connell Bridge waiting for the little Sandymount tram to take him home." "He was full of smouldering anger and revengefulness. He felt humiliated and discontented; he did not even feel drunk; and he had only two pence in his pocket. He cursed everything... he began to feel thirsty again and he longed to be back again in the hot, reeking public-house. He had lost his reputation as a strong man, having been defeated twice by a mere boy. His heart swelled with fury and, when he thought of the woman in the big hat who had brushed against him and said '*Pardon!*' his fury nearby chocked him."

Farrington alighted from the tram and aversely ran to his home and straight went to the empty kitchen where fire was nearly out. He called out to his wife: "Ada! Ada!" Ada was not at home, she had gone to the chapel. His son, Tom, came out and he harshly ordered him to light the lamp and raucously asked him: "What's for my dinner?" The dinner had not been cooked. Little boy Tom said he was going to cook his dinner. This reply mightily infuriated Farrington. He blasted at Tom: "On that fire! You let the fire out! By God, I'll teach you to do that again!" Farrington secured a walking-stick and began to whip Tom. "The little boy cried '*O, pa!*' and ran whimpering round the table, but the man followed him and caught him by the coat. The little boy looked about knees." Farrington had no compunction. He shouted "Now, you'll let the fire out the next time!" and began to beat him vigorously with the stick, pronouncing: "Take that, you little whelp!" The stick cut the boy's thigh and he uttered a sequel of cries. He clasped his hands together in the air and obsequiously begged to his father not to bit him, assuring his father that he would pray for him: "O, pa!", he cried, "Don't beat me, pa! And I'll.... I'll say a *Hail Mary* for you.... I'll say a *Hail Mary*...." [*Hail Mary* is a Christian prayer to the Blessed Mary that goes like this: "Hail

Mary, full of grace, our Lord is with thee, blessed art thou among woman, and blessed is the fruit of thy womb, Jesus. Holy Mary, Mother of God, pray for us sinners, now, and in the hour of our death. Amen."

(3)

In any critical appraisal of "Counterparts", no one should miss noticing the well-chosen title of the story "Counterparts." The term "counterpart" signifies both "an opposite" as well as "a duplicate" or "a double." In this story, both the meanings of the term may be found. In the former meaning, Farrington is a counterpart of Mr. Alleyne, because there is antagonism or hostility between the two; Farrington and his wife, Ada, are counterparts, because the two bullies each other, though in different moods; Farrington and Weathers are two counterparts in showing physical strength; and Farrington and his son Tom are counterparts, because Farrington is the punisher and Tom is the receiver of the punishment. In the second sense of the term "counterparts", i.e., in the sense of an original and a duplicate or in the sense of two identical units, Mr. Alleyne and Farrington are counterparts, in the sense that as Mr. Alleyne tyrannises Farrington so does Farrington his son Tom; and as Farrington's wife Ada seeks salvation in the Chapel so does Farrington seeks peace in drinks.

Robert Scholes has noticed that "Counterparts" offers us, in its little and in its plan, a major clue to the whole structure of *Dubliners*—to the almost musical fabric of themes and variations on the people of Dublin which Joyce has so carefully arranged for us. The title of this story ["Counterparts"] suggests both the harmonious balance of counterpointed musical parts and the anonymous interchangeability of cogs in a great machine. In the story itself, Mr. Alleyne bullies the shiftless Farrington, and Farrington bullies the hapless Tom.... And beyond this story, the brutal Farrington's return to his wifeless home and whining son is the counterpart of Little Chandler's encounter with his tiny son in the previous story, "A Little Cloud" (Scholes and Litz, 339-40). "Counterparts" and "A Little Cloud" are not the only two stories where Robert Scholes has found counterpart characters but among a few other stories of *Dubliners* as well. Scholes writes that "Connections like these, multiplied many times over, are the principal means by which Joyce has blended his separate stories into an imposing portrait of a city and a whole race of people" (*op. cit.*, 340).

The themes common in the other stories of *Dubliners*—paralysis and escaping fantasy—are also present in "Counterparts", albeit not in sharp accents. Dublin is a paralytic-like gloomy city. The expressions, such as "The *evening* was falling", "*dark* snug of O'Neill's shop", "the curate to grope for it in the *gloom*", "The *dark damn* night", "The fog had began to chill him", "the place in *darkness*" and "You let the *fire out*" (*emphases added*) in "Counterpart" are metaphorical of the paralytic state of Dublin. The escaping fantasy lies with the protagonist Farrington. He often leaves his desk and runs to the snug atmosphere of the public house. But, "Counterparts" has an additional theme which is not to be found in any other story of *Dubliners*: the theme of masculinity. In this story, Joyce satirises the traditional concept of masculinity. Farrington is addicted to wine, he leers at young woman, he takes part in wrestling trials, and he beats his wife and son masterfully.

10. Clay

(1)

"Clay" is the tenth story in *Dubliners*, though in order of composition it was the fourth. Again, "Clay" is the third story in the group of stories known as "maturity stories." This story had not been published anywhere before it was included in *Dubliners* in 1914. Joyce wrote "Clay" early in 1905 after he abandoned the story he was writing called "Christmas Eve." "Clay" has a difficult history of publication. "Joyce tried several times, unsuccessfully, to have 'Clay' (and the earlier version 'Hallow Eve') published before it finally appeared as part of the *Dubliners* collection in June 1914" (Fargnoli and Gillespie, 64).

(2)

The principal characters of "Clay" are the following:

1. Maria. Maria was an aged unmarried woman and the protagonist of the story. She was "a cook's assistant in a Protestant institution dedicated to the reformation of prostitutes." "Maria was a very, very small person indeed, but she had a very long nose and a very long chin. She talked a little through her nose, always soothingly: '*Yes, my dear*', and '*No, my dear.*'" She was known as a "veritable peace-maker". When she laughed, "the tip of her nose nearly met the tip of her chin." "Every one was so fond of Maria." Joe Donnelly called her "my proper mother." She served in *Dublin by lamplight* laundry.
2. Alphy Donnelly. There are two characters in the story with the identical name: one the uncle and the other the nephew. "The elder Alphy Donnelly, an offstage character, is the estranged brother of Joe Donnelly.... The younger Alphy Donnelly is Joe Donnelly's son, apparently named after the uncle in happier times."
3. Joe Donnelly. He is the father of younger Alphy Donnelly. It was in his house that the main event of the story, celebrating Hallow Eve, occurred.
4. Mrs. Donnelly. She is wife of Joe Donnelly.

The story begins in the evening and closes just before daybreak, next day. "The matron had given her leave to go out as soon as the women's tea was over, and Maria looked forward to her evening out." It was the Hallow Eve (or Allhalloween or All Hallow's Eve or All Saints' Eve that falls on 31st October) and so barmbracks (a kind of cake traditionally served in Ireland on Halloween, in which symbolic objects, such as a ring, are baked) have been prepared. The Hallow Eve celebration would be held in the house of Joe Donnelly. Maria thought she would be there before eight in the evening. Before that the women worker would have their tea and she would have to buy things for the children in the Hallow Eve celebration. She took out her purse that Alphy Donnelly presented her five years before and that bore the words, *A Present from Belfast*. She was imagining the past enjoyment in Joe Donnelly's house at Belfast when children would be singing.

The cook reported that everything was ready, Maria rang the bell and all the women, who worked there, came in for the tea. There were much joking and laughing. Lizzie Fleming said Maria "was sure to get the [wedding] ring" in the Hallow Eve and Maria in shyness "had to laugh and say she didn't want any ring or man either." She recalled the next day was Sunday and so she piled up her best attires on the bed for the morning mass. She then went out in the rain, with her brown waterproof on, towards Joe Donnelly's house in Belfast. She boarded a tram and, having "two half-crowns and some coppers" in her purse, was thinking "how much better it was to be independent and to have your own money in your pocket." She also thought that Alphy and Joe, the two Donnelly brothers, who were now estranged from one another, had once been very close to each other and that both of them would be delighted to see her. Maria alighted from the tram and went to Downes's cake-shop, but as it was full of people she just bought a dozen of penny cakes and came out and went to a shop in Henry Street to buy something nice. There a stylish lady behind the counter asked her if she wanted to buy some wedding cakes. Maria blushed but the stylish lady took it very seriously and "cut a thick slice of plumcake, parceled it up and said: 'Two-and-four, please.'" Maria obliged her. Maria then boarded a Drumcondra tram and an elderly gentleman made room for her. "He was a stout gentleman and he wore a brown hard hat; he had a square red face and a grayish moustache. Maria thought he was a colonel-looking gentleman and she reflected how much more polite he was than young men who simply stared straight before them."

"The gentleman began to chat with her about Hallow Eve and the rainy weather.... He was very nice with her and when he was getting out at the Canal Bridge she thanked him and bowed, and he bowed to her and raised his hat and smiled agreeably; and while she was going up along the terrace, bending her head under the rain, she thought how easy it was to know a gentleman even when he has a drop taken."

When Maria reached Joe Donnelly's house, she gave the bag of cakes to Alphy, the eldest boy, to distribute the cakes and the children thanked her. Then she was rummaging her pockets and other places for the plum cake that she bought for the "papa and mamma" of the children (for Joe Donnelly and his wife Mrs. Donnelly), but she could not find it out. Donnelly said that Maria had left the parcel of plum cake in the tram. "Maria, remembering how confused the gentleman with the grayish moustache had made her, coloured with shame and vexation and disappointment." However, Joe said it did not matter and the Hallow Eve celebration began. Mrs. Donnelly played the piano and the children danced and sang. Mrs. Donnelly asked Maria to drink a bottle of stout but she took nothing, in spite of Joe's insistence. Maria thought of compromising the two rival brothers, Alphy and Joe, but Joe was dead against any rapprochement. There were two grown-up next-door girls in the celebration and they arranged some games. In one such game, they "put some saucers on the table and then led the children up to the table, blind-folded." One of the children touched the prayer-book and three others touched the water. Then one of the two grown-up next-door girls picked up the ring—that symbolized marriage—and Mrs. Donnelly shook her finger to tell all around that she already knew all about the girl's marriage.

Next, all insisted on blindfolding Maria and she laughed. After she was blindfolded, "They led her up to the table amid laughing and joking, and she put her hand out in the air as she was told to do. She moved her hand about here and there in the air and descended on one of the saucers. She felt a soft wet substance with her fingers and was surprised nobody spoke or took off her bandage." Maria's performance was followed by "a great deal of scuffling and whispering." Mrs. Donnelly became angry (because the "soft wet substance" was a clod of clay that symbolized death) and asked one of the next-door girls to throw it away. Maria had another chance and this time she, blindfolded again, got the prayer-book. The children by now grew tired and sleepy and so to wrap up the celebration Joe asked Maria to sing some old little song. Mrs. Donnelly played the prelude of the song and Maria "began to sing in a tiny quavering voice":

> I dreamt that I dwelt in marble halls
> With vassals and serfs at my side,
> And of all who assembled within those walls
> That I was the hope and the pride.
>
> I had riches too great to count, could boast
> Of high ancestral name,
> But I also dreamt, which pleased me most,
> That you loved me still the same.

But Maria made a mistake in her song. The first verse (stanza: the first four lines of the above song) she sang all right but when she was to sing the next verse, she mistakenly sang the first verse once again (instead of the second verse: the last four lines of the song). (The second verse contained a reference to an unmaterialised love—"That you loved me still the same"—that contained a pathos. This was why Maria unconsciously shied away from the second verse or stanza.) No one tried to show her mistake (in order to not get her affected by her pathos of yore). But Joe understood why Maria made that mistake and himself suffered anguish. He said, "there was no time like the long ago and no music for him like poor Balfe." Joe's eyes gathered so much tears that he could not find what he was looking for [because he could not see clearly on account of the tears] and "he had to ask his wife to tell him where the corkscrew was."

(3)

Among the fifteen stories of *Dubliners*, "Clay" is the most mute and ambiguous. It leaves us in a state of little quandary as to why Maria made the "mistake" of singing the first verse twice. Was the "mistake" due to some love of her long ago or was the "colonel-looking gentleman" a new hint of love? What was her epiphany? This "mystery" about Maria aside, "Clay" is a simple story, in fact, like most of the stories of *Dubliners* but their endings. Maria was a poor middle-aged innocent spinster working as a scullery maid in the "Dublin by Lamplight" Laundry. She participated in the funny game in the Hallow Eve and then she was asked to sing "some little song"—"one of the old songs". She was supposed to sing the two verses or stanzas of the song "*I Dreamt that I Dwelt*" but, astonishingly, instead of singing the second stanza she sang the first twice. Why did she commit the "mistake"? Or, was it not a "mistake" of her but she unconsciously (or consciously?) refrained from singing the second stanza—"But I also dreamt, which pleased me most,/ That you love me still the same"—to stave off the pain of her unfructified love of yore.

However, this theme of "Clay" does not make it a loner among the other stories of *Dubliners*, for the four common and fundamental themes of the stories are also present in it: paralysis, pessimism, corruption and death, though rather subduedly. Firstly, Maria was absolutely impassive; she did only what she was asked to do and she could never refuse to do what she was asked to do. She was somewhat paralytic. Secondly, the story's atmosphere is full of gloominess, darkness and inclemency. The story begins in the evening, when darkness falls, and closes before the next daybreak, when darkness still prevails. Maria went to Joe Donnelly's house when it was raining (rain is a symbol here of inclemency or pessimism, as in the fictions of Ernest Hemingway). The gloomy or pessimistic atmosphere is also suggested by the name of the shop where Maria worked, "Dublin by *Lamplight* Laundry" (*emphasis added*). The laundry used to open at night when lamplight was necessary for it would be dark. And, lastly, death is an important theme in "Clay". In the funny game, the blindfolded Maria first touched clay (from which the little of the story derives) and clay suggests death ("Dust [clay] thou art, and to dust thou returnest."). In this sense, death is also a theme of "Clay". "Clay" is cognate with the last story of *Dubliners*, "The Dead", because like in "The Dead" the male lover of "Clay" was also perhaps dead or, at least, her love was lost. Lastly, the clause "the tip of her [Maria's] nose nearly met the tip of her chin" occurs thrice in the story. Why has Joyce so much emphasized this *clause*? This posture Maria's face took when she *laughed*. Has Joyce used this clause for a light-hearted risibility against the sombre atmosphere of the story to underscore the pathos of the story?

Or is this posture of Maria's face a picture of the face of Joyce himself?

11. A Painful Case

(1)

This is the eleventh story in *Dubliners*, but in the order of composition this story was the seventh. In the group of stories, conveniently marked as "maturity stories", it is the fourth or last story. The original title of this story was "A Painful Incident." Why Joyce changed the title of the story we do not know but, perhaps, he wanted to make the title a solemner. The term "incident" might refer to a violent event, but the event of the story, though *painful*, was not *violent*. In this sense, the present title is more appropriate. "A Painful Case" in draft was first completed in 1905 and then was "repeatedly revised, indicating Joyce's dissatisfaction with the story" (Fargnoli and Gillespie, 66). Whatever opinion of Joyce might have been about "A Painful Case", the story was well received by readers. We say this because of the fact that "Eight years after publication of *Dubliners*, "A Painful Case" was translated into French by Yva Fernandez, and it appeared in the March 1922 issue of the Swiss journal *Revue de Geneve*. An Italian translation of the story, done by Giacomo Prampolini, was published in the June 3, 1928 issue of the journal *Fiera Letteraria*" (Fargnoli and Gillespie, 66). However, it is believed that the story was based on a real life report of Joyce's brother, Stanislaus.

(2)

The principal characters of "A Painful Case" are two:

1. Mr. James Duffy. "Mr. Duffy abhorred anything which betokened physical or mental disorder. A medical doctor would have called him saturnine [gloomy]. His face, which carried the entire tale of his years, was of the brown tint of Dublin streets. On his long and rather large head grew dry black hair and a tawny moustache did not quite cover an unamiable mouth. His cheekbones also gave his face a harsh character; but there was no harshness in the eyes which, looking

at the world from under their tawny eyebrows, gave the impression of a man ever alert to greet a redeeming instinct in others but often disappointed. He lived at a distance from his body, regarding his own acts with doubtful side-glances. He had an odd autobiographical habit which led him to compose in his mind from time to time a short sentence about himself containing a subject in the third person and a predicate in the past tense. He never gave alms to beggars, and walked firmly, carrying a stout hazel." For many years, Mr. Duffy was a cashier in a private bank. He liked the simple lifestyle, was interested in William Wordsworth and Gerhart Hauptmann, and loved Motzart's music. He lived a spiritual life, lonely. He was somewhat misanthropic. He loved to write.

2. Mrs. Emily Sinico. She was forty-three years of age and was the wife of Captain Sinico. She had "an oval face with strongly marked features" and her "eyes were very dark blue and steady." Miss Mary Sinico was her daughter, her only issue.

Mr. James Duffy lived in Chapelizod, which was unpretentious and suburbane, because he was not comfortable with modern city. His house was devoid of all luxuries—a black iron bedstead, an iron wash-stand, a cane chair and such other things only were there in his house. But he had white wooden shelves for books where there was a copy of *Maynooth's Catechism* (a modified version of a Catechism drawn up in 1775 by Dr. James Butler, Archbishop of Cashel.) and "a manuscript translation of Hauptmann's *Michael Kramer* [Joyce perhaps translated this play in English in his young years]." Mr. James Duffy had been the cashier in a private bank in Baggot Street. He would come here from Chapelizod by tram. Lone as he was, he would take his lunch at Dan Burke's and after he would be free at four o'clock he would go to an eating-house in George's Street. "His evenings were spent either before his landlady's piano or roaming about the outskirts of the city. His liking for Mozart's music brought him sometimes to an opera or a concert: these were the only dissipations of his life." He had no friends and no companions; he lived a spiritual life. Sometimes he would visit relatives at Christmas and sometimes escorted them to the cemetery when they died.

One evening, he was sitting beside two ladies in the Rotunda. One of the ladies happened to initiate a conversation with him. A young girl was beside her, and considering this girl, Mr. Duffy thought that the lady would be "a year or so younger than himself." "Her face which must have been handsome, had remained intelligent." Her eyes suggested her defiance, great sensibility, and prudence. While they talked, Mr. Duffy "tried to fix her permanently in his memory."

A few weeks afterwards, Mr. Duffy and that lady, i.e., Mrs. Sinico, met at a concert in Earlsfort Terrace and both tried to become intimate with each other. Mrs. Sinico once or twice talked of her husband but that did not deter her from trying to be intimate with Mr. Duffy. They met a third time and on that occasion Mr. Duffy "found courage to make an appointment. She came. This was the first of many meetings; they met always in the evening and chose the most quiet quarters for their walks together." Mr. Duffy did not like to meet her stealthily and so "forced her to ask him to her house." Mrs. Sinico's husband, Captain Sinico, did not mind Mr. Duffy's visits to his house. "He had dismissed his wife so sincerely from his gallery of pleasures. He did not suspect that anyone else would take an interest in her. As the husband was often away and the daughter out giving music lessons, Mr. Duffy had many opportunities of enjoying the lady's society.... Little by little he entangled his thoughts with hers."

Mr. Duffy used to lend her books and talked to about his ideas, and Mrs. Sinico gave out to him some "fact of her own life". She would urge him to write out his thoughts but Mr. Duffy was not inclined to "compete with phrasemongers." "He went often to her little cottage outside Dublin; often they spent their evenings alone. Little by little, as their thoughts entangled, they spoke of subjects less remote. Her companionship was like a warm soil about an exotic. Many times she allowed the dark to fall upon them, refraining from lighting the lamp. The dark discreet room, their isolation, the music that still vibrated in their ears united them.... The end of these discourses was that one night, during which she had shown every sign of unusual excitement, Mrs. Sinico caught up his hand passionately and pressed it to her cheek." Mr. Duffy was very much surprised and did not meet her for a week. Then they met in a cakeshop near the Parkgate. "They agreed to break off their intercourse: every bond, he said, is a bond to sorrow. When they came out of the Park they walked in silence towards the tram; but here she began to tremble so violently that, fearing another collapse on her part, he bade her good-bye quickly and left her. A few days later he received a parcel containing his books and music."

After four years, Mr. Duffy returned to his life before his meeting with Mrs. Sinico. He bought some new music pieces and Friedrick Nietzsche's *Thus Spake Zarathustra* (which asks man to overcome himself, his sorrows, defeats, etc. and become an Overman) and his *The Gay Science* (also known as *The Joyful Wisdom* or *Joyous Science*, this book inspires man to say "yea" to life). Mr. Duffy wrote seldom. "One of the sentences, written two months after his last interview with Mrs. Sinico, read: Love between man and man is impossible because there must not be sexual intercourse, and friendship between man and woman is impossible because there must be sexual intercourse."

One evening, as he was eating his dinner, in George's Street, his attention was drawn by "a paragraph in the evening paper which he had propped against the water-carafe." He was struck by that paragraph, read it over and over, paid his bill and went out. He walked home, went to bedroom, took the paper out and read the paragraph in the dim light of the window, not loudly but like the priest reads the prayers *secreto* [prayers that priests read in low voice during religious services]. The paragraph was as follows:

"Death of a Lady at Sydney Parade

A Painful Case

To-day at the City of Dublin Hospital the Deputy Coroner (in the absence of Mr. Leverett) held an inquest on the body of Mrs. Emily Sinico, aged forty-three years, who was killed at

Sydney Parade Station yesterday evening. The evidence showed that the deceased lady, while attempting to cross the line, was knocked down by the engine of the ten o'clock slow train from Kingstown, thereby sustaining injuries of the head and right side which led to her death."

When the case was brought before the court, on behalf of the railway company Mr. H.B. Patterson Finlay expressed his deep regret at the incident. He also said that "The deceased [Mrs. Emily Sinico] had been in the habit of crossing the lines late at night from platform to platform and, in view of certain other circumstances of the case, he did not think the railway officials were to blame." Mrs. Emily Sinico's husband, Captain Sinico was not present in Dublin, he came to Dublin that morning hearing about the incident. He deposed that he and Mrs. Sinico "had been married for twenty-two years and had lived happily until about two years ego, when his wife began to be rather intemperate in her habits." Miss Mary Sinico told the jury that "her mother had been in the habit of going out at night to buy spirits. She, witness, had often tried to reason with her mother and had induced her to join a League. She was not at home until an hour after the accident." The jury exonerated James Lennon, the driver of the engine.

All the above Mr. Duffy read in the newspaper, sitting in his bedroom, and "gazed out of his window on the cheerless evening landscape." He apostrophied: "what an end!" He was sorry that he disclosed "what he held as sacred.... Not merely had she degraded herself; she had degraded him. He saw the squalid tract of her vice, miserable and malodorous. His soul's companion!" He opined about her: "Evidently she had been unfit to live, without any strength of purpose, an easy prey to habits, one of the wrecks on which civilisation has been reared." He loathed her: "But that she could have sunk so low!" He recalled the night when Mrs. Sinico had burst into extreme emotion and he judiciously kept himself under control.

Outside it was gathering darkness. The memory of her hand touching him returned to him. He was shocked more than earlier. He pulled over his overcoat, went to the public-house, and ordered a hot punch. Mr. Duffy was listlessly waiting a long while and then ordered another punch and then waited there in the quiet shop till late in the night. "He sat there, living over his life with her [Mrs. Emily Sinico] and evoking alternately the two images in which he now conceived her, he realised that she was dead, that she had ceased to exist, that she had become a memory. He began to feel ill at ease. He asked himself what else could he have done. He could not have carried on a comedy of deception with her; he could not have lived with her openly. He had done what seemed to him best. How was he to blame? Now that she was gone he understood how lonely her life must have been, sitting night after night alone in that room. His life would be lonely too until he, too, died, ceased to exist, become a memory—if anyone remembered him." Mr. Duffy left the shop after nine o'clock and began to walk through the Park in the cold and dark night. Mrs. Emily Sinico, he felt, was beside him in the darkness. He seemed to hear her voice and to feel the touch of her hand. "He stood still to listen. Why had he withheld life from her? Why had he sentenced her to death? He felt his moral nature falling to pieces."

He reached the crest of the Magazine Hill and looked at the river below where lights were burning redly and invitingly in the cold night. "He looked down the slope and, at the base, in the shadow of the wall of the Park, he saw some human figures lying. Those vernal and furtive loves filled him with despair. He gnawed the rectitude of life; he felt that he had been outcaste from life's feast. One human being had seemed to love him and he had denied her life and happiness: he had sentenced her to ignominy, a death of shame." Even the human beings engaged in "vernal furtive loves" in the shadow, Mr. Duffy thought, "wished him gone." No one wanted him; he was "outcaste from life's feast." Beyond the river, a goods train was moving slowly in the darkness. The laborious drone of the engine of the train he heard as the "syllables of her [Mrs. Emily Sinico's] name."

Mr. Duffy "began to doubt the reality of what memory told him" about the affairs between herself and himself. He halted under a tree for a moment and the drone of the engine died out. Perfect silence engulfed the surround. "He felt that he was alone."

(3)

Perhaps Joyce could not absolutely decide as to what to make with this story and so he had to have "repeatedly revised" (Fargnoli and Gillespie, 66) it. And for the same reason, no single interpretation of this story is possible: it is a complex story. Complex are also the two principal characters in it—Mr. Duffy and Mrs. Emily Sinico. Mr. Duffy is an ambiguous character. We hear that he led a "spiritual life" and "lived at a distance from his body" and sustained himself in the creature comfort of his household which was far from the city of Dublin. We hear that he had neither friends nor companions; he passed his days in loneliness. But we are also told—and this is contrary to the above—that he lived in the Dublin suburb of Chapelizod "a locale near Phoenix Park long associated with the mythical lovers Tristan and Isolde." Further, after Mrs. Sinico "caught up his hand passionately and pressed it to her cheek", Mr. Duffy was "disillusioned" and completely distanced himself from her for four years till her death. Nevertheless, he began to hear music—asceticism gone?—and read life-asserting books of Nietzsche: *Thus Spake Zarathustra* ("Life is a well of joy") and *The Gay Science* (be merry). And why did he writes two months after his last meeting with Mrs. Sinico that "friendship between man and woman is impossible because there must be sexual intercourse"? And, also, why did he intently view those "vernal furtive loves" "in the shadow of the wall of the Park", and why the view "filled him with despair"? Mr. Duffy is a wobbling and complex character.

Mrs. Sinico, on the other hand, is a steadfast, constant character. She was "a year and so younger" than Mr. Duffy; was "handsome" and "intelligent" and had, a teen-aged daughter (who used to go out to impart music lessons). Her husband lived in Leoville, Sydney Parade, far from Dublin. The moot question about her is why did she "caught up his [Mr. Duffy's] hand passionately and pressed it to her cheek"? She had her husband and, on her husband's admission, they "had been married for twenty-two years and had lived happily until about two years ego", i.e., before she became intimate with Mr. Duffy for two years. And when about she beveled from Mr. Duffy's company she grew into the habit of a drunkard. Why? We may reason that in Mr. Duffy she found a surrogate husband, Captain Sinico living far away from her. And this line of reasoning may lead us to take her to be an adultress. This may be confirmed by what the unnamed narrator tells us that Mrs. Sinico degraded both herself as well as Mr. Duffy: "Not merely had she degraded herself; she had degraded him." Mr. Duffy had a great hatred for her, and that even after her death! "He saw the squalid tract of her vice, miserable and malodorous."

12. Ivy Day in the Committee Room

(1)

This story is the twelfth in the sequence of the fifteen stories of *Dubliners*, but it was the eighth in the order of composition. Again, it is the first of the four stories of the group of stories related to public life. The "Ivy Day" in the tittle refers to the day on which the most beloved leader of Ireland's struggle for freedom from the English hegemony, Charles Stewart Parnell, died—6 Oct. 1891. The day is celebrated on the 6th October each year. The "Committee Room" in the tittle of this story refers to the Committee Room No. 15 in the House of Parliament in London. "Ivy day in the Committee Room" was a favourite story of Joyce. It is the third longest story of *Dubliners* after "The Dead" and "Grace." For some readers, this story is difficult for two reasons: one, it has a good number of Irish words and slangs; and two, it refers us to some terms, ideas and jargons related to the time of the Nationalist movement of Ireland.

The Irish Words and Slangs

cocks him up (slang) = encourages an inflated self-image.

a sup taken = a hard drink of alcohol.

bowsy (slang) = rogue.

tinker = gypsy.

shoreens = an Irish who imitates English custom and snobbery.

hunker-sliding (slang) = shirking.

spondulics or spondulix (slang) = money.

musha = expression of surprise or disbelief.

usha = contraction of musha.

shoeboy (slang) = a boot-licker or an insincere flatterer.

moya = bitter or exceptional.

had a tricky little black bottle up in a corner (slang) = sold liquor illegally.

a decent skin (Irish slang) = a good person underneath it all.

Knock it out = get along financially.

goster (Irish-English) = gossip.

yerra (Irish) = really.

wisha (Irish) = a variant of musha.

P.L.G. = Pro-Legit-Gamer (one who does not have to cheat to win.

vermin = malaproprism for ermine (a stoat coat used by judges, etc.)

Did the cow calve? (slang) = is there any reason to celebrate?

a loan of = influence got from somebody or something.

Terms and Jargons Related to Irish Nationalist Movement

[Ireland was under the rule of Great Britain since the 16th century. The first cogent rebellion against the British rule occurred in 1798. After that, under the mighty leadership of the great nationalist Charles Stewart Parnell—"the uncrowned King of Ireland"—the nationalist movement gathered powerful momentum. But when Parnell's affairs with Katherine ("Killy") O'Shea, a married woman, became a public knowledge in 1889, he had his irrevocable downfall, and consequently, the nationalist movement lost its steam, particularly after Parnell's death in 1891. About 25 years afterwards, in April 1916 the Irish republicans launched a potential movement against the British rule, known as Easter Rising or Easter Rebellion and proclaimed Ireland a Republic. Finally, on 21 January 1919, Sinn Fein declared Irish Independence.]

German monarch = "Edward VII (1841-1910); the King of Great Britain and Ireland (1901-1910), son of Queen Victoria and Prince Albert, both of whom were of German descent."

Nationalist = A member of the Irish Parliamentary Party which demanded full independence of Ireland.

Fenian = A member of the secret revolutionary party or group that was formed in New York with the objective of freeing Ireland from British rule. The Fenian movement was active from the 1860s to the end of WWI. The secret revolutionary party was called Irish Republican Brotherhood. The "fenian" means ancient inhabitant of Ireland. The word derived from the legendary Irish King Finn MacCool.

Castle hacks = The term refers to informers who gathered information about the British people who ruled over Ireland from the Castle in central Dublin.

Major Sirr = Henery Charles Sirr (1764-1841), an Irish, who was an officer in the British army and who put down Irish freedom movements in 1798 and 1803.

Mansion House = The official residence of Lord Mayor of Dublin.

Old Mother = Queen Victoria.

Chief, the = Charles Stewart Parnell (1846-91).

"*Hillside men*" = The term applied to the Fenians.

(2)

The principal characters of "Ivy Day in the Committee Room" are:

1. Old Jack. He is an old man, "very bony and hairy." He had "moist blue eyes" and "moist mouth." He had a nineteen years old impudent son. Old Jack was the caretaker of the Committee Room in Wicklow Street.
2. Mr. "Mat" O'Connor. Hynes addressed him as "Mat." He was a "grey-haired man, whose face was disfigured by many blotches and pimples." He was engaged by Mr. Richard Tierney's agent to canvass for Tierney. He used to wear an ivy (leaf) in his coat.
3. Mr. Richard Tierney. He was a P.L.G. (one who does not have to cheat to win) and a boozer.

4. Joe Hynes. He was a "tall, slender young man with a light brown moustache." In the Committee Room he recited the 44-line poem that began with the verse extolling Charles Stewart Parnell:
   He is dead. Our Uncrowned King is dead.
   O, Erin [Ireland], mourn with grief and woe
   For he lies dead whom the fell gang
   Of modern hypocrites laid low.
5. Colgan. He was "a working man" who also stood as a candidate in the Municipal Election.
6. Father Keon. A poor clergyman in shabby frock-coats. He had a long mouth and very bright blue eyes. His voice was velvety. A disrespectful man.
7. Mr. John Henchy. He had the habit of taking snuffling (breathing hard) and spitting copiously.
8. Mr. Crofton. He was a fat man with a sloping figure and a young ox's face. He had blue eyes and a grizzling moustache. He was canvassing for Mr. Tierney (a Nationalist), but before that he had been canvassing for Wilkins, a Conservative. He was an opportunist.
9. Lyons. A young man with a thin clean-shaven face. He wore a double collar and a wide brimmed bowler hat. He was canvassing for Mr. Tierney. He was a Nationalist.

Old Jack and Mr. O'Connor were sitting near the burning cinders. Old Jack raked up the fire with a piece of card-board. Mr. O'Connor put a cigarette in his mouth and took out a pack of thin pasteboard card and read out what was printed on it:

"Municipal Elections

Royal Exchange Ward

Mr. Richard J. Tierney, P.LG., respectfully solicits the
favour of your vote and influence at the
coming election in the Royal Exchange Ward."

Mr. O'Connor had been engaged by Tierney's agent to canvass. It was the 6th October—the day on which Charles Stewart Parnell died and the day, which was celebrated as the Ivy Day, was cold, dark and dismal. So, Mr. O'Connor and Old Jack were sitting idly in the Committee Room in the Withlow Street.

Old Jack, the caretaker of the Committee Room, told Mr. O'Connor that he wanted to make his nineteen-years-old son a decent youth and so had sent him to the Christian Brothers but his son went around boozing. Old Jack said that he would like to beat him for correction but his wife spoiled him doing something stupid ("The mother, you know, she cocks him up with this and that....") Mr. O'Connor opined that such things as his wife did to his son spoiled children. Old Jack said that as a result of his mother's putting him upright, or defending him, his son took the upper hand over him (the old man) whenever he took to drinking ("I've a sup taken"). Ruefully, the old man (Old Jack) wondered: "What's the world coming to when sons speaks the way to their fathers?" Mr. O'Connor asked the old man why he did not get a service for his son, and the old man replied that whenever his son got a job he spent all the money on wine ("he drinks it all.").

When they were talking thus, Joe Hynes ("Someone") entered the room and asked if it was a Freemason's meeting in that room (freemasonry is a secret fraternal order that preaches instinctive understanding and sympathy among members). Next moment Hynes asked how the canvassing for Mr. Tierney was going ("How goes it?"). Mr. O'Connor said that it was not going well ("shook his head."). Hynes asked if Mr. Tierney paid him for his canvassing and O'Connor said: "Not yet." Hynes satirically laughed. The old man interceded, saying Mr. Tierney might not have paid O'Connor but he would pay because Mr. Tierney was not like the working-class Colgan (who was another candidate in that election). The old man said this scornfully and so Hynes argued that there was no difference between a working-man and a publican and that a working-man had the right to be in the Municipal Corporation. Hynes also said that a working man was better than the Irish people who flaunt British customs and behaviour ("shoneens"), always holding hats in their hands. Mr. O'Connor agreed with him.

Hynes continued: "The working-man (Colgan) is not going to drag the honour of Dublin in the mud to please a German monarch (Queen Victoria or the British)." Mr. O'Connor said that their man, i.e., Mr. Tierney, would not go to kowtow before a foreign (British) King, Edward VII (Edward Rex) because he is a Nationalist. Mr. Hynes differed from Mr. O'Connor and satirically said that Mr. Tierney was a tricky man—"Tricky Dicky Tierney". Mr. O'Connor then said that Mr. Hines might be right but he wished Mr. Tierney returned there with money ("spondulics") to pay them. The three men—Mr. O'Connor, Mr. Hynes and the Old man (Old Jack)—then fell silent. Mr. Hynes took off his hat (a symbol of a *shoneen*) and then when he turned down the color of his coat an ivy leaf (a symbol of Ireland and Irish nationalism) appeared. Again a silence fell in the room.

At this moment, Mr. Henchy flew into the room, saying "No money, boys", meaning Mr. Tierney was not going to pay them, the canvassers, at that point of time. Mr. Hynes chucklingly told Mr. ("Mat") O'Connor: "What did I tell you, Mat?".... Tricky Dicky Tierney." Mr. Henchy then went further on Mr. Tierney: "He hasn't got those little pig's eyes for nothing. Blast his soul! Couldn't he pay up like a man instead of "O, now Mr. Henchy, I must speak to Mr. Fanning.... I've spent a lot of money." Mr. Henchy also said that Mr. Tierney's old father sold liquor illegally ("had a tricky little black bottle up in a corner"). Mr. Hynes went out slowly.

Mr. Henchy breathed hard and sat copiously and then told Mr. O'Connor that Joe Hynes's father, Larry Hynes, was a respectable man but Joe was "not nineteen carat" and that Joe was a spy of Colgan's. Old Jack dittoed Mr. Henchy's opinion about Joe Hynes. Mr. Henchy further said that "hillsiders and fenians", like Mr. Hynes, were secretly in the pay of the Castle (the Dublin Castle was the headquarters of the English rulers of Ireland) and that such hillsiders and fenians were "Castle hacks." They were, Mr. Henchy said, descendants of Major Sirr (Henry Charles Sirr suppressed the Irish rebellion of 1798, in spite of himself being an Irish man). Mr. Henchy interjected about "a certain little nobleman with a cock-eye" who was a lineal descendant of Major Sirr: "O, the heart's blood of a patriot! That's a fellow now that'd sell his country for fourpence—ay—and go down on his bended knees and thank the Almighty Christ he had a country to sell."

There was a "knock at the door" and then Father Keon appeared. Mr. Henchy asked him to sit down but as he was to go to the *Black Eagle* (a public house), he swiftly went away. Mr. Henchy and Mr. O'Connor doubted the exact nature of Keon. Mr. Henchy believed him to be a "black sheep" and told Mr. O'Connor that how Father Keon could have his two ends meet was a mystery. Both Mr. O'Connor and Mr. Henchy were feeling thirsty of drink and asked the little shoeboy (errand-boy) to bring a dozen of stout but the boy was in deep goster (gossip) with Alderman Cowley. Henchy said that the dwarf boy ("hop-o'-my-thumb") certainly had forgotten all about the drink. Mr. Connor and Mr. Henchy then entered into a conversation about the Irish peoples' ("Dubliners") indolence and monetary corruption. Mr O'Connor said that he had seen three men engaged hard at a game (including that dwarf boy). Mr. Henchy said he understood something of the game, and he explained it in some detail: "You must owe the City Father's money nowadays if you want to be made Lord Mayor. Then they'll make you Lord Mayor."

At that time there was yet another "knock at the door" and a boy entered and put down a basket full of bottles of liquors from O'Farrell's shop. The boy asked for the basket of empty bottles but the old man (Old Jack) told him to come the next day for that. Mr. Henchy asked the boy to bring a corkscrew and he obeyed. The old man opened three bottles for the three. Mr. Henchy then asked the boy:

> "Would you like a drink, boy?"
>
> "If you please, sir," said the boy.
>
> The old man opened another bottle grudgingly, and handed it to the boy.
>
> "What age are you?" he asked.
>
> "Seventeen," said the boy.

The boy took the bottle, drank its contents, and went away showing respects to Mr. Henchy and taking back the cork screw.

Now two new men entered the room, Mr. Crofton and Mr. Lyons. The second man sniffed the smell of the liquor in the room and enquired if there was something to celebrate in the room ("Did the cow calf?"). Mr. Lyons censoringly told everyone in the room: "Is that the way you chaps canvass," said Mr. Lyons, "and Crafton and I out in the cold and rain looking for votes?" Mr. Henchy threw a repartee: "Why, blast your soul," said Mr. Henchy, "I'd get more votes in five minutes than you two'd get in a week." Mr. O'Connor asked the old man, Jack, to bring two bottles of stout but the old man said that there was no cork-screw. Mr. Henchy got up quickly to show the trick of opening the cork of a bottle of liquor. "He took two bottles from the table and, carrying them to the fire, put them on the hob [a surface beside a fireplace on which anything may be kept to keep it hot]." "In a few minutes an apologetic 'Pok!' was heard as the cork flew out of Mr. Lyons' bottle [the heated liquor of the bottle pressurized the cork to go off]. Mr. Lyons jumped off the table, went to the fire, took his bottle and carried it back to the table."

At this time, Mr. Lyons raised the point of the visit (and Address) of King Edward VII (King of Great Britain and Ireland, and Emperor of India from 1901 to 1910, and the eldest son of Queen Victoria) to Ireland. Mr. Lyons, who was canvassing for Mr. Tierney, was against the King's visit, and this Mr. Henchy knew well. Mr. Henchy, therefore, was trying to persuade Mr. Lyons to abandon his objection to the visit of the King. "Listen to me," said Mr. Henchy. "What we want in this country, as I said to old Ward, is capital [finance or money]. The King's coming here will mean an influx of money into this country. The citizens of Dublin will benefit by it. Look at all the factories down by the quays there, idle! Look at all the money there is in the country! if we only worked the old industries, the mills, the ship-building yards and factories. It's capital we want." To Mr. Henchy the independence of Ireland was of secondary consideration after Ireland's material advancement. To fortify his point, Mr. Henchy went further: "Parnell," said Mr. Henchy, "is dead. Now, here's the way I look at it. Here's this chap [King Edward VII] come to the throne after his old mother keeping him out of it till the man was grey. He's a man of the world, and he means well by us. He's a jolly fine, decent fellow, if you ask me, and no damn nonsense about him. He just says to himself: 'The old one never went to see these wild Irish. By Christ, I'll go myself and see what they are like.' And are we going to insult the man when he comes over here on a friendly visit? Eh? Isn't that right, Crofton?" Mr. Crofton agreed with him.

But Mr. Lyons contradicted Mr. Henchy by hinting at some objectionable things said of the king. Mr. Henchy did not give up: he said, "Let's bygones be bygones." But Mr. Lyons stuck to his particular view: "What I mean," said Mr. Lyons, "is we have our ideals. Why, now, would we welcome a man like that [King Edward VII]? Do you think now after what he [King Edward VII] did Parnell was a fit man to lead us? And why, then, would we do it for Edward the Seventh?" Mr. O'Connor dowsed the hot controversy saying that that day was (Charles Stewart) Parnell's (death) anniversary and that they all, and even the Conservatives, respected him after he had been "dead and gone."

At this moment there was the third sound: "Pok!" The sound indicated that this time the cork of Mr. Crofton's bottle flew out and away. Mr. Crofton rushed to the fire, grabbed the bottle, came back, and said in a deep voice: "Our side of the house respects him [Parnell], because he was a gentleman." Mr. Henchy supported him loudly and said: "He [Parnell] was the only man that could keep the bag of cats in order. 'Down, ye dogs! Lie down, ye curs!' That's the way he treated them [the English]." Joe Hynes came in slowly. On seeing him, Mr. Henchy asked Old Jack to bring another bottle of stout and he put the bottle on the hob. Mr. O'Connor then asked Joe Hynes to sit down and told him that they were talking about Parnell—"the Chief." Mr. Hynes sat silently. Mr. Lyons thankfully told Joe Hynes that he (Joe) had not renounced the path of Parnell: "By God, I'll say for you, Joe! No, by God, you stuck to him like a man!"

Suddenly, Mr. O'Connor asked Joe Hynes to read out what he had written. Mr. Henchy seconded him and told Mr. Crofton that it was a "splendid thing." Mr. O'Connor shouted: "Fire away, Joe." But Mr. Hynes at once could not figure out what to fire and "after reflecting a while" said:

"O, that thing is it.... Sure, that's old now."

"Out with it, man!" said Mr. O'Connor.

"Sh, sh," said Mr. Henchy. "Now, Joe!"

Mr. Joe Hynes hesitated for a while, while he was rehearsing the poem he was to recite in his mind, and then announced: "THE DEATH OF PARNELL, 6 October 1891." He then "cleared his throat once or twice and then began to recite:

He is dead. Our Uncrowned King is dead.
O, Erin [Ireland], mourn with grief and woe
For he lies dead whom the fell gang
Of modern hypocrites laid low.
He lies slain by the coward hounds
He raised to glory from the mire;
And Erin's hopes and Erin's dreams
Perish upon her monarch's pire.
In palace, cabin or in cot
The Irish heart where'er it be
Is bowed with woe—for he is gone
Who would have wrought her destiny.
He would have had his Erin famed,
The green flag gloriously unfurled,
Her statesmen, bard and warriors raised
Before the nations of the World.
He dreamed (alas, 'twas but a dream!)
Of Liberty: but as he strove
To clutch that idol, treachery
Sundered him from the thing he loved.
Shame on the coward, caitiff hands
That smote their Lord or with a kiss
Betrayed him to the rabble-rout
Of fawning priests—no friends of his.
May everlasting shame consume
The memory of those who tried
To befoul and smear the exalted name
Of one who spurned them in his pride.
He fell as fall the mighty ones,

Nobly undaunted to the last,
And death has now united him
With Erin's heroes of the past.
No sound of strife disturb his sleep!
Calmly he rests: no human pain
Or high ambition spurs him now
The peak of glory to attain.
They had their way: they laid him low.
But Erin, list, his spirit may
Rise, like the Phoenix from the flames
When breaks the dawning of the day,
The day that brings us Freedom's reign.
And on that day may Erin well
Pledge in the cup she lifts to Joy
One grief—the memory of Parnell.

Recitation over, Mr. Hynes sat down on the table and there fell a short silence. Then the auditors applauded Mr. Hynes with a burst of clapping, "even Mr. Lyons clapped." And then all "drank from their bottles in silence." Suddenly, once again and for the last time, that very sound was heard: "Pok!" The sound was produced when the cork of Mr. Hynes's bottle went off. Mr. Hynes heard the sound sitting on the table, coolly. Mr. O'Connor cheered Mr. Joe Hynes saying "Good man, Joe!" and then to hide his jubilation took out his cigarette papers and tobacco pouch. Mr. John Henchy asked Mr. Crofton: "Isn't that fine? What?" And "Mr. Crofton said that it was a very fine piece of writing."

13. A Mother

(1)

This is the second of the four stories of *Dubliners* that relate matters of public life. "A Mother" was the tenth story that Joyce wrote for *Dubliners* sometime in September 1905, though it is the thirteen story in the published collection. Its predecessor, "Ivy Day in the Committee Room" was related to the political life of Dublin (or Ireland) but it—"A Mother"—is concerned with the cultural life of the people of Dublin (or Ireland): the Celtic Revival, the (Irish) language movement, and the paralysis in the social and cultural spheres of Dublin (or Ireland). There is yet another difference between the two stories: "Ivy Day" is concerned with masses or groups of Dubliners but "A Mother" focuses on a single woman—a mother.

(2)

The chief persons in "A Mother" are the following:

1. Mrs. Kearney. She, as a mother, is the eponym of the story. Before her marriage, she was Miss Devlin. She learned French and music and nursed a romantic life in future. She was naturally pale and of unbending nature. She married Mr. Kearney, a boot-maker, morganetically. She was the mother of Miss Kathleen Kearney who learned French and music in a high-class convent.
2. Mr. Holohan. Mr. Kearney and Mr. Holohan are the two most prominent characters in "A Mother." Mr. Holohan had a game leg (i.e., lame leg). People would call him Happy Holohan for his insoucience with any thing. He was the Assistant Secretary of the *Eire Aby* Society (a patriotic society whose motto *Eire Abu*) means "Ireland to Victory!"
3. Mr. Kearney. He was a boot-maker whom Miss Devlin married "out of spite" and became Mrs. Kearney. He was much older than Mrs. Kearney and a submissive husband to her. With a great brown beard, he was "sober, thrifty and pious." In temperament and aspiration, he was contrary to Mrs. Kearney. But, all the same, they made a tolerably good couple. Mr. Kearney was, though, a model father.
4. Miss Kathleen Kearney. She was the daughter of Mr. and Mrs. Kearney and was, supposedly, in her late teens. She was given to study the Irish Language under an Irish teacher and was trained in music. People thought her to be a "very nice girl." Like her father, Mr. Kearney, she was submissive to Mrs. Kearney. She was "a believer in the [Irish] language movement." Miss Kathleen had a younger sister.

5. Mr. Fitzpatrick. He was a little man with a vacant face and his accent was flat. He was the secretary of the *Eire Abu* Society.
6. Mr. Duggan. A first-rate bass singer and "a slender young man with a scattered black moustache."
7. Mr. Bell. The second tenor, "a fair-haired little man."
8. Miss Healy. She was the contralto in the final concert.
9. Madam Glynn. She was the soprano in the final concert.
10. Mr. O'Madden Burke. An elderly suave man, with an umbrella which was large and made of silk. He had an imposing body. "His magniloquent western name was the moral umbrella upon which he balanced...the fine problem of his finances. He was widely respected."

Mr. Holohan, the assistant secretary of the *Eire Abu* Society, was anxiously busy arranging for a series of concerts for the society for nearly one month. But "in the end it was Mrs. Kearney who arranged everything." Mrs. Kearney learned French and music in a high-class convent. Her "ivory manners" (elitist behaviour) and exclusiveness kept her prospective suitors at bay and so to have a taste of the romantically coloured life she would secretly frequent delicate Turkish eateries. Her suitors then began to tease her and to take vengeance on them she married Mr. Kearney, a boot-maker, who was far below herself in social status but much older than herself.

Mrs. Kearney did never walk away from her romanticism and yet she was a good wife to her old husband: when his cough grew troublesome she "put the eiderdown quilt over his feet and made a strong rum punch." On the other hand, Mr. Kearney would go in the summer to the holiday resort of Skerries or Howth or Greystones, near Dublin, along with his whole family. Mr. Kearney had sent Kathleen to a star convent where she learned French and music (to be *avant-garde*). Miss Kathleen was "very clever at music".

One day, Mr. Holohan visited the Kearneys and proposed that Miss Kathleen would be "the accompanist at a series of four grand concerts which his Society [the *Eire Abu* Society] was going to give in the Ancient Concert Rooms." Mrs. Kearney accepted the proposal and "a contract was drawn up by which Kathleen was to receive eight guineas for her services as accompanist at four grand concerts." As Mr. Holohan was a novice in matters related to the concerts, he came to Mrs. Kearney and she helped him with advices. Mrs. Kearney bought some lovely blush-pink charmeuse for Kathleen to wear during the concerts. Also she bought a dozen two-shilling tickets of the final concerts for her friends.

The four concerts were to be on Wednesday, Thursday, Friday and Saturday. On Wednesday, Mrs. Kearney went to Ancient Concert Rooms with her daughter for the first concert and was disappointed to see only a few young men in the auditorium who were not in evening dress. However, in the dressing-room she was introduced to the secretary of the *Eire Abu* Society, Mr. Fitzpatrick. When it was very late (the auditorium showing no sign of hope), Mr. Fitzpatrick announced: "Well, now, ladies and gentlemen, I suppose we'd better open the ball." Mrs. Kearney expressed her contempt at Mr. Fitzpatrick's "very flat final syllable." Mrs. Kearney expressed her dissatisfaction with the performances and Mr. Holohan, agreeing with her, said that the committee "had decided to let the first three concerts go as they pleased and reserve all the talent for Saturday night." "The concert expired shortly before ten, and every one went home quickly." "The concert on Thursday night was better attended, but Mrs. Kearney saw at once that the house was filled with paper. The audience behaved indecorously, as if the concert were an informal dress rehearsal." Mr. Fitzpatrick seemed jovial, nonetheless, but Mrs. Kearney was disappointed once more when she learned that the committee decided to skip the concert on Friday with the view to "secure a bumper house on Saturday night." Hearing this, Mrs. Kearney buttonholed Mr. Holohan and asked him if it was true. When Mr. Holohan said that it was true, Mrs. Kearney threw into his face the stern warning: "But, of course, that doesn't alter the contract", she said. "The contract was for four concerts."

"The night of the grand concert came. Mrs. Kearney, with her husband and daughter, arrived at the Ancient Concert Rooms three-quarter of an hour before the time at which the concert was to begin." Unluckily, it was a rainy evening. Mrs. Kearney asked Miss Beirne that she wanted to meet one of the secretaries of the society and Miss Beirne told her that they would arrive any moment. But none was in view and so Mrs. Kearney entered the dressing-room leaving her husband elsewhere with the charge of keeping her daughter's (Kathleen's) clothes and music.

The *artistes* were arriving: the bass singer Mr. Duggan, the second tenor Mr. Bell, the contralto Miss Healy, the soprano Madam Glynn, the first tenor singer and the baritone singer. Mrs. Kearney brought her daughter in the company of the *artistes* and talked with them amiably, always keeping a searching eye after the movements of the limping Mr. Holohan. At an opportune moment she demanded of Mr. Holohan "when was her daughter going to be paid." She reminded him that as per the contract her daughter was to be paid eight guineas. Mr. Holohan told her that it was not his responsibility but it was the responsibility of Mr. Fitzpatrick (the secretary of the *Eire Abu* Society). Mrs. Kearney sternly reminded him about the contract: "I don't know anything about Mr. Fitzpatrick", repeated Mrs. Kearney. "I have my contract, and I intend to see that it is carried out."

Mrs. Kearney came back to the dressing room where one *Freeman* man (a reporter for the daily newspaper *The Freeman's Journal*) and Mr. O'Madden Burke were conversing with Miss Healy and the baritone singer. Miss Healy stood in front of the *Freeman* man, Mr. Hendrick, and the "warmth, fragrance and color of her body appealed to his senses." But due to the imminent demand of his duty, he could stay no longer and so took leave of her regretfully. Then Mr. Hendrick, along with Mr. Holohan, went upstairs and entered into a secluded room and there found Mr. O'Madden Burke, the "suave, elderly man" with his umbrella. "While Mr. Holohan was entertaining the *Freeman* man Mrs. Kearney was speaking so animatedly to her husband that he had to ask her to lower her voice." Meanwhile

Mr. Bell, "the first item", stood ready for his performance but Miss Kathleen Kearney, showed no sign of readiness.

At this moment, Mr. Holohan and Mr. O'Madden Burke came into the dressing-room. Mr. Holohan very earnestly tried to persuade Mrs. Kearney to ask Miss Kathleen to begin her performance as the accompanist. He also appealed to Mr. Kearney and Miss Kearney, but Mrs. Kearney would not budge from her stand: "She won't go on without her money." "The noise in the auditorium had risen to a clamour when Mr. Fitzpatrick burst into the room, followed by Mr. Holohan, who was panting. The clapping and stamping in the hall were punctuated by whistling. Mr. Fitzpatrick held a few bank notes in his hand. He counted out four into Mrs. Kearney's hand and said she would get the other half at the interval. Mrs. Kearney said: "This is four shillings short." At once, Miss Kathleen Kearney urged Mr. Bell to start their performance. The noisy hall became silent on their appearance and they performed successfully. The first part of the concert was well done, only Madam Glynn's song—*Killarney*—was poor. [The song *Killarney* is a classic song about the natural beauty of the surround of the lake of Killarney.] The first part of it runs thus:

> By Killarney's lakes and fells
> Emerald isles and winding bays
> Mountain paths and woodland dells
> Memory ever fondly strays
> Bounteous nature loves all lands
> Beauty wanders everywhere
> Footprints leave on many strands
> But her home is surely there
> Angels fold their wings and rest
> In that Eden of the West
> Beauty's home, Killarney
> Heaven's reflex, Killarney.

Miss Kathleen "played a selection of Irish airs which was generously applauded." The first part of the concert was well appreciated by the audience. In the dressing-room, all the participants in the concert and in the management were full of excitement, excepting Mr. O'Madden Burke. Mr. Burke said:

"It was the most scandalous exhibition he had ever witnessed. Miss Kathleen Kearney's musical career was ended in Dublin after that, he said."

The second part of the exhibition was to begin after the interval. During the interval, the matter of the payment to Mrs. Kearney was being discussed. Miss Beirne definitely opined that she should not be paid anything further ("Pay her nothing."). Mrs. Kearney told Miss Healy, the young lady who was to recite the patriotic piece in the second part, and others that "the committee treated her scandalously." The committee thought that they could deal with her roughly. "But she would show them their mistake.... If they didn't pay her to the last farthing she would make Dublin ring."

Mr. Fitzpatrick and Mr. Holohan met Mrs. Kearney and "told her that the other four guineas would be paid after the committee meeting on the following Tuesday and that, in case her daughter did not play for the second part [of the concert] the committee would consider the contract broken and would pay nothing." This very much angered Mrs. Kearney and she blurted: "I haven't seen any committee", said Mrs. Kearney angrily. "My daughter has her contract. She will get four pounds eight into her hand or a foot she won't put on that platform." Mr. Holohan told her that he was surprised at her behaviour. Mrs. Kearney retorted that she was treated by him in no better way. "Her face was inundated with an angry colour and she looked as if she would attack some one with her hands." She told Mr. Holohan that she asked for her rights. Mr. Holohan, on the other hand told her that she should have shown some sense of decency. Mrs. Kearney told him that it was his, and not her, business to talk to the secretary Mr. Fitzpatrick about the payment, and that she was "a great fellow fol-the-diddle-I-do [a nonsense phrase]."

"After that Mrs. Kearney's conduct was condemned on all hands: every one approved of what the committee had done." Mrs. Kearney, "haggard with rage", stood there till the beginning of the second part of the performance, "arguing with her husband and daughter", "in the hope that the secretaries would approach her." But the secretaries were no more in view and so she stood there for an instant "like an angry stone image". And when the first sound of the song of the second part of the performance reached her ears, Mrs. Kearney "caught up her daughter's cloak and said to her husband: "Get a cab!" Her husband went out and she followed him. Stopping at the doorway, she "glared into Mr. Holohan's face" and "I'm not done with you yet", she said. But Mr. Holohan replied that he was done with her. Miss Kathleen "followed her mother meekly." And Mr. Holohan "began to pace up and down the room in order to cool himself, for he felt his skin on fire."

"That's a nice lady!" he said. "O, she's a nice lady!"

"You did the proper thing, Holohan", said Mr. O'Madden Burke, poised upon his umbrella in approval.

14. Grace

(1)

This 30-page long story is the second longest story in *Dubliners*, next only to "The Dead." If we take "The Dead" as the virtual coda, "Grace" is the 14th and last story of *Dubliners*. In order of composition, it is the 12th story, and it was never published before it was published in *Dubliners*. Joyce's brother Stanislaus reported that James Joyce planned this story on the structure of Dante's *Divine Comedy*. It was absolutely true, indeed, but Joyce treated his story not seriously as in *Divine Comedy* but absolutely satirically. The central character of this story is Mr. Tom Kernan who appears in Ulysses as well as in Finnegans wake. "Grace" reminds one of Shakespeare's *The Taming of the Shrew*. The story has three parts: in the first part, Mr. Kernan fell from a staircase in a lavatory due to being over-drunk, and injured himself (Hell); in the second part, Mr. Kernan's friends made him believe that his fall was due to his "sin" of boozing, and persuaded him to go for a retreat for his salvation (Purgetory); and in the third part, Mr. Kernan was redeemed out of his "sin" as a result of his prayers (Paradise). However, this story was also refused publication for the use of the word "bloody" twice in its body.

(2)

The principal characters of this story are:

1. Mr. Kernan. He was a Dublin tea-taster.
2. Mrs. Kernan. She was the wife of Mr. Kernan. She was "an active, practical woman of middle age."
3. Martin Cunningham, Jack Power, C.P.M'Coy and Mr. Fogarty (a Dublin grocer) were Mr. Kernan's friends.

Like in "Ivy Day in the Committee Room", in this story also there are some non-English (Irish) words: *sha* (Irish, meaning "yes"); *ulster* (Irish, meaning "a long, heavy overcoat with a belt"); *bostooms* (Irish, meaning "rogues"); *peloothered* (Irish, meaning "thoroughly drunk") and *omadhauns* (Irish, meaning "fools").

Mr. Tom Kernan had fallen at night, under the effect of a booze, from a flight of stairs in the lavatory in a pub. He was unconscious and blood oozed out from skull and gum in the mouth. People around informed the police, who came and noted the accident. Then Mr. Kernan was huddled into a car and taken to his house on the Glasnevin road.

In the second part of the story, we find Mr. Kernan on a bed in his own house. Mr. Kernan's wife came in and complained that he has "been drinking since Friday", implying that his fall was due to his uncontrolled attraction to drinking. Mr. Power, a young friend of Mr. Kernan, tried to persuade Mr. Kernan's wife to belive that the fall was just an accident, but Mrs. Kernan would not be convinced. She told Mr. Power: "O, you needn't tell me that, Mr. Power. I know you are a friend of his, not like some of the others he does be with. They're all right so long as he has money within his pocket to keep him out from his wife and family."

Mrs. Kernan, a woman of middle age, was in good terms with her husband immediately after marriage. She found him "a jovial well-fed man." But only after "three weeks she had found a wife's life irksome and, later on, when she was beginning to find it unbearable, she had become a mother. Since then for twenty-five years she had been caring for the family, her two eldest sons and other younger ones as well as her husband. Her husband has not been violent since the children have grown up. Mr. Kernan was sitting, propped up with pillows when his friends were ushered in. He was quite in the dark about the fact that his fall (from the flight of stairs) was the result of a plot. Among the friends of Mr. Kernan who saw him were Mr. Cunningham, Mr. M'Coy and Mr. Power. Mr. Cunningham was highly intelligent and knowledgeable, but in family life he was unhappy, mostly due to his wife, "an unpresentable woman who was an incurable drunkard."

The three friends, who met Mr. Kernan, divulged the plot behind Mr. Kernan's fall to Mrs. Kernan. Mr. Kernan simply said: "I leave it all in your hands, Mr. Cunningham." Mrs. Kernan had been disillusioned from her 25 years of married life. She knew though Mr. Kernan married her after converting to Catholicism, he would not be reformed. She also saw "a curious appropriateness" in her husband's fall, particularly in his biting off half of his tongue as a result of the fall—as a divine punishment for his non-compliance with Catholicism. She believed in the Sacred Heart, the Holy Ghost and the banshee, a mythical bird in Ireland that they believed to shriek before any death in a family, all these being Catholic beliefs. Meantime, Mrs. Kernan placed a tray of refreshments and said, "Help yourselves, gentlemen." Her husband asked:

> "And have you nothing for me, duckie?"
>
> "O, you! The back of my hand to you!" Said Mrs. Kernan tartly.

Her husband called after her: "Nothing for poor little hubby!" To save his face, Mr. Kernan assumed a humorous grimace. The guests fell into a religious conversation. Mr. Power said that the Jesuit Order was good, but Mr. M'Coy complained that the Jesuits cater only for the upper classes. Mr. Cunningham opined that the Irish priesthood was honoured all over the world.

Mrs. Kernan announced that Mr. Fogarty had arrived. Fogarty had pale, oval face and a "fair trailing moustache." He was "a modest grocer." Fogarty brought a bottle of whiskey for Mr. Kernan. However, Mr. Cunningham said that Pope Leo XIII wanted to unite the Latin and Greek churches and that he was a great scholar and a poet. Mr. Power said that "great minds can see things." On the other hand, Fogarty said "As the poet says: *Great minds are very near to madness*." Fogarty said that the Pope is infallible because he speaks *ex-cathedra*. Mr. Kernan kept him aloof from the debate, but Mrs. Kernan silently supported the infallibility theory and was glad. Mr. Kernan's friends then decided to take Mr. Kernan to the Jesuit Church for retreat. Mr. Power turned to Mrs. Kernan and said: "Well, Mrs. Kernan, we're going to make your man here a good holy pious and God-fearing Roman catholic." Mr. Kernan "swept his arm round the company inclusively", saying "I don't mind."

In the third part of the story, we find Mr. Kernan and his friends in the Jesuit Church. The transept of the Jesuit Church was full to the brim with visitors, who were well-dressed. "In one of the benches near the pulpit sat Mr. Cunningham and Mr. Kernan. In the bench behind sat Mr. M'Coy alone: and in the bench behind him sat Mr. Power and Mr. Fogarty. Mr. Kernan was seen in the unsettled congregation. The Priest was also seen. Father Purdon knelt down and prayed. The congregation followed Father Purdon and then resettled on the benches. He then "turned back each wide sleeve of his surplice with an elaborate gesture and slowly surveyed the array of faces." Then he said: "*For the children of this world are wiser in their generation than the children of light. Wherefore make unto yourselves friends out of the mammon of iniquity so that when you die they may receive you into everlasting dwellings*." Father Purdon explained this difficult quotation from the scripture properly. To a superficial glance, this quotation seem to be at variance with the "lofty morality elsewhere preached by Jesus Christ." Father Purdon said: "It [the quoted italisized sentence] was a text for business and professional men. Jesus Christ, with his divine understanding of every cranny of our human nature, understood that all men were not called to the religious life, that by far the vast majority were forced to live in the world, and, to a certain extent, for the world: and in this sentence He designed to give them a word of counsel, setting before them as exemplars in the religious life those very worshippers of Mammon who were of all men the least solicitous in matters religious." Father Purdon further told the congregation: "Jesus Christ was not a hard taskmaster. He understood our little failings, understood the weakness of our poor fallen nature, understood the temptations of this life. We might have had, we all had from time to time, our temptations: we might have, we all had, our failings. But one thing only, he said, he would ask of his hearers. And that was: to be straight and manly with God. If their accounts tallied in every point to say: "Well, I have verified my accounts. I find all well." But if, as might happen, there were some discrepancies, to admit the truth, to be frank and say like a man: "Well, I have looked into my accounts. I find this wrong and this wrong. But, with God's grace, I will rectify this and this. I will set right my accounts" (Father Purdon suggested the Catholic idea of Paradise).

15. The Dead

(1)

This is one of the best short stories that Joyce wrote. Some commentators call it not a short story but a novella, like, for instance, Ernest Hemingway's *The Old Man and the Sea*. Dan Barry (of *The New York Times*) called it "just about the finest story in the English language" and T.S. Eliot "called it one of the greatest short stories ever written." Joyce's official biographer, Richard Ellman wrote that "In its lyrical, melancholy acceptance of all that life and death offer, 'The Dead' is a linchpin in Joyce's work".

The popularity of "The Dead" may be gauged from the following list of its adaptations:

1. 1967= It was adapted as an one-act play of the same name by Hugh Leonard.
2. 1973= Joyce Carol Oates' story "The Dead" makes many references to Joyce's "The Dead".
3. 1987= Adapted as a film, *The Dead*, directed by John Huston, starring Angelica Huston, as Gretta Conroy and Donal Mc Cann as Gabriel Conroy.

4. 1999= Adapted into a Broadway musical by Richard Nelson and Shaun Davey, which won a Tony Award for Best Book of a Musical.
5. 2019= Adapted into a Bengali film titled "Basu Paribar", starring Soumitra Chatterjee and Aparna Sen and directed by Suman Ghosh.

"The Dead" is the final story in the collection, *Dubliners*. It is the longest story in the collection with 15,952 words. Its theme is love and loss of love. It has been treated highly passionately. Richard Ellmann has found autobiographical elements in "The Dead." According to him, Nora Barnacle (1884-1951) in her adolescence fell in love with one Michael Bodkin, a student at University College at Galway. In "The Dead", Michael Bodkin is the model of Michael Furey. Nora had another love affair, during her nubility, with one Willy Mulvey who is the model of his namesake in *Ulysses* (Fargnoli and Gillespie, 244).

"The Dead" was completed in 1907 but was not published before it was included in *Dubliners* in 1914. "The Dead" is not only Joyce's longest short story but of all Joyce's short stories it also contains the greatest number of characters (it comprises at least 12 characters).

(2)

The characters of "The Dead":

1. Gabriel Conroy and Gretta Conroy. Gabriel and his wife Gretta (Conroy) are the two principal characters round whom the spiel unwinds. Gabriel is educated, sophisticated, and is a teacher and book reviewer (teacher, like Joyce once had been). "Sexuality and sexual appetites come to dominate his consciousness...." (Fargnoli, 75). Gabriel and Gretta went to Julia Morkan and Kate Morkan's dinner party where Gabriel saw her to be unmindful. Coming back to Gresham Hotel he asked her the reason of her being unmindful. Gretta said in her young age she loved a youth—and the youth loved her—and that youth, Michael Furey, used to sing that song which she heard in the dinner from Mr. D'Arcy. For the first

time, Gabriel realized that "he had never experienced a love as profound as that which Gretta describes" (Fargnoli, 75).

2. Michael Furey. A student of the University College at Galway where Gretta, before her marriage, lived. Furey was now dead but his memory dominates the whole of the story, or rather the song he used to sing—"*The Lass of Aughrim*":

    If you be the lass of Aughrim
    As I suppose you to be
    Tell me the last token
    That passed between you and me
    The rain falls on my yellow locks
    And the dew, it wets my skin
    My babe lies cold within my arms
    Lord Gregory let me in
    Oh Gregory, don't you remember
    One night on the hill
    When we swapped rings off each other's hands
    Sorely against my will?
    Mine was of beaten gold
    Yours it was but tin.
    Mine was of beaten gold
    Yours it was but tin.
    If you be the lass of Aughrim
    As I suppose you to be
    Tell me the last token
    That passed between you and me
    Oh Gregory don't you remember
    One night on the hill
    When you swapped smocks off each other's backs
    Sorely against my will?
    Mine was the Holland fine
    Yours was but scotch cloth
    Mine was the Holland fine
    Yours was but scotch cloth.

3. Julia Morkan and Kate Morkan. Both of them were aunt to Gabriel Conroy. Kate was younger than Julia.

Both of them were of advanced years. It was they that had hosted the annual Christmas party, like previous years (where we see Gabriel and Gretta Conroy at the opening of the story).

4. Lily. She was the "caretaker's daughter"—the caretaker of the house of Julia and Kate.
5. Bartell D'Arcy. A fussy and insecure minor character, but his role was of immense importance. It was he who sang the song: "The Lass of Aughrim" that brought to Gretta's mind the memories of her dead lover Michael Furey who used to sing the same song in Galway, when she was in her early teens.
6. Mervyn Archdale Browne, Miss Molly Ivors, Freddy Malins, Mary Jane, Miss O' Callaghan, Miss Daly, Miss Power, Miss Daly, Miss Power, T.I. Conroy, Mr. Bergin, Mr. Kerrigan, Miss Furlongand and Mr. Browne are minor characters.

(3)

Like in previous years, that year the two old ladies Julia Morkan and Kate Morkan, both aunt of Gabriel Conroy, would play hosts to a number of guests, including Gabriel and his wife Gretta, in the annual Christmas feast. It was a cold day, snow falling again. The Christmas celebration would be elaborate, with waltz, song, and an address by Gabriel. In time, Julia Morkan and Kate Morkan received Gabriel very delightedly because Gabriel was the son of their dead older sister Ellen who had married T.I. Conroy.

Meantime the on-going waltz ceased on the upper storey as well as the playing on the piano. It was Mary Jane who was playing on the piano. She was a music teacher, unmarried. Each year she organized a concert in the Ancient Concert Rooms. However, Gabriel did not miss Miss Mary Jane's performance. He was interested in listening to her playing on the piano but he did not find any melody in her performance. However, in course of time Miss Jane's performance came to an end, and applause followed.

Gabriel now found himself beside Miss Ivor, and the two entered into a conversation. Miss Ivor invited Gabriel to stay with them in the Aran Isles for some time. Gabriel was not interested in the Aran Isles, not even in Ireland and Irish language—he was a sort of West Britain, meaning, pro-British and none of the Irish nationalists. He suddenly burst out to Miss Ivor: "I'm sick of my own country, sick of it!" He was dancing with Miss Ivor and he noticed in her eyes signs of disgust at his blunt declaration.

In the meantime, supper arrived, after which Gabriel was to deliver his speech. He was thinking about his speech anxiously. Suddenly, he got courage from a new idea: "He would say, alluding to Aunt Kate and Aunt Julia: 'Ladies and Gentlemen, the generation which is now on the wane among us may have had its faults, but for my part I think it had certain qualities of hospitality, of humour, of humanity, which the new and very serious and hypereducated generation that is growing up around us seems to me to lack.'" Miss Ivor appreciated it. Then Aunt Julia sang the old song—*Arrayed for the Bridal*. At the end of the song, Gabriel "applauded loudly". Aunt Julia meekly but with pride said: "Thirty years ago I hadn't a bad voice as voices go." "*Arrayed for the Bridal*" is a song written by George Linley based on Bellini's Italian Opera I Puritani. The song can be categorized as an epithalamium. It runs as below:

> Arrayed for the bridal, in beauty behold her,
> A white wreath entwineth a forehead more fair;
> I envy the zephyrs that softly enfold her, enfold her,
> And play with the locks of her beautiful hair.
> May life to her prove full of sunshine and love,
> of love, yes! yes! yes!
> Who would not love her?
> Sweet star of the morning! Shining so bright
> Earth's circle adorning, fair creature of light!

[George Linley (1797-1865), English verse-writer and musical composer] (This song has relevance to *The Lass of Aughrim*)]

Miss Ivor was very eager to go home. Mrs. Gretta Conroy and Mary Jane tried to persuade her to take the supper, but she

Gabriel, next, lamented that "we are living in a skeptical and, if I may use the phrase, a thought-tormented age; and sometimes I fear that this new generation, educated or hypereducated as it is, will lack those qualities of humanity, of hospitality, of kindly humour which belonged to an older day." He was mourning for those olden "specious days." However, he soon rescued himself and others from the grief of the loss by pointing out that all gathered there in a spirit of camaraderie and that they were blessed by "the Three Graces of the Dublin musical world", meaning, Aunt Julia, Aunt Kate and Mary Jane. All burst into loud laughter.

At last Gabriel proposed a toast to the "Three Graces": "Let us toast them all together." All stood up, glass in hand, and three ladies sang in unison, with Mr. Browne as leader:

"For they are jolly gay fellows.
Which nobody can deny."

And with emphasis they sang:

"Unless he tells a lie,
Unless he tells a lie."

Lastly, turning towards the hostesses, they sang the refrain: "Which nobody can deny." Now, here is the critical turn in the story. The wee hours of the night was about to be over. Piercingly, cold air was pushing through the half ajar door. Someone said "Close the door, somebody." Mr. Browne came in from out the door. Gabriel was pulling over his overcoat and looking around the hall. He asked "Gretta not down yet?"

"She's getting on her things, Gabriel," said Aunt Kate.

"Who's playing up there?" asked Gabriel.

"Nobody. They are all gone."

"O no, Aunt Kate," said Mary Jane. "Bartell D'Arcy and Miss O'Callaghan aren't gone yet."

"Some one is fooling at the piano anyhow"; said Gabriel.

The conversation unexpectedly veered back towards the memory of Patrick Morkan, grandfather of Gabriel and his famous horse, Johnny. Patrick Morkan, Gabriel began to narrate, was generally known by his epithet “glue-boiler”, because he used to make glue or starch in his mill. The mill would be driven by the horse, Johnny, who would be “walking round and round in order to drive the mill.” One day Patrick Morkan went out on that horse from his mansion. Johnny moved well until he came before the statue of King Billy. Whether Johnny fell in love with the statue or not, he “began to walk round the statue” over and over again. Patrick Morkan, the old grandfather, became “highly indignant” and went on: “Go on, sir! What do you mean, sir? Johnny! Johnny! Most extraordinary conduct! Can't understand the horse!” There followed peals of laughter. [The horse is a symbol: he is circumnavigating a statue—a dead thing (Gretta; dead to Gabriel)—like Gabriel (horse).]

It was now time for the guests to depart. Freddy Malins rushed into the hall and reported that he could secure only one cab. Freddy Malins, Mrs. Malins and Mr. Browne got into the cab, and the cabman drove off. Gabriel had not seen them off, like others but “He was in a dark part of the hall gazing up the staircase. A woman was standing near the top of the first flight, in the shadow also.” Gabriel could well recognize her: “It was his wife. She was leaning on the banisters, listening to something. Gabriel was surprised at her stillness and strained his ear to listen also. But he could hear little save the noise of laughter and dispute on the front steps, a few chords struck on the piano and a few notes of a man's voice singing.” “There was grace and mystery in her attitude as if she was a symbol of something. He asked himself what is a woman standing on the stairs in the shadow, listening to distant music a symbol of. If he were a painter he would paint her in that attitude. Distant Music he would call the picture if he were a painter.

Now Aunt Kate, Julia and Mary Jane came into the hall, laughing, and closed the door so that the singing voice and the piano could be more clearly heard. Gabriel was still listening to the music spell-bound. The song in the upper storey “seemed to be in the old Irish tonality” and the song expressed grief of yore and the singer was Bartell Darcy who sang:

"O, the rain falls on my heavy locks
And the dew wets my skin,
My baby lies cold..."

Now Gretta, Gabriel's wife, was coming down. Behind her were Mr. Bartell D'Arcy and Miss O'Callaghan. That year there was heavy snow-fall all over Ireland, unlike in the past thirty years. Mr. D'Arcy, to protect him from cold, hastily put on his overcoat. Miss O'Callaghan appreciated the snow. She said Christmas was never really Christmas without snow. But Aunt Julia was not so delighted of the snow; she only loved the look of snow.

Gabriel saw her wife in profile, still "in the same attitude and seem unaware of the talk about her." Gretta then turned and Gabriel "saw that there was color on her cheeks and her eyes were shining. A sudden joy went leaping out of his heart." Gretta asked Mr. D'Arcy: "what is the name of that song you were singing?" Mr. D'Arcy told her it was called "*The Lass of Aughrim*". "*The Lass of Aughrim*", Gretta repeated.

Gabriel and Gretta now departed, saying "Good Night" to all. "The morning was still dark. A dull, yellow light brooded over the houses and the river; and the sky seemed to be descending." Gretta was walking on, before Gabriel, with Mr. D'Arcy "her shoes in a brown parcel tucked under one arm and her hands holding her skirt up from the slush [cf. the birdgirl in *A Portrait of the Artist As a Young Man*]." "She had no longer any grace of attitude, but Gabriel's eyes were still bright with happiness." "She [Gretta] was walking before him [Gabriel] so lightly and so erect that he longed to run after her noiselessly, catch her by the shoulders and say something foolish and affectionate into her ear. She seemed to him so frail that he longed to defend her against something and then to be alone with her. Moments of their secret life together burst like stars upon his memory". Gabriel "longed to recall to her those moments, to make her forget the years of their dull existence together and remember only their moments of ecstasy." He "longed to be alone with her."

At the corner of Winetavern street they took a cab. Gretta was looking out of the window of the cab. She "seemed tired". The horse galloped along in the fresh morning and Gabriel was wishing a honeymoon soon with her. The cab reached the hotel and Gabriel and Gretta were walking towards it. "She leaned lightly on his arm, as lightly as when she had danced with him a few hours before. He had felt proud and happy then, happy that she was his, proud of her grace and wifely carriage. But now, after the kindling again of so many memories, the first touch of her body, musical and strange and perfumed, sent through him a keen pang of lust."

"An old man was dozing at entrance of the hall of the hotel. He lit a candle and led them to the stairs." It was then eight o'clock. Gabriel locked the door and was leaning against a chest of drawers. Gretta was unhooking her waist. Gabriel called out, "Gretta!" She turned away from the mirror slowly moved to him but said, "No, it was not the moment yet." He asked if she did feel ill or weak and she answered: "No, tired: that's all." "She went on to the window and stood there, looking out. The street lights were till then burning. Gabriel was falsely suspicious. He suddenly asked:

"By the way, Gretta!"

"What is it?"

"You know that poor fellow Malins?" he said quickly.

"Yes. What about him?"

Gabriel was seething in rage, about to break out into brutal language about the "sottish Malins", but he restrained himself because Malins was not so bad a person; his only fault was that he kept company with Browne. Gretta slid away from the window, looked at Gabriel strangely, and then suddenly raised herself tiptoe and kissed him, saying "You are a very generous person, Gabriel." Gabriel came down from the height of rage and swelled with extreme happiness. He thought: "Perhaps she had felt the impetuous desire that was in him, and then, the yielding mood had come upon her." He was standing holding her hand and now drew her close to himself and asked her: "Gretta, dear, what are you thinking about?" Gretta did not answer immediately. Then she burst out with tears in her eyes: "O, I am thinking about that song, *The Lass of Aughrim.*" "She broke loose from him and ran to the bed and, throwing her arms across the bed-rail, hid her face. Gabriel stood stock-still for a moment in astonishment and then followed her." He stopped a few paces from her, and asked: "What about the song? Why does that make you cry?"

Gretta dried her eyes and said, "I am thinking about a person long ago who used to sing that song."

> "'And who was the person long ago?' asked Gabriel, smiling?"
>
> "It was a person I used to know in Galway when I was living with my grandmother", she said.

Gabriel's smile gave place to rage and now he asked, "Someone you were in love with?" he asked ironically.

"It was a young boy I used to know," she answered, "named Michael Furey. He used to sing, that song, *The Lass of Aughrim.* He was very delicate."

Gabriel was silent. "I can see him so plainly," she said, after a moment. "Such eyes as he had big, dark eyes! And such an expression in them—an expression!"

> "O, then, you are in love with him?" said Gabriel.
>
> "I used to go out walking with him," she said, "when I was in Galway."

Gabriel coldly asked her if that was the reason why she wanted to go to Galway with Miss Molly Ivor. Gretta replied that the boy was no more; he died when he was only seventeen. She told he was working in the gas factory. Gabriel felt humiliated, ashamed, for her love of a gas worker.

> "I suppose you were in love with Michael Fuery, Gretta," he said.
>
> "I was great with him at that time," she said.

Her voice was veiled and sad. Gabriel asked:

> "And what did he die of so young, Gretta? Consumption was it?"

> "I think he died for me," she answered. "A vague terror seized Gabriel at this answer.... But he shook himself free of it with an effort of reason and continued to caress her hand.... Her hand was warm and moist: it did not respond to his touch, but he continued to caress it."

Gretta resumed her narration of Michael Furey. It was a winter when she was going to leave her grandmother's home at Galway to come up here to the convent [at Dublin] that she heard of the declining health of Furey. Saying so far she paused for a moment and then sighed and continued:

"Poor Fellow," she said. "He was fond of me and he was such a gentle boy. We used to go out together, walking, you know, Gabriel, like the way they do in the country. He was going to study singing only for his health. He had a very good voice poor Michael Furey."

As Gretta was readying to come to Dublin, she wrote a letter to Michael Furey telling him that in the summer she would be back to Galway and that she hoped by then he would come round. However, the night she was to leave Galway she heard Michael Furey shivering and throwing stones at the window. She went to the garden from where he was pelting and implored him to go back home for the rain would bring death to him. But he said he did not want to live. Within a week Furey died and was interned in Oughterard. Gretta apostrophized: "O, the day I heard that, that he was dead!" Gretta was chocking with sobs and then flung herself on the bed, "sobbing in the quilt."

"Gabriel held her hand for a moment longer, irresolutely, and then, shy of intruding on her grief, let it fall gently and walked quietly to the window." Gretta almost instantaneously fell asleep. Coming back from the window, "Gabriel, leaning on his elbow, looked for a few moments unresentfully on her tangled hair and half-open mouth, listening to her deep-drawn breath. So she had had that romance in her life: a man died for her sake. It hardly pained him now to think how poor a part he, her husband, had played in her life. He watched her while she slept, as though he and she had never lived together as man and wife." His curious eyes surveyed her previous girlish beauty when "a strange, friendly pity for her entered his soul."

Gabriel was thinking of Michael Furey's death, and then thought that everyone—poor Aunt Julia, who sang *Arrayed for the Bridal*, and Aunt Kate, and everyone would die one day or the other and would become shades. He "lay down beside his wife" and was philosophising: "Better pass into that other world, in the full glory of some passion, than fade and wither dismally with age. He thought how she who lay beside him had locked in her heart for so many years that image of her lover's eyes when he had told her that he did not wish to live." "Generous tears filled Gabriel's eyes. He had never felt like that himself towards any woman, but he knew that such a feeling must be love. The tears gathered more thickly in his eyes and in the partial darkness he imagined he saw the form of a young man standing under a dripping tree. Other forms were near. His soul had approached that region where dwell the vast hosts of the dead." The dead Michael Furey brought in Gabriel's imagination "the vast hosts of the dead." He thought, "The time had come for him to set out on his journey westward."

Now snow began to fall. Gabriel went to the window and saw snowflakes falling. He thought the newspapers were right: "snow was general all over Ireland." He thought snow was falling also "on the hill where Michael Furey was buried.... His soul swooned slowly as he heard the snow falling faintly through the universe and faintly falling, like the descent of their last end, upon all the living and the dead."

******

The title of the story Joyce took from the first line of a poem of the Irish poet Thomas Moore's *Irish Melodies*. The first stanza of the poem runs thus:

> "Oh, ye dead! oh, ye dead! whom we know by the light you give
> From your cold gleaming eyes, though you move like men who live.
> Why leave you thus your graves,
> In far off fields and waves,
> Where the worm and the sea-bird only know your bed,
> To haunt this spot where all

Those eyes that wept your fall,
And the hearts that wail'd you, like your own, lie dead?"

(The words "dead" and "snow" of this stanza appear in "The Dead" with great significances.)

"The Dead" bears a shadow of Joyce's relation to Nora, in the sense that like Nora, Gretta came from Galway and like her she had a relation with a young man before she eloped with Joyce.

A few symbols are obvious in "The Dead." Lily, the first name, that begins the story, is a symbol. Lily is white and the colour has an association with death. Gabriel, the name of the protagonist, refers to the Archangel Gabriel who is the guardian of the gates of death—death that is the central theme of the story. In the concluding paragraph of the story, Gabriel says that "The time had come for him to set out on his journey westward." Journeying to the west symbolizes death because of its similarity with the sun's going to the west to disappear.

Drawing some characters of his stories based on real persons of Dublin was a peculiar knack of Joyce. In "The Dead", thus Joyce modelled Miss Kate and Miss Julia on two real persons of Dublin, Misses Flynn, who actually presided over a musical academy. Of course, he drew the character of Miss Kate following his own aunt Callahan.

Like in some other stories of *Dubliners*, the ending of "The Dead" is ambiguous, for while near the end of the story, Gabriel was frantically trying to take the place of Michael Furey for the love of Gretta, at the close of it he was thinking not of love but of death. Why? Is it because to take the place of Furey he also must die or because being defeated by Furey he did not like to live? [In fact, Michael Furey did not die for Gretta but he died of tuberculosis. In the story, Joyce changed the cause of Furey's death for paying homage to W.B. Yeats. In Yeats' *Cathleen ni Houlihan* an old woman represents Ireland. When one patriot of Ireland is martyred by hanging, she laments that he died for love of her.]

"The Dead" is one of the most anthologized short story, and the final paragraph of it is famously one of the most emotionally charged finely crafted paragraph of any fiction ever written. Look at the analogy, for instance, between Furey's throwing stones at Gretta's window with pebbles and snow flecks tapping the window of the hotel where Gabriel was imagining Gretta's bygone young romance.

Long after Joyce's "The Dead", one of his admirers, Jocye Carol Oates (b. June 16, 1938) wrote a story "The Dead", perhaps as a homage to Joyce, but Oates' story differs widely from Joyce's story of the same title.

Lastly, the master scholar of Joyce, William York Tindall, very rightly said that Joyce wrote but only one work with different titles at different times. To prove his point, Tindall says that in *Finnegans Wake* Joyce refers to the titles of all the fifteen stories of *Dubliners*, jocularly, such as "Eveline" is "eveling"; "An Encounter" is "wrong countered"; "The Boarding House" is "boarded house" and "A Painful Case" is "the painful sake'.

****

SOME MORE FEATURES OF *DUBLINERS*

1. SPACE AND TIME IN THE STORIES

Joyce wrote *Dubliners* having two professed targets in view: to create a daguerreotype of his "dear, dirty Dublin" "so complete that if the city one day suddenly disappeared from the earth it could be reconstructed out of my book", and to write about the (debased) "moral history" of his city or nation. For the first target, he has produced an album of the 15 stories of *Dubliners* where he has presented a Baedeker of Dublin. The 15 stories of *Dubliners* (each one a stand-alone story) are short stories nonpareil, but they are not mere stories, they are stuffed with many things, one of which is a guide for roads, lanes, cul-de-sacs, eateries, distilleries, reputed buildings, public places, etc., in short, a complete Baedeker of Dublin or almost a complete cartography of the city.

At a quick count, there are not less than 60 street and road names and place names in *Dubliners*, most of them being concentrated in "Two Gallants" (21) and "Counterparts" (10).

The distribution of street names and place names are as shown below.

1. "The Sisters": Great Britain St., Irishtown.
2. "An Encounter": Canal Bridge, Wharf Rd., Pigeon House, North Strand Rd., quay on the bank of river Liffey, Ringsend.
3. "Araby": North Richmond St., Westland Row Station.
4. "Eveline": Nil.
5. "After the Race": Naas Rd., Dame St., Stephen's Green, Grafton St., Westland Row, Kingstown.
6. "Two Gallants": Rutland Square, Dorset St., Dame St., Baggot St., South Circular, Trinity College, Nassau St., Kildare St., Stephen's Green, Hume St., Merrion St., Duke's St., Westmoreland St., College of Surgeons, City Markets, Ely Place.
7. "The Boarding House": George's Church, Marlborough St.
8. "A Little Cloud": King's Inns, Capel St., Grattan Bridge, Henrietta St.
9. "Counterparts": O' Neill's shop, Fleet St., Terry Kelly's pawn-office, Temple Bar, Westmoreland, St., Duke St., Ballast Office, Scotch House, Poolbeg St., Shelbourne Rd.
10. "Clay": Downes's cake-shop, Henry St.
11. "A Painful Case": Chapelizod, Rotunda, Magazine Hill, Sydney Parade.
12. "Ivy Day in the Committee Room": Royal Exchange Ward.
13. "A Mother": Ormond Quay, Ancient Concert Room, Howth, Greystones, Skerries.
14. "Grace": Jesuit Church in Gardiner St.
15. "The Dead": Galway, Oughterard, Bog of Allen.

Joyce has also shown directions, compass-like, in some of the stories. For instance, "Araby" points towards the east; the young narrator boy in it is attracted by the fantastic Eastern bazaar—Araby. And in "A Little Cloud", Little Chandler dreams of going to London, that lies to the east of Ireland, where Gallahar has immensely prospered. On the other hand, in "An Encounter" Joe Dillon has mesmerized the narrator and his friends with the adventures of the Wild West; in "Eveline" the protagonist dreams of going to Buenos Ayres in the west; and in "The Dead" Gretta mourns for Furey who lies buried in Galway in the west and Gabriel is all set to go westward, at the close of the story.

Roads, streets and prominent places are spaces which we have mentioned before, are used by Joyce in *Dubliners*, but he has not forgotten *time*. In *Dubliners*, he has directed the reader, in each one of the stories, to notice the time. Joyce believed in Giambattista Vico's (1668-1744) theory of repetition and circularity, which is grounded on the flow of time, as expostulated in Vico's *Scienza Nuova*. According to Vico, historical events occur in a repetitive and circular manner—what has happened will happen again and again in the unending course of time in a pattern of circularity. Joyce in *Dubliners* is always time-conscious. The parallel courses of time and events as are indicated in the stories of *Dubliners* are shown below:

1. "The Sisters": Rev. James Flynn dies on "July 1st, 1895."
2. "An Encounter":
   (i) At the beginning of the story, the narrator tells us that "His parents went to mass every morning...."
   (ii) The narrator, along with his friends, would embark on an adventure the next day and so the earlier night he slept badly.
   (iii) The band of youngsters were to be back visiting the Pigeon House "before four o'clock.
3. "Araby":
   (i) The narrator will go to the bazaar (Araby) on Sunday, at night.
   (ii) His uncle came home at "nine o'clock" in the evening.
   (iii) The bazaar closed as the lights were switched off at night.

4. "Eveline": The story begins with a suggestion of time: "She [Eveline] sat at the window watching the evening invade the avenue."

5. "After the Race": The story ends at the break of day: "Day break, gentlemen!"

6. "Two Gallants": Like "The Sisters", this story begins with an indication of time: the adventures of the two gallants begin in a "grey warm evening of August on a Sunday".

7. "The Boarding House":

(i) Mrs. Mooney was thinking about making Mr. Doran marry Polly under duress. She thought: "It was seventeen minutes past eleven: she would have lots of time to have the matter out with Mr. Doran and then catch short twelve at Marlborough Street."

(ii) "On nights when he [Mr. Doran] came in very late it was she [Polly] who warmed up his dinner."

8. "A Little Cloud": Like "The Sisters" and "Two Gallants", this story begins with a reference to time: Eight years. Eight years ago Gallahar left Dublin and went to England.

9. "Counterparts": Farrington was tasked with copying out the contract papers "by four o'clock".

10. "Clay": Many thought of joining the Christmas celebration in the house of Joe Donnelly "before eight" (in the evening).

11. "A Painful Case":

(i) "Four years passed. Mr. Duffy returned to his even way life."

(ii) Mrs. Emily Sinico "was knocked down by the engine of the ten o'clock train from Kingstown."

(iii) After reading of the death of Mrs. Emily Sinico in the newspaper in the eatery, Mr. Duffy was mournfully shocked. "It was after nine o'clock when he left the shop."

12. "Ivy Day in the Committee Room": Mr. O'Connor and others were sitting in the room to discuss about the Municipal

Elections. "It was sixth of October, dismal and cold out of doors."

13. "A Mother":

(i) On Wednesday, Mrs. Kearney went to the Ancient Concert Room and saw that the performance did not begin. "At first she wondered had she mistaken the hour. No, it was twenty minutes to eight."

(ii) Even after a long time since then the performance did not ensue. "When it was nearly half-past eight, the few people in the hall began to express their desire to be entertained."

14. "Grace": The injured Karnan "was hoisted on to the car" and "The car drove off towards Westmoreland Street. As it passed the Ballast Office the clock showed half-past nine."

15. "The Dead": Near the beginning of the story only once do we hear of time: "Of course, they had good reason to be fussy on such a night. And then it was long after ten o'clock and yet there was no sign of Gabriel and his wife."

2. THE STORIES ARE IMPRESSIONISTIC

Joyce was a devoted follower of Henrik Ibsen, the acknowledged "father of realism" but then in the stories of *Dubliners* he is perspicuously impressionist. Joyce is a complex artist; on the surface his story looks realistic but underneath the realism impressionism lies hidden. "The term [impressionism], as it is used in literary discourse, was borrowed from the impressionistic movement in painting, in the vanguard of which movement were Edgar Degas ["The Dance Class"] and Claude Monet ["Water Lily"].... The impressionist painters were trying to capture momentary subjective impression of an object from a particular point of view rather than showing the real object or giving a sharp and idealized representation of the form and colours of the object" (Sarker, 86-87).

Following the foot-steps of the impressionist painters, impressionist writers concentrate on the inner lives and experiences of the principal characters of their short stories, novels, or dramatic works instead of focusing on the external reality that surrounds them. Impressionist writing is highly personal in the sense that the writer describes characters and scenes as they appear to them, not as they really are. Noted impressionist writers are: Dorothy Richardson, Virginia Woolf, Marcel Proust and Joyce. To consider how far Joyce was an impressionist writer, let us briefly analyse three or four stories of *Dubliners* to see how he has revealed the inner lives and experiences of the principal characters in them.

1. "Araby": The unnamed narrator's delight at seeing the girl was boundless: "When she came out on the doorstep my heart leaped." He tells us: "Her image accompanied me even in places the most hostile to romance." On Sunday evenings, the narrator boy used to accompany his aunt. On such an evening, he heard street-singers chant in nasal voice "come-all-you about O' Donovan Rosa" (Rosa or Rossa was an Irish Fenian leader who suffered much for freedom of Ireland). The song reminded him of the girl he loved. He tells us: "Her name sprang to my lips at moments in strange prayers and praises which I myself did not understand. My eyes were often full of tears (I could not tell why).... I did not know whether I would ever speak to her or not or, if I spoke to her, how I could tell her of my confused adoration. But my body was like a harp and her words and gestures were like fingers running upon the wires."

And one evening, while it was raining, the young narrator saw a faint distant light coming from the direction where the girl lived below. He tells us: "All my senses seemed to desire to veil themselves and, feeling that I was about to slip from them, I pressed the palms of my hands together until they trembled, murmuring: 'O love! O love!' many times."

The narrator told the girl: "I will bring you something." But in the bazaar, when the lights went out and he could not buy anything, he stood there stupefied. He says: "Gazing up into the darkness, I saw myself as a creature driven and derided by vanity; and my eyes burned with anguish and anger."

2. "Eveline." Just at the beginning of the story, we understand that Eveline was "going to go away like the others, to leave her home." The word "Home!" (like the word "Forlorn!" in Keats' "Ode to a Nightingale") whipped up in her mind a turbulent

debate: should she escape her home to be happy in Buenos Ayres or should she hang around her home to do the "categorical imperatives" that her mother had charged her with. She was weighing her duty against her "right to happiness" from the start of the story to its end.

3. "A Little Cloud." Little Chandler's mind is fully occupied, since almost the beginning of the story, with the gulf of difference between Gallaher's flourishing life in London after he left his "dear, dirty Dublin" and his sorry plight in Dublin.

4. "Grace." This three-part Dantesque story retells the Catholic philosophy of Fall, Purgation and Paradise, or the philosophy of inner purity. Whatever is dramatised throughout the story ultimately converges in the enlightened consciousness of Kernan: "Well, I have verified my accounts. I find all well." He repeats (at close the story): "Well, I have looked into my accounts. I find this wrong (of boozing) and this wrong (denigration of Pope's infallibility). But with God's grace, I will rectify this and this. I will set right my accounts."

5. "The Dead." Of all the fifteen stories in *Dubliners*, "The Dead" presents the deepest tragic inner drama that can draw a man's consciousness in pitch-black darkness. Gabriel, the protagonist, got an inkling of the impending tragedy when he saw "Mrs. [Gretta] Conroy leaned over the banisters [in the house of the Morkans] to listen for the hall-door." And he saw, all at the same time, Miss Ivor getting down the flight of steps, smirking meaningfully. Going back to the hotel, Gabriel understood the mystery behind Gretta's leaning over the banister and Miss Ivor's giggling: Gretta had a romantic passion for Michael Furey who, she believed, died for her in Galway. Nowhere in the story before this revelation were we given to understand the heartrending inner tragic consciousness of Gabriel. The revelation gave Gabriel a smart shattering blow: "His soul swooned slowly as he heard the snow falling faintly through the universe and faintly falling, like the descent of their last end, upon all the living and the dead." Gabriel wished to get frozen in that frozen universe.

Impressionism is also present in "Counterparts", "Clay" and "A Painful Case." In "Counterparts", Farrington is disgusted with his job at "Crosbie & Alleyne" and drowned his repugnance in alcohol. His life is a life of inner struggle: to keep his job and suppress his animosity against his boss Mr. Alleyne or to give vent to his grudge. In "Clay", Maria's love for Joe lied buried in her 'unconscious', from where it popped out in her unconscious avoidance of the second stanza of the song. And in "A Painful Case", Mr. James Duffy had entered the love life of Mrs. Emily Sinico but left her impudently forever. The result was she committed suicide under the impact of alcohol. The news of her tragic death rolled out the past relation between the two kaleidoscopically before Mr. Duffy's consciousness. The drama of 'to love or not to love' was going on in the consciousness of both Mrs. Sinico and Mr. Duffy.

3. UNHAPPY FAMILY LIFE IN *DUBLINERS*

Among the fifteen stories of *Dubliners*, there are at least five where we hear of unhappy family lives:

1. Stories of Childhood (upto 10 years): NIL
2. Stories of Adolescence (11 years to 21 years): "Eveline"
3. Stories of Maturity (21 years and beyond): "A Little Cloud", "A Painful Case" and "The Dead"
4. Stories of Public Life: "Ivy Day in the Committee Room"

1. "Eveline." Joyce was a very careful writer: he rightly avoided treating of familial unhappiness in childhood. However, we first encounter unhappy family life in "Eveline" where Eveline, over nineteen years of age, had to endure "her father's violence. She knew it was that that had given her the palpitations." Her brother Ernest was dead and another brother Harry was away from home and so "now she had nobody to protect her." She always gave her father all her earnings, but whenever she asked money from him he snubbed her saying "she used to squander the money, that she had no head...." "She had hard work to keep the house together and to see that the two young children who had been left to her charge went to school regularly and got their meals regularly. It was hard work—a hard life—."

2. "A Little Cloud." Little Chandler, in "A Little Cloud", was doubly depressed when he met Ignatius Gallaher who had come back to Ireland on a visit after eight years. Gallaher was a rising journalist on the London Press while Little Chandler was smarting under pecuniary constraints, though intellectually he was superior to Gallaher. Little Chandler's ambition soared while thinking of Gallaher's rise and becoming aware of his poetic rage. He was not old but only thirty-two. He was watching children "run screaming along the gravel path." "He watched the scene [buoyant and lively] and thought of life; and (as always happened when he thought of life) he became sad. A gentle melancholy took possession of him." But his sunken elan vital suddenly sprang up as he thought that he might transform his melancholy into poetry that "men would listen" and then he could be an achiever. Little Chandler's elaborate musing suddenly stopped as soon as he became aware of the iron net in which he was enmeshed immobile—the net of his family: his little child; his dull, passionless and irritating wife Annie; and his miserably low existence. "Could he not escape from his little house?"—he asked himself.

A volume of Byron's poems that lay on the table he opened and began to read the melancholy first poem in it—"Hushed are the winds and still the evening gloom...." The sleeping child woke up and began to cry. He stopped reading: "It was useless. He couldn't read. He couldn't do anything. The wailing of the child pierced the drum of his ear. It was useless, useless! He was a prisoner for life." Little Chandler shouted at the child: "Stop!" Annie, his wife, admonished him sternly. "Little Chandler felt his cheeks suffused with shame and he stood back out of the lamplight. He listened while the paroxysm of the child's sobbing grew less and less; and tears of remorse started to his eyes."

The unhappy family life of Little Chandler is expressed in his lamenting regret: "He was a prisoner of life."

3. "A Painful Case." "A Painful Case" relates the unhappy family life of Mrs. Sinico, who was forty-three years of age and had been married to captain Sinico twenty years ago. She had only a daughter. Her husband lived away from home at Leoville,

Sydney Parade. She had been living happily until two years ago since when she "began to be rather intemperate in her habits."

The cause of her intemperance had a history. Her husband lived far away at Leoville, Sydney Parade while she stayed in Capelizod almost lonely with her only daughter Miss Mary Sinico. One evening in a musical soiree she met a reclusive bachelor, about one year older than she, and the two were instantly drawn to each other. As Mrs. Sinico was leading a high and dry life so the reclusive bachelor, Mr. Duffy, was bearing a passionless soul. So the bond between the two was quick.

They met many times and in "one night, during which she had shown every sign of unusual excitement, Mrs. Sinico caught up his hand passionately and pressed it to her cheek." Conscious of their unnatural exchange of passions, they agreed to put an end to it: "They agreed to break off their intercourse: every bond, he said, is a bond to sorrow." "A few days later he received a parcel containing his books and music."

"Four years passed." Then one day in an eatery, Mr. Duffy read about the tragic death of Mrs. Sinico being knocked down by a slowly moving train. Investigations revealed that Mr. and Mrs. Sinico "had been married for twenty-two years and had lived happily until about two years ago, when his [Mr. Sinico] wife began to be rather intemperate in her habits." "Miss Mary Sinico said that of late her mother had been in the habit of going out at night to buy spirits."

Loneliness and lack of emotional support in the family ultimately drove Mrs. Sinico to her tragic death.

4. "The Dead." Gabriel's happy union with Gretta on a sudden was smashed into smithereens when in the hotel he saw her sob and "flung herself face downward on the bed" for Furey, her teenage boyfriend, who, she believed, died for her. Gabriel's grave unhappiness in his family may be gauged from the concluding sentence of the story: "His soul swooned slowly as he heard the snow falling faintly through the universe and faintly falling, like the descent of their last end, upon all the living and the dead." Gabriel wished to freeze in the snow and become a zombie.

5. "Ivy Day in the Committee Room." In this story, the unhappy family life belonged to the "old man" whose nineteen years old son was a ragamuffin drunkard. The old man laments to Mr. O'Connor: "Only I'm an old man now I'd change his tune for him. I'd take the stick to his back and beat him while I could stand over him—as I done many a time before. The mother, you know, she cocks him up with this and that."

4. ESCAPE MOTIVE IN *DUBLINERS*

From the very day of the dawning of his consciousness, Joyce could not adjust himself with the conservative religion, nationality (the on-going independence movement), and language (revival of the ancient language of Hibernia or Ireland) of his land of birth—all for which he suffered much angst and anguish. It is for this reason that he wished to leave Ireland for some liberal air of an alien land (Europe). And it is for this reason that the theme of escape is present in his very first book, *Dubliners*. And in the last but one closing sentence of his second book, *A Portrait of the Artist as a Young Man*, Joyce really (not only fictionally) avowed his escape motive: "Welcome, O life! I go to encounter for the millionth time the reality of experience and to forge in the smithy of my soul the uncreated conscience of my race." And very true to his avowal, on 8 October 1904, Joyce left Ireland (Dublin) virtually for ever, holding Nara's hand tightly, for Paris and Triesle (Italy).

Joyce's secret wish to escape Ireland (Dublin) is reflected in six stories of *Dubliners*: "The Sisters", "Araby", "Eveline", "After the Race", "A Little Cloud", and "The Dead."

1. "The Sisters". After the death of the priest, Rev. James Flynn, the unnamed narrator boy surprisingly tells us: "I found it strange that neither I nor the day seemed in a mourning mood and I felt even annoyed at discovering in myself *a sensation of freedom as if I had been freed from something by his death*" (*italics mine*). The boy tells us that his uncle "had studied in the Irish college in Rome and he had taught me to pronounce Latin properly [a suggestion of his escaping into Italy]. He had told me stories about the catacombs and about Napoleon Bonaparte [also a suggestion of escaping into Paris]...."

2. "Araby." On Saturday evenings, the unnamed narrator boy used to accompany his aunt going to the market for carrying some parcels. On one such occasion he heard street singers singing "'*come-all-you*' about O' Donovan Rossa, a ballad about the troubles in our native land" (*italics mine*). This trouble contributed to his wish to leave his native land for elsewhere. The narrator boy had a romantic attraction for Mangan's sister. When the festivities of Araby was going on, the boy told the girl he would go to Araby and would bring something for her. Since then, the narrator boy tells us "The syllables of the word Araby were called to me through the silence in which *my soul luxuriated and cast an Eastern enchantment over me*" (*italics mine*). The expression "troubles in my native land" suggests the boy's apathy towards his native land, and the expression "my soul luxuriated and cast an Eastern enchantment over me" implies his romantic dream of escaping his nation.

3. "Eveline." Tired with the hardship of her home and anguished for her father's ill treatment on one hand and lured by Frank of a happy home in Buenos Ayres on the other hand, Eveline sought her "right to happiness". And enticed by her romantic fancy to escape her home to be the wife of Frank, she even went so far as to be ready to board the boat bound for Buenos Ayres only to stop suddenly at the last moment being pulled back by her mother's moral imperative.

4. "After the Race." In this story, there is no explicit wish on the part of Jimmy Doyle, the protagonist, to escape Ireland for the Continent, but there are certain suggestions to that effect. Four friends of Jimmy, and Jimmy himself, did carnival-like jubilations at car-racing, dinner, music and waltz, and at games of cards. Of the four friends of Jimmy, two were French (Segouin and Riviere), one Hungarian (Villona) and one English (Ruth). Jimmy was the only Irish participant. He attended a Catholic college in England with the lavish money of his rich merchant father, and there in England he was attracted to the excited life of the French and Continental culture demonstrated and described by Segouin and Riviere. The dull Jimmy Doyle was a big failure in both education and business, but he was also dampened by the dull life in the poor Ireland. So in the

spree of youthful jubilations, Jimmy wanted to rub shoulders with his French friends, hoping to find some opportunity of enjoying the rich life in France. He felt himself inferior to his friends but covered his sense of inferiority with exaggerated excitement only to be deeply drowned in mental darkness when he found himself the greatest looser in the game of cards on the yacht. Jimmy Doyle's wish to escape Ireland is suppressed in this story but is not absolutely opaque.

5. "A Little Cloud." Like in "After the Race", in this story also the escape motive is hazed. Little Chandler's escape motive sprang up when he met Gallaher, his junior and inferior, after eight years. Gallaher had left Dublin eight years ago and now was a flourishing journalist there on the pay of London Press. Little Chandler, after he saw the sea change in Gallaher, mused that he, too, could be an achiever like him but for the inescapable trap of his family. He imagined the lush lively life of Paris that Gallaher spoke of to him and the vibrant life of London from where Gallaher pooh-poohed his native land saying "dear dirty Dublin." It is here that we understand Little Chandler's escape wish.

6. "The Dead." The most tragic escape motive we find in "The Dead." Gabriel Conroy had a happy married life with Gretta for some years. They participated in Kate and Julia Markan's (Gabriel's aunts) Christmas dinner party where Gretta listened to Bartell D'Arcy's singing "The Lass of Aughrim." Back to hotel, Gabriel passionately advanced to Gretta but she was quite impassive. On enquiry Gretta confessed she wished to visit her childhood home in Galway (far west of Dublin) where Michael Furey fell in love with her and, she believed, he died for her. Gabriel had had an epiphany: Gretta's love for Furey continued to live in her heart for so long, even after her marriage! The dead is still alive in herself! Gabriel understood that this was the affirmation of immortality: there was no difference between the living and the dead. He wanted to be dead, like Furey, to be immortal in the shining love of Gretta: he wanted soon to go westward (in Galway): "The time had come for him to set out on his journey westward." This is Gabriel's wish to escape not Dublin, not love, but life for love.

5. INTER-TEXTUALITY IN AND INFLUENCES ON *DUBLINERS*

No great writer's external influences on him is always and entirely visible in his works, even to himself. Sometimes the influences are openly acknowledged by him, sometimes they are deliberately ignored or hazed, and sometimes they peep out through the chinks in their works. However, let us have a quick survey of intertextuality in Dubliners and external influences on Joyce.

Intertextuality in *Dubliners*

I. Shakespeare: A. "Ivy Day in the Committee Room": About the middle of the story, Father Keon's "knock at the door" reminds us of Shakespeare's Macbeth (II, ii and III iii).

Bi. "Grace": The narrator tells us, in the second section of the story, that Martin Cunningham's "face was like Shakespeare's."

Bii. "Grace": In the second section, again, of the story, Mr. Power (a character) twice refers to Shakespeare's *All's Well That Ends Well*: "Ah, well, all's well that ends well" and "All's well that ends well."

C. "The Dead": In the first section of the story, Gabriel Conroy sees on the wall "A picture of the balcony scene in *Romeo and Juliet* [of Shakespeare]...."

II. Byron: In the second part of "A Little Cloud", Little Chandler reads Byron's poem "On the Death of a Young Lady":

> Hushed are the winds and still the evening gloom,
> Not e'en a zephyr wanders through the grove,
> Whilst I return to view my Margaret's tomb
> And scatter flowers on the dust I love....

III. Wordsworth: In the very first paragraph of "A Painful Case", we are told that "A complete Wordsworth stood at one end of the lowest shelf [of books] of Mr. James Duffy."

Influences on *Dubliners*

1. Gambatista Vico: Joyce was much influenced in his conception of the course of human history or civilization by Vico's (1668-1744) *Scienza Nuova* where Vico said that the

Heap of broken images, where the sun beats,
And the dead tree gives no shelter, the cricket no relief,
And the dry stones no sound of water.

("The Burial of the Dead" in *The Waste Land*)

This new cognition grew out of the aftermath of the two World Wars; first the inner world of man splintered and then his outer world got fragmented. All this led to the new novel's new manifestations: inner-worldliness, non-chronologicality, psychological analysis, pessimism, etc. Modern novel now tends to be but jumbles of disjointed perceptions, feelings, memories and stream of consciousness. The plot of the novel is now a matter of the past.

The new shape of the modern fiction is no one's fancy, it is a legitimate demand of the *zeit geist*. Virginia Woolf, in her essay "Modern Fiction" justifies the advent of the new fiction: "Look within and life, it seems, is very far from being 'like this.' The mind receives a myriad of impressions—trivial, fantastic, evanescent, or engraved with the sharpness of steel. From all sides they come, an incessant shower of innumerable atoms; and as they fall, as they shape themselves into the life of Monday or Tuesday, *the accent falls differently from the old*; the moment the importance came not here but there; so that, if a writer were a free man and not slave, if he could write what he choose, not what he must, if he could base his work upon his own feeling and not upon convention, *there would be no plot, no comedy, no tragedy, no love interest or catastrophe in the accepted style, and perhaps not a single button sewn on as the Bond street tailors would have it. Life is not a series of gig-lamps symmetrically arranged; life is a luminous halo, a semi transparent envelope surrounding us from the beginning of consciousness to the end. Is not the task of the novelist to convey this varying, this unknown and uncircumscribed spirit, whatever aberration or complexity it may display, with as little mixture of the alien and external as possible? We are not pleading merely for courage and sincerity; we are suggesting that the proper stuff of fiction is a little other than custom would have us believe it*" (*italics mine*) (McNeille, 160-61). So why *Dubliners* cannot claim to be a novel (or fiction) in the modernist sense of the term?

7. THE QUOTIDIAN FOR THE UNIVERSAL AND THE MOMENTARY FOR THE PERPETUAL IN *DUBLINERS*

Joyce himself said that he wrote the stories with "scrupulous meanness." Here "mean" does not mean "average" but "low in rank or birth" or "base" or "sordid" (*Chambers Twentieth Century Dictionary*, 1981). The "seeds" of Joyce's stories are not high-falutin but ordinary, paltry, quotidian. And this device Joyce voluntarily chose carefully, conscientiously, scrupulously. Joyce's stories grow around petty, paltry matters but they ultimately lead us to enormous, weighty meanings. Not only in *Dubliners* does this happen but in *Ulysses* and *Finnegans Wake*, the two fictions of epic length. In *Ulysses*, an ordinary *hombre*, a commercial advertiser, Leopold Bloom's ordinary one day's circular peregrination is narrated to show Man's—universal man's—life's burlesque trajectory; and in *Finnegans Wake*, one night's dream of Finnegan, a hod carrier, shows us the circular history of human civilization. This creative art or technique of growing an oak out of an acorn is Joyce's unique and superb artistry.

Let us briefly look into a few stories in *Dubliners* to see how in them under trivial and ephemeral matters lie grave, and sustained or perpetual human concerns.

1. "The Sisters." From the beginning to the end of "The Sisters" we hear of Father Flynn's queer corpse which symbolizes the paralysis of Dublin. Father Flynn's death or his corpse is not something of great concern, but the paralysis of Dublin is.

2. "Araby." The theme of "Araby" is a small thing: frustration of a small boy from his unability to buy something for his beloved girl. In his frustration, he felt himself "as a creature" that is paralysed, again this is a symbol of the paralysed Dublin.

3. "Eveline." And so was the protagonist of "Eveline", a simple, common girl, who, when the boat began steaming away, felt "like a helpless animal"—felt, as if, paralysed.

4. "Clay." Come to "Clay" and think of Maria's love-generated pain. She is a common woman. But when she refrains from singing the second verse, holding, perhaps, her tears

back, her suffering, as if, irradiates across the universe and her momentary pain to us seem perpetual.

5. "A Painful Case." In this story, Mr. Duffy's subconscious love of Mrs. Sinico was not so extraordinary an event. Mr. Duffy had always been a voluntary recluse. He had never before felt lonely, though lonely he had been. It was only after the death of Mrs. Sinico that he for the first time tasted what it was to feel lonely—"He felt he was alone." No, not only he but with him each one of us also feels the pang of being a loner. The particular, becomes universal; the momentary becomes eternal.

6. "The Dead." And, lastly, in "The Death" Joyce us how the quotidian may be magnified by the artist into the universal and the momentary into the perpetual. Joyce clearly shows us how one man's quotidian and ephemeral sorrow (of Gabriel) may disseminate across the whole humanity and across the whole universe.

8. THE TITLES OF THE STORIES IN DUBLINERS

Joyce is a very crafty or cunning artist, and very complex at that, and he has applied his cunning in all the nooks and corners of all his creations. We are thinking here about his cunning in crafting the titles of his stories (and also his novels). Ulrich Schneider's article "Titles in *Dubliners*" (Bosinelli and Mosher, 189-204) has a somewhat detailed discussion on the strategy behind Joyce's entitling the stories. We cannot, here, do better than making a summary of the 10-odd-page article below, with some of our observations on them in parentheses.

1. Joyce "preferred the shortest, most prosaic, and most noncommittal title possible. (But "Ivy Day in the Committee Room" is egregiously longish, like the title of his first novel, *A Portrait of the Artist as a Young Man.*)

2. "Joyce's title does not reveal anything about his attitude toward his character." (The title "Two Gallants" is an exception, for Joyce used it in a satiric vein about Corley and Lenehan.)

3. Only one story is entitled after the name of its protagonist—"Eveline." [By the bye, the name of Eveline may be interpreted as a conjugation of "Eve" (evening), and "line"

(the line that on the horizon separates the day from the night), symbolizing Eveline's situation or her psychological state.]

4. Nine titles, each one of them, consist of single nouns or names ("The Sisters," "An Encounter," "Araby," "Eveline," "Counterparts," "Clay," "A Mother," "Grace," "The Dead"); one title consists of a compound ("The Boarding House"); and four titles just add an adjective, or a preposition, or a numeral to the nouns ("After the Race," "Two Gallants," "A Little Cloud," "A Painful Case"); and only one title runs upto six words, four of them monosyllabic ("Ivy Day in the Committee Room").

5. Some of the titles point toward the social roles that the individual characters play ("The Sisters," "Two Gallants," "A Mother").

6. Two titles refer to the setting of the stories but they transcend their realistic circumference and point toward qualities that are conspicuous by absence. For instance, "Araby" is much more than a place-name; the word means "an Eastern enchantment." "Ivy Day in the Committee Room" conjures up a state of affairs in which the fatal split of the Irish Nationalist Party and its decline happened after Parnell's downfall.

7. The titles that have perplexed readers most in *Dubliners* are probably "Clay" and "A Little Cloud." The clay of the title may refer to Maria's death (cf. "Dust thou art, to dust returnest.") but we may also infer from the clay ("soft wet substance") her psychical death. Hence we suffer perplexities of the meaning of the title. Another perplexing term is 'grace', in the title "Grace." 'Grace' may connote theologically as well as aesthetically in the story "Grace." In the penultimate sentence of the story, Mr. Kernan promises: "But, with God's grace, I will rectify this and this." Here 'grace' means God's free gift or agape (giving something to someone as a token of love without expecting anything in return). This is the theological connotation of the term. But, as Ulrich Schneider writes, "The word 'grace', however, is not restricted to the sphere of theology but plays an equally important role in aesthetics. A silk hat can be balanced 'gracefully' on Mr. Kernan's arm, a poet can have the '*gift of easy and graceful verse*', and three musical ladies

may be called the 'Three Graces of the Dublin musical world' [all the three allusions are from the story 'Grace']" (Bosinelli, 202). And hence another perplexity with the word "grace".

However, Ulrich Schneider says that "A Little Cloud" is the most difficult title of stories in *Dubliners* to discern its meaning: "No matter how we try to come to grips with the title, we can understand why 'A Little Cloud' has been called 'the most perplexing title of all the stories in *Dubliners*' (Weir, 301), although some other titles come fairly close" (Bosinelli, 200). What in the story is signified by the signifier 'cloud' is almost quite obfuscated.

****

Now, let us not go any further with the special features of *Dubliners* but briskly touch on some others important points about *Dubliners*.

1. Joyce's technique of describing Mr. Duffy of "A Painful Case" deserves attention. Joyce does not tell us about Mr. Duffy's personality traits or his lifestyle but gives us a clear and lively picture of his by furnishing some details of his milieu. This indirect portrait painting of Joyce is interesting. In the long beginning paragraph of "A Painful Case", Joyce tells us that Mr. Duffy lived in an "old sombre house" and that "he wished to live as far as possible from the city" and that he lived in an "uncarpeted room." Mr. Duffy had a "black iron bedstead", a "little hand mirror" and on his book shelf "A complete Wordsworth", "a copy of the *Maynooth Catechism*" and "a manuscript translation of Hauptmann's *Michael Kramer.*" With these few stochastic brush strokes Joyce has drawn a Zeuxian portrait of the lonely stoic Mr. Duffy. This cunning technique is not repeated anywhere else in *Dubliners*.

2. Contrary to common knowledge that Joyce lived miles away from theology, the Bible was a favourite of his next only to Dante's *Divine Comedy*. This is the reason of *Dubliners* being stuffed with 'inter texual markers' between the Bible and *Dubliners*. For one thing, in the very first paragraph of the first story of *Dubliners*, "The Sisters", there is the biblical word "*paralysis.*" Secondly, while writing the story, Joyce was

often influenced by the Bible or matters biblical. For instance, whatever may be the theme of "The Sisters", the story revolves around the death of a Father, the Rev. James Flynn, who is connected with the Bible. And so is the story "Grace" which closes with Mr. Kernan's avowal: "*But, with God's grace, I will rectify this and this. I will set right my accounts.*" In "Clay", Maria participates in the *Hallow Eve* games and Joe had brought the (prized) purse for Maria five years ago when he had gone to Belfast on a *Whit Monday*. In "Eveline", we see "the coloured print of the promises made to *Blessed Margaret Mary Alacoque*." In "Araby", Mangan's sister would not be able to go to Araby "because there would be a retreat in her convent." In "A Painful Case", we see "a copy of the *Maynooth Catechism*" on one end of Mr. Duffy's shelf. Mr. Kernan, at the close of "Grace", takes shelter in "*God's grace*." Lastly, Gabriel and Gretta participated with others in the *Christmastime dinner* party in the house of Miss Kate Morkan and Miss Julia Morkan (*all emphases are mine*). So, a potential presence of the biblical or liturgical tradition in *Dubliners* is obvious. Not for nothing has Joyce written the word 'God' 37 times, the word 'priest' 24 times and the word 'catholic' nine times, the name of Christ 20 times and the word 'retreat' seven times in *Dubliners*.

3. At its surface, *Dubliners* may seem sombre and pessimistic but the book, at places, is quite vibrant with song, music and dance, especially in the most tragic of the 15 stories—"The Dead." In "After the Race", there is waltz on the yacht to the music of a piano; in "The Boarding House", Polly Mooney used to sing in boarding house '*I'm a naughty girl*'; in "Clay", Mrs. Donnelly played the piano for the children and they danced and sang; and concerts and singing were there in "A Mother." But the most lively and vibrant setting Joyce made is in "The Dead." In this story, there were waltzes (twice), quadrilles, music (more than once), lancers (lancer is a sequence of quadrilles) and songs. There were also a speech by Gabriel Conroy, eulogizing past hospitality, humours, a toasting by the guests "glass in hand", and singing in honour of Miss Kate Morkan, Miss Julia Morkan and Mary Jane:

'For they are jolly gay fellows,
. . . .
Which nobody can deny.' etc.

4. Interestingly, paralysis is a core theme of *Dubliners* though the term appears only once in the whole book, to be specific, in "The Sisters" (and only once the word 'paralytic' in the same story). Also curious it is that while the term 'rain' is used 39 times in the whole body of *Dubliners*, it is employed only twice in the longest (57 pages) story "The Dead", and that the word 'snow' is used 21 times in the single story, "The Dead", and nowhere in the rest of the book.

5. Colour was a favourite thing to Joyce and he has employed it in *Dubliners* rather liberally:

1. "The Sisters": yellow ("discolored teeth" of the priest) and black.
2. "An Encounter": green.
3. "Araby": violet, yellow.
4. "Eveline": brown, black.
5. "After the Race": blue.
6. "Two Gallants": grey.
7. "The Boarding House": white.
8. "A Little Cloud": NIL.
9. "Counterparts": NIL.
10. "Clay": NIL.
11. "A Painful Case": NIL.
12. "Ivy Day in the Committee Room": black
13. "A Mother": NIL.
14. "Grace": black, white, green.
15. "The Dead": black, yellow, white (Lily).

6. Joyce is famous for coining words and use of foreign and nonsense words in *Ulysses* and *Finnegans Wake*. A faint glimpse of his fad for these may be discerned in *Dubliners*. In the second section of "Grace", we come across the term 'peloothered' which Joyce coined as an English word from the rare and informal Hiberno-English 'peloothered.' The word means highly drunk

or intoxicated. Joyce wrote in English where Irish is a foreign language. In this sense, he has used many Irish words, slangs and phrases, such as *beannacht* (goodbye), *bostoons* (rogues), *bowsy* (rogue), *deoc an doruis* (last round of drink), *Eire Abu* (Ireland to Victory), *goster* (gossip), *lambabaun* (lamb child), *moya* (as it were), *musha* (indeed), *amadhauns* (fools), *sha* (yes), *smahan* (smattering), *usha and wisha* (indeed), *yerra* (really) and *tinker* (gypsy), etc. Some other foreign words are: *cocottes* (French, meaning prostitutes), *credo* (Latin, I believe), *gnomon* (Latin, a perpendicular pin on a sundial whose shadow indicates the time of day), *parole d'honneur* (French, word of honour), etc. Nonsense words or phrases in *Dubliners* are two: "Derevaun Seraun! Derevaun Seraun!" in "Eveline" and "fol-the-diddle-I do" in "A Mother."

Besides, there are a good number of rare words, phrases, slangs, etc. in the book, e.g., 'curates' (barman), 'instanter' (without delay), 'josser' (fellow, guy), 'a loan of' (influence on), 'a little of the ready' (with money available), 'spondulics' (money).

All these, and such others, have made *Dubliners* a more difficult book to engage with. The meanings of the stories are like Chinese boxes—one inside the other, which is inside another, and so on. Sometimes place names or settings contribute to the meanings, sometimes meanings are to be gathered from allusions, and sometimes meanings are hidden in the *gnomons* and the reader has to guess what is what. So, so much is the complexity of *Dubliners* that William York Tindall was but right when he commented about the book: "It is clear (as well,) that although we know a thing or two about *Dubliners*, we know little yet" (Tindall, 8).

DUBLINERS: APPRECIATIONS

In the middle of January 1914, Joyce sent the final manuscript of *Dubliners*, along with the first chapter of *A Portrait of the Artist as a Young Man* to Ezra Pound (*Dubliners* was published, for the first time, by Grant Richards on 15 June 1914). In his letter of 18 February 1915, Pound wrote to H.L. Mencken: "The prose writer I am really interested in is James Joyce.... His

Dubliners, a book of short stories, has succeeded since I first wrote to him" (Deming, 78). A fuller review of *Dubliners* by Pound is to be found in his article "*Dubliners* and Mr. James Joyce" published in *Egoist*, I, No. 14 (15 July 1914). To know Ezra Pound's opinion about *Dubliners*, perhaps some quotes from the above-mentioned article will suffice (Deming, 66-68):

1. "Freedom from sloppiness is so rare in contemporary English prose that one might well say simply, 'Mr. Joyce's book of short stories is prose free from sloppiness', and leave the intelligent reader ready to run from his study, immediately to spend three and six pence on the volume."

2. "Mr. Joyce writes a clear hard prose. He deals with subjective things, but he presents them with such clarity of outline that he might be dealing with locomotives or with builders' specifications. For that reason one can read Mr. Joyce without feeling that one is conferring a favour."

3. "I can lay down a good piece of French writing and pick up a piece of writing by Mr. Joyce without feeling as if my head were being stuffed through a cushion. There are still impressionists about and I dare say they claim Mr. Joyce. I admire impressionist writers. English prose writers who haven't got as far as impressionism (that is to say, 95 per cent of English writers of prose and verse) are a bore...."

4. "Mr. Joyce's merit, I will not say his chief merit but his most engaging merit, is that he carefully avoids telling you a lot that you don't want to know. He presents his people swiftly and vividly, he does not sentimentalise over them, he does not weave convolutions. He is a realist."

5. "He [Joyce] gives us Dublin as it presumably is. He does not descend to farce. He does not rely upon Dickensian caricature. He gives us things as they are, not only for Dublin, but for every city. Erase the local names and a few specifically local allusions, and a few historic events of the past, and substitute a few different local names, allusions and events, and these stories could be retold of any town."

6. "Mr. Joyce does not present 'types' but individuals. I mean he deals with common emotions which run through all

races.... He is classic in that he deals with normal things and with normal people."

7. "Francis Jammes, Charles Vildrac and D.H. Lawrence have written short narratives in verse, trying, it would seem, to present situations as clearly as prose writers have done, yet more briefly. Mr. Joyce is engaged in a similar condensation. He has kept to prose not needing the privilege supposedly accorded to verse to justify his method."

8. "I think that he [Joyce] excels most of the impressionist writers because of his more rigorous selection, because of his exclusion of all unnecessary details." Pound concludes: "At any rate these stories [the stories in *Dubliners*] and the novel [*A Portrait of the Artist as a Young Man*] now appearing in serial form are such as to win for Mr. Joyce a very definite place among English contemporary prose writers."

W.B. Yeats, Joyce's compatriot, also had some commendatory words for Joyce's works. In his letter of 24 July 1915 to Edmund Gosse, Yeats wrote about Joyce: "I believe him to be a man of genius.... He has written *Dubliners* a book of satiric stories of great subtlety, a little like Russian work..." (Deming, 79). Again, in his letter of 29 July 1915 to the Secretary of the Royal Literary Fund, Yeats wrote about Joyce's *Dubliners*: "I think that his [Joyce's] book of short stories *Dubliners* has the promise of a great novelist and a great novelist of a new kind. There is not enough foreground, it is all atmosphere perhaps, but I look upon that as a sign of an original study of life" (Deming, 79-80). George Moore, another compatriot of Joyce, praised *Dubliners* with some reservation. On 3 August 1916, he wrote a letter to Edward Marsh, Asquith's secretary, in which he commented on *Dubliners*: "The only book of Joyce's that I have read is a collection of stories called *Dubliners*, some of them are trivial and disagreeable, but all are written by a clever man, and the book contains one story, the longest story in the book and the last story which seemed to me perfection whilst I read it! I regretted that I was not the author of it ['The Dead'] (*sic*)" (Deming, 80).

One virtuoso component in Joyce's artistry, demonstrated in *Dubliners*, is to be found in "A Painful Case." In this story, Joyce paints the character of Mr. Duffy not using any adjectives, not mentioning any traits of him, not even telling us what he does or how he behaves but simply by giving us a photograph of the circumstance or habitation in which he lives. The very first paragraph of "A Painful Case" gives us a daguerorotyped portrait of the old self-willed cynic bachelor Mr. Duffy: "Mr. James Duffy lived in Chapelizod because he wished to live as far as possible from the city of which he was a citizen because he found all the other suburbs of Dublin mean, modern and pretentious. He lived in an old somber house, and from his windows he could look into the disused distillery or upwards along the shallow river on which Dublin is built. The lofty walls of his uncarpeted room were free from pictures. He had himself bought every article of furniture in the room: black iron bedstead, an iron wash-stand, four cane chairs, a clothes-rack, a coal-scuttle, a fender and irons and a square table on which lay a double desk. A bookcase had been made in an alcove by means of shelves of white wood. The bed was clothed with white bed-clothes and a black and scarlet rug covered the foot. A little hand-mirror hung above the wash-stand and during the day a white-shaded lamp stood as the sole ornament of the mantelpiece...."

And another distinguished credit of Joyce is hidden in his famous phrase that he pronounced about the craft in *Dubliners*—"scrupulous meanness"—by which he meant that he wrote the stories using mean or lowly materials, though he purported to mean grave matters (the same thing he has done also in *Ulysses* and *Finnegans Wake*). And lastly, true to the demand of his age (but certainly he was never a time server), he was truly a realistic artist writing tongue in cheek.

DUBLINERS: CRITICISMS

1. One serious criticism of Joyce's works is that they are inordinately stuffed with too much of allusions, and *Dubliners* is no exception. All the fifteen stories of *Dubliners* contain allusions—some highly stuffed with them. Moreover, some

of the allusions are so distant and hazy that the stories are beyond the comprehension of even the moderately intelligent and knowledgeable readers. Take a few instances. Even the first page of "The Sisters", the first story of the book, presents difficult allusions to readers: "gnomon in the Euclid", "simony" and "faints and worms" and then, one page down, comes the term "Rosicrucian." "A Painful Case", we cannot read without any knowledge of "Chapelizod", "complete Wordsworth", "Maynooth Catechism", "Hauptmann's *Michael Kramer*" and the more distant "faint fragrance." And no one can well appreciate "Grace" without some knowledge of Dante's *Divine Comedy* or realise the pathetic irony of "The Dead" without understanding the burdens of the songs: "*Arrayed for the Bridal*", "*Let me like a soldier fall*", "O, the rain falls on my heavy locks/ And the dew wets my skin,/ My babe lies cold..." and "*The Lass of Aughrim.*"

2. Obnoxious sexual frankness in "A Painful Case", even against the background of modern cultural code of sexuality, is overmuch to some critics: "Love between man and man is impossible because there must not be sexual intercourse, and friendship between man and woman is impossible because there must be sexual intercourse."

3. Like Ernest Hemingway, James Joyce is sometimes rather hard to read for his using pronouns continually without reverting to the nominative case. Look, for instance, at the beginning of the second paragraph of "Two Gallants":

"Two young men came down the hill of Rutland Square. One of them was just bringing a long monologue to a close. The other, *who* walked on the verge of the path and was at times obliged to step on to the road, owing to his companion's rudeness, wore an amused, listening face. He was squat and ruddy. A yachting cap was shoved far back from *his* forehead, and the narrative to which *he* listened made constant waves of expression break forth over *his* nose and eyes and mouth. Little jets of wheezing laughter followed one another out of *his* convulsed body. *His* eyes, twinkling with cunning enjoyment, glanced at every moment towards *his* companion's face. Once or twice he rearranged the light waterproof which he had slung over one shoulder in toreador fashion. *His* breeches, *his* white rubber shoes and *his* jauntily slung waterproof expressed youth. But *his* figure fell onto rotundity at the waist, *his* hair was scant and grey, and his face, when the waves of expression had passed over it, had a ravaged look" (*italics mine*).

In the above paragraph, the "long monologue" belongs to Lenehan, and his companion is Corley, the "other", The most part of the paragraph describes Corley. But without mentioning Corley's name for once, Joyce has used sixteen pronouns, which may confuse the reader between Lenehan and Corley—the pronouns may obfuscate the identity of the noun they stand for.

4. Much credit has been given to Joyce's cunning use of epiphany but Stephen Koch, in his *A Guide to the Craft of Fiction*, devalues Joyce's use of epiphany, saying epiphany is "just a bore" (p. 188). Even if we do not agree with Koch, we may say that Joyce has employed epiphany in its widest (and sometimes confusing) sense rather too much, as he has done gnomon.

5. Objection has been raised against Joyce's sadistic portrayal of some of his characters. Joyce has really shown callousness while delineating some of his characters, such as Eveline, Mrs. Sinico, Mr. Doran, Little Chandler and Farrington.

6. Lastly, objections has been raised the stories of *Dubliners* for being loosely sewn sequence of events, which straightaway rejects the claim of some scholars that *Dubliners* may be treated as a novella.

3

A Portrait of the Artist as a Young Man

(Abridged, Elucidated, and Evaluated)

This 288-pages, long novel (Penguin) is the second of the four artistic marvels of James Joyce: *Dubliners*, *A Portrait of the Artist as a Young Man* (henceforth *A Portrait*), *Ulysses* and *Finnegans Wake*, in that chronological order and in that order of increasing complexity. *A Portrait* is a *bildungsroman* or, better, a *kunstlerroman*, for it is a history of Joyce's literary development, hazed as a novel. Interestingly, from the very early years of his literary apprenticeship, Joyce was confident of becoming a *great literary artist* as may be apparent from the title of the novel—*A Portrait of the Artist as a Young Man* (notice the word 'Artist')—and from the title of the novel's predecessor, or 'ur-*A Portrait*', "Stephen Hero", that Joyce began in 1903 but abandoned in 1905 (notice the name 'Stephen' which suggests 'crown' or 'crowned' or 'great'). Joyce was so confident about his literary capability that long ago when in August 1904 (he was 22 years old) he submitted "The Sisters" to the *Irish Homestead* for publication, he signed the item as "Stephen Daedalus", supposedly meaning that he was like the mythic sculptor (artist) Daedalus, with a 'crown' ('Stephen') on his head.

But the road to his literary eminence was not at all smooth. His first literary output, *Dubliners*, was fabulously rejected by, some say, as many as around 20 publishers, for various reasons.

He had to suffer so much haggling with publishers. But in the case of *A Portrait* he had to suffer not from publishers but with himself, for he could not decide how to proceed with the story of the novel (or of his life). First, he started with what he called "Stephen Hero" in 1903, but after composing some seven chapters he dropped it and wrote a narrative reorientation in his essay "A Portrait of the Artist", a "fictional narrative and philosophical exposition", supposedly on the theme on which *A Portrait* was written, and submitted it to the Dublin literary magazine *Dana* in 1904. But the authority of *Dana* rejected it. Joyce then went back to "Stephen Hero" and completed 25 out of the projected 63 chapters. But, for reasons unknown (but, perhaps, because he was not satisfied with his compositions), Joyce put aside "Stephen Hero" and finally decided to write *A Portrait* in September 1907, planning to complete the novel in just five sections or chapters. And *A Portrait* he completed in 1913 or 1914. So, the novel took him, in one count, around 10 or 11 years (1903-13/14). Hans Walter Gabler, in his essay "The Genesis of *A Portrait of the Artist as a Young Man*" has given us a detailed history of the composition of *A Portrait* (Brady and Carens, pp. 83-110).

Though the writing process of *A Portrait* was full of hazards, unlike that of *Dubliners*, its publication did not entail any such, again, unlike *Dubliners*. In January 1914, when the manuscript of *A Portrait* was not yet complete, Joyce sent the first chapter of it to Ezra Pound, along with *Dubliners*, and it began to be serially published in *The Egoist* from 2 February 1914 to August 1914 under the insistence of Ezra Pound and under the aegis of Joyce-admirer Harriet Shaw Weaver.

The title of *A Portrait* itself speaks enough about the central theme of the novel: it is a sort of Joyce's autobiography—a realistic portrayal of the early years of his choosing the profession of the literary artist for life and the hazards and blocks in his way to that end, which he had to superate.

The hero or protagonist of *A Portrait* is Stephen Dedalus (same as Daedalus), Joyce's alter ego, whose tormenting experiences from school days to the day of leaving his fatherland—Ireland—cover the 288 pages of *A Portrait*. As a young boy, Stephen grew up in the straightjacket of the Catholic environment of Clongowes Wood College (a school), where Father Dolan treated him most cruelly and his classmate, Wells, used to bully him and taunt him because Stephen used to kiss his mother before going to bed. All such things would put him to the rack and he would feel severe anguish.

Next, we see him in the renowned day school called Belvedre School, where his latent literary potential began to blossom and where he first, at the age of 16, visited the red light area and felt penitent for the sin committed. Earlier he repudiated the Chatholic piety but now he began to attend the retreats and to go regularly to the Mass. But the conflict or tussell between the two contradictory forces of attraction—the sensual pull on one hand and the haul of the high value—was tearing him apart. At this time he was also painfully critical of the submissive attitude of his countrymen towards British over-lordship over Ireland or their puerile nostalgia for Ireland's hoary past.

Ultimately, he cut across everything—every externally imposed bindings that so long kept him arrested and subdued, and got absolutely free. He discarded Catholicism, shunned his sense of guilt for carnal enjoyments, and made himself a free individual, free to decide his own destiny without being encumbered by any religious or political servility or social injunctions.

But, what was the superior impulse that did force him to be so self-dependent—absolutely independent? It was his inescapeable and overpowering love and desire of *Beauty*. Like P.B. Shelley, he held beauty as his loadstar. This sea-change came to him suddenly one particular day, as if providentially, in the shape of what he called 'epiphany.' On that momentous day, Joyce went to the sea beach near Howth, where he suddenly saw that "A girl stood before him in midstream, alone and still, gazing out to sea." From a distance, this girl seemed to him a lonely "strange and beautiful seabird." This was his first ever epiphany. "--------Heavenly God!" cried Joyce, alias Stephen. His vacillation about what should be his life's loadstar went away and forever. He stood fixed and creation of beauty, would be his guiding star of life. He went home and wrote in his diary:

"O life! I go to encounter for the millionth time the reality of experience and to forge in the smithy of my soul the uncreated conscience of my race." And on the very next day, in the diary he asseverated that he would dedicate his life to the pursuit of creating literary beauty. And here ends the story of how Stephen (Joyce) came to be a great artist, and here also ends the novel, *A Portrait*.

A Portrait is divided into five sections or chapters: Section I (66 pages), Section II (49 pages), Section III (48 pages), Section IV (30 pages) and Section V (91 pages). Section I is divided into four parts, Section II into five parts, Section III into two parts, Section IV into three parts, and Section V into four parts.

The epitaph of *A Portrait* Joyce has taken from Ovid's *Metamorphosis* (VIII, 18): "*Et ignotas animum dimittit in artes.*" [*Et*=and; *ignotas*=unknown; *animum*=mind or soul; *dimittit*= dismiss; *in artes*=in arts] which means "And he turned hid mind to unknown arts." This is an appropriate epitaph for *A Portrait*, indeed!

Before entering into the novel, let us have quick acquaintances with 12 out of some 30 characters in it.

1. Stephen Dedalus. He is the central character in *A Portrait* (and a minor character in *Ulysses*). According to Chapt. 7:55-60 of the Bible, Stephen was the first Christian martyr who was stoned to death. Stephen also means 'crown'. Dedaulus (or Daedalus) was the fabulous artificer who made wings of wax for himself and his son Icarus and escaped their imprisonment on the island of Crete. *A Portrait* is the story of the development of Stephen as an artist and his escaping the cribbing circumstances of Ireland. In this sense, the name of the protagonist of *A Portrait* is justified.

2. Simon Dedalaus. He is Stephen Dedalus' father—improvident and roguish.

3. Emma Clery. She is the object of Stephen dedalus' romantic fantasy and his idealized vision of Irish womanhood (he once imagined her as Virgin Mary). In "Stephen Hero", her name is explicitly stated but in *A Portrait* her name is initialized as E...C....

4. Katey Dedalus. Stephen Dedalus' younger sister.

5. Cranley. He is modeled on Joyce's close friend John Francis Byrne. Cranley was Stephen Dedalus' classmate at University College, Dublin, and was his confidant.

6. Father Dolan. He was the prefect of studies and dean of discipline at Clongowes Wood College (a school). He pandied Stephen for breaking his eyeglasses.

7. Davin. He is Stephen's close friend and classmate at University College, Dublin. He was a foil to Stephen, in that he was a devout Catholic and a nationalist.

8. Vincent Heron. He was a "putative school friend" of Stephen Dedalus at Belvedere College. He was his sworn rival. Stephen used to satirise him saying that Heron had a "mobile face beaked like a bird" (heron is a screaming and wading bird).

9. Vincent Lynch. He was modelled on Vincent Cosgrave, James Joyce's actual friend at University College, Dublin. It was with Vincent Lynch that Stephen Dedalus discussed his disquisition on aesthetics and his views on the Catholic Church and on women.

10. Rev. Charles Ghezzi, S J. A real person, he was a Jesuit priest and professor of Italian at University College, Dublin. He taught Stephen Italian and discussed with him Dante Alighieri, Gabriel D'Anunzio and other Italian writers, and also discussed with him Giordano Bruno and the aesthetics of St. Thomas Aquinas. In *A Portrait*, Joyce has employed the real name of Rev, Ghezzi but, earlier, in "Stephen Hero" he used the fictional name of Father Artifoni for Rev. Ghezzi.

11. Dante. Dante is a corruption of "auntie." The young Joyce called her by the name of "auntie." In *A Portrait,* her fictional name is Mrs. Riordan and is affectionately called Dante. She was the governess in the Dedalus household and she epitomized a harsh and menacing authority. She was modelled on Mrs. Hearn Conroy who came to the Joyce household from Cork. She was an orthodox Catholic and a hater of Parnell.

12. Eileen Vance. She appears only in *A Portrait*, and not in "Stephen Hero." In his younger ages, Stephen was attracted

In the Catholics-dominated Clongowes Wood College (Stephen's first school), Stephen had to reside in the boarding and willy-nilly behave like a true Catholic with trembling fingers so "he might not go to hell when he died." Christmas came near and he was to go home to the delight of his father and mother and all, but he was taken to the infirmary for illness. Stephen had passionately imagined boarding the train and speeding home with the sound "click, click: click, click", the telegraph poles running to the opposite direction. But that was not to be. He wrote to his mother: impatiently: "Dear Mother, I am sick. I want to go home. Please come and take me home. I am in the infirmary. ...Your fond son, Stephen." In the infirmary, too, Nasty. Roche and Athy kept teasing him (jesting with him) badly. It was queer that they had not given him any medicine" (p. 29). Just at this time, Charles Parnell, the nationalist died and the people were mourning. Dante was in *high spirit*.

Part 3. In this part, we see Stephen at home and saying "the grace before meals" at the dinner table, as per Christian injunction. It was Stephen's ever first Christian dinner in which the point of national politics arose. Dante said that politics should come from the pulpit. Supporting her, Mr. Casey said, "We are all sinners, black sinners." At one point, Dante said, "I'll defend my church and my religion when it is insulted and spit on by-renegade catholics." She heaped aspersions on Parnell for the Kitty O'Shea scandal (Parnell secretly continued to have carnal relation with the married O'Shea). Stephen's father, Mr. Dedalus, was saying "crooning and swaying his head":

> O, come all you Roman Catholics
> That never went to mass.

Mr. Casey who was disgusted with the on-going religious controversy in Ireland said:

"...No God for Ireland! he cried. We have had too much God in Ireland. Away with God!

...Blasphemer! Devil! screamed Dante, starting to her feet and almost spitting in his face."

Part 4. The Catholics believed that the Blessed Virgin was the 'Tower of Ivory' and the 'House of Gold.' The Protestants made fun of this: "How could a woman be a tower of ivory or a house of gold?" Stephen was thinking of Eileen Vance: "Eileen had long thin cool white hands too because she was a girl. They were like ivory; only soft. That was the meaning of Tower of Ivory but protestants could not understand it and made fun of it." He thought of Eileen's hair: "Her fair hair had streamed out behind her gold in the sun. Tower of Ivory. House of Gold." Thus, Stephen understood religion in terms of artistic beauty. And this was his first leaning towards aesthetics.

After the Christmas, Stephen went back to school at Clongowes. One day, Father Arnall, a Jesuit, found in class that Fleming was unable to decline the Latin noun *mare* and asked him to kneel down, and also informed Father Dolan, the dean of punishment, about him. Father Dolan came and pandied both arms of Fleming and asked him to kneel down again. Then Father Dolan asked Father Arnall why Stephen was not writing like others. Father Arnall informed him that Stephen had broken his eyeglasses. Father Dolan wrongly thought that it was a trick of Stephen and pandied him severely. Stephen prayed, tears rolled down while he was crying, but the pandibat did not stop.

This was Stephen's first cognition of great fear and punishment and shame and humiliation. He decided to tell Father Conmee, the rector about what happened. He told the Father that he had broken his glasses and so could not write his theme, and this was why Father Dolan pandied him. The rector showed Stephen sympathy and told him that Father Dolan could not understand the matter and so was the mistake on Father Dolan's part. The rector assured Stephen that he would talk with father Dolan. Stephen was satisfied and thanked the rector.

SECTION II

Part 1. In this part, there is a psychological change in Stephen. He is searching within the gloomy darkness of his soul the means of transforming himself, from his passivity to an active tryst with the real world. Now Stephen would not be sent back to school at Clongowes, due to his father's financial constraints. He now had enough time to learn the ways of the world with his naked eyes and through 'words'—"Words which he did not understand he said over and over to himself till he had learnt them by heart: and through them he had glimpses of the real world about them." He believed it was time for him to prepare himself to proactively participate in "the life of the world" that "seemed drawing near and in secret he began to make ready for the great part which he felt awaited him the nature of which he only dimly apprehended." "For some time he had felt the slight change in his house; and those changes in what he had deemed unchangeable were so many slight shocks to his boyish conception of the world. The ambition which he felt astir at times in the darkness of his soul sought no outlet." He wanted to meet in the real world the unsubstantial image which his soul so constantly beheld." Perhaps, this was the moment in his life when he was imagining himself as a great writer.

Part 2. In this part, we see Stephen shrouded with melancholy and loneliness. He was now interested in the Irish politics which he thought he was to enter not very long afterwards. During this time, one day he saw his aunt reading the evening paper in the kitchen. Bending over the paper his aunt was looking at the picture of the beautiful Mabel Hunter for a long time. At this moment Eileen Vance came there and gazed at the picture, spell-bound and exclaimed: "Isn't she an exquisite creature?" There Stephen was sitting gloomily amid a children's party. The party being over, he and Eileen went together to catch a tram.

In the tram, Eileen came to him from her seat to tell him a phrase or two and went back. "His heart danced upon movements like a cork upon a tide." Later on he recalled the day when he and Eileen "had stood looking into the hotel grounds, watching waiters running up a trail of bunting." However, in the tram, he fancied "...She too wants me to catch hold of her, he thought...I could hold her and kiss her." But his timidity stood in the way. This was his libidinal egging. Next day, alone, he tried to write a poem for her, "To E...C..." (Emma Clay), but in spite of all his efforts he could only write at the top of the paper the Jesuit moto: A.M.D.G. (*Ad Majorem Dei Glorium*, meaning for the greater glory of God). Stephen's excruciating mental conflict may be apparent here—the conflict between his infirm Jesuit belief and his instinct's insistent promptings.

Part 3. Whitsuntide (White+Sunday: the seventh Sunday after Easter, when the converts to the primitive church wore white robes.) All young boys were astir, joyous, mobile. In this ambience of merriment, Stephen was teased and mocked by Vincent Heron. He asked Stephen to smoke but Stephen said: "...I don't smoke." Being at his crisp reply, Heron satirized him: "...No, said Heron. Dedalus is a model youth. He doesn't smoke and doesn't go to bazaars and doesn't flirt and doesn't damn anything or damn all". Stephen shook his head to rescue himself from the mockery. He noticed that not only Heron's name reminds one of a species of birds but he, with his "flushed and mobile face" and "narrow and bony and thin hooked nose", looks like a bird of that species. Heron was angry. He nudged Stephen and called him "a sly dog." "The old restless moodiness had again filled his breast as it had done on the night of the party, but had not found an outlet in verse". Heron told Stephen that his false or fake saintliness had been exposed because he and Wallis had seen his girlfriend (E-c-or Eileen). Heron and Wallis laughed. Heron asked Stephen to confess his supposed flirting with that girl: "—Admit!" and stroke on the leg with his cane. Stephen was bearing the pain. Heron again admonished Stephen with: "—Admit!" "It was towards the close of his first term on the college [a school, in fact] when he was in number six. His sensitive nature was still smarting under the lashes of an undivided and squalid way of life. His soul was still disquitted and cast down by the dull phenomenon of Dublin.

Stephen's psychological grilling did not end there. One day Mr. Tate, his English master, accused him of heresy in his essay. All the other students in the class were dumbfounded. Mr. Tate read the portion of his essay that he called heresy: "—Here. It's about the Creator and the soul. Rrm...rrm...rrm.... *Ah! without a possibility of* ever approaching nearer. That's heresy." Stephen was enough chided.

After a few days, when Stephen was sauntering in the night he was halted by Heron, who was carrying a cane. Heron was accompanied by Boland and Nash. He asked Stephen:

"Who is the greatest poet?" Stephen answered: Byron. Heron sarcastically said: "Byron the greatest poet! He is a poet for uneducated people." Heron further went—

"—In any case Byron was a heretic and immoral too." Stephen's reaction was adamantine: "I don't care what he was, cried Stephen hotly." After a few more such exchanges, Heron suddenly cautioned Stephen: "—Behave yourself! cried Heron, cutting at Stephen's legs with cane." Stephen became hardened. When he was ordered to agree with his tormentor to say that Byron was no good poet, Stephen did not bend:

"Admit that Byron was no good.
—No.
—Admit.
—No.
—Admit.
—No. No."

At last Stephen went his own way, embittered, and crying, and his tormentors went the other way, laughing and jeering at him.

Part 4. Stephen went to Cork with his father by train to join Belvedere College. In that college, he and his father entered the anatomy theatre to find out Stephen's initial on a certain desk. Suddenly, Stephen noticed the word FOETUS cut on a desk and had an epiphany: "On the desk he read the word FOETUS cut several times in the dark stained wood. The sudden legend startled his blood: he seemed to feel the absent students of the college about him and to shrink from their company. A vision of their life, which his father's words had been powerless to evoke, sprang up before him out of the word cut in the desk. A broad-shouldered student with a moustache was cutting the letters with a jackknife, seriously." Stephen came down from the anatomy theatre but the "vision" of the word "foetus" remained with him: "But word and the vision capered before his eyes as he walked back across the quadrangle and towards the college gate. It shocked him to find in the outer world a trace of what he had deemed till then a brutish and individual malady of his own mind. His monstrous reveries came thronging into his memory. They too had sprung up before him, suddenly and furiously, out of mere words. He had soon given in to them and allowed them to sweep across and abase his intellect, wandering always where they came from, from what den of monstrous images, and always weak and humble towards others, restless and sickened of himself when they swept over him."

Stephen was walking beside his father. "He recalled his own equivocal position in Belvedere, a free boy, a leader afraid of his own authority, proud and sensitive and superstitious, battling against the squalor of his life and against the riot of his mind. The letters cut in the stained wood of the desk stared upon him, mocking his bodily weakness and futile enthusiasms and making him loathe himself for his own mad and filthy orgies."

Stephen's father found two cronies of his on the way and with them entered a bar, Stephen following. Stephen saw the three—his father and the two cronies—raising three glasses to the memories of their sweet past. But Stephen was gloomy, nevertheless. "He had known neither the pleasure of companionship with others nor the vigour of rude male health nor filial piety. *Nothing stirred within his soul but a cold and cruel and loveless lust*. His childhood was dead or lost and with it his soul capable of simple joys and he was drifting amid life like the barren shell of the moon.

Art thou pale for weariness
Of climbing heaven and gazing on the earth,
Wandering companionless...?

He repeated to himself the lines of Shelley's fragment. Its alternation of sad human ineffectiveness with vast inhuman cycles of activity chilled him and he forgot his own human and ineffectual grieving."

Part 5. Stephen was feeling the pressure of his life of loneliness. He would wander along the long footpaths while he would look within himself. "He turned to appease the fierce longings of his heart before which everything else was idle and alien. He cared little that he was in mortal sin, that his life had grown to be a tissue of subterfuge and falsehood. Beside the savage desire within him to realise the enormities which he brooded on nothing was sacred.... By day and night he moved among the distorted images of the outer world. A figure that had seemed to him by day demure and innocent came towards him by night through the winding darkness of sleep, her face transfigured by lecherous cunning, her eyes bright with brutish joy. Only the morning pained him with its dim memory of dark orgiastic riot, its keen and humiliating sense of transgression."

Stephen felt cribbed by the familial, social and political injunctions. But though he wanted to get free of all these, his timidity, weakness and inexperience stood on the way of his "holy encounter" with the reality. "His blood was in revolt. He wanted to sin with another of his kind, to force another of his kind, to force another being to sin with him and to exult with her in sin." His flesh revolted religion. One day, as he was sauntering alone along the roadway, his wistful imagination came to fruition. "A woman, dressed in a long pink gown laid her hand on his arm to detain him and gazed into his face. She said gaily: "...Good night, Willie dear!" She took him to her room and embraced "him gaily and gravely." Stephen was overwhelmingly touched by her soft affection. "Tears of joy and relief shone in his delighted eyes and his lips parted though they would not speak."

"She passed her tinkling hand through his hair, calling him a little rascal."

"—Give me a kiss", she said.

"His lips would not bend to kiss her. He wanted to be held firmly in her arms, to be caressed slowly, slowly, slowly. In her arms he felt that he had suddenly become strong and fearless and sure of himself. But his lips would not bend to kiss her.

"With a sudden movement she bowed her head and joined her lips to his and he read the meaning of her movements in her frank uplifted eyes. It was too much for him. He closed his eyes, surrendering himself to her, body and mind, conscious of nothing in the world but the dark pressure of her softly parting lips. They pressed upon his brain as upon his lips though they were the vehicle of a vague speech; and between them he felt an unknown and timid pressure, darker than the swoon of sin, softer than sound or colour."

SECTION III

Part 1. Part 1 begins with Stephen's (he was then 16 or so years of age) experience in the brothel. He was revolting against the smothering, atrocious, life-denying, and anti-aesthetic injunctions of Catholicism. He wanted to moult off the baggage of his religious past with a jerk and to do all that as "his sin-loving soul" dictated—to visit the whoredom. There, he was greeted:

"—Hello, Bertie, any good in your mind?

—Is that you, pigeon?

Number ten. Nelly is waiting on you.

—Good night, husband! Coming in to have a short time?"

The unreal life of religion faded out at once before Stephen—the life of loneliness and boredom. "The vast cycle of starry life bore his weary mind outward to its verge and inward to its centre, a distant music accompanying him outward and inward.... The stars began to crumble and a cloud of fine stardust fell through space." Stephen was defiantly going to meet sin after sin, to make his self free of all constraints. "It was his own soul going forth to experience, unfolding itself sin by sin, spreading abroad the balefire of its burning stars and folding back upon itself, fading slowly, quenching its own lights and fires. They were quenched: and the cold darkness filled chaos." Before his maiden carnal sin, Stephen had apprehended that all his reserve vitality would leave him but his encounter with the sin proved otherwise. "At his first violent sin he had felt a wave of vitality pass out of him and had feared to find his body or his soul maimed by the excess. Instead the vital wave had carried him on its bosom out of himself and back again when it receded: and no part of body or soul had been maimed but a dark peace had been established between them."

Stephen sinned thus not once but "many times." Nevertheless he had no atonement or repentance, no compunction, no contrition; and no shame nor no fear. He spurned prayer for his guilt: "What did it avail to pray when he knew that his soul lusted after its own destruction?" He rather mocked the church and the worshippers at the church. He thought "His sin, which has covered him from the sight of God, had led him nearer to the refuge of sinners." Stephen was devising questions to himself about the belief in the church: if a youth had stolen pound and amassed a huge amount of wealth long afterwards was he to give back only one pound or the whole amount grown on that pound to save himself? Is baptism valid when it is done with mineral water? Stephen went further: "Why was the sacrament of the eucharist instituted under the two species of bread and wine if Jesus Christ be present body and blood, soul and divinity, in the bread alone and in the wine alone? Does a tiny particle of the consecrated bread contain all the body and blood of Jesus Christ or a part only of the body and blood? If the wine change into vinegar and the host crumble into corruption after they have been consecrated, is Jesus Christ still present under their species as God and as man?"

On Wednesday was the retreat in honour of Saint Francis Xavier. The rector, in his lecture, narrated the illustrious life of Xavier who converted ten thousand idolaters in one month and whose right hand had grown powerless "from having been raised so often over the heads of these whom he baptized." Stephen was there. His "heart had withered up like a flower of the desert that feels the simoom coming from afar." His atheism's foundation was shaken for the moment.

Part 2. The annual retreat of Belvedere college was being celebrated in which Saint Francis Xavier would be honoured (Xavier, the patron saint of the college). Father Arnall was delivering the sermon in the chapel. He said retreat meant "a withdrawal for a while from the cares of our life of this workaday world, in order to examine the state of our conscience, to reflect on the mysteries of holy religion and to understand better why we are here in this world." He asked the assembled boys to remember four last things of life for the benefit of our souls—death, judgment, hell and heven. Father Arnall added: "And remember, my dear boys, that we have been sent into this world for one thing and for one thing alone: to do God's holy will and to save our immortal souls. All else is worthless." He urged them "to shun all loud unseemly pleasures." Then he drew a daguerreotyped picture of human beings' last moment: "And while the friends were still standing in tears by the bedside the soul of the sinner was judged. At the last moment of consciousness the whole earthly life passed before the vision of the soul and, ere it had time to reflect, the body had died and the soul stood terrified before the judgment seat."

It was also announced by him that "The last day had come. The doomsday was at hand. ....The archangel Michael, the prince of the heavenly host, appeared glorious and terrible against the sky. With one foot on the sea and one foot on the land he blew from the arch-angelical trumpet the brazen death of time.... No longer the lowly Lamb of God, no longer the meek Jesus of Nazareth, no longer the Man of Sorrows, no longer the Good Shepherd, He is seen now coming upon the clouds, the power and majesty, attended by nine choirs of angels, angels and archangels, principalities, powers and virtues, thrones and dominations, cherubim and seraphim, God Omnipotent, God Everlasting." Father Arnall also cited an actual example of a pious Christian—that of the English writer Addison: "Was it not Addison, the great English writer, who, when on his deathbed, sent for the wicked young earl of Warwick to let him see how a Christian can meet his end? He it is and he alone, the pious and believing Christian, who can say in his heart:

O grave, where is thy victory?
O death, where is thy sting?"

Stephen understood that every word of the sermon was meant for him. And he thought: "Yes, the preacher was right."

Nevertheless, when he was walking towards home, "the light laughter of a girl" brought before his mental eyes the image of his childhood girlfriend Emma: "The image of Emma appeared before him, and under her eyes the flood of shame rushed forth from his heart." Stephen fabricated a compromise between what the preacher said about the life after death and his present life with Emma. He thought: "God and the Blessed Virgin were too far from him. God was too great and stern and the Blessed Virgin too pure and holy. But he imagined that he stood near Emma in a too wide land and, humbly in tears, bent and kissed the elbow of her sleeve." Stephen fancied that the Blessed Virgin exonerated him and Emma because they were her children. He thought "Their error had offended deeply God's majesty though it was the error of two children; but it had not offended her [Emma] whose beauty *is not like earthly beauty, dangerous to look upon, but like the morning star which is its emblem, bright and musical.* The eyes were not offended which she turned upon him nor reproachful. She placed their hands together, hand in hand, and said, speaking to their hearts: "—Take hands, Stephen and Emma, It is a beautiful evening now in heaven. You have erred but you are always my children. It is one heart that loves another heart. Take hands together, my dear children, and you will be happy together and your hearts will love each other."

On another day, Father Arnoll, the preacher and Stephen's Latin teacher, lectured about Adam and Eve; the fruit of the forbidden tree; the only son of God the Virgin Mary; the Blessed Trinity; and the Eternal Word. He also spoke about how Jesus was seized and bound and tortured by "jewish rabble and Roman soldiery" and then hanged upon a gibbet. Father Arnoll also narrated the hill of Calvary on top of which Jesus founded the holy catholic church and from where he showed pity for mankind. He said that the walls of the hell were four thousand miles thick, and there was tortuous livid fire but absolutely no light. He said in the Hell there was no law whatever and no sense of humanity. Arnoll (the Father) paused and went to his seat (from the lectern of church, like podium desk). But just before going to his seat tremblingly, he shrieked out: Hell! Hell! Hell! Hell! Hell!

After a while, the preacher went back to the podium and the English lesson began. He began with the history of the dead royal personages. The burden of the introduction was that all life was a long wait for death: "...a whole life, every hour of life. Only wait." Then he resumed the torments in hell-physical and spiritual-consequent upon commitment of sinful acts:

"—Sin, remember, is a twofold enormity. It is a base consent to promptings of our corrupt nature to the lower instincts, to that which is gross and beastlike; and it is also a turning away from the counsel of our higher nature, from all that is pure and holy, from the Holy God Himself. For this reason mortal sin is punished in hell by two different forms of punishment, physical and spiritual.

"Now of all these spiritual pains by far the greatest is the pain of loss, so great, in fact, that in itself it is a torment greater than all others. Saint Thomas,..., says that the worst damnation consists in this, that the understanding of a man is totally deprived of divine light and his affection obstinately turned away from the goodness of God."

The preaching went on: "The second pain which will afflict the souls of the damned in hell is the pain of conscience. Just as in dead bodies worms are engendered by putrefaction, so in the souls of the lost there arises a perpetual remorse from the putrefaction of sin, the sting of conscience, the worm, as Pope Innocent the Third calls it, the triple sting." The three stings of conscience were:

(i) "memory post pleasures"—the dreadful memory. The king would recall his pomp of court, "the lover of artistic pleasures his marbles and pictures and other treasures", etc.

(ii) the sinners would "rage and fume to think that they have lost the bliss of heaven for the dross of earth."

(iii) and now though they repent the most and weep as much "all that sea of repentance would not gain for you what a single tear of true repentance shed during your moral life would have gained for you."

The preacher continued: "...The next spiritual pain to which the damned are subjected is the pain of extension. Man, in this earthly life, though he be capable of manly evils, is not capable of them all at once, in as much as one evil corrects and counteracts another. In hell, on the contrary, one torment, instead of counteracting another, lends it still greater force; and moreover, as the internal faculties are more perfect than the external senses, so are they more capable of suffering." Further, "—Opposed to this pain of extension and yet coexistent with it we have the pain of intensity." The preacher explained this pain of extension thus: "in hell the torments cannot be overcome by habit, for while they are of terrible intensity they are at the same time of continual variety, each pain, so to speak, taking fire from another and reendowing that which has kindled it with a still fiercer flame." And, lastly, said the preacher: "—Last and crowning torture of all tortures of that awful place is the eternity of hell. Eternity! O, dread and dire word. Eternity!" The priest (or preacher) told the assembled students in the chapel: "I pray to God, and do you pray with me, that we may repent our sins." Then he went towards the alter and knelt to pray. And "Stephen, his tongue cleaving to his plate, bowed his head, praying with his heart.

—O my God!—
—O my God!—
—I am heartily sorry—
—I am heartily sorry— Etc.

Stephen swiftly went to his room, closed the door, and climbed into the bed. Being alone now he began "to examine his conscience, to meet his sins face to face, to recall their times and manners and circumstances, to weep over them. He could not weep. He could not summon them to his memory." He questioned himself if he actually committed any sin, "How came it that God had not struck him down?" He saw wild creatures roaring hither and thither in the field. Goatish creatures with human faces, soft language issuing forth from their "spittleless lips." It was a terrifying vision. Stephen cried out "Help!" and "flung the blankets from him madly to free his face and neck. That was his hell." He cried out "Air! The air of heven!" He was tottering in sickness and then "vomited profusely in agony."

When he recovered, Stephen prayed with his heart to the Blessed Mary: "*And now thy very face and form, dear mother, speak to us of the Eternal; not like earthly beauty, dangerous to look upon, but like the morning star which is thy emblem, bright and musical*". Stephen begged to the Blessed Mary to take him to Lord Jesus. He "wept for the innocence he had lost." He again knelt and confessed. He questioned himself was he inhuman and beastly when he was moved by a lower self and committed the sins. "He cowered in the shadow of the thought, abasing himself in the awe of God Who had made all things and all men." Why such thoughts did come to him? Was he now mad? He asked himself. He thought that some demon was whispering these thoughts into his ears. He felt an urge to confess all his sins.

Stephen rushed to the streets and walked on and on "through illicit streets." He thought: "How beautiful must be a soul in the state of grace when God looked upon it with love!" As he walked, he saw some unkempt and frowsy girls on the curbstones with baskets. He thought if God would see their souls in grace, they would look beautiful. An old woman was crossing the street. He asked her whether there was a chapel nearby. She showed him a church. Stephen entered the church and prayed with others. He felt a gripping, shattering shame for his act of sin. He thought had it been a murder he would not feel so much of the same. He beat his breast and promised he would, thenceforth, be one with God and pray to Him and do what He commanded. Back to his room, he prayed lonely to the suspended crucifix and whimpered: "—Sorry! Sorry! Sorry!" Then he "prayed of the priest to bless him for he had sinned. And he repeated the *Confiteor* [Latin="I confess"—"*Mea culpa, mea culpa, /mea maxima culpa*—, meaning: I confess to almighty God—that I have greatly sinned]. The priest then asked him:

—With women, my child?

—Yes, father.

—Were they married women, my child?

"Stephen bowed his head, overcome."

—How old are you, my child?

—Sixteen, father.

Stephen went homeward. He believed God had pardoned him. He understood: "How simple and beautiful was life after all! And life lay all before him." "In a dream he fell asleep. In a dream he rose and saw that it was morning. In a waking dream he went through the quiet morning towards the college."

SECTION IV

Part 1. This is the shortest section of *A Portrait* and in this section Stephen has his most crucial turning of all his life: his turning from religion (Catholicism) to literary aestheticism (beauty). This turning happens in the third or last part of this section.

At the beginning of Part 1 of this section, we see Stephen still under the spell of the priest's hortatory homily. "Every morning he hallowed himself anew in the presence of some holy image or mystery. His day began with an heroic offering of its every moment of thought or action for the intentions of the sovereign pontiff and with an early mass." His life was full of devotion and all the while he was afraid of the purgatorial fire. "Every part of his day, divided by what he regarded now as the duties of his station in life, circled about its own centre of spiritual energy." Stephen was indeed head over ears in Christian piety. He regularly said his rosaries, and for that end he carried his rosaries in the pockets of his trousers.

Stephen "offered up each of his three daily chaplets that his soul might grow strong in each of the three theological virtues, in faith in the Father Who had created him, in hope in the Son Who had redeemed him and in love of the Holy Ghost Who had sanctified him; and this thrice triple prayers he offered to the Three Persons through Mary in the name of her joyful and sorrowful and glorious mysteries." And "On each of the seven days of the week he further prayed that one of the seven gifts of the Holy Ghost might descend upon his soul and drive out of it day by day the seven deadly sins which had defiled it in the past…."

Nevertheless, Stephen could not forget the reality of earthly love. "He could no longer disbelieve in the reality of love, since God Himself had loved his individual soul with divine love from all eternity. Gradually, as his soul was enriched with spiritual knowledge, he saw the whole world forming one vast symmetrical expression of God's power and love…. The world for all its solid substance and complexity no longer existed for his soul save as a theorem of divine power and love and universality." And nevertheless "Each of his senses was brought under a rigorous discipline. In order to mortify the senses of sight he made it his rule to walk in the street with downcast eyes, glancing neither to the right nor left and never behind him. His eyes shunned every encounter with the eyes of women."

But all the religious practices of Stephen failed to deliver his desired effects. He wanted to suppress absolutely the promptings of his flesh but the whisperings of his flesh frequently interfered in his voluntary engagements in devotional functions. His intellect and will were stemmed by the demand of his flesh. "It surprised him however to find that at the end of his course of intricate piety and self-restraint he was so easily at the mercy of childish and unworthy imperfections. His prayers and fasts availed him little for the suppressions of anger at hearing his mother sneeze or at being disturbed in his devotions." These were but small instances of his tottering, unsteady will to devotion. Stephen felt his soul seduced by some unholy force. "An inaudible voice seemed to caress the soul, telling her names and glories, bidding her arise as for espousal and come away, biding her look forth, a spouse, from Amana ["apparently a mountain in or near Lebanon" (Smith, 25)] and from the mountains of the leopards; and the soul seemed to answer with the same inaudible voice, surrendering himself: *Inter ubera mea commorabitur* [the lure of flesh]."

"This idea of surrender had a perilous attraction for his mind now that he felt his soul beset once again by the insistent voices of the flesh which began to murmur to him again during his prayers and meditations." Stephen had fallen into the grey area of uncertainties. His doubt about his progress in the way of purity and salvation was growing in force. "When he had eluded the flood of temptation many times in this way he grew troubled and wondered whether the grace which he had refused to lose was not being filched from him little by little. The clear certitude of his own immunity grew dim and to it succeeded a vague fear that his soul had really fallen unawares." In his *aporia* he questioned himself: "...I have amended my life, have I not?"

Part 2. In this part, we see the director of the college at Belvedere, and a priest, persuading Stephen to join the order of the Jesuit Church. The priest had called for Stephen and Stephen met the priest who initiated the conversation by telling him that "—Victor Hugo had never written half so well when he had turned against the church as he had written when he was a Catholic." After this, the priest turned to the point for which he wanted to talk to Stephen. The priest told him:

"—I sent for you today, Stephen, because I wished to speak to you on a very important subject.

—Yes, sir.

—[the priest asked him] Have you ever felt that you had a vocation?

—[the priest explained] I mean, have you ever felt within yourself, in your soul, a desire to join the order? Think.

—I have sometimes thought of it, said Stephen.

—In a college like this, he [the priest] said at length, there is one boy or perhaps two or three boys whom God calls to the religious life.... And you, Stephen, have been such a boy in this college, prefect of Our Blessed Lady's sodality. Perhaps you are the boy in this college whom God designs to call to himself." Stephen was imbued. The priest doubled the lucre: "No king or emperor on this earth has the power of the priest of God. No angel or archangel in heaven, no saint, not even the Blessed Virgin herself, has the power of a priest of God.... What an awful power, Stephen."

"A flame began to flutter again on Stephen's check as he heard in this proud address an echo of his own proud musings.... His soul loved to muse in secret on this desire." The images of the chasuble (a sleeveless vestment worn by the priest while celebrating mass) and thurible (cerser) and dalmatic (a loose-fitting, wide-slaved ecclesiastical vestment worn specially by deacons) of cloth of gold floated in the air before his eyes. But his mind was swinging this way and that because some other string was pulling him to the contrary way. Its pull was more potential than that of the Church. The string was tied to his past memories of love and beauty and the warmth of the flesh. "Some instinct, waking at these memories, stronger than education or piety, quickened within him at every near approach to that life [of flesh], an instinct subtle and hostile, armed him against acquiescence. The chill and order of the life repelled him."

But the immediately next moment, the pull of the church came to him. If he joined the order, he would be "The Reverend Stephen Dedalus, S.J." What a glory! Stephen wondered. He was then passing by the Jesuit house in the Garden Street. Casually and vaguely he thought which window would be his if he joined the order. But that was a fleeting phenomenon. He did not feel even the slightest impulse to associate himself with the Jesuit order (or for that matter to any form of religion or piety). He was not for going to the Jesuit house in the Garden Street nor for listening to the exhortation of the priest. "His destiny was to be elusive of social or religious orders. The wisdom of the priest's appeal did not touch him to the quick. He was destined to learn his own wisdom apart from others or to learn the wisdom of others himself wandering among the snares of the world. The snares of the world were its ways of sin. He would fall. He had not yet fallen but would fall silently, in an instant. Not to fall was too hard, too hard; and he felt the silent lapse of his soul, as it would be at some instant to come, falling, falling, but not yet fallen, but about to fall." He felt that his life fell into disorder and that his life was a stagnant "vegetable life." A sudden instinct of remorse arose in Stephen's heart when he entered into the kitchen of the house where his brothers and sisters were sitting round a table over tea. Stephen asked one of them where his father and mother were. One answered: "—Goneboro toboro lookboro atboro aboro houseboro [the 'boro' is a nonsense addition to each word]." Stephen was moving away from the sphere of the Jesuits and now this family is moving to another house. He ejaculated: "Still another removal!" Stephen asked one of these sitting around the table why his family is again moving elsewhere. The answer came: "Because boro theboro landboro lordboro willboro putboro outboro." The group of sisters and brothers then sang Thomas Moore's song: *Oft, in the Stilly Night* in a chorus in which Stephen also joined.

[Oft in the stilly night,
Ere slumber's chain has bound me,
Fond memory brings the light
Of the other days around me;
Sad memory brings the light
Of other days around me.]

In that chorus, Stephen felt a sense of weariness and pain that overcast the singers. "He heard the choir of voices in the kitchen echoed and multiplied through an endless reverberation of the choirs of endless generations of children and heard in all the echoes an echo also of the recurring note of weariness and pain." All seemed weary of life even before entering upon it. "And he remembered that Newman had heard this note also in the broken lines of Virgil, *giving utterance, like the voice of Nature herself, to that pain and weariness yet hope of better things which has been the experience of her children in every time.*"

Part 3. This part is a sort of prolegomena to Joyce's theory of aesthetics which virtually occupies the whole of Section V. However, Stephen's father had gone out with Stephen's tutor, Dan Crosby, for gathering information about the University College of Dublin to consider Stephen's study there. Stephen, on the other hand, was sauntering to and fro from Byron's public house to Clontarf chapel and back, and thus anxiously waiting for his father to return. While his father was considering his study in the university, his mother was against the idea. Stephen's faith in Christianity during that time was slowly sinking in his soul. He was thinking that the "end had been born to serve" and was beaconing him. It seemed to him that he was hearing notes of music of that end. That end, he felt, was leaping like "triple-branching flames." He knew "the oils of ordination would never anoint his body." He asked himself: "Why?"

He was walking over the wooden bridge where he saw a squad of "christian brothers". He avoided them and forgot to answer his own "Why?" and began to think that the Christian commandment of loving one's neighbour does not mean what most men mean by that commandment. He argued to himself that "the commandment of love bade us not to love our neighbour as ourselves with the same amount and intensity of love but to love him as ourselves with the same kind of love."

After the dilemma between the delighting prospect of studying in the university and the feeling of guilt from leaving the door of the church, Stephen's consciousness now floated freely. Suddenly, he began to dally with the strange phrase that arrived in his consciousness:

> "...A day of dappled seaborne clouds." He wondered that "The phrase and the day and the scene harmonized in a cord." He was curious to know what was there in that phrase or in the words that gave him so much of delight. He was curious to know if it was his love of words, or his love of the rhythm in the phrase, or of his love of the meaning of the phrase. He began to reflect on the words: "Words. Was it their colours? He allowed them to glow and fade, hue after hue: sunrise gold, the russet and green of apple orchards, azure of waves, the grey fringed fleece of clouds. No, it was not their colours: it was the poise and balance of the period itself. Did he then love the rhythmic rise and fall of words better than their associations of legend and colour? Or was it that, being weak of sight as he was shy of mind, he drew less pleasure from the reflection of the glowing sensible world through the prism of a language many coloured and richly and richly storied than from the contemplation of an inner world of individual emotions mirrored perfectly in a lucid supple periodic prose?"

Such was the train of Stephen's thought when he walked over that wooden bridge toward the firm land. He looked down and saw the slow-flowing river Liffey and inhaled the "cold infrahuman odour of the sea." In the short distance, he saw "slender masts" of boats and canoes on the Liffey crowded the sky, and in the distance he dimly saw the city of Dublin that appeared to him like the hoary thingmote [the 'earthen terraced mount (that) was in all senses an outstanding monument of unknown antiquity in Dublin.']: "Like a scene on some vague arras, old as man's weariness, the image of the seventh city of christendom [Dublin was the mythical 7th city of Christendom] was visible to him across the timeless air, no older nor more weary nor less patient of subjection than the days of the thingmote."

The view (or vision) of Dublin as the mythical seventh city of Christendom disheartened him. He looked at the seaborne dappled clouds that were coming from westwards (from Italy?). He heard "a confused music within him of memories...then the music seemed to recede, to recede, to recede...." Then he heard "A voice from beyond the world was calling: ...Hello, Stephenos!" He again heard the call: "—Stephenos Dedalus! Bous Stephanoumenos! Bous Stepheneferos!" He thought the call that pronounced his name "Dedalus"—"the fabulous artificer"—was a prophecy for him. But he asked himself: was it a prophecy that he would be an artist: "a prophecy of the end he had been born to serve and had been following through the mist of childhood and beyond, a symbol of the artist forgoing anew in his workshop out of the sluggish matter of the earth a new soaring impalpable imperishable being?" Stephen was extremely delighted: "His soul was soaring in an air beyond the world and the body he knew was purified in a breath and delivered of incertitude and made radiant and commingled with the element of the spirit. An ecstasy of flight made radiant his eyes and wild his breath and tremulous and wild and radiant his wind-swept limbs."

Stephen looked towards Howth. "The sea had fallen below the line of seawrack [sea weeds] on the shallow side of the breakwater and already the tide was running out fast along the foreshore." On the beach he saw some light-clad persons who were wading and delving. "In a few moments he was barefoot, his stockings folded in his pockets and his canvas shoes dangling by their knotted laces over his shoulders and, picking a pointed salteaten stick out of the jetsam among the rocks, he clambered down the slope of the breakwater." Stephen now asked himself: "Where was his boyhood now? Where was the soul that had hung back from her destiny, to brood alone upon the shame of her wounds and in her house of squalor and subterfuge to queen it in faded cerements and in wreaths that withered at the touch? Or where was he?" "He was alone. He was unheeded, happy and near to the wild heart of life. He was alone and young and willful and wildhearted, alone amid a waste of wild air and brackish waters and the seaharvest of shells and tangle and veiled grey sunlight and gayclad lightclad figures of children and girls and voices childish and girlish in the air."

"A girl stood before him in midstream, alone and still, gazing out to sea she seemed like one whom magic had changed into the likeness of a strange and beautiful seabird. Her long slender bare legs were delicate as a crane's and pure save where an emerald trail of seaweed had fashioned itself as a sign upon the flesh. Her thighs, fuller and soft-hued as ivory, were bared almost to the hips, where the fringes of her drawers were like feathering of soft white down. Her slate-blue skirts were kilted boldly about her waist and dovetailed behind her. Her bosom was as a bird's, soft and slight, slight and soft as the breast of some dark-plumed dove. But her long fair hair was girlish: and girlish, and touched with the wonder of mortal beauty, her face.

"She was alone and still, gazing out to sea; and when she felt his presence and the worship of his eyes her eyes turned to him in quiet sufferance of his gaze, without shame or wantonness. Long, long she suffered his gaze and then quietly withdrew her eyes from his and bent them towards the stream, gently stirring the water with her foot hither and thither. The first faint noise of gently moving water broke the silence, low and faint and whispering, faint as the bells of sleep; hither and thither, hither and thither; and faint flame trembled on her check." To Stephen, the girl looked like a *beaute du diable*, the seabird. "—Heavenly God! Cried Stephen's soul, in an outburst of profane joy."

Stephen suddenly looked away from her, his cheek aflame, body aglow, limbs tremulous. "On and on and on and on he strode, far out over the sands, singing wildly to the sea, crying to greet the event of life that had cried to him." Though Stephen moved away from the girl, her glow did not dim. "Her image had passed into his soul for ever and no word had broken the holy silence of his ecstasy. Her eyes had called him and his soul had leaped at the call. To live, to err, to fall, to triumph, to create life out of life! A wild angel had appeared to him, the angel of mortal youth and beauty, an envoy from the fair courts of life, to throw open before him in an instant of ecstasy the gates of all the ways of error and glory. On and on and on and on!" "He halted suddenly and heard his heart in the silence. How far had he walked? What hour was it?"

The disoriented Stephen saw that there was no human being now near him, as "the day was on the wane." "He closed his eyes in the languor of sleep. His eye lids trembled as if they felt the vast cyclic movement of the earth and her watchers, trembled as if they felt the strange light of some new world. His soul was swooning into some new world, fantastic, dim, uncertain as under sea, traversed by cloudy shapes and beings. A world, a glimmer or a flower? Glimmering and trembling, trembling and unfolding, a breaking light, an opening flower, it spread in endless succession to itself, breaking in full crimson and unfolding and fading to palest rose, leaf by leaf and wave of light by wave of light, flooding all the heavens with its soft flushes, every flush deeper than other. "Evening had fallen when he woke and the sand and arid grosses of his bed glowed no longer. He rose slowly and, recalling the rapture of his sleep, sighed at its joy. "He climbed to the crest of the sandhill and gazed about him. Evening had fallen. A rim of the young moon clept the pale waste of skyline, the rim of a silver hoop embedded in grey sand; and the tide was flowing in fast to the land with a low whisper of her waves, islanding a few last figures in distant pools."

SECTION V

[Section V, with some 91 pages, is the longest of all the five sections of *A Portrait*. In this section Joyce has given us an exposition of his theory of aesthetics.]

Part 1. However, in the next morning, Stephen woke and "drained his third cup of watery tea to the dregs." The yellow colour of the tea in which "crusts of fried bread" he dipped "brought back to his memory the dark turf-coloured water of the bath in Clongowes." It was "twenty past ten" in the morning. Stephen was now to go to the University College of Dublin but he was late. His angry father shrilly shouted to one of Stephen's sisters: "Is your lazy bitch of a brother gone out yet?" Stephen laughed at his father's wrong knowledge of gender in saying "bitch" instead of "dog" and his mother scolded him for being late and for laughing: "Ah, it's a scandalous shame for you, Stephen." At last, Stephen left for the college, his heart full of bitterness from his father's rough language and his mother's mutterings. But when he felt the grey morning light around him, he forgot his bitterness and then came to him the "memories of the girls and women in the plays of Gerhart Hauptmann". His train of thought did not stop there. He recalled the "silverveined prose of Newman", the "dark humour of Guido Cavalcanti", and Ibsen, and "passing a grimy marine dealer's shop beyond the Liffey he would repeat the song by Ben Jonson which begins: '*I was not wearier where I lay.*'"

Stephen was very interested in knowing what actually beauty was, was thinking of Aristotle and Thomas Aquinas for edification, but being wearied of them turned to the "dainty songs of the Elizabethans" for finding there the essence of beauty. He was walking and by then he reached Hopkin's rector at Dublin and a political activist. MacCann told him: "—Dedalus, you're an antisocial being, wrapped up in yourself, I'm not. I'm a democrat and I'll work and act for social liberty and equality among all classes and sexes". Stephen saw it was eleven o'clock and knew that it was Thursday. He thought he had to attend the English class from ten to eleven and then to attend his French and physics classes. "He fancied to himself the English lecture and felt, even at that distance, restless and helpless." He was imagining the on-going class in which he too was present. There in the class he saw "before him like the phantom of a dream, the face of a severed head or death-mask.... It was a priest-like face...the face of a guilty priest who heard confessions of those whom he had not power to absolve but that he felt again in memory the gaze of its dark womanish eyes."

Stephen was now walking through the lane, along the sides of which there were shops. In the legends of the shops he saw "heaps of dead language" and his consciousness was offended by the wayward misuse of language. He recalled that the rector at Clongowes taught him Ovid's *Metamorphoses* which was in

Latin. He read Horace's lyric poems (odes), which were in Latin and which were warm, fragrant, and inspiring to him though he was a "poor Latinist". It "wounded him to think that he would never be but a shy guest at the feast of the world's culture and that the monkish learning, in terms of which he was striving to forge out an esthetic philosophy, was held no higher by the age he lived in than the subtle and curious jargons of heraldry and falconry."

"Stephen went on walking, now the grey block of Trinity being on the left. He looked at the droll statue of William Butler Yeats, without anger because the origin of the drolled statue, he thought, was "humbly conscious of its indignity." The statue of Yeats seemed a Firbolg (a medieval Irish peasant who left for Europe, especially Greece, but afterwards came back to Ireland) particularly for his Milesian (of Miletus in Greece) clock. The statue brought to his mind the memory of his friend Davin (a jesting name, between them), a young peasant. Once, at night, when he and Davin were slowly walking towards Davin's room he had a strange vision inspired by what Davin told him. Davin told him that once he was returning from seeing a hurling match at Buttevant. Finding no conveyance he was walking on and on in the almost pitch darkness. At last he found a cottage with a light in the window. He knocked at the door and asked for a glass of water. Davin told Stephen: "After a while a young woman opened the door and brought me out a mug of milk. She was half undressed as if she was going to bed when I knocked and she had her hair hanging and I thought by her figure and by something in the look of her eyes that she must be carrying a child. She kept me in talk a long while at the door and I thought it strange because her breast and shoulders were bare. She asked me I was tired and would like to stop the night there. She said she was alone in the house and that her husband had gone that morning to Queenstown with his sister to see her off. And the time she was talking, Stevie [Stephen], she had her eyes fixed on my face and she stood so close to me I could hear her breathing. When I handed her back the mug at last she took my hand to draw me in over the threshold and said: '*Come in and stay the night here. You have no call to be frightened. There's no one in it but ourselves....*' I did not go in, Stievie. I thanked her and went on my way again, all in a fever. At the first the bend of the road I looked back and she was standing at the door." The last words of Davin's story sang in Stephen's memory.

Immediately afterwards, a young flower girl with hoydenish face insisted him to buy her blue flowers: "—Do, gentleman! Don't forget your own girl, sir!" "—I have no money, said Stephen." And he left her quickly and walked through Grafton Street and at last reached his college, University College, Dublin. He thought it was too late to upstairs to the French class, and so went to the physics theatre. The dean of studies and the priest were there, and the priest was making a fire. Stephen approached the priest and asked him:

"—Good morning, sir! Can I help you?"

The priest looked up and said: "—One moment now, Mr. Dedalus, and you will see. There is an art in lighting a fire. We have the liberal arts and we have the useful arts. This is one of the useful arts."

"—I will try to learn it, said Stephen."

The fire having been made, the priest squatted down before the alter and there fell a silence. And then Stephen and the priest entered into a conversation, initiated by Stephen:

"—I am sure I could not light a fire.

—You are an artist, are you not, Mr. Deadlus? said the dean, glancing up and blinking his pale eyes. The object of the artist is the creation of the beautiful. What the beautiful is, is another question.

He rubbed his hands slowly and drily over the difficulty.

—Can you solve the question now? He asked.

—Aquinas, answered Stephen, says *pulcra sunt quae visa placent* [beautiful is that which pleases].

—This fire before us, said the dean, will be pleasing to the eye. Will it therefore be beautiful?

—In so far as it is apprehended by the sight, which I suppose means here esthetic intellection, it will be beautiful. But Aquinas also says *Boneem est in quod tendit appetites* [the good is that toward which the appetite tends]. In so far as it satisfies the animal craving for warmth fire is good. In hell, however, it is an evil.

—Quite so, said the dean, you have certainly hit the nail on the head."

The dean went out but soon returned and resumed the esthetic conversation with Stephen:

"—When may we expect to have something from you on the esthetic question? he asked.

—From me! said Stephen in astonishment. I stumble on an idea once a fortnight if I am lucky.

—These questions are very profound, Mr. Dedalus, said the dean."

Stephen said that presently he was being guided by two ideas of Aristotle and (Thomas) Aquinas as regards the question of esthetics. He said that one difficulty "in esthetic discussion is to know whether words are being used according to the literary tradition or according to the tradition of the marketplace. I remember a sentence of Newman's in which he says of the Blessed Virgin that she was detained in full company of the saints. The use of the word in the marketplace is quite different. I hope I am not detaining you."

Next, when the dean was pouring oil in lamp, he said that one should only pour that much oil that the funnel can contain. The word 'funnel' struck the ear of Stephen. He said that in Lower Drumcondra of Ireland, the people who spoke the best English, called the funnel 'tundish'. A moment afterwards, Stephen resumed the earlier conversation about beauty when the dean told him that the word 'tundish' was interesting. "—The question you asked me a moment ago seems to me more interesting. What is that beauty which the artist struggles to express from lumps of earth, said Stephen coldly." Stephen knew that the dean was from the country of the dramatist Ben Jonson—England. He thought: "The language in which we are speaking is his before mine. How different are the words 'home' [in Irish *bhaile*], Christ [in Irish *baiste*], ale [in Irish *leann*], master [in Irish *maistir*] on his lips and on mine! I cannot speak or write these words without unrest of spirit. His language, so familiar and so foreign, will always be for me an acquired speech. I have not made or accepted its words. My voice holds them at bay. My soul frets in the shadow of his language."

After this, the dean wanted to discuss the distinction between 'the beautiful' and 'the sublime' and to distinguish between 'moral beauty' and 'material beauty' but he said that speculation on these things may lead one to 'the danger of perishing of inanition'—of facing vacuity or emptiness. Nevertheless, the dean advised Stephen not to be despondent about understanding these things, for, he said "We never can say what is in us. *Per aspera ad astra* [through adversity to the stars]." The dean left for seeing the first arts class.

The physics professor entered the class and was calling the rolls. When he called the name of Cranley there was no answer and a "smile flew across Stephen's face as he thought of his friend's studies." Another friend of Stephen scribbled a calculation on a page and handed it down to him from behind. Stephen "had heard some say that the old professor was an atheist free mason." The bell rang and the class ended. Stephen came out and saw Cranley and asked him if he had signed. Cranley answered:

"—*Ego habeo* [I have].

—What is it for?

—Quod [what]?

—What is it for?

Cranley turned his pale face to Stephen and said blandly and bitterly:

—*Per pax universalis* [for universal peace].

Stephen pointed to the Tsar's photograph and said:

—He has the face of a besotted Christ.

The scorn and anger in his voice brought Cranly's eyes back from a calm survey of the walls of the hall.

—Are you annoyed? He asked.

—No, answered Stephen.

—Are you in bad humour?

—No.

—*Credo ut vos sanguinarius mendax estis*, said Cranly, *quia facies vostra monstrat ut vos in damno malo humore estis* [I believe that you are a bloody liar because your face looks as though you're in a damned bad mood]."

Moynihan, MacCann and the gipsy-like Temple joined Stephen and Cranly. MacCann began to speak in favour of the Tsar's rescript, general disarmament and "new humanity and the new gospel." Temple, at one point, shouted "—Three cheers for universal brotherhood!" And again "Marx is only a bloody cod." And once again: "Socialism was founded by an Irishman and the first man in Europe who preached the freedom of thought was Collins. Two hundred years ago. He denounced priestcraft, the philosopher of Middlesex. Three cheers for John Anthony Collins [English philosopher (1676-1729) from Middlesex, who strongly believed in deism]!" Cranly wanted to dowse the fire of the battle of beliefs. He interfered saying: "—*Pax super tatum sanguinarium globum* [Peace through the whole bloody world]." Stephen, whom MacCann earlier thought to be a reactionary, angrily reacted: "—Keep your icon. If we must have a Jesus let us have a legitimate Jesus." MacCann said it was a fine expression (he said this approvingly), and asked Stephen: "—Do you believe in Jesus? I believe in man. Of course, I don't know if you believe in man. I admire you, sir. I admire the mind of a man independent of all religions. Is that your opinion about the mind of Jesus?" Cranly again interfered: "—*Nos ad manum ballum jacobimus* [Let us go play handball]." (Cranly wanted to draw the debate to a conclusion and drew Stephen away.) Stephen, while going away, told MacCann:

"—My signature is of no account, he said politely. You are right to go your way. Leave me to go mine.

—Dedalus, said MacCann crisply, I believe you are a good fellow but you have yet to learn the dignity of altruism and the responsibility of human individual."

The three students—Cranly, Stephen and Temple—walked off through the inner hall and the garden and found Davin watching the game. Temple asked Stephen if he believed that Jean Jaques Rousseau was a sincere man? "—He was like you, I fancy, said Stephen, an emotional man." Temple accepted the opinion of Stephen: "—I'm an emotional man, said Temple. That's quite rightly expressed. And I'm proud that I'm an emotionalist." Davin was immersed in the game; he did not hear the talks. Stephen wanted to know if Davin signed the petition for universal peace. Davin said he did sign and asked Stephen if he did sign too. Stephen shook his head. Davin called him a terrible man for not signing. He declared: —I'm an Irish nationalist, first and foremost." Stephen responded jocularly:

"—When you make the next rebellion with hurley sticks, said Stephen, and want the indispensible informer, tell me. I can find you a few in this college.

—I cannot understand you, said David. One time I hear you talk against English literature. Now you talk against the Irish reformers. What with your name and your ideas.... Are you Irish at all?"

"A tide began to surge beneath the calm surface of Stephen's friendliness.

—This race and this country and this life produced me, he said. I shall express myself as I am" "—Try to be one of us, repeated Davin. In heart you are an Irishman but your pride is too powerful."

"—My ancestors threw off their language and look another, Stephen said. They allowed a handful of foreigners to subject them. Do you fancy I am going to pay in my own life and person debts they made? What for?

—For your freedom, said Davin.

—No honourable and sincere man, said Stephen, has given up to you his life and his youth and his affections from the days of Tone [Theobald Wolfe Tone (1763-98) was a leading Irish revolutionary and one of the founders of United Irishmen that revolted against the British rule] to those of Parnell [Charles Stewart Parnell (1846-91) was an Irish nationalist politician], but you sold him to the enemy or failed him in need or reviled him and left him for another. And you invite me to be one of you. I'd see you damned first.

—They died for their ideals, Stevie, said Davin. Our day will come yet, believe me.

Stephen, following his own thought, was silent for an instant.

—The soul is born, he said vaguely, first in those moments I told you of. It has a slow and dark birth, more mysterious than the birth of the body. When the soul of a man is born in this country there are nets flung at it to hold it back from flight. You talk to me of nationality, language and religion. I shall fly by those nets.

Davin knocked the ashes from his pipe.

—Too deep for me, Stevie, he said. But a man's country comes first. Ireland, first, Stevie. You can be a poet or a mystic after.

—Do you know what Ireland is? asked Stephen with cold violence. Ireland is the old sow that eats her farrow."

Stephen and Davin rose and, as the game was over, took Cranly and Lynch with them, and passed back through the garden and out through the hall. As they walked, Stephen suddenly said that Aristotle had not defined piety and terror but he could do that. And he went on: "—Pity is the feeling which arrests the mind in the presence of whatever is grave and constant in human sufferings and unites it with human sufferer. Terror is the feeling which arrests the mind in the presence of whatever is grave and constant in human sufferings and unites it with the secret cause." Tragedy happens to be where there are both pity and terror. Stephen explained his definition of tragedy with the help of a girl's death by accident. Newspapers might call it a tragic death but said Stephen, it was not because here the pity is not aligned with terror or with the "secret cause" of the incident.

Stephen did not stop there. He went on explaining tragic emotion:

"—The tragic emotion, in fact, is a face looking two ways, towards terror and towards pity, both of which are phases of it. You see I use the word *arrest*. I mean the tragic emotion is static. Or rather the dramatic emotion is. The feelings excited by improper art are kinetic, desire or loathing. Desire urges us to possess, to go to something. The arts which excite them, pornographical or didactic, are therefore improper arts. The esthetic emotion (I use the general term) is therefore static. The mind is arrested and raised above desire and loathing.

—You say that art must not excite desire, said Lynch. I told you that when you were a boy in that charming carmelite school you ate pieces of dried cow dung. Lynch broke into a whining laughter...." And then he agreed, still laughing: "—O, I did! I did! He cried."

Stephen came up to explaining Lynch's eating cow dung:

"—As for that, Stephen said in polite parenthesis, we are all animals. I also am an animal.

—You are, said Lynch.

—But we are just now in a mental world, Stephen continued. The desire and loathing excited by improper esthetic means are really not esthetic emotions not only because they are kinetic in character but also because they are not more than physical. Our flesh shrinks from what it dreads and responds to stimulus of what it desires by a purely reflex action of the nervous system. Our eyelid closes before we are aware that the fly is about to enter our eye.

—Not always, said Lynch critically.

—In the same way, said Stephen, your flesh responded to the stimulus of a naked statue, but it was, I say, simply a reflex action of the nerves. Beauty expressed by the artist cannot awaken in us an emotion which is kinetic or a sensation which is purely physical. It awakens, or ought to awaken, or induces, or ought to induce, an esthetic stasis, an ideal pity or an ideal terror, a stasis called forth, prolonged and at last dissolved by what I call the rhythm of beauty.

—What is that exactly? Asked Lynch.

—Rhythm, said Stephen, is the first esthetic relation of part to part in any esthetic whole or of an esthetic whole to its parts or of any part to the esthetic whole of which it is a part."

Lynch asked if that is true, what is beauty then? Stephen told him that "—to press out again, from the gross earth or what it brings forth, from sound and shape and colour which are the prison gates of our soul, an image of the beauty we have come to understand—that is art."

By now Stephen and Lynch reached the canal bridge and turned and walked on by the trees. Lynch continued the conversation:

"—But you have not answered my question, said lynch. What is art? What is the beauty it expresses?"

"—Art, said Stephen, is the human disposition of sensible or intelligible matter for esthetic end."

"—Aquinas [St. Thomas Aquinas (1225-74)], said Stephen, says that is beautiful the apprehension of which pleases."

Lynch nodded.

"—I remember that, he said, *pulcra sunt quae visa placent.*"

"—He [Aquinas] uses the *visa,* said Stephen, to cover esthetic apprehensions of all kinds, whether through sight or hearing or through any other avenue of apprehension. This word, though it is vague, is clear enough to keep away good and evil which excite desire and loathing. It means certainly a stasis and not a kinesis."

Stephen brought in the point of the relation between beauty and truth, with a view to further explain beauty.

"—Static therefore, said Stephen. Plato, I believe, said that beauty is the splendor of truth [cf. Shelley] I don't think that it has a meaning, but the true and the beautiful are akin. Truth is beheld by the intellect which is appeased by the most satisfying relations of the intelligible; beauty is beheld by the imagination which is appeased by the most satisfying relations of the sensible. The first step in the direction of truth is to understand the frame and scope of the intellect itself, to comprehend the act itself of intellection. Aristotle's entire system of philosophy rests upon his book of psychology and that, I think, rests on his statement that the same attribute cannot at the same time and in the same connexion belong to and not belong to the same subject. The first step in the direction of beauty is to understand the frame and scope of the imagination, to comprehend the act itself of esthetic apprehension. Is that clear?

—But what is beauty? Asked Lynch impatiently. Out with another definition. Something we see and like! Is that the best you and Aquinas can do?"

To explain beauty further, Stephen cited the different concepts of beauty of different peoples of different countries. He told Lynch to take the example of women: "—The Greek, the Turk, the Chinese, the Copt, the Hottentot, said Stephen, all admire a different type of female beauty. That seems to be a maze out of which we cannot escape. I see, however, two ways out. One is this hypothesis: that every physical quality admired by men in women is in direct connexion with manifold functions of women for the propagation of the species.... For my part I dislike that out. It leads to eugenics rather than to esthetics...." Stephen said there was another hypothesis about beauty:

"—This hypothesis, Stephen repeated, is the other way out: that though the same object may not seem beautiful to all people, all people who admire a beautiful object find in it certain relations which satisfy and coincide with the stages themselves of all esthetic apprehension. These relations of the sensible, visible to you through one form and to me through another, must be therefore the necessary qualities of beauty. Now, we can return to our old friend saint Thomas [St. Thomas Aquinas] for another pennyworth of wisdom." Stephen said that Thomas Aquinas was a poet and that he wrote a hymn which he liked. It began with the words *Pange lingua gloriosi* [celebrate with a boastful language]. But, said Stephen, no hymn could be compared with "that mournful and majestic processional song, the *Vexilla Regis* [the royal or king's standard or flag of Venantious Fortunatus]. And then "Lynch began to sing softly and solemnly [four verses of the song] in a deep bass voice."

They—Stephen, Lynch and Donovan—turned into lower Mount Street. After a while, Donovan asked Stephen:

"—I hear you are writing some essay about esthetics.

Stephen made a vague gesture of denial.

—Goethe and Lessing, said Donovan, have written a lot on that subject, the classical school and the romantic school and all that. The Laocoon interested me very much when I read it. Of course it is idealistic, German, ultra-profound."

Donovan went away after taking leave of them urbanely. Then Stephen went back to his topic of beauty that earlier he left:

"—To finish what I was saying about beauty, said Stephen, the most satisfying relations of the sensible must correspond to the necessary phases of artistic apprehension. Find these and you find the qualities of universal beauty. Aquinas says: *Ad pulcritudinem triarequiruntur integritas, consonnentia, claritas.* I translate it so: Three things are needed for beauty, wholeness, harmony and radiance."

"Stephen pointed to a basket which a butcher's boy had slung inverted on his head.

—Look at that basket, he said.

—I see it, said Lynch.

—In order to see the basket, said Stephen, your mind first of all separates the basket from the rest of the visible universe which is not the basket. The first phase of apprehension is a bounding line drawn about the object to be apprehended. An esthetic image is presented to us either in space or in time. What is audible is presented in time, what is visible is presented in space. But temporal or spatial, the esthetic image is first luminously apprehended as self-bounded and self-contained upon the immeasurable background of space or time which is not it. You apprehended it as *one* thing. You see it as one whole. You apprehended its wholeness. That is *integritas*.

—Bull's eye! said Lynch, laughing. Go on.

—Then, said Stephen, you pass from point to point, led by its formal lines; you apprehend it as balanced part against part within its limits; you feel the rhythm of its structure. In other words, the synthesis of immediate perception is followed by the analysis of apprehension. Having first felt that it is *one* thing you feel now that it is a *thing*. You apprehend it as complex, multiple, divisible, separable, made up of its parts, the result of its parts and their sum, harmonious. That is *consonantia*.

—Bull's eye again! said lynch wittily. Tell me now what is *clarita* and you win the cigar.

—The connotation of the word, Stephen said, is rather vague. Aquinas uses a term which seems to be inexact. It baffled me...that he had in mind symbolism or idealism, the supreme quality of beauty being a light from some other world, the idea of which the matter is but the shadow, the reality of which it is but the symbol. I thought he might mean that *claritus* is the artistic discovery and representation of the divine purpose in anything or a force of generalization which would make the esthetic image a universal one, make it outshine its proper conditions. But that is literary talk. I understand it so. When you have apprehended that basket as one thing and have then analysed it according to its form and apprehended it as a thing you make the only synthesis which is logically and esthetically permissible. You see that it is that thing which it is and no other thing. The radiance of which he speaks in the scholastic *quidditas,* the *whatness* of a thing. This supreme quality is felt by the artist when the esthetic image is first conceived in his imagination. The mind in that mysterious instant Shelley likened beautifully to a fading coal. The instant wherein that supreme quality of beauty, the clear radiance of the esthetic image, is apprehended luminously by the mind which has been arrested by its wholeness and fascinated by its harmony is the luminous silent stasis of esthetic pleasure, a spiritual state very like to that cardiac condition which the Italian physiologist Luigi Galvani, using a phrase almost as beautiful as Shelley's called the enchantment of the heart."

Stephen continued:

"—What I have said, he began again, refers to beauty in the wider sense of the word, in the sense which the word has in the literary tradition. In the market place it was another sense. When we speak of beauty in the second sense of the term our judgment is influenced in the first place by the art itself and by the form of that art. The image, it is clear, must be set between the mind or senses of the artist himself and the mind or senses of others. If you bear this in memory you will see that art necessarily divides itself into three forms progressing from one to the next. These forms are: the lyrical form, the form wherein the artist presents his image in immediate relation to himself: the epical form, the form wherein he presents his image in mediate relation to himself and to others; the dramatic form, the form wherein he presents his image in immediate relation to others."

Stephen then produced before Lynch a few queer and humorous but legitimate esthetic questions: "*Is a chair finely made tragic or comic? Is the portrait of Mona Lisa good if I desire to see it? Is the bust of sir Philip Crampton lyrical, epical, or dramatic? If not, why not?*"

"—Why not, indeed? Said Lynch, laughing.

—*If a man hacking in fury at a block of wood*, Stephen continued, *make there an image of a cow, is that image a work of art? If not, why not?*

—That's a lovely one, said Lynch, laughing again. That has the true scholastic stink.

—Lessing, said Stephen, should not have taken a group of statues to write of. The art, being inferior, does not present the forms I spoke of distinguished clearly one from another. Even in literature, the highest and most spiritual art, the forms are confused. The lyrical form is in fact the simplest verbal vesture of an instant of emotion, a rhythmical cry such as ages ago cheered on the man who pulled at the oar or dragged stones up a slope. He who utters it is more conscious of the instant of emotion than of himself as feeling emotion. The simplest epical form is seen emerging out of lyrical literature when the artist prolongs and broods upon himself as the centre of an epical event and this form progresses till the centre of emotional gravity is equidistant from the artist himself and from others. The narrative is no longer purely personal. The personality of the artist passes into the narration itself, flowing round and round the persons and the action like a vital sea. This progress you will see easily in that old English ballad *Turpin Hero* [the ballad *Turpin Hero* refers to Richard Dick Turpin (1705-39), a Robinhood-like English highway man. The ballad begins thus: 'On Hounslow Heath as I rode out/ I spied a lawyer riding about:/ "Now sir," I said, "Run all you can/ From Turpin that mischievous man."' And ends with the two verses: 'Whose legacy is a strong rope,/ For the shooting of a dunghill cock.'] which begins in the first person and ends in the third person. The dramatic form is reached when the vitality which has flowed and eddied round each person fills every person with such vital force that he or she assumes a proper and intangible esthetic life. The personality of the artist, at first a cry or a cadence or a mood and then a fluid and lambent narrative, finally refines itself out of existence, impersonalizes itself, so to speak. The esthetic image in the dramatic form is life purified in and reprojected from the human imagination. The mystery of esthetic, like that of material creation, is accomplished. The artist, like the God of creation, remains within or behind or beyond or above his handiwork, invisible, refined out of existence, indifferent, paring his fingernails."

A fine rain began to fall. Stephen and Lynch went through duke's lawn, reached national library, passed through the passage beside Kildare house and to avoid the rain took shelter under the arcade of the library. There they found some girls. They were talking about their future. One of them said that medical practice was in the countryside of Ireland than on ocean liners. The other said that medical practice is no better than midwifery. The former student said that Hynes had "no brains", he "got through by stewing, pure stewing."

The girl, Stephen was interested in, was leaving the place along with other girls "holding their umbrellas at cunning angles against the few last raindrops, closing them again, holding their skirts demurely. "And if he [Stephen] had judged her harshly [the narrator wondered]? If her life were a simple rosary of hours, her life simple and strange as a bird's life, gay in the morning, restless all day, tired at sundown? Her heart simple and wilful as a bird's heart?"

Part 2. In the early morning, next day, Stephen woke to a beautiful musical morning, sweet and dewy. "Over his limbs in sleep pale cool waves of light had passed. He lay still, as if his soul lay amid cool waters, conscious of faint sweet music. His mind was waking slowly to a tremulous morning knowledge, a morning inspiration." "An enchantment of the heart! The night had been enchanted. In a dream or vision he had known the ecstasy of seraphic life. Was it an instant of enchantment only or long hours and years and ages?" "The instant flashed forth like a point of light and now from cloud on cloud of vague circumstance confused form was veiling softly its afterglow. O! In the virgin womb of the imagination the word was made flesh. Gabriel the seraph had come to the virgin's chamber." Stephen felt that "lured by that ardent roselike glow the choirs of the seraphim were falling from heaven" [Stephen, as if, heard the villanelle that slyly refers to Emma Clery, his ideal female beauty]:

> "*Are you not weary of ardent ways,*
> Lure of the fallen seraphim?
> Tell no more of enchanted days."

The "veiled windless hour" of the morning passed and the morning revealed its dazzling brightness. A bell rang at a distance and birds twittered. Stephen rose and "began to write out the stanzas of the villanelle in small neat letters on the rough cardboard surface" of a cigarette packet with a pencil. He then lay back on the "lumpy pillow, murmuring the verses. The lumps of knotted flock under his head [when he laid his head on *the* lumpy pillow] reminded him of the lumps of knotted horse hair on the sofa of her parlour on which he used to sit [cf. Marcel Proust's *Remembrance of Things Past*] smiling or serious, asking himself why he had come, displeased with her and with himself, confounded by the print of the Sacred Heart above the untenanted sideboard. He saw her approach him in a lull of the talk and beg him to sing one of his curious songs. Then he saw himself sitting at the old piano, striking chords softly from its speckled keys and singing, amid the talk which had risen again in the room, to her who leaned beside the mantelpiece a dainty song of the Elizabethans, a sad and sweet loth to depart, the victory chant of Agincourt, the happy air of Greensleeves. While he sang and she listened, or feigned to listen, his heart was at rest but when the quaint old songs had ended and he heard the voices in the room he remembered his own sarcasm; the house where young men are called by their Christian names a little too soon."

"She [Emma] passed now dancing lightly across his memory as she had been that night at the carnival ball, her white dress a little lifted, a white spray nodding in her hair. She danced lightly in the round. She was dancing towards him and, as she came, her eyes were a little averted and a faint glow was on her cheek. At the pause in the chain of hands her hand had lain in his an instant, a soft merchandise.

—You are a great stranger now.
—Yes. I was born to be a monk.
—I am afraid you are a heretic.
—Are you much afraid?

For an answer she had danced away from him along the chain of hands, dancing lightly and discreetly, giving herself to none. The white spray nodded to her dancing and when she was in shadow the glow was deeper on her cheek."

Stephen, coming out of his vision or daydream, confusedly asked himself if the image of the girl was his. He replied to himself: "No, it was not his image. It was like the image of the young priest in whose company he had seen her last, looking at him out of dove's eyes, toying with the pages of her Irish phrasebook." He then thought that he was wise in leaving her company: "Bah! He had done well to leave the room in disdain. He had done well not to salute her on the steps of the library! He had done well to leave her to flirt with her priest, to toy with a church which was the scullery-maid of christendom."

"Rude brutal anger routed the last lingering instant of ecstasy from his soul. It broke up violently her fair image and flung the fragments on all sides." And with the image of that girl, he had discarded the images of all other girls who at one time or the other drew his attention. And yet he thought all his malignity of the girls was a sort of adoration of them. Stephen now also felt, after denouncing the image of the girl, that his pride was wounded by himself when he railed against her and her paramour. Stephen recalled: "To him [the priest] she would unveil her shy nakedness, to one who was but schooled in the discharging of a formal rite rather than to him, a priest of the eternal imagination, transmuting the daily bread of experience into the radiant body of ever-living life."

In a sort of jealousy (at the young priest with whom, Stephen now imagines, Emma flirts), Stephen instantly recited the hymn of thanksgiving (to God for His kindness in creating the beautiful earth, etc.):

> "Our broken cries and mournful lays
> Rise in one eucharistic hymn
> Are you not weary of ardent [passionate] ways?
> While sacrificing hands upraise
> The chalice flowing to the brim.
> Tell no more of enchanted days."
>
> (From Joyce's poem "Villanelle of the Temptress")

He not only recited the verse, but copied and looked at them in order "to feel them the better by seeing them". (All this he did to outdo that young priest, to be more full of piety than him.)

The morning is now much brighter. The noises of the quotidian life were audible. Now there was a feeling of weariness in him from those ardent [passionate] ways. Ignoring the humdrum of the morning, Stephen turned towards the path of piety: "Shrinking from that life he turned towards the wall, making a cowl of the blanket and staring at the great overblown scarlet flowers of the tattered wall-paper. He tried to warm his perishing joy in their scarlet glow, imagining a rose-way from where he lay upwards to heaven all strewn with scarlet flowers. Weary! Weary! He too was weary of ardent ways." "A gradual warmth, a languorous weariness passed over him descending along his spine from his closely cowled head. He felt it descend and, seeing himself as he lay, smiled. Soon he would sleep."

Stephen recalled his childhood folly with the girl [Emma] he loved: "He had written verses for her again after ten years. Ten years before she had worn her shawl cowl-wise about her head, sending sprays of her warm breath into the night air, tapping her foot upon the glossy road. It was the last tram.... They stood on the steps of the tram, he on the upper, she on the lower. She came up to his step many times between their phrases and went down again and once or twice remained beside him forgetting to go down and then went down. Let be! Let be!"

Stephen now thought that all that were "Folly indeed!" He also thought that by doing what he did to her "he had wronged her. He now felt pity for her and believed that he had sinned from wronging her. And then "a tender compassion filled his heart as he remembered her frail pallor and her eyes, humbled and saddened by the dark shame of womanhood." Stephen fell into a reverie. He saw her beside him, just waking from sleep. "A glow of desire kindled again in his soul and fired and fulfilled all his body. Conscious of his desire she was waking from odorous sleep, the temptress of his villanelle. [Emma was both his transcendental ideal womanhood and his fleshy temptress of the earth.] "Her eyes, dark and a look of languor, were opening to his eyes. Her nakedness yielded to him, radiant, warm, odorous and lavish-limbed, enfolded him like a shining cloud, enfolded him like water with a liquid life; and like a cloud of vapour or like waters circumfluent in space the liquid letters of speech, symbols of the element of mystery, flowed forth over his brain.

Are you not weary of ardent ways,
Lure of the fallen seraphim?
Tell no more of enchanted days.
Your eyes have set man's heart ablaze
And you have had your will of him.
Are you not weary of ardent ways?
Above the flame the smoke of praise
Goes up from ocean rim to rim.
Tell no more of enchanted days.

Our broken cries and mournful lays
Rise in one Eucharistic hymn.
Are you not weary of ardent ways?

While sacrificing hands upraise
The chalice flowing to the brim.
Tell no more of enchanted days.

And still you hold our longing gaze
With languorous look and lavish limb!

Are you not weary of ardent ways?
Tell no more of enchanted days."

Part 3. Stephen stood on the steps of the library, "leaning wearily on his ashplant" and saw an assemblage of birds wheeling over a house in the Molesworth Street. In the delighting evening blue sky of March they were sporting "circling about a temple of air" and were chirping. The "airy temple of the tenuous sky soothed his eyes which still saw the image of his mother's face." Why was he gazing at those wheeling birds? He asked himself. Memories of the German mystic Heinrich Cornelius Agrippa (1486-1535) and the Swedish mystic Emanuel Swedenborg (1688-1772) flew across his mind—did the flights of the birds portend anything? He recalled the thoughts of Swedenborg "on the correspondence of birds to things of the intellect and of how the creatures of the air have their knowledge and know their times and seasons because they, unlike man, are in the order of their life and have not perverted that order by reason."

Stephen became apprehensive of some possible presage. "A sense of fear of the unknown moved in the heart of his weariness, a fear of symbols and portents, of the hawk-like man [Thoth] whose name he bore soaring out of his captivity on osierwoven wings, of Thoth [Egyptian God (identical with Greek God Hermes) with power over, and patron of, science, literature, wisdom, and invention], the God of writers, writing with a reed upon a table and bearing on his narrow ibis head the cusped moon." The birds came back nearer circling. Stephen thought that they must be swallows, coming from the south and that they were birds "building ever an unlasting home under the eaves of men's houses and ever leaving the homes they had built to wander." In overflowing joy and excitement, he recited:

> *"Bend down your faces, Oona and Aleel.*
> *I gaze upon them as the swallow gazes*
> *Upon the nest under the eave before*
> *He wonder the loud waters."*

(Oona and Aleel are characters in W.B. Yeats's play *The Countess Kathleen*)

Stephen was delighted. A soft liquid joy "like the noise of many waters flowed over his memory" and he "felt that the augury he had sought in the wheeling darting birds and in the pale space of sky above him had come from his heart like a bird from a turret, quietly and softly." He thought his heart rightly responded to his mind's desire. The wheeling birds were a symbol of that truth. But was that the symbol of his flight, like those birds, from his family and his native land, like those birds flying from the eaves of houses or was it a symbol of his loneliness? "Symbol of departure or of loneliness?" He recalled his experience "of the hall on the night of the opening of the national theatre." There he was alone and he heard the "catcalls and hisses." The catcalls were against Yeats's play because it had a sense of nationalism. Stephen decried the protests.

The electric lamps of the reading room were switched on and Stephen went upstairs and into the reading room. He found there Cranly, a medical student, and a priest who was engaged with a copy of *The Tablet* (an ultra right-wing English Catholic paper) but felt disturbed and stood up to go. Stephen, Dixon and Cranly went along through a lane of tables across the hall when "a man of dwarfish stature", with a "monkey-puckered face" which was full of stubbles, and with melancholy eyes met them. Addressing him as captain, Dixon asked the dwarfish monkey-faced man what he had been reading then and whether it was *The Bride of Lammermoor* [Sir Walter Scott's novel of tragic love]. The captain replied: "—I love old Scott...I think he writes something lovely. There is no writer can touch sir Walter Scott."

The park trees by the lake were drenched with rain. "A game of swans flew there and the water and the shore beneath were fouled with their green-white slime. They embraced softly, impelled by the grey rainy light, the wet silent trees, the shield-like witnessing lake, the swans." Just at this instant Stephen had a vision—a vision of Davin and his sister: "They embraced without joy or passion, his arm about his sister's neck. A grey woolen clock was wrapped athwart her from her shoulder to her waist and her fair head was bent in willing shame. He had loose red-brown hair and tender shapely strong freckled hands. Face? There was no face seen. The brother's face was bent upon her fair rain fragrant hair. The hand freckled and strong and shapely and caressing was Davin's [Davin is a foil to sexually chaste Stephen] hand."

Stephen "frowned angrily upon his thought" and brushed his thought aside and questioned himself: Why were they not Cranly's hands? Had Davin's simplicity and innocence stung him more secretly?" They walked across the hall—Stephen, Temple, Dixon and others, O'Keefe and Cranly discussing various light subjects. At one point, Goggins, the stout student, "farted briefly". "Dixon turned towards him, saying in a soft voice: "—Did an angel speak?" Cranly snubbed him. Then Temple asked Stephen if he believed in the law of heredity. Temple, and not Stephen: "Reproduction is the beginning of death." Cranly slyly told Stephen: "—Do you feel how profound that is because you are a poet?" But, next, he showed his cynical contempt for Temple (a student) pointing his finger at him for others: "Look at Ireland's hope!" Goggins, the stout student, shouted at Temple to leave the place. Temple felt defeated: "I'm a bollocks, he said, shaking his head in despair." And he also called Cranly a bollocks: "—But he, Temple said, pointing to Cranly, he is a bullocks, too, like me. Only he doesn't know it. And that's the only difference I see." "A burst of laughter covered his words. But he turned to Stephen and said with a sudden eagerness:

—That word is a most interesting word. That's the only English dual number. Did you know?

—Is it? Stephen said vaguely."

The image (or vision) of the girl (Emma Clery) appeared again before Stephen (Dedalus). "She passed out from the porch of the library and bowed across Stephen in reply to Cranly's greeting. He also? Was there not a slight flush in Cranly's cheek? .... The light had waned. He could not see." "He [Stephen] lifted up his arms and spoken in ecstasy to the somber nave of the trees, knowing that he stood on holy ground and in a holy hour. And a bend in a gloomy road he had broken off his prayer to whistle loudly an air from the last pantomime."

The phantom of the girl did not vanish from Stephen's view. "She had passed through the dusk. And therefore the air was silent save for one soft hiss that fell. And therefore the tongues about him had ceased their babble. Darkness was falling.

Darkness falls from the air."

"A trembling joy, lambent as a faint light, played like a fairy host around him. But why? Her passage through the darkening air or the verse with its black vowels and its opening sound, rich and lute like?" Stephen "walked away slowly towards the deeper shadows of the end of the colonnade, beating the stone softly with his stick to hide his revery from the students whom he had left: and allowed his mind to summon back to itself the age of Dowland and Byrd and Nash."

"The images he had summoned gave him no pleasure. They were secret and inflaming but her image was not entangled by them. That was not the way to think of her. Could his mind then not trust itself?" The presence (or apprehension) of the girl was neither mental nor visual but tactile—sensual. "It was not thought nor vision though he knew vaguely that her figure was passing homeward through the city. Vaguely first and then more sharply he smelt her body. A conscious unrest seethed in his blood. Yes, it was her body he smelt, a wild and languid smell, the tepid limbs over which his music had flowed desirously and the secret soft linen upon which her flesh distilled odour and a dew."

A louse was irritatingly crawling on his neck; he caught it and let it fall to the ground and wondered whether it would live or die. A curious phrase, phrase of Cornelious à Lapide [a Flemish Catholic priest 1567-1637] came to his mind—Cornelious who said that "the lice born of human sweat were not created by God with the other animals on the sixth day." Suddenly, the molested body of the louse made him think about his own body and he despaired. "The life of his body, ill clad, ill fed, louse-eaten, made him close his eyelids in a sudden spasm of despair and in the darkness he saw the brittle bright bodies of the lice falling from the air and turning often as they fell. Yes, it was not darkness that fell from the air. It was brightness: *Brightness falls from the air.*" [This is the third line of the third verse or stanza of the poem "A Litany in Time of Plague" by the Elizabethan playwright and poet Thomas Nash (1567-1601). The third stanza of this pessimistic poem runs thus: "Beauty is but a flower/ Which wrinkles will devour;/ Brightness falls from the air;/ Queens have died young and fair;/ Dust hath closed Helen's eye./ I am sick, I must die./ Lord, have mercy on us!"] Stephen actually could not rightly recall the verses of Nash's poetry. And all the images that the poem of Nash aroused in him were false: "His mind bred vermin. His thoughts were lice born of the sweat of sloth."

Stephen walked along the colonnade of the Library and towards the group of students. He was trying to drive away the memory of the girl: "Well then, let her go and be damned to her! She could love some athlete who washed himself every morning to the waist and had black hair on his chest. Let her." He moved to where there were Cranly, Temple, Dixon, O'Keefe and Glynn and Goggins. The group of Stephen and others soon entered into a religious debate. Temple asked Glynn: "if Jesus suffered the children to come why does the church send them all to hell if they die unbaptised? Why is that?" Glynn avoided the question, but Temple answered:

> "—Because the church is cruel like old sinners, Temple said.
>
> —Are you quite orthodox on that point, Temple? Dixon said suavely.
>
> —Saint Augustine says that about unbaptized children going to hell, Temple answered, because he was a cruel old sinner too.

—I bow to you, Dixon said, but I had the impression that limbo existed for such cases.

. . . .

—Limbo! Temple cried. That's a fine invention, too. Like hell.

—Hell, Temple said. I can respect that invention of the grey spouse of Satan. Hell is Roman, like the walls of the Romans, strong and ugly. But what is limbo?

. . . .

—Neither my arse nor my elbow! Temple cried out scornfully. And that's what I call limbo."

They crossed the quadrangle together without speaking. Then they "parleyed in shouts" "about a game of billiards to be played in the Adelphi hotel." Stephen walking alone stood in the quiet of Kildare Street opposite Maple's hotel. He stood lugubriously and imagined that the patricians of Ireland, who had sleek lives, frequented that hotel—Maple's hotel. He imagined: "They thought of army commissions and land agents: peasants greeted them along the roads in the country; they knew the names of certain French dishes and gave orders to jarvices in high pitched provincial voices which pierced through their skintight accents." He thought: "How could he hit their conscience or how cast his shadow over the imaginations of their daughters, before their squares begat upon them, that they might breed a race less ignoble than their own? And under the deepened dusk he felt the thoughts and desires of the race to which he belonged flitting like bats across the dark country lanes, under trees by the edges of streams and near the pool mottled bogs." Stephen thought not only of the rich daughters but also at that very instant thought of the poor woman who offered Davin a cup of milk and all hinted to lie with her: "A woman had waited in the doorway as Davin had passed by at night and, offering him a cup of milk had all but wooed him to her bed; for Davin had the mild eyes of one who could be secret. But him no woman's eyes had wooed."

Cranly took Stephen's hand and walked on in silence. When they turned left, Stephen broke the silence:

"—Cranly, I had an unpleasant quarrel this evening.
—With your people? Cranly asked.
—With my mother.
—About religion?
—Yes, Stephen answerd.

After a pause Cranly asked:

—What age is your mother?
—Not old, Stephen said. She wishes me to make my easter duty.
—And will you?
—I will not, Stephen said.
—Why not? Cranly said.
—I will not serve, answered Stephen."

Cranly asked him to cool down and affably told him that he was an irascible, excitable man. Stephen laughingly admitted. Then:

"—Do you believe in the eucharist? Cranley said.
—I do not, Stephen said.
—Do you disbelieve then?
—I neither believe in it nor disbelieve in it, Stephen answered."

After a pause, Cranly took Stephen's hand and asked him:

"—Do you not fear that those words may be spoken to you on the day of judgment?"
Stephen did not budge. Then:
"—It is a curious thing, do you know, Cranly said dispassionately, how your mind is supersaturated with the religion in which you say you disbelieve. Did you believe in it when you were at school? I bet you did.
—I did, Stephen answered.
—And were you happier then? Cranly asked softly, happier than you are now, for instance?
—Often happy, Stephen said, and often unhappy. I was someone else then.
—How someone else? What do you mean by that statement?

—I mean, said Stephen, that I was not myself as I am now, as I had to become.

—Not as you are now, not as you had to become, Cranly repeated. Let me ask you a question. Do you love your mother?

Stephen shook his head slowly.

—I don't know what your words mean, he said simply.

—Have you never loved anyone? Cranly asked.

—Do you mean women?

—I ask you if you ever felt love towards anyone or anything?"

Stephen walked on beside his friend, staring gloomily at the footpath.

"—I tried to love God, he said at length. It seems now I failed. It is very difficult. I tried to unite my will with the will of God instant by instant. In that I did not always fail. I could perhaps do that still....

Cranly cut him short by asking:

—Has your mother had a happy life?

—How do I know? Stephen said.

—How many children had she?

—Nine or ten, Stephen answered. Some died."

Cranly asked Stephen if his father was well-to-do when he had been growing up. Stephen answered in the positive. Cranly then asked what his father's attributes were. Stephen began to enumerate and then said:

"—A medical student, an oarsman, a tenor, an amateur actor, a shouting politician, a small landlord, a small investor, a drinker, a good fellow, a story-teller, somebody's secretary, something in a distillery, a tax-gatherer, a bankrupt and a present praiser of his past."

Cranley then enquired of Stephen's mother:

"—Your mother must have gone through a good deal of suffering, he said then. Would you not try to save her from suffering even if...or would you?

—If I could, Stephen said, that would cost me very little.

—Then do so, Cranly said. Do as she wishes you to do."

Both Cranly and Stephen remained silent for a while and then Stephen said:

> "—Whatever else is unsure in this stinking dunghill of a world, a mother's love is not. Your mother brings you into the world, carries you first in her body. What do we know about what she feels? But whatever she feels, it, at least, must be real. It must be." Stephen, after a moment, continued:
>
> —Pascal, if I remember rightly, would not suffer his mother to kiss him as he feared to contact her sex.
>
> —Pascal was a pig, said Cranly.
>
> —Aloysius Gonzaga [an Italian aristocrat and a member of the Society of Jesus], I think, was of the same mind, Stephen said.
>
> —And he was another pig then, said Cranly.
>
> —The church calls him a saint, Stephen objected."

Still Cranly called Aloysius Gonzaga a pig.

Stephen was arranging the words he would deliver to Cranly and then said: "Jesus, too, seems to have treated his mother with scant courtesy in public but Suarez, a Jesuit theologian and Spanish gentleman, has apologized for him."

> "—Did the idea ever occur to you, Cranly asked, that was not what he pretended to be?
>
> —The first person to whom the idea occurred, Stephen answered, was Jesus himself.
>
> —I mean, Cranly said, hardening in his speech, did the idea ever occur to you that he was himself a conscious hypocrite, what he called the jews of his time, a whited sepulcher? Or to put it more plainly, that he was a blackguard?"

Stephen simply said he did not think about that any time. Cranly then asked whether Stephen believed that Christianity is a false religion and that Jesus was not the son of God. Stephen said:

> "—I am not at all sure of it, Stephen said. He [Jesus] is more like a son of God than a son of Mary.

> —And is that why you will not communicate, Cranly asked, because you are not sure of that too, because you feel that the host, too, may be the body and blood of the son of God and not a wafer of bread? And because you fear that it may be?
>
> —Yes, Stephen said quietly, I feel that and also fear it."

A short while afterwards, Cranley asked if Stephen would not be a Protestant. Stephen replied:

> "—I said that I had lost the faith, Stephen answered, but not that I had lost self-respect. What kind of liberation would that be to forsake an absurdity which is logical and coherent and to embrace one which is illogical and incoherent?"

Stephen and Cranly were now walking towards the township of Pembroke. The trees of the avenue and the lights of the villas comforted them. When they neared the kitchen behind a hedge of laurel, they heard a female servant singing in broken voice the song "Rosie O' Grady". The soft beauty of the song was more touching than the touch of a woman's hand. "The figure of a woman as she appears in the liturgy of the church passed silently through the darkness: a white robed figure, small and slender as a boy, and with a falling girdle. Her voice, frail and high as a boy's, was heard intoning from a distant choir the first words of a woman which pierce the gloom and clamour of the first chanting of the passion: "*—Et tu cum Jesu Galileo eras* [and you were with Jesus the Galilian." The song touched all the hearts.

"The singing ceased. They went together, Cranly repeating in strongly stressed rhythm the end of the refrain:

> And when we are married,
> O' how happy we'll be
> For I love sweet Rosie O' Grady
> And Rosie O' Grady loves me.
> [Rosie O'Grady was an Irish Vaudeville performer.]
> —There's real poetry for you, he [Cranly] said. There's real love.

> He glanced sideways at Stephen with a strange smile and said:
> —Do you consider that poetry? Or do you know what the words mean?
> —I want to see Rosie first, said Stephen.
> —She is easy to find, Cranly said."

Stephen looked at strong-bodied, large dark-eyed, handsome Cranly and saw his friend's pale face. "Away then: it is time to go. A voice spoke softly to Stephen's lonely heart, bidding him go and telling him that his friendship was coming to an end. Yes; he would go. He could not strive against another. He knew his part." Stephen told Cranly that he might depart:

> "—Probably I shall go away, he said.
> —Where? Cranly asked.
> —Where I can, Stephen said.
> —Yes, Cranly said. It might be difficult for you to live here now. But is it that makes you go?
> —I have to go, Stephen answered.
> . . . .
> —I don't know what you wish to do in life. Is it what you told me the night we were standing outside Harcourt Street?"

Stephen agreed and asked Cranly:

> "—Well? Stephen said. Do you remember the rest?
> —What you said, is it? Cranly asked. Yes, I remember it. To discover the mode of life or of art whereby your spirit could express itself in unfettered freedom."

Stephen raised his hat in acknowledgment.

Cranly understood that Stephen was after unfettered freedom of life and expression through art. But to make the point clearer from Stephen, he asked what his "point of view" was. Stephen responded:

> "—Look here, Cranly, he said. You have asked me what I would do and what I would not do. I will tell you what I will do and what I will not do. I will not serve that in which I do no longer believe, whether you call itself my home, my fatherland, or my church: and I

will try to express myself in some mode of life or art as freely as I can and as wholly as I can, using for my defence the only arms I allow myself to use—silence, exile, and cunning.

Cranly seized his arm and steered him round so as to lead him towards Leeson Park. He laughed almost slyly and pressed Stephen's arm with an elder's affection.

—Cunning indeed! he said. Is it you? You poor poet? You!

—And you made me confess to you, Stephen said, thrilled by his touch, as I have confessed to you so many other things, have I not?

—Yes, my child, Cranly said, still gaily.

—You made me confess the fears that I have. But I will tell you also what I do not fear. I do not fear to be alone or to be spurned for another or to leave whatever I have to leave. And I am not afraid to make a mistake, even a great mistake, a lifelong mistake, and perhaps as long as eternity too.

Cranly, now grave again, slowed his pace and said:

—Alone, quite alone. You have no fear of that. And you know what that word means? Not only to be separate from all others but to have not even one friend.

—I will take the risk, said Stephen.

—And not to have any one person, Cranly said, who would be more than a friend, more even than the noblest and truest friend a man ever had."

"His words seemed to have struck some deep cord in his nature. Had he spoken of himself, of himself as he was or wished to be? Stephen watched his face for some moments in silence. A cold sadness was there. He had spoken of himself, of his own loneliness which he feared.

—Of whom are you speaking? Stephen asked at length.

Cranly did not answer."

Part 4. [This part is simply some pages from Stephen's diary entries from March 20 to April 27 (thirty-nine days), the year being unknown. These are disconnected, scattered entries, that may somehow be a precursory mode of *Finnegans Wake*.]

"*March 20*. Long talk with Cranly on the subject of my revolt.

He had his grand manner on. I supple and suave. Attacked me on the score of love for one's mother. Tried to imagine his mother: cannot...his father was sixty-one when he was born.... Sometimes [Cranly] talks to girls after nightfall. But his mother? Very young or very old? Hardly the first. If so, Cranly would not have spoken as he did. Old then. Probably, and neglected. Hence Cranly's despair of soul: the child of exhausted loins."

"*March 21*, morning.... The exhausted loins are those of Elizabeth and Zaccchary.... Also, when thinking of him [Cranly], saw always a stern severed head or death mask as if outlined on a grey curtain or veronica [cloth impressed with an image of Christ's face]. Decollation [decapitated] they call it in the fold. Puzzled for the moment by saint John at the Latin gate [St. John was the governor of all churches of Asia. Around the year 95 AD, the Roman Emperor had him thrown in a cauldron of boiling oil. By the grace of God, St. John came out of the cauldron only refreshed. This miracle happened without the gate of Rome called Latina]."

"*March 21*, night. Free. Soul free and fancy free. Let the dead bury the dead. Ay. And let the dead marry the dead."

"*March 22*. In company with Lynch followed a sizable hospital nurse. Lynch's idea. Dislike it. Two lean greyhounds walking after a heifer."

"*March 23*. Have not seen her [Emma Clery] since that night. Unwell? Sits at the fire perhaps with mamma's shawl on her shoulders. But not peevish. A nice bowl of gruel? Won't you now?"

"*March 24*. Began with a discussion with my mother. Subject: B.V.M. [the Blessed Virgin Mary]. Handicapped by my sex and youth. To escape held up relations between Jesus and Papa against those between Mary and her son. Said religion was not a lying-in hospital. Mother indulgent. Said I have a queer mind and have read too much. Not true. Have read little and understood less. Then she said I would come back to faith because I had a restless mind. This means to leave church by backdoor of sin and reenter through the skylight of repentance. Cannot repent. Told so and asked for sixpence. Got three pence.

"Then went to college. Other wrangle with little round head rogue's eye Ghezzi [Joyce's teacher of Italian and Father]. This time about Bruno the Nolan. Began in Italian and ended in pidgin English. He said Bruno was a terrible heretic. I said he was terribly burned. He agreed to this with some sorrow. Then gave me recipe for what he calls *risotto alla bergamasca* [a rice dish made with cheese and either a fish or chicken stock, prepared in the style of Bergamo in Italy]....

"Crossing Stephen's, that is, my green, remembered that his countrymen and not mine had invented what Crany the other night called our religion. A quartet of them, soldiers of the ninety-seven infantry regiment, sat at the foot of the cross and tossed up dice for the overcoat of the crucified.

Went to library. Tried to read three reviews. Useless. She [Emma Clery?] is not out yet. Am I alarmed? About what? That she will never be out again.

Blake wrote:

I wonder if William Bond will die
For assuredly he is very ill.

[The two lines are from William Blake's (1757-1827) poem "William Bond" (c. 1803)—a 52-line poem in four-line stanzas. The quote is the last two lines of the first stanza that runs thus: "I wonder whether the Girls are mad/ And I wonder whether they mean to kill/ And I wonder if William Bond will die/ For assuredly he is very ill." But the reference may be to the four lines of the seventh stanza: "Yes Mary I do another Love/ Another I Love far better than thee/ And Another I will have for my wife/ Then what have I to do with thee.]

Alas, poor William!

I was once at a diorama in Rotunda. At the end were pictures of big nobs. Among them William Ewart Gladstone, just then dead. Orchestra played O *Willie, we have missed you.*

A race of clodhoppers!

[William Ewart Gladstone (1809-1998), English born but of Irish descent, served as Prime Minister of the United Kingdom for 12 years.]"

"*March 25, morning.* A troubled night of dreams. Want to get them off my chest.

A long curving gallery. From the floor ascend pillars of dark vapours. It is peopled by the images of fabulous Kings, set in stone. Their hands are folded upon their knees in token of weariness and their eyes are darkened for the errors of men go up before them for ever as dark vapours.

Strange figures advance as from a cave. They are not as tall as men. One does not seem to stand quite apart from another. Their faces are phosphorescent, with darker streaks. They peer at me and make their eyes seem to ask me something, They do not speak. [Epiphany?]"

"*March 30.* This evening Cranly was in the Porch of the library, proposing a problem to Dixon and her brother. A mother let her child fall into the Nile. Still harping on the mother. A crocodile seized the child. Mother asked it back. *Crocodile* said all right if she told him what he was going to do with the child, eat or not eat it.

This mentality, Lepidus [Marcus Aemilius Lepidus (89 B.C.-12 B.C.), second Roman triumvirate with Octavius and Mark Antony, a weak man, given to folly, fickleness and indecision] would say, is indeed bred out of your mud by the operation of your sun.

And mine? Is it not too? Then into Nile mud with it!" (*emphasis mine*)

"*April 1.* Disapprove of this last phrase."

"*April 2.* Saw her [Emma Clery] drinking tea and eating cakes in Johnson's, Mooney and O' Brien's. Rather, lynxeyed Lynch saw her [Emma] as we passed. He tells me Cranly was invited there by brother. Did he bring his *crocodile*?..." (*emphasis mine*)

"*April 3.* Met Davin at the cigar shop opposite. Find later's church.... Wants me to read law. Says I was cut out for that. More mud, more *crocodiles*." (*emphasis mine*)

"*April 5.* Wild spring. Scudding clouds. O life! Dark stream of swirling bogwater on which apple trees have cast down their delicate flowers. Eyes of girls among the leaves. Girls demure and romping. All fair or auburn: no dark ones. They blush better. Houpla!"

"*April 6.* Certainly she [Emma] remembers her past. Lynch says all women do. Then she remembers the time of her childhood—and mine, if I was ever a child. The past is consumed in the present and the present is living only because it brings forth the future. Statues of women, if Lynch be right, should always be fully draped, one hand of the woman feeling regretfully her own hinder parts."

"*April 6, later.* Michael Robertes [English poet, writer and critic] remembers forgotten beauty and, when his arms wrap her round, he presses in his arms the loveliness which has long faded from the world. Not this. Not at all. I desire to press in my arms the loveliness which has not yet come into the world."

"*April 10.* [The entry is a jabbering about Joyce's fantasy of one on horse-back coursing through the silent night and sleeping fields.]—to what journey's end—what heart?—bearing what tidings?"

"*April 11.* Read what I wrote last night. Vague words for a vague emotion. Would she [Emma?] like it? I think so? Then I should have to like it also."

"*April 13.* That tundish has been on my mind for a long time. I looked it up and find it English and good old blunt English too. Damn the dean of studies and his funnel! What did he come here for to teach us his own language or to learn it from us. Damn him one way or the other!"

"*April 14.* John Alphinsus Mulrennan [either an active member of the Gaelic Union, or a fellow student of Joyce's father, or an invented person of Joyce (see "James Joyce Online Notes" in www)] has just returned from the west of Ireland.... He told us he met an old man there in a mountain cabin....

Mulrennan spoke to him about universe and stars. The old man sat, listened, smoked, spat. Then said:

> —Ah, there must be terrible queer creatures at the latter end of the world.

I fear him. I fear his red-rimmed horny eyes. It is with him I must struggle.... Till he yield to me? No. I mean no harm."

"***April 15.*** Met her [Emma] today point blank in Grafton Street. The crowd brought us together. We both stopped. She asked me why I never came, said she had heard all sorts of stories about me. This was only to gain time. Asked me was I writing poems? About whom? I asked her. This confused her more and I felt sorry and mean. Turned off that valve at once and opened the spiritual-heroic refrigerating apparatus, invented and patented in all countries by Dante Alighieri [(c. 1265-1321), Italian poet and author of *Divine Comedy*]. Talked rapidly of myself and my plans. In the midst of it unluckily I made a sudden gesture of a revolutionary nature. I must have looked like a fellow throwing a handful of peas into the air. People began to look at us. She shook hands a moment after and, in going away, said she hoped I would do what I said.

Now I call that friendly, don't you?

Yes, I liked her today. A little or much? Don't know.

I liked her and it seems a new feeling to me. Then, in that case, all the rest, all that I thought I thought and all that I felt I felt, all the rest before now, in fact...[*sic*] O, give it up, old chap! Sleep it off!"

"***April 16.*** Away! Away!

The spell of arms and voices: the white arms of roads, their promise of close embraces and the black arms of tall ships [cf. "Eveline"] that stand against the moon, their tale of distant nations. They are held out to say: We are alone—come. And the voices say with them: We are your kinsmen. And the air is thick with their company as they call to me, their kinsmen, making ready to go, shaking the wings of their exultant and terrible youth [like Icarus, son of Daedalus]."

"*April 26.* Mother is putting my new secondhand clothes in order. She prays now, she says, that I may learn in my own life and away from home and friends what the heart is and what it feels. Amen. So be it. Welcome, O life! I go to encounter for the millionth time the reality of experience and to forge in the smithy of my soul the uncreated conscience of my race."

"*April 27.* Old father, old artificer [Daedalus], stand me now and ever in good stead."

Dublin, 1904
Trieste (Pola), 1914

DISCUSSION

In *A Portrait*, Joyce has fictionally chronicled his life roughly from 1885, when he was about three years old, to 1900, when he was about eighteen years old—his life of nearly fifteen years. In the first section of the novel, Joyce (Stephen Dedalus the hero of the novel) remembers his childhood days when his father would affectionately call him "baby tuckoo" and when he used to "wet the bed." This is a very rare beginning of a novel. In this section, we find some of Joyce's autobiographical experiences, many of which informed his personal ideas and opinions later on: Dante's (Mrs. Riordan's) threat, his attraction to Eileen Vance, his being ragged by his seniors in the Clongowes Wood College (a school), his knowledge that the Catholics hated Parnell just for his love of Kitty O'Shea, his being severely pandied for a slight fault, etc.

In the second section of *A Portrait*, we are told that Stephen (Joyce) entered the prestigious Belvedere College where, again, he was assailed by other students. Nevertheless, Stephen somehow felt comfortable here and here in the night of Whitsuntide he acted in a play. But soon the situation changed for the worse when Mr. Tate, the English master, found in Stephen's essay his heretic inclination. From that time on Stephen felt utterly alienated and lonely. In such a hapless state, he once entered a brothel and surrendered himself to a prostitute: "He wanted to be held firmly in her arms, to be caressed slowly, slowly, slowly. In her arms he felt that he had suddenly become strong and fearless and sure of himself. But his lips would not bend to kiss her." This was his ever first experience of carnal comfort. He was then sixteen.

In third section of *A Portrait* has no reference to any events in the life of Joyce nor are we told about any significant event in the fictional life of his save that now he was between tenterhooks—between two contrary pulls. On the one hand, he could not avoid the lure of brothels and on the other his "sin loving soul" was restless to get salvation. The most part of this section (the whole of part 2 of this section) is devoted to the teaching of the book of Ecclesiastes: the fear of Hell and the path of salvation. Here we find Stephen very devotedly inclining towards retreat and salvation.

Even at the beginning of the fourth section, Stephen is yearning for salvation, escaping the "ardent ways"—the ways of passion for flesh. He is even carrying the rosaries "in his trouser's pockets" with that aim in view. But the lure of the flesh is not letting him go. He was in a bind. "Every part of his day, divided by what he regarded now as the duties of his station in life, circled about its own centre of spiritual energy." Nevertheless, earthly love or passion allured him to the other way, which he rationalized thus: if God's love encompasses the whole universe why should he be bereft of earthly love? This query drag him away from the path of prayers and meditations, from the path of piety and self-restraint. He "grew troubled." And at the fag end of the fourth section, when at Howth Stephen saw the girl (the "seabird") in the midstream his trouble, his indecision left him. "Her image had passed into his soul for ever and no word had broken the holy silence of his ecstasy. Her eyes had called him and his soul had leaped at the call". Stephen accepted Tennyson's charge: "To live, to err, to fall, to triumph, to create life out of life!" He determined to devote his life on the creation of the life of art out of the life he lived—he determined to be an artist.

The fifth or last section of *A Portrait* is devoted principally to a long discourse on theories of beauty, mostly that of Thomas Aquinas, like in the third section we saw a long discourse on Christian piety. But in the fourth or last part of the fifth section, Stephen suddenly turned away from the high-flown philosophical deliberation and condescended to his quotidian diary entries, beginning 20 March (year NA). In the twenty-one diary entries, Stephen recounted the various memorable events of his life of some fifteen years. In the last three entries, he indicated his vision of departure from his land of birth and his determination to materialize his vision. In the entry of 16th April Stephen wrote that in a vision he saw the white arms of Ireland's roads lovingly embraced him, meaning Ireland, as if, did not want to let him go away. In the entry of 26th April he wrote that his mother prayed so that he might learn "what the heart is and what it feels" and that he said 'Amen' to it. There he inscribed: "Welcome, O life! I go to encounter for the millionth time the reality of experience and to forge in the smithy of my soul the uncreated conscience of my race." And in last entry of 27th April, Stephen, like Icarus begged his father Dedalus to help him fly away from the prison of Crete in the distant past, begged Dedalus ("Old father, old artificer") to help him now to escape his land of birth and help him always: "Old father, old artificer, stand me now and ever in good stead."

Now, we may compress the above summarization of the matter of the novel into the following nutshells:

Section I : Stephen perceived the world through senses.

Section II : Stephen showed his sexuality.

Section III : Stephen went to and fro about religion.

Section IV : Stephen's epiphany (profane or secular) of the beauty of the 'seabird.'

Section V : (a) Stephen discussed with the Dean of Studies about language and art.

(b) Stephen discussed with Davin about politics.

(c) Stephen discussed with Lynch about theory of art.

(d) Stephen discussed with Cranley about love and apostasy.

(e) Stephen's diary (he prepared to fly away).

Any discussion on *A Portrait* should begin with a mention of the epigraph of the novel: *Et ignotas animum dimittit in artes* (Ovid, *Metamorphoses*, VIII, 18).

The Latin epigraph has been rendered into English as follows:

> "(He spoke) and turned his mind to unknown arts (tr. Gilbert Hight)"; and
>
> "(This said) to uncouth arts he bent the force of all his wits (tr. Arthur Golding)."

Joyce had similarity with Ovid on at least one point: both went into exile. In 8 AD, the Roman Emperor Augustus banished Ovid from Italy and ordered him to live at Tomi on the Black Sea for his immoral poetic compositions. And in 1904 Joyce went into exile in Italy on his own. This might have prompted him to choose the above quote as the epigraph of *A Portrait*. Further, the quote has some relevance to the novel. Ovid's character, to whom the quote refers, turned to "unknown arts" or "uncouth arts" and *A Portrait* is a novel that presents "unknown" or "uncouth" art. Its beginning is amazingly unprecedented: "Once upon a time and a very good time it was there was a moocow coming down along the road and this moocow that was coming down along the road met a nicens little boy named baby tuckoo..." and the novel closes with pages of a diary, which too is bewilderingly strange.

The title of the novel, *A Portrait of the Artist as a Young Man,* also deserve some attention. The novel is a pen-picture of the protagonist who is destined to be a great artist. This is reflected in his name—Stephen Dedalus. 'Stephen' is derived from Greek 'Stephanos' which means 'wealth' or 'crown'. Dedalus or Daedalus is a legendary builder of a labyrinth (and so an artist). When Dedalus and his son Icarus were imprisoned in Crete, he devised wings of wax for them to fly away from there. Stephen Dedalus, the protagonist, or the alter ego or doppelganger of Joyce, was confident of becoming a great artist and the novel is a kaleidoscopic show of his progression towards that end since his boyhood to his prime manhood. In this regard, the title of the novel is all justified.

Some Features of *A Portrait of the Artist as a Young Man*

It is sometimes said that Joyce has written only one novel (William York Tindall) and this was once admitted by Joyce himself when he said that one could write only one novel in one's life. If we look closely through the sequence of his works—from *Dubliners* through *A Portrait*, through *Exiles*, through *Stephen Hero* to *Ulysses* (for the time being forget *Finnegans Wake* which is a dream), we will find that in each of these works there is Joyce present. *A Portrait* may be said to start from the last story in *Dubliners*, "The Dead", because in both the novel and the short story the protagonist is alone—a desolate man—surrounded by inclement milieu. In the same way, the trouble of love that is there in "The Dead" (a shadow of Joyce's "bad marriage") runs through *Exiles* and *Ulysses*.

A Portrait is closer to *Dubliners* than to any other works of Joyce. As *A Portrait* is autobiographical so are the stories of *Dubliners*; as *A Portrait* portrays the protagonist's (Joyce's) life from boyhood to adulthood so do the 15 stories of *Dubliners* show Dubliners' life from boyhood to (early) adulthood. On the other hand, as *Dubliners* is a collection of short stories so *A Portrait* may well be conceived of as a sequence of short stories. A good number of good short stories may be excerpted from *A Portrait*: Say, the story of the little boy, Stephen, and Dante (Mrs. Riordan); the story of the boy, Stephen, and his beloved girl Eileen Vance; the story of the teenager Stephen flogged by Father Dolan; the story of the teenage Stephen's visiting the prostitute and then his bearing rosaries in the pocket of his pantaloon; the story of the pre-adult Stephen's epiphany of the "seabird"; and Davin's (the peasant student) story of the married poor woman's affection for him, etc. In fact, almost all the 18 parts of the five sections of *A Portrait* can be metamorphosed into short stories. So, William York Tindall very rightly writes that "A good story, *A Portrait* is composed of good stories" (Tindall, 51).

Going by the same way, William York Tindall further says that the "stories" within the "story" that is *A Portrait* are not knitted back to back but there are *gaps* between the "stories" and no "transitions." Tindall writes, for instance, about the "stories" or "parts" of the first section or chapter of *A Portrait*: "The first chapter consists of four parts, connected by idea and theme, but separated by gaps without transitions. The first and shortest of these parts is Stephen's infancy. Suddenly, skipping years, we find Stephen at school, on playground, in classroom, dormitory, and infirmary. The third part finds him back at home for the Christmas dinner. He suddenly reappears on the playground and in refectory, complains in the rector's study, and, on playground again, enjoys social success" (Tindall, 60). Tindall calls this cinematographic method (a method much used in post-modern literature) or "montage" (a term coined by Eisenstein) in which disparate things are juxtaposed for enhanced effect.

William York Tindall has found in the five chapters or sections of *A Portrait* Gustav Freytag's pyramid of Aristotlean dramatic pattern: "This five-part structure, with climax in the fourth and resolution in the fifth, is that of classical drama, Joyce's model may be" (Tindall, 59). Tindall has rightly discovered the pattern of Freytag's pyramid in the novel—the first chapter is the exposition of the novel; the second and third chapters represent the rising action; the fourth is the climax because here Stephen stood on the brink of his indecision and then gradually he was bracing himself for fleeing Dublin; and, lastly, he determined in the fifth chapter to escape Dublin (or Ireland) like Icarus resolved to fly away from Crete. So far so good. But seeing Fretag's pyramid in an autobiographical novel is perhaps, seeing a white elephant in a patch of cloud. But Tindall justly writes that "Chapters three and four of *A Portrait* are almost as straight forward as chapters of a common novel, but chapters one, two, and five, intricate in structure, puzzle many readers. The symphony or the poem affords a good analogy for such structures, but the cinema is a better" (Tindall, 60).

The five sections of *A Portrait* are, however, rhythmically arranged. But what is rhythm in an art object? In 1903, Joyce himself defined rhythm in an art object thus: "Rhythm seems to be the first or formal relation of part to part in any whole or of a whole to its part or parts, or of a part to the whole of which it is a part.... Parts constitute a whole as far as they have a common end" (Gorman, 98). The five chapters of *A Portrait* are so patterned that the first chapter leads to the second, the second to the third, the third to the fourth, and the fourth to the last. While a section is related to its successor, each section is also related to the whole, i.e., to *A Portrait* as a whole. See, for instance, Stephen's experiences in the first section are linked to the last section where he avouches his departure from Dublin (or Ireland). The novel is therefore an integrated whole with a rhythmic pattern of its parts in each of which Stephen is recurrently betrayed by external forces, as a result of which he resolves to escape those antagonistic forces for ever.

Betrayal is a central theme of *A Portrait*. From the first part of the first section of the novel down to the first part of the last section of it we hear of Stephen's being betrayed (deceived, or treated treacherously, not loyally but perfidiously) by his family, by the religious members of his family, by his teachers and schoolmates, and by his compatriots who lacked in the will to political independence of Ireland and abused Parnell. Being thus betrayed on all sides, Stephen felt like a prisoner in Dublin (or Ireland) and desperately desired freedom, independence, and one day on a sudden he broke the prison gate and flew away from "dear, dirty Dublin" ("A Little Cloud"), like Icarus did from the Cretan prison, and landed in Italy to refresh himself in the free air of Europe.

In the first part of the first section of *A Portrait*, we hear that in his boyhood Stephen was betrayed by Dante (Mrs. Riordan) for his love of Eileen Vance. He expressed his wish to marry her when he would grow up but Dante threatened him with dire consequences if he did that, for Eileen, Dante said, was accursed as a Protestant. Dante warned him if he did wish that sacrilege eagles would pull out his eyes. Dante was dittoed by Stephen's mother. Secondly, in the fourth part of the second section of the novel, we see Stephen betrayed by his father. It was in Cork where his father was flirting with barmaids. There when some friends of his father said that Stephen "had a great look of his grandfather" his father carped that Stephen had but "an ugly likeness." Thirdly, when Stephen was at school in Belvedere, his father once very badly shouted at his sisters, insinuating at his supposed delay in reaching the school: "Is your lazy bitch of a brother gone out [to school] yet?" Stephen just laughed at the "curious idea of genders" of his father. On another occasion, Stephen's father made Stephen the butt of his joke at Clongowes school when he narrated before some persons how severely Father Dolan pandied Stephen. Stephen grudged his mother not because she actively betrayed him but because she had been passive while his father or Dante abuse him, betrayed him.

Outside the family circle, Stephen was much betrayed in the school. At Clongowes Wood College (school), once, for example, as told by his father to his acquaintances (*supra*) Father Dolan very cruelly flogged Stephen for a trifling fault of his. And while in Belvedere College (school), he was many times ragged by his senior students.

Stephen was also betrayed by his countrymen—by their Catholic pursuance and political preference or predilection towards the English subjugation. Stephen nursed in his breast the idea of Ireland's absolute freedom but the majority of his compatriots were cosily nestled in the slavish idea of living under the dominion of the English. Not only the high-ups of the Irish society but even the pedestrian Irish people were impassive to the idea of Ireland's independence. To take an example from *A Portrait* (Section I, Part 3), Stephen was sitting for his first Christians dinner at home, when Dante (Mrs. Riordian), targeting Charles Parnell, the leader of the Irish nationalist movement for absolute freedom, fumed: "It would be better for him [Parnell] that a millstone were tied about his neck and that he were cast into the depths of the sea.... That is the language of the Holy Ghost." Stephen also protested against English as the language of the overlords of Ireland but his protest received no encouragements from his compatriots.

All these betrayals so much hardened his heart that Stephen became an abhorrer of his land of birth. In the first part of the fifth section, he expresses his detestation of Ireland to Davin, the peasant student: "—The soul is born, he said vaguely, first in those moments I told you of. It has a slow and dark birth, more mysterious than the birth of the body. When the soul of a man is born in this country there are nets flung at it to hold it back from flight. You talk to me of nationality, language, religion. I shall try to fly by those nets." And then: "—Do you know what Ireland is? asked Stephen with cold violence. Ireland is the old sow that eats her farrow."

A Portrait is obviously a *Bildungsroman* (formation-novel) because it narrates the troubled course of the central character Stephen's growing up from childhood to pre-adulthood and achieving his identity. In this regard, it may be placed beside many 19th and 20th century *Bildungsromans* such as Goethe's *Wilhelm Meister*, Dickens' *David Copperfield*, Maugham's *Of Human Bondage*, D.H. Lawrence's *Sons and Lovers*, Thomas Mann's *The Magic Mountain* (in a broader sense), Thomas Wolfe's *Look Homeward Angel*, George Moore's *Confession of a Young Man*, etc. But all the same, *A Portrait* is also a *Kunstlerroman* (artist-novel), for it's hero develops into a literary artist, and so it may be clubbed together with other *Kunstlerromans* as Thomas Mann's *Doctor Faustus* and Zola's *L'Oeuvre*.

One controversy that till now arises about *A Portrait* is whether the novel is autobiographical, meaning its protagonist, Stephen, is the alter ego or *doppelganger* of Joyce himself, or the novel is absolutely a fictional creation, though one may find traces of Joyce's life in it. From the very first sentence of the novel through the diary entries of Stephen in the last section of it we hear about many things that well tally with those of Joyce's real-life events. For a few instances, we know that Joyce's father really endearingly called him "tuckoo" when he was a little child, that he grew up in a tyrannically Catholic environment of his family, that his father treated him badly, that he was ill-treated at school by the teachers and senior students, that in his heart he worshipped Parnell, that he could not but resent the language of the English (he regretted that he had to speak the language of Shakespeare), and that being quite exasperated on all sides by the inclement and stuffy environment one day in a trice he left behind the "dear, dirty Dublin", holding Nara Barnacle's hand and reached Italy to breath in the free air of Europe. We may therefore legitimately say that *A Portrait* is an autobiographical novel. Further, Joyce himself once said that the novel was his "curve of emotion". So the autobiographical nature of *A Portrait* should be kept above any doubt.

But some scholars' doubt still lingers. William York Tindall, for one believes that *A Portrait* should not be treated as an autobiographical novel. Tindall writes: "Not autobiography, *A Portrait* is work of art. The word *Portrait* in the little is significant, and it is no less significant that the article preceding this word is A, not The. This novel, like a painter's work, is one of several possible interpretations of a subject. Not representational, the distortions and arrangements, like those on canvas, are expressive" (Tindall, 53). It is undeniable that Joyce based his first novel on his personal history but, writes Tindall, he decanted the materials that he got from his personal history and depersonalised them to suit his artistic purpose. Tindal writes: "Events and characters are distorted, rearranged, and invented to serve a novelist's purpose. A Portrait is less record than invention" (Tindall, 52). When we regard *A Portrait* as an autobiographical novel, we forget the robust creative imagination of Joyce working in it altogether, and the inventions are so verisimilar to their donnees that we are prone to take them as real. The epiphanic seabird episode in the third part of the fourth section of the novel, for instance, is so vivid and life-like that we are beguiled to take it as real. If, however, Joyce has ever written anything autobiographical, it is his unfinished and discarded novel *Stephen Hero* which is, plainly, autobiography done in the shape of a novel.

In *A Portrait*, the point of view, or perspective, is mostly through its central character Stephen. It is through him that we witness the events of the novel. The character of Stephen is, therefore, (internally) focalised. In the novel Joyce has adopted the third-person (objective) point of view all over. To take an instance of the third-person point of view, let us go to the very beginning of the narrative: "Once upon a time and a very good time it was a moocow...met a nicens boy named baby tuckoo...."

Here Joyce stands away from Stephen and looks straight at him. But Joyce also enters into the being of Stephen and acts as a surrogate of him, that is feels, thinks and acts like him. Here Joyce's narrative is not object but is subjective. To take just one instance, in the second part of the first section of *A Portrait*, Stephen, in the infirmary, imagined of being dead and his dead body being carried away in a catafalque for burying. He even heard the tolling of the bell and the song that Brigid once had sung: "Dingdong! The castle bell!/ Farewell, my mother!...." So far Joyce is a third-person objective narrator. But no sooner the song is over, Joyce pops into the being of Stephen and makes exclamations that Stephen himself would do: "How beautiful and sad that was! How beautiful the words were where they said *Bury me in the old churchyard*!" Here Joyce's point-of-view or perspective is not objective but quite subjective. Throughout the whole length of the novel thus Joyce, many times, pops into and pops out of Stephen.

Epiphany is a preferred concept and useful device of Joyce and, as in *Dubliners*, he has also employed this manoeuvre in several places of *A Portrait*; at least one in each section of the novel. In the first part of the first section of *A Portrait*, Stephen, the little child, expressed his wish to marry Eileen, the Protestant girl, when he would be grown up, and then "hid under the table" when his mother asked him to apologise. Dante then went further: "—O, if not, the eagles will come and pull out his eyes." This sudden knowledge of cruel divine dispensation for an innocent romantic wish of his was to him an epiphany. In the second part of the second section, there is an eerie experience of Stephen. He was sitting in his aunt's kitchen and she was engrossed in the picture of the beautiful Mabel Hunter. A "ringletted girl" and a boy came there, saw the picture and appreciated it. An old burstling woman was making tea and saying what the priest and the doctor told about her. Stephen was listening to her and surveying the changes in the fire of the coal. At that moment the epiphenomenon—the epiphany—happened to Stephen.

> "Suddenly he [Stephen] became aware of something in the doorway. A skull appeared suspended in the gloom

> of the doorway. A feeble creature like a monkey was there, drawn thither by the sound of the voices at the fire. A whining voice came from the door asking:
>
> —Is that Josephine? The burstling woman answered cheerily from the fireplace:
>
> —No, Ellen, it's Stephen.
>
> O...O, good evening, Stephen.
>
> He answered the greeting and saw a silly smile break over the face in the doorway.
>
> —Do you want anything, Ellen? Asked the old woman at the fire.
>
> But she did not answer the question and said: —I thought it was Josephine. I thought you were Josephine, Stephen.
>
> And, repeating this several times, she fell to laughing feebly."

The third—and it was a major—epiphany of Stephen we come across in the second part of the third section. At the end of the second section, Stephen succumbed to the call of his flesh and went to a brothel, and now he was atoning for his sin. At that moment "the senses of his soul closed. They closed for an instant and then opened. He saw." He saw:

> "A field of stiff weeds and thistles and tufted nettle-bunches. Thick among the tufts of rank stiff growth lay battered canisters and clots and coils of solid excrement. A faint marshlight struggling upwards from all the ordure through the bristling greygreen weeds. An evil smell, faint and foul as the light, curled upwards sluggishly out of the canisters and from the stale crusted dung."
>
> "Creatures were in the field: one, three, six: creatures were moving in the field, hither and thither. Goatish creatures with human faces, hornybrowed, lightly bearded and grey as India rubber.... Soft language issued from their spittleless lips as they swished in slow circles round and round the field, winding hither and thither through the weeds, dragging their long

> tails amid the rattling canisters. They moved in slow circles, circling closer and closer to enclose, to enclose soft language issuing from their lips, their long swishing tails besmeared with stale shit, thrusting upwards their terrific faces...."

Stephen cried out: "Help!" "That was his hell." "He sprang from the bed, the reeking odour pouring down his throat, clogging and revolting his entrails. Air! The air of heaven! He stumbled towards the window, groaning and almost fainting with sickness. At the washstand a convulsion seized him within; and, clasping his cold forehead wildly, he vomited profusely in agony."

Stephen fourth—and it was another major—epiphany occurs in the third part of the fourth section. In this part Stephen had come away from the religious path and was beckoned by an "unseen path"—the secular or profane path. "He turned seaward from the road at Dolly mouth and as he passed on to the thin wooden bridge he felt the planks shaking with the tramp of heavily shod feet. A squad of Christian brothers was on its way back from the Bull and had began to pass, two by two, across the bridge. Soon the whole bridge was trembling and resounding." Stephen avoided the four clerics near the bridge and recalled a choice phrase of his: "A day of dappled seabourne clouds." "His soul was soaring in the air...."

"He looked northward towards Howth." The sea came into view. The sparkling beach beckoned him. Barefoot, shoes dangling from the shoulder, stockings in pockets, Stephen "clambered down the slope of the breakwater." "He was alone. He was unheeded, happy and near to the wild heart of life." Children and girls in the distance came to view and their clamouring voices were heard. Just at this moment he had an epiphany. Out there a beautiful girl stood in the midstream—"alone and still, gazing out to sea." "She seemed like one whom magic had changed into the likeness of a strange and beautiful seabird." "—Heavenly God! Cried Stephen's soul, in an outburst of prophane joy."

And, lastly, in the last part of the last section of *A Portrait*, there are two oneiric epiphanies in Stephen's diary entry of 25th morning. The first epiphany was as follows:

> "*March 25, morning*" "A troubled night of dreams. Want to get them off my chest." "A long curving gallery. From the floor ascend pillars of dark vapours. It is peopled by the images of fabulous kings, set in stone. Their hands are folded upon their knees in token of weariness and their eyes are darkened for the errors of men go up before them for ever as dark vapours."

And the second epiphany as below:

> "Strange figures advance as from a cave. They are not as tall as men. One does not seem to stand quite apart from another. Their faces are phosphorescent, with darker streaks. They peer at me and their eyes seem to ask me something. They do not speak."

What do these two dreams mean? How to interpret them? We have no answer. However, perhaps William York Tindall may be right when he writes: "Like any work of art—indeed, like life itself—*A Portrait* remains a riddle or an unanswerable question. Maybe that is why Athy in the infirmary [in the second part of the first section of *A Portrait*] puts a riddle to Stephen, who cannot find an answer. Maybe that is why riddles figure in most of Joyce's works" (Tindall, 100).

Or did Joyce purported to make *A Portrait*, like his all other works, difficult (like life itself) to understand? Otherwise why did he stuffed it with so many Latin phrases and so many references to recondite literary works and biblical mythologies, for instance, and with so many difficult or uncommon words.

However, a short list of the Latin words and phrases in *A Portrait* is being given below:

Latin phrases (select): *Ad Mejorem Dei Glorium* (for the greater glory of God), *Lous Deo Semper* (praise to God always), *Tempora mutantur nos et mutamur in illis* (times change and we change in them), *Quasi cedrus exaltata sum in Libanon et quasi cupressus in monte Sion. Quasi palma exaltata sum in Gades et quasi plantatio rosae in Jerico. Quasi uliva speciosa in campis et quasi plantanus exaltata sum juxta aquam in plateis. Sicut cinnamomum et balsamum aromatizans odorem dedi et quasi myrrha electa dedi suavitatem odoris* (I am exalted as the cedar in Lebanon and as the Cyprus on Mount Sion. I am exalted as the palm tree in Cadiz and as the rose in Jerico. I am exalted as a beautiful olive tree in the plains and as a plane-tree by the water in the streets. I gave forth a sweet fragrance like cinnamon and aromatic balm. I yielded a sweet smell like choicest myrrh), *Corpus Domini nostril* (the Body of our Lord), *Pulcra sunt quae visa placent* (those things are beautiful which please the sight), *Bonam est in quod tendit appetites* (good is that to which an appetite tends), *Per aspera ad astra* (through difficulties to the stars) and *Ad pulcritudinem tria requiruntur: integritos, consonantia, claritas* (for beauty, three things are required: integrity, consonance, and clarity).

Of diametrically opposite to Earnest Hemingway, who claimed that no reader of his works required to keep a dictionary by himself, was Joyce, who, while composing his works, was all oblivious of the intellectual level of his readers, and consequently, he being an accomplished linguist, difficult words—even of different tongues—stealthily crept into his works. In *A Portrait*, there are many such difficult words as (a selection only): soutane, capuchin, scullion, tundish (Irish: a large funnel), monstrance, cerement, muff, chasuble, dubitation, paraclele, ciborium, rictus, collywobbles, sacristy, simoon, cultus, drisheen (Irish, a sausage made of sheep's milk, blood, and seasonings), hoyden, hansel, vervain (a herbaceous plant having magical power and medicinal use), denarious (silver coin in ancient Rome), chine, prelatic, ephod, dray and Carmelite.

APPRECIATION Of *A PORTRAIT*

Joyce's contemporary English novelist H.G. Wells has some reservations about *A Portrait*, particularly for Joyce's "cloacal obsession" (meaning, moral filth) in it. But he is, nevertheless, not niggardly in appreciating the novel. In 1917, the year in which the novel was published in Britain, Wells wrote in *Nation* about *A Portrait*: "The value of Mr. Joyce's book has little to do with its incidental insanitary condition. Like some of the best novels in the world it is the story of an education; it is by far the most living and convincing picture that exists of an Irish Catholic upbringing. It is a mosaic of jagged fragments that does altogether render with extreme completeness the growth of a rather secretive, imaginative boy in Dublin. The technique is startling, but on the whole it succeeds" (Fargnoli and Gillespie, 150).

Joyce long endured jactitation in publishing *Dubliners* and the book did not fetch immediate renown, but *A Portrait* proved almost instant success after its serialisation in *The Egoist* in 1914 and publications in U.S.A. in 1916 and in Britain in 1917. Morris Beja writes in this regard: "The response to the publication of the *Portrait* must have been immensely gratifying; it received a great deal of attention, especially for a first novel.... It is true that a number of reviewers could not stomach either James' method or his world.... [Nevertheless] Irish reviewers were in fact the exception; the anonymous reviewer in the *Freeman's Journal* lamented that 'English critics are already hailing the author as a typical Irishman, and his book as a faithful picture of Irish life.' On the other hand Ernest Boyd, in 1923 wrote that "'the simple truth is that *A Portrait of the Artist as a Young Man* is to the Irish novel what *The Wanderings of Oisin* was to Irish poetry and *The Playboy of the Western World* to Irish drama, the unique and significant work which lifts the *genre* out of the commonplace into the national literature.' Generally most of even the first reviewers and critics were excited and impressed, and many recognised that here was a major new author" (Beja, 62).

Two other important contemporaries of Joyce—one, his compatriot W.B. Yeats and the other, Ezra Pound—could recognise the worth of *A Portrait* and the high merit of Joyce much earlier than other connoisseurs of literary art, to wit, in 1915. In that year, Yeats wrote about *A Portrait*: "I have read in a paper called *The Egoist* certain chapters of a new novel, a disguised autobiography [*The Portrait of the Artist*] [*sic.*], which increases my convictions that he is the most remarkable new talent in Ireland today" (Deming, 80). In the same year, Ezra Pound delivered his judgment on *A Portrait:* "It's damn well written" (Deming, 78). Two years latter, in 1917, Pound doubly asserted his earlier judgment on the novel: "It is unlikely that I shall say anything new about Mr. Joyce's novel, *A Portrait of the Artist as a Young Man*. I have already stated that it is a book worth reading and that it is written in good prose. In using these terms I do not employ the looseness of the half-crown reviewer" (Deming, 82). Pound, was at one point, much irritated by the Dublin and English publishers who declined to publish *A Portrait* but he prophesied a good future for the novel and the novelist: "Now, despite the jabbing of bigots and their sectarian publishing houses...and the initial objections of the Dublin publishers and the later unwillingness of the English publishers, Mr. Joyce's novel appears in book form, and intelligent readers gathering few by few will read it, and it will remain a permanent part of English literature written by an Irishman in Triste and first published in New York city" (Deming, 83). Pound also reasoned why *A Portrait* would "remain a permanent part of English literature." He wrote: "Apart from Mr. Joyce's realism—the school life, the life in the University, the family dinner with the discussion of Parnell depicted in the novel—apart from, or of a piece with, all this is the style, the actual writing: hard, clear-cut, with no waste of words, no bundling up of useless phrases, no filling in with pages of slosh" (Deming, 84).

Ford Maddox Ford it seems has his highest praise for a novelist—for James Joyce. In 1922, he wrote: "The *Portrait of the Artist as a Young Man* (*sic.*) is a book of such beauty of writing, such clarity of perception, such a serene love and interest in life, and such clarity that, being the ungenerous creature man is, one was inclined to say: 'This surely must be a peak! It is unlikely that this man will climb higher!'" (Deming, 128-29). To illustrate his point, Ford compared Joyce with another great novelist, Miss Dorothy Richardson: "And Mr. Joyce is a writer of very beautiful, composed English. To read *The Portrait of the Artist as a Young Man* (*sic.*) as against, say, *Interim* [the fifth volume of *Pilgrimage*] of Miss Dorothy Richardson is to recognize the difference between singularly fussy inclusiveness and absolutely aloof selection. There is really more enlightenment as to childhood and youth in the first three pages of Mr. Joyce's book—there is more light thrown on the nature of man—than in all Miss Richardson's volumes" (Deming, 128).

Like Ford Maddox Ford, William York Tindall is also ebullient in his praise of *A Portrait*, particularly about its scenes and episodes, brilliantly sketched. Ford says that any reader's even cursory attention will be glued to these scenes and episodes that make up the most part of the novel. Tindall writes: "What detains the most casual eye is an abundance of brilliant scenes and episodes, not only immediate in effect but persistent in memory. No eye could be more casual or innocent than mine when I first picked this great novel up, and I cannot forget my impression of the first two pages, which by selection, tone, and rhythm create a child's world. The scene of the wading girl is memorable; and there are the unforgettable sermons on hell, which emerge from their Catholic setting to inflame the infidel, or even the Protestant heart. But most striking of all is the Christmas dinner, which might have found a place beside the first three stories of *Dubliners*.... A good story, *A Portrait* is composed of good stories" (Tindall, 50-51).

CRITICISM

A Portrait was "criticized" even before it was published: it was rejected by publishers and printers. In 1916, "The Egoist Press had intended to publish *A Portrait of the Artist as a Young Man* in London this year [1916] also but Joyce's old enemy, the Moral British Printer, intervened again. The Editors of the Egoist Press tried printer after printer but the result was always the same, a demand for deletion or a simple refusal to print the book" (Gorman, 233). At least seven firms refused to print the book and their common reason of refusing to print the book was "objectionable passages" or "objectionable matter" or such. In this regard, *A Portrait* had almost the same fate at the hands of publishers as *Dubliners* earlier had had. Joyce, of course, had a little "cloacal obsession." Many critics and writers, including Rebeca West, have also voiced their objections to Joyce's use of obscene words and scenes.

Difficult or uncommon words in the book and, perhaps, needless insertion of Latin phrases (instances of which we have given above)—and they are not few—have made the novel a difficult reading. We know that Joyce read *Skeat's Etymological Dictionary* by the hour (as he states in *Stephen Hero*) and his advanced knowledge of etymology might have crept unawares into his artistic creation only to make it somewhat cumbersome.

These objections belong to the surface of the novel. But there are grave, shattering criticisms against it. In 1937, Windham Lewis accused *A Portrait* as being sentimental and so devalued it: "*Some* pages of the *Portrait* I had read, when it first appeared as a serial in the *Egoist*.... But I took very little interest. At that time, it was of far too tenuous an elegance for my taste. Its flavor was altogether too literary. And as to its emotional content, that I condemned at once as sentimental-Irish. Even now, for that matter, I feel much the same about the *Portrait of the Artist*, with the important difference that I have obliged myself to read a great many more books, in the meanwhile, many of which suffer from the same shortcomings, as I see it. So I do recognize the *A Portrait of the Artist as a Young Man* to be one only of a large class, and of its kind a very excellent example" (Deming, 120). Rebeca West dittoed Windham Lewis, though she admired Joyce "tremendously". William Carlos Williams, in his article "A Point for American Criticism" writes about Rebeca West's displeasure with Joyce's sentimental writing: "'But the sentimental artist (Joyce) is becoming nothing.' She criticizes the drawing of Stephen Dedalus. 'He rolls his eyes, he wobbles on his base with suffering, like a Guido Reni [1575-1642: Italian painter]...a consequence of Mr. Joyce's sentimental habit of using his writing as a means for gratifying certain compulsions under which he labors, without making the first effort towards lifting them over the threshold that divides life from art'" (Slingsby and Dixon, 81).

Joyce, we understand, wanted to make *A Portrait* a *Bildungsroman*—a narrative of a character's development, unfolding, evolution or maturation in the line of Goethe's *Wilhelm Meister* that in 1796 inaugurated the *Bildungsroman* tradition. It was with this aim in view that he abandoned his unartistic autobiographical novel *Stephen Hero*, which he called "rubbish". In 1905, after engaging in it for over two years and setting it aside Joyce set out to write *A Portrait*. *Stephen Hero* was visibly an exercise in autobiography in the garb of a novel and Joyce wanted to make his new novel [*A Portrait*] a developmental novel or formation-novel. But some critics have rightly raised the question: where is Stephen's development in *A Portrait*? When we open the novel we find the boy Stephen in an inclement or harsh situation which he ardently desired to escape and, as the novel progresses and Stephen grew up with the passage of time, we see him in identical situations at different places with the same desire to escape them. Where is Stephen's mental or spiritual development then? When we open the book we see him alone and when we close it we see him alone. Where then is the developed of Stephen? Some have categorised *A Portrait* as a *Kunstlerroman* or artist-novel but nowhere in the book do we find in Stephen as an artist save in his name—Stephen Dedalus (the mythological Dedalus was an artist). So Tobias Boes justly writes in his article "*A Portrait of the Artist as a Young Man* and the 'Individuating Rhythm' of Modernity": "'the merit of *Potrait* lies in its being an unmistakable failure' as a novel of development" (Moretti, 243).

Tobias Boes' opinion is fortified by Hugh Kenner in his article "The *Portrait* in Perspective" (Kenner, 416). Joyce wanted to show that Stephen rejected the church and his country and then became an artist or, rather, his rejection of the church and his country contributed to his becoming an artist. True, we do not see Stephen as an artist before he left the church and the country but certainly there was no causal connectivity between the two events. Unfortunately, *A Portrait* tends to suggest such a connectivity. Hugh Kenner writes in the above-mentioned article: "Stephen does not, as the careless reader may suppose, become an artist by rejecting church and country. Stephen does not become an artist at all." But then why *A Portrait of an Artist as a Young Man* instead of "A Portrait of a Young Man"?

Barring the some seven-page long fourth part of the fifth or last section of *A Portrait*, the whole of the fifth section of the novel that encompasses eighty-five odd pages, Joyce needlessly utilised as a space for an exposition of his theory of aesthetics. This has considerably reduced the tenor of the narrative and consequently the interest of the reader in the fate of Stephen. This is certainly not a minor fault in the novel.

Howbeit, Fran O'Rourke, of the University of Dublin, claims that in his exposition of his theory of beauty *a la* Thomas Aquinas, Joyce has confused the real Thomistic theory of aesthetics. In his 18-page article "Joyce's Early Aesthetic" [*Journal of Modern Literature*, Vol. 3, No. 2, January 2011, University College Dublin, pp. 97-120], Fran O'Rourke has tried to explain his point. He says that for his own theory or understanding of goodness, beauty, and truth (in *A Portrait*), Joyce depended on Thomas Aquinas' theory of goodness, beauty, and truth as enunciated in Aquinas' *Summa Theologica*. But when Joyce wrote his first novel *A Portrait* (or *Stephen Hero*) at the age of around 22, he did not go directly to *Summa Theologica* but acquainted himself with Aquinas' theory through his reading of Barnard Bosanquet. The consequence of this was that Joyce's knowledge of Aquinas' theory of goodness, beauty, and truth was flawed, at that time. It is not possible here, for paucity of space, to discuss O'Rourke's "Joyce's Early Aesthetic" and, therefore, we can only quote a few sentences from that article to show an instance of Joyce's misunderstanding of Aquinas' theory of aesthetics. O'Rourke writes that Joyce utilised Aquinas' theory from his memory, which was faulty: "Two 'errors' in Joyce's quotation from Aquinas on beauty confirm that he was working from memory rather than from the text of *Summa Theologica*. Instead of '*Pulchra* dicuntur *quae visa placent*' ('those things are *called* beautiful which please when seen'), he [Joyce] wrote '*Pulcra* (sic*) sunt quae visa placent*' ('those things are beautiful which please when seen'). The misspelling of 'pulchra' in itself is unimportant—an 'error' that persisted through later citations (*Stephen Hero*, 95, *Portrait*, 186). The interpretive implications of the second error—substituting '*dicuntur*' [meaning called] for '*sunt*' [read 'sunt' for 'dicuntur'] are not inconsiderable: by defining beauty as that which is called beautiful, Aquinas assigns a role to the *subjective element* of experience [which Joyce missed]" (*emphases added*). This mistake of Joyce in

A Portrait has to an extent damaged his whole narrative on Aquinas' theory of beauty.

From near the beginning of *A Portrait* to near the close of it we find Stephen a weak personality. He never changes, never grows. He suffers ambivalence towards his family, religion and nation, but chiefly towards religion and towards Jesuitism. He committed "sin" while he was a boy and he apologized for this (section I, part 1); he entered into a brothel and prayed for God's forgiveness (section II, part 5 and section III, part 1); he was secularly (sexually) attracted to the bird-girl (section IV, part 3) and was carnally aroused by Davin's story of the "half undressed" woman (section V, part 1) and then was tempted by the image of Emma Clarey (section V, part 2). All through Stephen was weak in mind, undecided, ambivalent and lonely. This long journey of Stephen through painful ambivalence and indecision seems to be the result of Joyce's own indecision as to how to close the novel. Hugh Kenner, in his article "The *Portrait* in Perspective" (*supra*) cannot accept this procrastination on the part of Joyce on the point of Stephen's ambivalence, instability and moral ambiguity. Kenner writes: "The Stephen of the end of the fourth chapter [or section], however, is still unstable; he had to be brought into a final balance, and shown at some length as a being whose development was virtually ended. Unfortunately, the last chapter makes the book a peculiarly difficult one for the reader to focus, because Joyce had to close it on a suspended cord. As a lyric, it is finished in its own terms; but the themes of the last forty pages, though they give the illusion of focusing, don't really focus until we have read well into *Ulysses*. The final chapter, which in respect to the juggernaut of *Ulysses* must be a vulnerable flank, in respect to what has gone before must be a conclusion. This problem Joyce didn't wholly solve; there remains a moral ambiguity (how seriously are we to take Stephen?) which makes the last forty pages painful reading" (Kenner, *Dubliner's Joyce* ch. 8).

However, to close our discussion on *A Portrait*, we may say that Joyce is an extremely complex writer in this book as in his other ones. Sometimes it seems that he in *A Portrait* has even intentionally made it labyrinthine and cumbersome with *labor improbus* but he never forgets his lyricism, picturesqueness, artisty in form and, of course, his swelling emotion. Call it a *Bildungsroman* or *Kunstlerroman* or simply an autobiographical novel, *A Portrat* is unique in its own terms, and as such stands away from so many autobiographical novels, such as Maugham's *Of Human Bondage*; D.H. Lawrence's *Sons and Lovers*; Thomas Mann's *Magic Mountain;* Goethe's *The Sorrow's of Young Werther*; Samul Butler's *The Way of All Flesh*; George Meredith's *Richard Fiverel*; J.M. Coetzee's *Boyhood Scenes from Provincial Life*, *Youth Scenes from Provincial Life* and *Summertime*. Why do we call *A Portrait* unique as an autobiographical novel or a *Bildungsroman* or a *Kunstlerroman* or whatever? It is unique in the sense that it is a "curve of emotion" as Joyce himself dubbed it. This emotional curvature of it has given it a sense of poetry. If we cannot get the rhythmic poetic sense and swelling passion of art and freedom in it, we have not understood it. And, lastly, we echo William York Tindall's warning before nursing a fancy to comprehend *A Portrait* in the totality of its meaning: "Like any work of art—indeed, like life itself—*A Portrait* remains a riddle or an unanswerable question. May be that is why Athy in the infirmary puts a riddle to Stephen, who cannot find an answer" (Tindall, 100).

In the second part of the first section of *A Portrait*, Athy asked Stephen in the infirmary:

> "—Are you good at riddles?
> —Not very good.
> —Can you answer me this one? Why is the country Kildre like a leg of a fellow's breeches?
> Stephen thought what could be the answer and then said:
> —I give it up."

We are like Stephen. No better.

STEPHEN HERO: A NOTE

Stephen Hero is the earlier version of *A Portrait of the Artist as a Young Man*. *A Portrait* has a torturous history. In January 1904, Joyce wrote an essay of some two thousand words, gave it the title "A Portrait of the Artist", and sent it to the Irish periodical *Dana*. The essay was an unusual work: "part manifesto, part narrative; a story with only one character, a portrait without descriptive detail; an attempt to chart 'an individuating rhythm...the curve of emotion'" (Scholes and Kain, 56). The essay was rejected. Almost immediately Joyce planned to translate the essay into a long novel and put out about 1,000 manuscript pages between 1904 and 1906 (about 26 chapters of the projected 52 chapters of the novel) and titled it *A Portrait of the Artist as a Young Man* (the original title of *Stephen Hero*).

For unknown reasons, Joyce suddenly stopped going ahead with the about 1,000 pages manuscript, perhaps being displeased with the looseness of the form and prolixity of the narrative of the novel, and began it *ab novo* with the same title: *A Portrait of the Artist as a Young Man*, which is the present novel (the about 1,000 pages of the discarded fragmentary novel is now known as *Stephen Hero*, though its earlier title was also *A Portrait of the Artist as a Young Man*). So we may take *Stephen Hero* as Joyce's transitional work.

Joyce was not only displeased with the bulky manuscript of *Stephen Hero*, he was exasperated with it; so much so that in a moment of conniption he had thrown the whole of it into fire but luckily for us, 383 pages of it was somehow promptly saved by Mrs. Joyce at the risk of burning her hands, the rest of the manuscript being consumed by the fire. So, at present, of the 1,000-odd pages, we have only 383 pages (519 to 902 pages) under the rubric *Stephen Hero*. There is another story about the loss of some 617 pages of the 1000-odd pages of the manuscript of "Stephen Hero". The remaining pages of the manuscript, some say, were stolen and sold to different institutions. However, Joyce himself gave the rescued part of the manuscript to Sylvia Beach who in 1938 sold it to Harvard College Library. And in 1944, with the permission of Harvard College Library the manuscript (edited by Joyce's executor Theodore Spencer) was published by New Directions, with the title *Stephen Hero*.

The extent fragmentary *Stephen Hero* begins at page 23 with a broken sentence: "anyone spoke to him mingled a too polite disbelief with its expectancy." This is most probably from Ch. XV. At page 32 begins Ch. XVI which is followed by 10 consecutive chapters (XVII to XXVI) at the end of which the manuscript ends. In *Stephen Hero*, Joyce planned to write an autobiographical novel, realistic, with less embellishment, and based on his own life history, a novel quite unlike *A Portrait* which is not autobiographical but is an artistic creation. Nevertheless, in *A Portrait* he used the fragments of *Stephen Hero* as raw material. Further, some of the characters of *Stephen Hero* have found places in *A Portrait*: Stephen Daedalus (in *A Portrait* as Stephen Dedalus), Simon Daedalus (in *A Portrait* as Simon Dedalus), Emma Clery (in *A Portrait* as E—C—) and Cranly. Joyce heavily reduced the puffedness of *Stephen Hero* and confined it within only five sections or part, which may remind one of the five-act dramatic device or even of Freytag's pyramid which may be found in the basic structure of *A Portrait*.

Now, we have only 11 chapters (most of the pages of which are now missing) of *Stephen Hero,* from Ch. XVI to Ch. XXVI. In Ch. XVI, we read about Stephen's uneasy relations with schoolmates and his struggle to be a writer. At this time he is being influenced by stalwart Continental writers—Ibsen, Strindberg, Maeterlinck, Tugenev, etc. Ch. XVII shows us Stephen's life at home, his sense of nationalism, and his attraction to Emma Clery. Ch. XVIII and Ch. XIX narrate Stephen's meeting with Charles Wells (who in *A Portrait* pushes Stephen into a square ditch). Here we hear of Stephen's essay "Drama and Life" and of his discussions with friends on aesthetics. Ch. XX deals with the discussion between Cranly and Stephen about Catholicism.

In Ch. XXI, we find Stephen gradually growing aloof from friends (which is graphically detailed in *A Portrait*) and directly being involved in conflict with his mother. In Ch. XXII, we see Stephen's nonchalant interest in Emma Clery and his firm belief in his own theory of aesthetics. Stephen shows angst as a result of his alienation from his father in Ch. XXIII and in Ch. XXIV he is alienated also from his source of emotional support from Emma due to her conservative attitude to matters sexual. In Ch. XXV, we read that Stephen is more alienated from his father. He has an epiphany here, about his ambivalence between flesh and piety, which prompts him to compose the "Villanelle of the Temptress": "Are you not weary of the ardent ways,/ Lure of the fallen Seraphim?/ Tell no more of enchanted days./..." (which reappears at the end of the second part of the fifth or last section of *A Portrait*). Ch. XXVI largely corresponds to the fourth part of the last section of *A Portrait*—Stephen is planning to swiftly slip away from his fatherland.

Let us now compare between *Stephen Hero* and *A Portrait* to see if there are any similarities between the discarded fragment of a novel and the finished novel chiseled out the fragment. The similarities are: both are novelistic creations; both grow out of the (real) life of their common protagonist, (Joyce) Stephen; in both Stephen aspires to be an artist; and in both he struggles against the forces that betray him—his family, the church, and his nation.

But the differences are more significant. Firstly, *Stephen Hero* is an artless matter but in *A Portrait* that artless matter is transmogrified into a super art object. Secondly, Joyce has rigorously compressed the huge bulk of *Stephen Hero* to make it *A Portrait*, whittling away all the needless matters from it. Thirdly, *A Portrait* is a well-constructed novel but *Stephen Hero* is not what *A Portrait* is but a mere chronicle of Stephen. And fourthly, in *A Portrait* Stephen is a victim but in *Stephen Hero* he is a hero.

4
Exiles
James Joyce
(Abridged, Elucidated, and Evaluated)

INTRODUCTION

James Joyce will certainly go down for long in the history of English novel but he also tried his hand in writing poems (*Chamber Music* and *Pomes Penyeach*) and plays (*A Brilliant Career* and *Dream Stuff* and *Exiles*). *Chamber Music* was published in 1907—Joyce's first published creative work. *Pomes Penyeach* was published much later, in 1927. Both these works are extant, but the two dramatic works—*A Brilliant Career* and *Dream Stuff* are lost entirely, save only a few tiny fragments of them. *A Brilliant Career* was written in 1900, and Joyce very quizzically dedicated it to himself: "To my own Soul I dedicate the first true work of my life." It may be noted here that Joyce considered this first dramatic work of his—*A Brilliant Career*—as his "first true work", which may hint that he might have aspired to be a playwright in his early creative life. This hint may be corroborated by the fact that during the time he was writing this play he was much bemused by the dramatic brilliance of the great Norwegian playwright Henrick Ibsen (1828-1906) and even began to learn Norwegian language to enable himself to read Ibsen's plays in the original language of Norway.

To assess the dramatic worth of *A Brilliant Career*, Joyce sent the play to William Archer with the request: "'I am most anxious to hear your judgment upon it'" (Ellmann, 78). Archer's letter of 15 September 1900 to Joyce was instructive: "I have at last found time to read your play. It has interested me and puzzled me a great deal—indeed, I scarcely know what to say of it. You seem to me to have talent—and yet I cannot say that I think this play a success. For the stage, of course—the commercial stage—it is wildly impossible.... On the other hand, you have certainly a gift of easy, natural and yet effective dialogue, and a certain amount of scenic picturesqueness.... On the whole, however you seem to me to be deficient as yet in the power of projecting characters so as to seize upon the reader's attention and kindle his imagination. It is true that you unduly handicap yourself in this respect by crowding your stage with such a multitude of figures that Shakespeare himself could scarcely individualize them" (Ellmann, 79).

Joyce's enthusiasm for writing plays might have been temporarily dampened by the harsh criticism of Archer for about two years since then he did not write any play. Archer in his criticism rightly pointed out a flaw in Joyce's play. He said that Joyce began with many supernumerary characters only ultimately to conclude with a few. Richard Ellmann says that this ideosyncracy of Joyce runs through *Dubliners*, *Ulysses* and *Finnegans Wake*. However, after reading Archer's opinion on his *A Brilliant Career*, Joyce undauntedly wrote back that "he himself disliked the play" (Ellmann, 80). Howbeit, the play is now in its entirety lost to limbo save the following four lines of a gypsy song of it to be sung during a merrymaking:

> We will leave the village behind,
> Merrily, you and I,
> Tramp it smart and throw to the wind,
> With the Romany Rye.

Joyce's second dramatic oeuvre was *Dream Stuff*, a verse play, composed in 1902 (*circa*). This play is also now lost for good, except the following one stanza of seven lines of a song in it:

> In the soft night fall
> Hear thy lover call,
> Hearken the Guitar!

Lady, lady fair
Snatch a cloak in haste,
Let thy lover taste
The sweetness of thy hair.

That Joyce had genuine interest in plays and the theatre is beyond doubt. He voraciously read the plays of Ibsen, Maeterlinck, Chekhov, Hauptmann and others, and, of course, of Shakespeare and other English playwrights. He also wanted to translate Hauptmann's plays into English. Joyce had eagerly watched such performances as of Sudermann's *Magda*, D'Annunzio's *Chitta Morta*, Synge's *Riders to the Sea*, Wedekind's and Strindberg's plays and, of course, the plays of Ibsen, including his *Ghost*. Not only this, at one time along with Claud Sykes Joyce formed a company of players to produce English plays in Zurich which, at his suggestion, was named English Players. And in the third part of the second section or chapter of *A Portrait*, we see Stephen acting in the theatrical performance in the Whitsuntide night. This may reflect Joyce's interest in the theatre. In fact, before writing his great short and long fictions, Joyce had shown his interest in poetry and play and tried his hand in both. Not only this, his enchantment with these two genres ever continued to inform his later fictional works slyly, almost invisible. That this is true is evinced by the fact that long after *Dream Stuff* (1902) Joyce wrote another, and his last, play *Exiles* (1918).

Joyce wrote *Exiles* simultaneously with the last story of *Dubliners*, "The Dead", *A Portrait* and the beginning pages of *Ulysses*. This may be one of the reasons why the same shadows of betrayal and loneliness passes over all the four works of his and also why this play could not achieve the expected level of excellence at his hand. Joyce wrote *Exiles* in Trieste during 1914-15 and it faced the same luckless lot of rejection from publishers as did *Dubliners* years ago. He could neither easily publish it nor could stage it (of course Joyce himself as well wanted it to be published after *A Portrait*, in case this novel had been printed in book form, and the novel was published in New York in 1916). But staging of *Exiles* was far more onerous than getting it published. W.B. Yeats rejected it in August 1917 for

Dublin's Abbey Theatre. Ezra Pound rejected it, saying it was unsuitable for the stage. Interesting it is that the first performance of *Exiles* was done not in its English version but in its German version, titled *Verbannte* (meaning 'exiled' or 'banished') at the Munchener Theatre in Munich in August 1919. And it is more interesting that *Exiles*, whose setting is Dublin, was not staged in Dublin "until the Gaity Theatre presented it on January 18, 1948, seven years after Joyce's death" (Fargnolli and Gillespie, 86).

Exiles: The Play

William York Tindall's observation on *Exiles* is noteworthy: "However simple its surface, *Exiles* is one of the more difficult of Joyce's works. Questions of theme, motive, and general meaning plague audience or readers, whatever their chairs, in pit or closet" (Tindall, 104). Joyce said that *Exiles* was a "three cat and mouse acts"; yes, but the difficult in it is how to explain the moves and motives of the cats and the mouse (or mice)? It is a play that has shunned actions, crisp dialogues are its only materials. Its theme is studiedly hazed, its externality is trivial, its setting is narrow as its time is short—from one evening to the next morning. But it doggedly follows Joyce's philosophy of creativity—to seek the big meaning in small things (*a la* Joyce's "scrupulous meanness"). And, above all, it shows Joyce's penchant for metagrobolization.

Exiles works with four principal and three minor characters. Of the total seven characters, three belong to a family: Richard Rowan, his wife Bertha and their eight-year-old son Archie. Brigid is the family's old servant. The three other characters are: Robert Hand, his cousin Beatrice Justice and a very insignificant character without a proper name—Fishwoman. The four principal characters are: Richard Rowan, Bertha, Robert Hand and Beatrice Justice.

Richard Rowan. Richard is the protagonist and he reflects the character of Joyce himself, at least in the point that he self-exiled and went to the Continent along with Bertha more than eight years ago (like Joyce went into self-exile taking Nora's hand about twelve years previously). Richard now has come back to

Ireland or Dublin along with Bertha, whom he had "married", and their eight-year-old son Archie. Richard is a writer, again like Joyce. He is intellectual, artistic and emotional. But he has queer sexual relation with Bertha, which is most problematic in interpreting the play. While his friend and Bertha's former lover Robert Hand tries to seduce her and win her away from him, he does not intervene, though he suffers mortally. In his note on the character of Richard, Joyce identified him as "an atomistic."

Bertha. Her surname, either previous to or after her "marriage" with Richard Rowan is not given in the play. She is Archie's mother. From her being sexually attractive arises the complexity of the plot. Before the play begins, she had been Robert Hand's fiancée but Richard Rowan snatched her away and "married" her and in the play we see Robert trying to seduce her back away. Richard willingly pushes her towards Robert (perhaps to weigh her fidelity and give her freedom) and she plays the role of a doll at Richard's hand. Robert does everything with her in passion but does not consummate his love. Bertha takes all this only as a play while Richard suffers internally being in doubt about the consummation.

Robert Hand. A journalist by profession, Robert is a friend to Richard and his neighbor. Robert's cousin Beatrice Justice once had been an object of love of both Robert and Richard, later on Bertha was installed by both in Beatrice's place. Beatrice is still intellectually and emotionally attached to Richard even after his "marriage" with Bertha, though at a lower level of desire. Robert, on the other hand, is in deep love of Bertha, even after more than eight years of her "marriage." Joyce thought of Robert as a disciple of Judas and "the elder brother in the fable of the Prodigal Son" (Fargnoli and Gillespie, 86). And in his note Joyce called Robert "an automobile." Robert "*is a middlesized, rather stout man between thirty and forty. He is clean-shaven, with mobile features. His hair and eyes are dark and his complexion sallow. His gait and speech are rather slow.*"

Beatrice Justice. She is a twenty-seven-year-old spinster who gives piano lessons to Archie. She is not blond like Bertha, but unlike Bertha she is intellectually of higher grade. Once she had been the beloved of both Richard and Robert, but as the play opens both her lovers have distanced themselves from Beatrice, though she continues to be intellectually attached to Richard (as Robert continues to be desiring Bertha). Nicholas Fargnoli and Michael Gillespie write about Beatrice: "Although Joyce modelled the other main characters in *Exiles* on recognizable Dublin friends and acquaintances, no critic has suggested an analogue for Beatrice. This absence in itself may account for the woodenness of her actions and attitudes. Joyce does, however, outline attributes of her character in his notes for *Exiles*: "Beatrice's mind is an abandoned cold temple in which hymns have risen heavenward in a distant past but where now a doddering priest offers alone and hopelessly prayers to the Most High" (Fargnoli and Gillespie, 87). "Joyce goes on to articulate the need to keep the image of Beatrice in the minds of the audience during the second act [she appears only in the first], despite the fact that she does not appear on stage then" (Fargnoli and Gillespie, 87). But why? We shall discuss about this later on when we comment on the play.

Archie. He is an eight-year-old son of Richard and Bertha. Archie is modelled on Joyce's son George Joyce.

Brigid. She is an old servant of the Rowan family.

Fishwoman. We meet her only for a little while when both Richard and Robert are reflecting on Bertha and on the possibility of reviving their friendship. She hawks outside Richard's house: "Fresh Dublin Bay herrings!..." and goes away. The herring signifies Bertha—the red hering. The Fishwoman's crying is a satirical humour to the scene.

The Theme. The theme is intentionally veiled, foggy, controversial. Perhaps it is Richard Rowan's experiment on faith and freedom, or on carnality and spirituality in conjugal love. But Richard Ellmann, in his *James Joyce*, assures us that the themes of *Exiles* are "return [from exile], friendship, and cuckoldry" (Ellmann, 355-56). And, we may add to all these probable themes two others: doubt and guilt. Richard's "wound" is due to his doubt about what happened in that "secret night" and his sense of guilt is due to his doubting Bertha.

The Plot. On the surface the plot is simple but underneath it is harboured deep complexity of feeling, desire and emotion. Both Richard and Robert loved Beatrice, but Beatrice became more attracted to Richard. Robert then became enamoured of the sexually attractive Bertha whom Richard loved. Richard suddenly eloped with Bertha and reached Rome. There she gave birth to Archie. After more than eight years Richard and his family return to his house in Ireland. Here Bertha's former lover Robert and Richard's former beloved Beatrice meet them. Even in his first meeting Robert, the ("*insomma*" lover as Richard calls him) plants a kiss on Bertha and invites her to meet him in the evening at his cottage. Bertha asks Richard if she should go to Robert's cottage and Richard leaves it to her own judgment.

Bertha arrives at Robert's cottage in the evening. Robert asks her if she loves him. Bertha replies: "I like you, Robert. I think you are good.... Are you satisfied?" Robert kisses her hair and again asks her if she also loves him (besides Richard). Berths returns home late in the night.

When Bertha reached home early morning, Richard tells her that he has been suffering from a deep wound in his soul arising from her stay at Robert's cottage the previous night. Bertha holds his hand still and tells him softly: "Forget me, Dick. Forget me and love me again as you did the first time. I want my lover. To meet him, to go to him, to give myself to him. You Dick. O, my strong wild lover, come back to me again!"

The Scenes. Richard Rowan's house at Merrion (Acts I and III) and Robert.

Hand's cottage at Ranelagh (Act II).

The Time. Summer of 1912 (one afternoon of June to the morning of next day).

Act I

(*The drawing room in Richard Rowan's house at Merrion, a suburb of Dublin.... It is a warm afternoon in June and the room is filled with soft sunlight which is waning.*)

Beatrice Justice, Archie's music teacher, has come to teach Archie a lesson, after a long absence.

"Brigid. The mistress and Master Archie is [sic.] at the bath. They never expected you. Did you send word you were back?

Beatrice. I arrived just now."

Mr. Richard Rowan was in the study writing something. He comes to the drawing room and shakes hands with Beatrice. Brigid brings Italian newspapers from the letterbox [Mr. Rowan, with wife Bertha and son Archie were in Italy for eight years.] and put them on the desk. Beatrice at one point of her conversation with Mr. Richard Rowan asks: "Why do you think I come here?"

"Richard. Why? Many reasons. To give Archie lessons. We have known one another so many years, from childhood, You, Robert and I—haven't we? You have always been interested in me, before I went away and while I was away [in Rome]. Then letters to each other about my book. Now it is published. I am here again. Perhaps you feel that some new thing is gathering in my brain; perhaps you feel that you should know it. Is that the reason?

Beatrice. No."

Richard knows that Beatrice loves Robert Hand, a journalist, though she has yet some love for himself. Richard asks her: "Do you love him [Robert] still?"

"Beatrice. I do not even know.

Richard. It was that that made me so reserved with you—then—even though I felt your interest in me, even though I felt that I too was something in your life.

Beatrice. You were.

Richard. Yet that separated me from you. I was a third person I felt. Your names were spoken together, Robert and Beatrice, as long as I can remember. It seemed to me, to everyone....

Beatrice. We were first cousins. It is not strange that we were often together."

Beatrice argued that her relation with Robert then was merely childish, that she was then a child. Richard rebutted: "[*Smiles maliciously*.] A child? Are you sure? It was in the garden of his mother's house. No? [*He points towards the garden*.] Over there. You plighted your troth, as they say, with a kiss. And you gave him your garter. Is it allowed to mention that?"

Richard tells her that when, in Rome, he got her first letter he understood that she was a changed woman due to his going away (to Rome). On the other hand, as she changed, says Beatrice, Robert also changed. Beatrice tells him that since then she was "near to death" and that "It made me see things differently." She also fell ill but now is convalescent. She now thinks that she could find peace in some convent. Richard tells her that she could not find peace there but could find it if she could give herself to Robert "freely and wholly."

> "Beatrice. [*Looking at him*.] I would try.
>
> Richard. You would try, yes. You were drawn to him as your mind was drawn towards mine. You held back from him. From me, too, in a different way. You cannot give yourself freely and wholly.
>
> Beatrice. [*Joints her hands softly*.] It is a terribly hard thing to do, Mr. Rowan—to give oneself freely and wholly—and be happy."

Richard saw her heart was as hard as his mother's. Before her death his mother had sent for him but he did not meet her. Richard tells Beatrice that his present sufferance is perhaps a punishment of his disobedience. He tells her his mother also turned away from his wife Bertha and his son Archie.

> "Richard. She drove me away. On account of her I lived years in exile and poverty too, or near it. I never accepted the doles she sent me through the bank. I waited, too, not for her death but for some understanding of me, her own son, her own flesh and blood; that never came.
>
> Beatrice. Not even after Archie...?
>
> Richard. [Rudely.] My son, you think? A child of sin and shame!.... There were tongues here ready to tell her

> all, to embitter her withering mind still more against me and Bertha and our godless nameless child...."

Richard says his father was different: he loved him all right. On the day his father died, he knew that Richard wanted "to go to the theatre to hear *Carmen*." His father gave him a shilling. He kissed his father and went out. Richard said it was "something sweet and noble."

Suddenly, a knock is heard. Richard is apprehensive it must be his old mother's spirit, then suspects it is Robert Hand, not Bertha, because she has a key.

> "Richard. O, probably Robert. I am going out through the garden. I cannot see him now.
>
> Say I have gone to the post. Goodbye."

Richard goes out telling Beatrice to ask Robert to wait. Brigid enters and after a few seconds Brigid and Robert Hand come in. Robert, with a "large bunch of red roses", advances towards Beatrice "*with outstretched hand which she takes*" and addresses her as "My dear coz." "I brought them to the mistress of the house. [Critically.] I am afraid they are not mine.

> "Brigid. O, they are lovely, sir. The mistress will be delighted with them.
>
> Robert. [lays the roses carelessly on a chair out of sight.] Is nobody in?
>
> Brigid. Yes, sir. Sit down, sir. They'll be here now any moment. The master was here."

[*A noise is heard at the window and a boy's voice is heard calling, 'Mr. Hand!' Robert turns.*] Archie enters and Beatrice welcomes him. Archie advances towards Robert.

> "Archie. [*Shakes hands.*] Good evening. We saw you on the top of the tram, and I shouted *Mr. Hand*! But you did not see me. But we saw you, mamma and I. She will be here in a minute. I ran."

Beatrice talked with the unwilling Archie about music [piano] lessons and asked him to study now after a long gap of ten days. Then Robert talks with him.

"Robert. Were you at the bath?

Archie. Yes.

Robert. Are you a good swimmer now?

Archie. [*Leans against the davenport*.] No. Mamma won't let me into the deep place.

Can you swim well, Mr. Hand?

Robert. Splendidly. Like a stone.

Archie. [*Laughs*.] Like a stone! [*Pointing down*.] Down that way?

Robert. [*Pointing*.] Yes, down; strait down. How do you say that over in Italy?

Archie. That? *Giu*. [*Pointing down and up*.] That is *giu* and this is *su*. Do you want to speak to my pappie?

Robert. Yes I came to see him.

Archie. [*Going towards the study*.] I will tell him. He is there, writing.

Beatrice. [*Comely, looking at Robert*.] No, he is out. He is gone to the post with some Letters."

Bertha comes in along with Archie. "Bertha is a young woman of graceful build. She has dark grey eyes, patient in expression, and soft features. Her manner is cordial and self-possessed." Bertha shakes hands with Beatrice. And then with Robert Hand.

"Bertha. [*Bows*.] Good evening, Mr. Hand.

Robert. [*Bowing*.] Good evening, signora!...."

Robert tells (introduces himself to) Bertha that he is a journalist and a first cousin of Beatrice. Bertha insists on Robert to have a cup of tea. Beatrice actually went down to see her father, but Robert light-heartedly explains her absence differently: "She goes there on retreat, when the Protestant strain in her prevails—gloom, seriousness, righteousness." Bertha tells Beatrice that she may give Archie piano lessons but not to fatigue herself and Beatrice and Archie "*go out together by the door on the left*."

Now, Bertha "[*opens a drawer of the davenport, takes out a slip of paper and closes the drawer again. Robert stands watching her.*]"

"Bertha. [*Coming towards him with the paper in her hand.*] You put this into my hand last night. What does it mean?

Robert. Do you not know?

Bertha. [*Reads.*] There is one word which I have never dared to say you. What is the word?

Robert. That I have a deep liking for you.

[*A short pause. A piano is heard faintly from the upper room.*]

Robert. [*Takes the bunch of roses from the chair.*] I brought these for you. Will you take them from me?

Bertha. [*taking them.*] Thank you. [*she lays them on the table and unfolds the paper again.*] Why did you not dare to say it last night?"

Robert explains that he could not say it because "There were too many people on the lawn." Robert tells her that the previous night Bertha seemed to him "like the moon."

"Bertha. [*laughs*] Why like the moon?

Robert. In that dress, with your slim body, walking with little even steps. I saw the moon passing in the dusk till you passed and left my sight."

After a while, Robert sits beside her and asks her: "Are you annoyed with me?"

"Bertha. No.

Robert. I thought you were. You put away my poor flowers so quickly.

Bertha. [*Takes them from the table and holds them close to her face.*] Is this what you wish me to do with them?

Robert. [*Watching her.*] Your face is a flower too—but more beautiful. A wild blowing in a hedge. [*Moving his chair closer to her.*] Why are you smiling? At my words?

Bertha. [*Laying the flowers in her lap.*] I am wondering if that is what you say—to the others.

Robert. [*Surprised.*] What others?

Bertha. The other women. I hear you have so many admirers."

Robert feels offended and says: "Did you not like me to speak to you in that way?"

"Bertha. What you said was very kind. [*She looks at him for a moment.*] Thank you for saying it—and thinking it.

Robert. [*Leaning forward.*] Bertha!

Bertha. Yes?

Robert. I have the right to call you by your name. From old times—nine years ago. We were Bertha—and Robert—then. Can we not be so now, too?

Bertha. [*Readily*] O yes. Why should we not?"

After a while, Bertha tells Robert that she believes that men speak to women eulogizingly and affectionately—lovingly—as Robert does to her. Robert pleads that there are exceptions or at least one exception. He asks her if he is different.

"Bertha. [*Looks into his eyes.*] Different."

Being assured of Bartha's love (or affection) for him, Robert becomes emboldened. "Robert. [Suddenly.] Bertha, may I kiss your hand? Let me. May I?

Bertha. If you wish.

[*He lifts her hand to his lips slowly. She rises suddenly and listens.*]

Bertha hears the sound of the garden gate. Piano also can be heard faintly from the upper room. Bertha starts to go away. Robert urges her not to: "Do not go away. You must never go away now. Your life is here. I came for that too today—to speak to him [Richard]—to urge him to accept this position. [Robert will still love Bertha, though she is now wife to Richard]. He must. And you must persuade him too. You have a great influence over him." Bertha reminds him of what Richard told him last night. Robert tells her that Richard quoted from Our Father ("Our Father" is also called "The Lord's Prayer": "...lead us not to temptation,/ But deliver us from evil;/ etc.") but said that "to take care for the future is to destroy hope and love in the world." Robert tells Bertha that in loving her Richard and he both are mad.

> "Robert. You must not go away. I will not let you.
>
> Bertha. [*Looks full at him.*] You?
>
> Robert. Those eyes must not go away. [*He takes her hands.*] May I kiss your eyes?
>
> Bertha. Do so.
>
> [*He kisses her eyes and then passes his hand over her hair.*]
>
> Robert. Little Bertha!
>
> Bertha. [*Smiling.*] But I am not so little. Why do you call me little?
>
> Robert. Little Bertha! One embrace? [*He puts his arm around her.*] Look into my eyes again.
>
> Bertha. [*Looks.*] I can see the little gold spots. So many you have.
>
> Robert. [*Delighted.*] Your voice! Give me a kiss, a kiss with your mouth.
>
> Bertha. Take it.
>
> Robert. I am afraid. [*He kisses her mouth and passes his hand many times over her hair.*] At last I hold you in my arms!
>
> Bertha. And are you satisfied?
>
> Robert. Let me feel your lips touch mine.
>
> Bertha. And then you will be satisfied?
>
> Robert. [*Murmurs.*] Your lips, Bertha!
>
> Bertha. [*Closes her eyes and kisses him quickly.*] There. [*Puts her hands on his shoulders.*] Why don't you say: thanks?
>
> Robert. [*Sighs.*] My life is finished—over."

Bertha asks him not to speak like that but he turns his deaf ear to her. He presses her to him and says: "To end it all—death. To fall from great high cliff, down, right down into the sea."

Robert does not relent but continues pampering her. Bertha asks him to listen to the music of piano. Robert responds: "Listening to music and in the arms of the woman I love—the sea, music and death."

> "Bertha. [*Looks at him for a moment.*] The woman you love?
>
> Robert. [*Hurriedly.*] I want to speak to you Bertha—alone—not here. Will you come?
>
> Bertha. [*With downcast eyes.*] I too want to speak to you.
>
> Robert. [*Tenderly.*] Yes, dear, I knew. [*He kisses her again.*] I will speak to you; tell you all; Then. I will kiss you, then, long long kisses—when you come to me—long long sweet kisses.
>
> Bertha. Where?
>
> Robert. [*In tone of passion.*] Your eyes. Your lips. All your body.
>
> Bertha. [*Repelling his embrace, confused.*] I meant where do you wish me to come?
>
> Robert. To my house. Not my mother's over there. I will write the address for you. Will you come?
>
> Bertha. When?
>
> Robert. Tonight. Between eight and nine. Come. I will wait for you tonight. And every night. You will?

[*He kisses her with passion, holding her head between his hands. After a few instants she breaks from him. He sits down.*]

> Bertha, [*Listening.*] The gate opened.
>
> Robert. [*Intensely.*] I will wait for you.

[*He takes the slip from the table. Bertha moves away from him slowly. Richard comes in from the garden.*]

> "Richard. [*Advancing, takes off his hat.*] Good afternoon.

Robert. [*Rises, with nervous friendliness.*] Good afternoon.

Bertha. [*At the table, taking the roses.*] Look what lovely roses Mr. Hand brought for me.

Robert. I am afraid they are overblown.

Richard. [*Suddenly.*] Excuse me for a moment, will you?

[*He turns and goes into his study quickly. Robert takes a pencil from his pocket and writes a few words on the slip; then hands it quickly to Bertha.*]

Robert. [*Rapidly.*] The address. Take the tram at Lansdowne Road and ask to be let down near there.

Bertha. [*Takes it.*] I promise nothing.

Robert. I will wait.

[*Richard comes back from the study.*]

Bertha. [*Going.*] I must put these roses in water.

Bertha bows before them (Richard and Robert) and goes out, leaving them to themselves.

Richard. [*After a slight pause.*] Have you any news?

Robert. [*In a different voice.*] Yes. I want to speak to you seriously. Today may be an important day for you—or rather, tonight. I saw the vice chancellor this morning. He has the highest opinion of you, Richard. He has read your book, he said."

Robert tells him that he has a fair chance of getting the "chair of romance literature" (in the university) and that Robert will work for him, as a journalist, might and main. The conversation between Robert and Richard took a sharp turn to an "act of impulse" on the part of Richard, in the past:

"Richard. [*Looks fixedly at him.*] You called it an act of folly, then—nine years ago. You told me I was hanging a weight about my neck.

Robert. I was wrong. [*Suavely.*] Here is how the matter stands, Richard. Everyone knows that you ran away years ago with a young girl.... How shall I put it?... With

> a young girl!... How shall I put it?... With a young girl! Not exactly your equal. [Kindly.] Excuse me, Richard, that is not my opinion, not my language. I am simply using the language of people whose opinions I don't share."

Richard asks him if he (through his journalism) can spread the rumour—the opinion of the people (about his elopement with Bertha). Robert replies: "I will. God help me." Robert further tells him: "Not only for your sake. Also for the sake of—your present partner in life. [Bertha]" Richard leans forward and questions Robert:

> "Richard. Why for her sake?
>
> Robert. [*Also leans forward, quietly.*] Richard, have you been quite fair to her? It was her own free choice, you will say. But was she really free to choose? She was a mere girl. She accepted all that you proposed."

They drink whisky. Robert, during their drinking, recalls and tells about an event—an event of "old times"—in which the participants behaved wildly. With loving memories, Robert interjects: "Lord, when I think of our wild nights long ago—talks by the hour, plans, carouses, revelry...." It was in the house of Robert, which earlier belonged to Richard.

> "Richard. It was not only a house of revelry; it was to be the hearth of a new life. [*Musing.*] And in that name all our sins were committed.
>
> Robert. Sins! Drinking and blasphemy [*he points.*] by me. And drinking and heresy, much worse, [*he points again.*] by you—are those the sins you mean?
>
> Richard. And some others.
>
> Robert. [*Lightly, uneasily.*] You mean the women. I have no remorse of conscience. May be you have. We had two keys on those occasions. [*Maliciously.*] Have you?
>
> Richard. [*Irritated.*] For you it was all quite natural?
>
> Robert. For me it is quite natural to kiss a woman whom I like. Why not? She is beautiful for me."

Richard asks him if he kisses everything that is beautiful. Robert says he does. Even a beautiful stone. He tells that "A kiss is an act of homage." Richard goes further and says that "It is an act of union between man and woman." He asks Robert: "Even if we are often led to desire through the sense of beauty can you say that the beautiful is what we desire?" Robert says to think about this question will give him headache. He raises the other question: "What is the most attractive in even the most beautiful woman?" And he answers his own question: "Not those qualities which she has and other women have not but the qualities which she has in common with them. I mean... the commonest."

After a while, Robert veered the conversation to a different direction. He informed Richard that the vice-chancellor has invited him tonight to a dinner in his house. The invitation, says Robert, has been extended to Richard through himself. Richard jocularly says that he can almost see his statue installed a hundred years afterwards. Robert also humorously says that statues are of two kinds: one kind asks, "*How shall I get down*?"; the other kind says, "*In my time the dunghill was so high*."

They drink once again. Robert tells Richard as if to toast: "Then to yourself, the way you loll on that lounge: then your boy's voice and also—Bertha herself. Do you allow me to call her that, Richard? I mean as an old friend of both of you." Richard has no objection: "O why not?" Robert with animation, tells Richard: "You have that fierce indignation which lacerated the heart of Swift. You have fallen from a higher world, Richard, and you are filled with fierce indignation, when you find that life is cowardly and ignoble." And he says of himself, archly: "I have come up from a lower world and I am filled with astonishment when I find that people have any redeeming virtue at all." But Robert bears no grudge against Richard, on that account. He tells Richard: "I fought for you all the time you were away. I fought to bring you back. I fought your place for you here. I will fight for you still because I have faith in you, the faith of a disciple in his master.... It may seem strange to you...." Richard, in turn tells him: "There is a faith still stranger than the faith of the disciple in his master." And he explains such a faith thus: "The faith of a master in the disciple who will betray him." Robert responds: "The church lost a theologian in you, Richard. But I think you look too deeply into life.... Be gay. Life is not worth it."

Archie and Beatrice come in. Robert tells her that he has own over Richard. Beatrice Justice is about to depart. Bertha enters with a bowl of roses. Robert informs Beatrice that "Richard is coming tonight to the vice-chancellor's dinner." As Richard Rowan meets them, Robert offers him his hand, saying: "Good afternoon, Richard. We shall meet tonight." Richard touches his hand, slyly saying: "At Philippi [Philippi was that city in Greece where in 42 B.C. Antony and Octavia fought against Brutus and Longinus and won].

> "Beatrice. [*Shakes hands also*.] Accept my best wishes, Mr. Rawan.
>
> Richard. Thanks. But do not believe him.
>
> Robert. [*Vivaciously*.] Believe me, believe me. [*To Bertha*.] Good afternoon, Mrs. Rowan." (Bertha sees Robert off.)

Richard teaches Archie the difference between giving and robbing. He says: "When you have a thing it can be taken from you." Further, says Richard: "But when you give it, you have given it. No robber can take it from you. [*He bends his head and presses his son's hand against his cheek*.] It is yours then for ever when you have given it. It will be your always. That is to give." At this moment, Bertha enters, fingering the petals of the roses that Robert gave her.

> "Richard. [*Watching her*.] Well?
>
> Bertha. [*Absently*.] Well. He says he likes me.
>
> Richard. [*Leans his chin in his hand*.] You showed him his note?
>
> Bertha. Yes. I asked him what it meant.
>
> Richard. What did he say it meant?"

Bertha frankly and unreservedly tells him what Robert told her and what he asked her to do and what he did with her.

Robert told her that he loved her always but more after she came back, and "He said I was like the moon in this lavender dress." And Robert, with her consent, held her hand and, without waiting for consent, put his arm around her. And then he said her eyes were beautiful and asked if he could kiss them and then, with her consent, did it. Now Bertha wants to know Richards's reaction to what went between herself and Robert. Bertha asks: "Tell me, Dick, does all this disturb you? Because I told you I don't want that. I think you are only pretending you don't mind. I don't mind."

"Richard. [*Quietly.*] I know, dear. But I want to find out what he means or feels just as you do."

Bertha is now somewhat irritated after this cascade of enquiries. She says everything has been told but yet Richard does not relent: "And then?"

> "Bertha. He asked for a kiss. I said: *Take it.*
>
> Richard. And then?
>
> Bertha. [*Crumpling a handful of petals.*] He kissed me.
>
> Richard. Your mouth?
>
> Bertha. Once or twice.
>
> Richard. Long kisses?
>
> Bertha. Fairly long. [*Reflects.*] Yes, the last time.
>
> Richard. [*Rubs his hands slowly; then.*] With his lips? Or...the other way?
>
> Bertha. Yes, the last time.
>
> Richard. Did he ask you to kiss him?
>
> Bertha. He did.
>
> Richard. Did you?
>
> Bertha. [*Hesitates, then looking straight at him.*] I did. I kissed him.
>
> Richard. What way?
>
> Bertha. [*With a shrug.*] O simply.
>
> Richard. Were you excited?

Bertha. Well, you can imagine. [*Frowning suddenly.*] Not much. He has not nice lips... Still I was excited, of course. But not like you, Dick.

Richard. Was he?

Bertha. Excited? Yes, I think he was. He sighed. He dreadfully nervous.

Richard. [*Resting his forehead on his hand.*] I see.

Bertha. [*Crosses towards the lounge and stands near him.*] Are you jealous?

Richard. [*As before.*] No.

Bertha. [*Quietly.*] You are, Dick.

Richard. I am not. Jealous of what?

Bertha. Because he kissed me.

Richard. [*Looks up.*] Is that all?

Bertha. Yes, that's all. Except that he asked me would I meet him.

Richard. Out somewhere?

Bertha. No. In his house."

Bertha gives him the address slip that Robert gave her and now Richard recognizes the house. Richard tells her that previously the house belonged to him but at present it is Robert's. Richard tells her that it is the house "Where we used to hold our wild nights, talking, drinking, planning—at that time. Wild nights; yes. He [Robert] and I together.... And sometimes alone. [*Stares at her.*] But not quite alone. I told you. You remember?" Bertha is shocked. Richard asks her when Robert asked her to meet him and what answer she did give him.

"Bertha. No answer. He said he would wait.

Richard. Tonight?

Bertha. Every night, he said. Between eight and nine.

Richard. And so I am to go tonight to interview—the professor. About the appointment I am to beg for. [*Looking at her.*] The interview is arranged for tonight by him [Robert]—between eight and nine. Curious, isn't it? The same hour."

The evil scheme of Robert soon appears clear before Richard's mind's eye.

> "Richard. [*Striding to and fro.*] A liar, a thief, a fool! Quite clear! A common thief! What else? [*With harsh laugh.*] My great friend! A patriot too! A thief—nothing else! [*He halts, thrusting his hands into his pockets.*] But a fool also!
>
> Bertha. [*Looking at him.*] What are you going to do?
>
> Richard. [*Shortly.*] Follow him. Find him. Tell him. [*Calmly.*] A few words will do. Thief and fool.
>
> Bertha. [*Flings the slip on the couch.*] I see it all!
>
> Richard. [*Turning.*] Eh!
>
> Bertha. [*Hotly.*] The work of a devil.
>
> Richard. He?
>
> Bertha. [*Turning on him.*] No, you! The work of a devil to turn him against me as you tried to turn my own child against me. Only you did not succeed.
>
> Richard. How? In God's name, how?"

Bertha now angrily accuses Richard of spoiling their son, Archie, giving him liberty and, at the same time curbing her disciplinary action on Archie. As a result of this, Bertha tells him, Archie took herself to be a cruel mother and him as a loving father. Though Richard denies the accusation, Bertha escalates her charging: "Because you never loved your own mother. A mother is always a mother, no matter what. I never heard of any human being that did not love the mother that brought him into the world, except you." Then Bertha tells Richard that it was she who taught Archie to love his father. She inculpates him of turning everyone against herself, taking the advantage of her "simplicity."

> Richard. [*Violently.*] And you have the courage to say that to me?
>
> Bertha. [*Facing him.*] Yes, I have! Both then and now. Because I am simple you think you can do what you like with me. [*Gesticulating.*] Follow him [Robert] now.

Call him names. Make him be humble before you and make him despise me. Follow him!

Richard. [*Controlling himself.*] You forget that I have allowed you complete liberty—and allow it still.

Bertha. [*Scornfully.*] Liberty!

Richard. Yes, complete. But he must know that I know. [*More calmly.*] I will speak to him [Robert] quietly. [*Appealing.*] Bertha, believe me, dear! It is not jealousy. You have complete liberty to do as you wish—you and he. But not in this way. He will not despise you. You don't wish to deceive me or to pretend to deceive me—with him, do you?

Bertha. No, I do not. [*Looking full at him.*] Which of us two is the deceiver?

Richard. Of us? You and me?

Bertha. [*In a calm decided tone.*] I know why you have allowed me what you call complete liberty.

Richard. Why?

Bertha. To have complete liberty with—that girl [Beatrice].

Richard. [*Irritated.*] But, good God, you know about that this long time. I never did it.

Bertha. You did. I thought it was a kind of friendship between you—till we came back, and then I saw."

Bertha produces further evidences in support of the close relationship between Richard and Beatrice. She tells Richard that he gives her "complete liberty" in order to enjoy "complete liberty" with that girl (Beatrice). And she tells him that he writes "things" about her, sitting up at night. She asks: "You call that friendship?" Bertha does not stop there. She charges him: "And that is why you allow him [Robert] to go on. Of course! It does not affect you. You love her."

Richard denies he loves Beatrice but she will not believe his word. She accuses him of hypocrisy: "You, who talk so much of the high kind of feeling you have for me, expressing yourself in that way to another woman. If he [Robert] did it, or other men, I could understand because they are all false pretenders. But you, Dick! Why do you not tell him [Robert] then [about Richard's affairs with Beatrice]? Unlike Richard, Bertha says, Robert "is honest in his own way." She repeats her objection to Richard's writing "long letters to her [Beatrice] for years." She had not understood this earlier but only after she came here (at Richard's house at Merrion).

Richard tells her that she does not understand the thing. Bertha sarcastically carps at him: "Neither he [Robert] nor I can understand it. Only she [Beatrice] can. Because it is such a deep thing!" With bitterness Bertha calls Beatrice "The diseased woman!"

> "Richard. [*Gravely.*] Bertha, take care of uttering words like that!
>
> Bertha. [*Turning, excitedly.*] I don't mean any harm! I feel for her more than you can because I am a woman. I do, sincerely. But what I say is true."

Bertha comes nearer to Richard and somewhat advisingly tells him: "You have given that woman very much, Dick. And she may be worthy of it. And she may understand it all, too. I know she is that kind." Bertha, again, counsels him: "But I believe you will get very little from her in return—or from any of her clan. Remember my words, Dick. Because she is not generous and they are not generous. Is it all wrong what I am saying? Is it?" Richard demurely agrees: "No. Not at all."

Brigid reports that tea is ready. Bertha asks her to call Archie in from the garden. Bertha takes the slip of address of Robert and asks Richard:

> "Bertha. Am I to go to this place?
>
> Richard. Do you want to go?
>
> Bertha. I want to find out what he means. Am I to go?
>
> Richard. Why do you ask me? Decide yourself.
>
> Bertha. Do you tell me to go?
>
> Richard. No.
>
> Bertha. Do you forbid me to go? Richard. No."

Brigid calls in the garden: "Come quickly, Master Archie!"

Bertha. Tell me not to go and I will not.

Richard. [*Without looking at her.*] Decide yourself.

Bertha. Will you blame me then?

Richard. [*Excitedly.*] No, no! I will not blame you. You are free. I cannot blame you.

Bertha. I did not deceive you.

Bertha goes out. Richard remains standing. Archie runs down to Richard. Richard "*puts his arm round his son's shoulders and looks down at him fondly.*"

Act II

(*A room in Robert Hand's cottage at Ranelagh.... It is evening of the same day.*)

[*Robert Hand, in evening dress, is seated at the piano. The candles are not lit but the lamp on the table is lit. He plays softly in the bass the first bars of Wolfram's [Wolfram is a musical group] song in the last act of "Tannhauser".... He sits down on a chair near the table and, smoothing his hair carefully, sighs once or twice.... A knock is heard at the street door. He rises quickly.*]

[*Tannhauser* is an opera by Richard Wagner, divided into three acts and based on the fight between pure and carnal love. Tannhauser was a 13th century German minnesinger who sought papal absolution after years spent in revelry with Venus.]

Robert goes out and, expecting Bertha, exclaims: "Bertha!" But it is not Bertha; it is Richard. After a few moments they enter the room.

"Robert. [*Pulling round a chair.*] Here you are. You are lucky to find me.... I was just wondering how you and the vice-chancellor were getting on together. [*With exaggerated alarm.*] But are you going in that suit? O well, it doesn't make much odds, I suppose. But how goes the time? [*He takes out his watch.*] Twenty past eight already, I declare!

Richard. Have you an appointment?

Robert. [*Laughs nervously.*] Suspicious to the last!

Richard. Then I may sit down?

Robert. Of course, of course. [*They both sit down.*] For a few minutes, anyhow.... Twenty past eight, yes.

Richard. [*Wearily, sadly.*] Your appointment also was for the same hour. Here.

Robert. What appointment?

Richard. With Bertha.

Robert. [*Stares at him.*] Are you mad?

Richard. Are you?

Robert. [*After a long pause.*] Who told you?

Richard. She."

Robert tells Richard that he feels greatly relieved on Richard's coming here and that he was thinking about how to break the news (of his relation with Bertha) and also that he was thinking of writing to him about that news. But Richard tells him that he knows everything since the affair between him (Robert) and Bertha began. Caught inescapably by Richard, Robert now admits his mistakes.

"Robert. [*Again rapidly.*] Yes, I was mad. But it was merely lightheartedness. I admit to have asked her here this evening was a mistake. I can explain everything to you. And I will. Truly.

Richard. Explain to me what is the word you longed and never dared to say to her. If you can or will.

Robert. [*Looks down, then raises his head.*] Yes. I will. I admire very much the personality of your...of your... your wife. That is the word. I can say it. It is no secret.

Richard. Then why did you wish to keep secret your wooing?

Robert. Wooing?

Richard. Your advances to her, little by little, day after day, looks, whispers. [*With a nervous movement of the hands.*] *Insomma*, wooing.

Robert. [*Bewildered.*] But how do you know all this?

Richard. She told me.

Robert. This afternoon?"

Richard told Robert that he was watching him and Robert asks Richard if he therefore hates him. Richard does not answer. Then Robert says that Richard definitely hates him. Richard says he felt very sad at the sight of that "great mass of overblown roses." Robert asks him if Richard felt sad because the roses were "too old or common?" Richard this time also gives no answer but only says, "The whole thing made me sad all at once." Robert muses that what Richard is hinting at is real—it is happening. But he tells Richard something different:

"Robert. And she, too, was trying me; making an experiment with me for your sake!

Richard. You know women better than I do. She says she felt pity for you.

Robert. [*Brooding.*] Pitied me, because I am no longer... an ideal lover. Like my roses. Common, old.

Richard. Like all men you have a foolish wandering heart."

In a tone like that of a counselor, Richard tells Robert that at their age what Robert is doing is not acceptable. Friendship is allowable or desirable throughout long life, but not love-making, and never "like thieves—at night." Robert confesses that he is now relieved because "the danger is passed." He explains. If Richard would not notice his wooing of Bertha and would not counsel him like this ignoring everything, "it might have been too late while it is not too late now."

Richard tells Robert, slyly hinting, or referring to, his night rendezvous with Bertha, that he could not take her either stealing by night or using violence: "Steal you could not in my house because the doors were open: nor take by violence if there were no resistance." In response, Robert pontificates: "You forget that the kingdom of heaven suffers violence: and the kingdom of heaven is like a woman." Robert tells Richard that the heavenly kingdom of a woman cannot be had with the aid of violence. He goes further and tells Richard about Bertha: "You love this woman. I remember all you told me long ago. She is yours, your work. [*Suddenly*.] And that is why I, too, was drawn to her. You are so strong that you attract me even through her."

Robert tells Richard that he is "the incarnation of strength". But it is not physical strength; it is a strength of another kind. When a man feels an intense passion for a woman, he wants to possess her, if need arise even brutally, bestially. But, he asks Richard, "But if you love.... What else is it?" Richard votes for Robert's implied answer embedded in his question: "To wish her well." Richard says never a man and a woman can be both physically and mentally united, such that one will feel with the other's body, and think with the other's brain. However, Richard suddenly asks Robert to go to Bertha: "Go away. You, and not I, would be necessary to her. Alone as I was before I met her." Robert comments: "A nice little load on my conscience!" Whatever Robert has done with Bertha, so far, has not actually corrupted him. He wishes that on the last day of the world when men will assemble together before the Almighty, "We will say that we lived chastely with one other creature...." Or, says he, "Or that we tried to." But in the same breath, he tells Richard what the Almighty will tell them: "And He will say to us: Fools! Who told you that you were to give yourselves to one being only? You were made to give yourselves to many freely. I wrote that law with My finger on your hearts."

Robert says that union between men and women must end in bodily union and that by the law of the Almighty, like men, women are also required to give themselves to many freely. Robert tells Richard: "...a woman, too, has the right to try with many men until she finds love. An immoral idea, is it not? I wanted to write a book about it. I began it..."

> "Robert. Because I knew a woman who seemed to me to be doing that—carrying out the idea in her own life. She interested me very much.
>
> Richard. When was this?"

Robert tells Richard that the experience he got when he was away. Robert says the woman was a stock broker's wife whom he knew intimately. Abruptly he asks Richard if he has never had such an experience—if he has ever betrayed a woman, not in love but carnally. Richard simply says that he has fully opened his character before his wife, Bertha.

> "Richard. I tried to give her a new life.
>
> Robert. And you have. A new and rich life."

Robert tells Richard: "And of course, Richard, I felt and knew all the time that you were a man of great talent—of something more than talent. And that was your excuse—a valid one in my eyes." Richard, in his turn tells him: "Have you thought that it is perhaps now—at this moment—that I am neglecting her?... I may be silent still. And she may yield to you at last—wholly and many times."

> "Robert. [*Draws back at once.*] My dear Richard, my dear friend, I swear to you I could not make you suffer.
>
> Richard. [*Continuing.*] You may then know in soul and body, in a hundred forms, ever restlessly, what some old theologian, Dun Scotus, I think, called a death of the spirit.
>
> Robert. [*Eagerly.*] A death. No; its affirmation! A death! The supreme instant of life from which all coming life proceeds, the eternal law of nature herself."

Richard regrets that he has maltreated Bertha's body and so he has a compunction for her and so also he has a moral fear. He tells Robert: "She is dead. She lies on my bed. I look at her body which I betrayed—grossly and many times. And loved, too, and wept over. And I know that her body was always my loyal slave. To me, to me only she gave.... [*He breaks off and turns aside, unable to speak.*]

> "Robert. [*Softly.*] Do not suffer, Richard. There is no need. She is loyal to you, body and soul. Why do you fear?
>
> Richard. [*Turns towards him, almost fiercely.*] Not that fear. But that I will reproach myself then for having

> taken all for myself because I would not suffer her to give to another what was hers and not mine to give, because I accepted from her loyalty and made her life poorer in love. That is my fear."

A moment afterwards, Richard told Robert of his feeling that they two are united in brotherhood, and friendship, and so not to cheat him.

> "Richard. [*Struggling with himself.*] I told you that I wished you not to do anything false and secret against me—against our friendship, against her; not to steal her from me craftily, secretly, meanly—in the dark, in the night—you Robert, my friend.
>
> Robert. I know. And it was noble of you.
>
> Richard. [*Looks up at him with a steady gaze.*] No. Not noble. Ignoble.
>
> Robert. [*Makes an involuntary gesture.*] How? Why?
>
> Richard. [*Looks away again: in a lower voice.*] That is what I must tell you too. Because in the core of my ignoble heart I longed to be betrayed by you and by her—in the dark, in the night—secretly, meanly, craftily. By you, my best friend, and by her. I longed for that passionately and ignobly, to be dishonoured for ever in love and in lust, to be...."

After this Richard tells Robert that he wants "to build up my soul again out of the ruins of its shame." Richard tells him about Bertha and himself: "She has spoken always of her innocence, as I have spoken always of my guilt, humbling me." Robert asks if he has humbly spoken of his guilt out of pride. And Richard mystically and mystifyingly replies: "From pride and from ignoble longing. And from a motive deeper still." Robert understands the mystery: "I understand you." Richard asks Robert to free themselves from both morality and from the bond of friendship between them. Richard confesses that so far he has acted secretly in the dark but will do no more. Robert reminds Richard that in his youth Richard believed that "The blinding instant of passion alone—passion, free, unashamed, irresistible—that is the only gate by which we can escape from the misery of what slaves call life." Robert tells him that "She [Bertha] and I [Robert] have only obeyed your will. And he asks for Richard's permission: "Shall we? Freely? Together?" Richard [*mastering his emotion.*] Together no. Fight your part alone. I will not free you. Leave me to fight mine."

A knock at the hall door is heard. Both recognise it is Bertha. Robert says: "Richard, I appeal to you.... She is yours. Keep her and forgive me, both of you." Robert goes out. Bertha enters. (Robert goes to the garden.)

Richard welcomes her: "Welcome back to old Ireland!" He tells her: "I told him [Robert] I knew everything, that I had known for a long time. He asked how. I said from you." Bertha tells him that Robert hates her, and that rightly: "He hates me. He is right to hate me. I have treated him badly, shamefully." Richard is not happy with this response: "What a fool you were to tell me! It would have been so nice if you had kept it secret."

Bertha veers the conversation to another direction. She asks if Richard is going to meet Beatrice Justice to "have an intellectual conversation!" Richard expresses his hatred for her: "To meet the devil's father!" To counter this, Bertha says that Richard has no respect for her but Beatrice has as Robert, too, has. Bertha charges him: "Great respect for me she has! Why did you not ask her to come away with you nine years ago?" Bertha tells Richard that in spite of everything that has happened, she still has trust in him. But she grumbles that Richard did not defend her against Robert. Obsequiously she asks Richard: "Dick, my God, tell me what you wish me to do?" Richard is overly delighted at this sweet entreaty of Bertha and tells her: "I have a wild delight in my soul, Bertha, as I look at you. I see as you are yourself.... You may be his more than mine."

> "Bertha. I am not. Only I feel for him, too.
>
> Richard. And I do too. You may be his and mine. I will trust you, Bertha, and him too. I must. ...You have drawn us together.... Bertha, love him, be his, give yourself to him if you desire—or if you can.
>
> Bertha. [*Dreamily.*] I will remain."

Richard departs, saying "Goodbye" to Bertha. Bertha remains sitting.

Bertha calls out: "Is anyone out there?" Robert comes away from the garden. Bertha discovers him: "Robert!" and Robert asks her if Richard told her that he was waiting in the garden for her. She says, he did.

> "Bertha. [*Looks down.*] Do you hate me now?
>
> Robert. I fear you. [*Clasping his hands at his back, quietly but a little defiantly.*] I fear a new torture—a new trap.
>
> Bertha. [*As before.*] For what do you blame me?
>
> Robert. [*Comes forward a few steps, halts: then impulsively.*] Why did you lead me on? Day after day, more and more Why did you not stop me?... Did you want me to?"

Robert asks her if she has told Richard everything. Bertha tells him she did. Robert, with an effort smiling, tells her: "I see. You were making an experiment for his sake. On me. Well, why not? It seems I was a good subject. Still, it was a little cruel of you." Bertha notices Robert's clothes are drenched with rain water and asks him to change and put on the clothes he earlier left in the room. Robert changes and lights a lamp of pink colour.

> Robert. [...] Do you like the effect of the light?
>
> Bertha. O, yes.
>
> Robert. Can you admire it from where you are?
>
> Bertha. Yes, quite well.
>
> Robert. It was for you.
>
> Bertha. [*Confused.*] I am not worthy even of that.
>
> Robert. Love's labour lost."

Bertha is afraid of something and is trembling. Robert holds her and asks if it has passed.

> "Bertha. Now you are here. I can see you. Now it has past.

Robert. [*With resignation.*] Passed. Yes. Love's labour lost.

Bertha. [*Looks up at him.*] Listen, Robert. I want to explain to you about that. I could not deceive Dick. Never. In nothing. I told him everything—from the first. Then it went on and on; and still you never spoke or asked me. I wanted you to."

Robert asks if she has divulged everything to Richard, including their kissing episodes. Bertha replies: "of course. I told him all."

"Robert. [*Shakes his head slowly.*] Extraordinary little person! Were you not ashamed?

Bertha. No.

Robert. Not a bit?

Bertha. No. Why? Is that terrible?

Robert. And how did he take it? Tell me. I want to know everything.

Bertha. [*Laughs.*] It excited him. More than usual.

Robert. Why? Is he excitable—still?

Bertha. [*Archly.*] Yes, very. When he is not lost in his philosophy."

Robert asks Bertha if she is angry with him for asking her to be here. Bertha says, no. Robert tells her that Richard already told him about all things touching them.

"Bertha. I try to forget it.

Robert. It does not trouble you?

Bertha. Not now. Only I dislike to think of it.

Robert. It is merely something brutal, you think? Of little importance?

Bertha. It does not trouble me—now."

A moment afterwards Robert turns towards her and asks: "If it were not only something brutal with this person or that—for a few moments. If it were something fine and spiritual—with one person only—with one woman. [*Smiles.*] And perhaps brutal too.... Would you try to forget and forgive that?" Bertha produces no direct answer but tells him to let Richard to be free as Richard leaves her to be free. Robert reminds her that Richard gave her freedom nine years ago. Bertha, slightly miffed, asks him: "But why do you ask me such a lot of questions, Robert?"

> "Robert. [*Stretches out both hands to her.*] Because I had another gift to offer you—a common simple gift—like myself. If you want to know it I will tell you.
>
> Bertha. [*Looking at her watch.*] Past is past, Robert. And I think I ought to go now. It is nine almost."

Robert persuades her to stay because he has one more confession (besides that he loves her) to make. Bertha says: "You need not confess any more tonight." Robert unrelentingly says that she "slighted" his (first) gift—the gift of being his beloved—and thus "condemned" him to his present life. Bertha is astonished. Robert tells her: "Yes when you slighted the common simple gift I had to offer you—and took his gift instead." It was then, Robert confesses, that he did a treason against Richard. Robert explains the treason: "I advised him to go alone [to Italy]—not to take you with him—to live alone in order to see if what he felt for you was a passing thing which might ruin your happiness and his career."

> "Bertha. Well, Robert. It was unkind of you towards me. But I forgive you because you were thinking of his happiness and mine.
>
> Robert. [*Bending closer to her.*] No, Bertha. I was not. And that was my treason. I was thinking of myself—that you might turn from him when he had gone and he from you. Then I would have offered you my gift. You know what it was now. The simple common gift that men offer to women. Not the best perhaps. Best or worst—it would have been yours."

Bertha now asks Robert: "Why did you not forget me?" In the same manner Robert asks her: "But why did you choose him? Did you not like me at all?" Bertha tells him: "Yes, I liked you because you were his friend."

Robert apostrophizes: "Nine years. Nine times more beautiful!"

Bertha. [*Smiling.*] But am I? What do you see in me?

Robert. [*Gazing at her.*] A strange and beautiful lady.

Bertha. [*Almost disgusted.*] O, please don't call me such a thing!

Robert. [*Earnestly.*] You are more. A young and beautiful queen."

Bertha. [*With a sudden laugh.*] O, Robert!

Robert. [*Lowering his voice and bending nearer to her.*] But do you not know that you are a beautiful human being? Do you not know that you have a beautiful body? Beautiful and young?

Bertha. [*Gravely.*] Some day I will be old.

Robert. [*Shakes his head.*] I cannot imagine it. Tonight you are young and beautiful. Tonight you have come back to me. [*With passion.*] Who knows what will be tomorrow? I may never see you again or never see you as I do now.

Bertha. Would you suffer?

Robert. [*Looks around the room, without answering.*] This room and this hour were made for your coming. When you have gone—all is gone.

Bertha. [*Anxiously.*] But you will see me again, Robert... as before.

Robert. [*Looks full at her.*] To make him—Richard—suffer.

Bertha. He does not suffer.

Robert. [*Bowing his head.*] Yes, yes. He does.

Bertha. He knows we like each other. Is there any harm, then?

Robert. [*Raising his head.*] No there is no harm.... He has left us alone here at night, at this hour, because he longs to know it [that the two are together here at this time and at this situation]—he longs to be delivered.

Bertha. From what?

Robert. [*Moves closer to her and presses her arms as he speaks.*] From every law, Bertha, from every bond. All his life he has sought to deliver himself. Every chain but one he has broken and that one we are to break. Bertha—you and I.

Bertha. [*Almost inaudibly.*] Are you sure?

Robert. [*Still more warmly.*] I am sure that no law made by man is sacred before the impulse of passion. [*Almost fiercely.*] Who made us for one only? It is a crime against our own being if we are so. There is no law against impulse. Laws are for slaves. Bertha, say my name! Let me hear you voice it. Softly!

Bertha. [*Softly.*] Robert!

Robert. [*Puts his arm about her shoulder.*] Only the impulse towards youth and beauty does not die. [*He points towards the porch.*] Listen!

Bertha. [*In alarm.*] What?

Robert. The rain falling. Summer rain on the earth. Night rain. The darkness and warmth and flood of passion. Tonight the earth is loved—loved and possessed. Her lover's arms around her; and she is silent. Speak, dearest!

Bertha. [*Suddenly leans forward and listens intently.*] Hush! Robert. [*Listening, smiles.*] Nothing. Nobody. We are alone."

A gust of wind blows. The flame of the lamp is down and leaping. The rain is understandably continuing. The room is now drowned in darkness. Robert asks Bertha: "Are you happy? Tell me."

"Bertha. I am going now, Robert. It is very late. Be satisfied.

Robert. [*Caressing her hair.*] Not yet. Not yet. Tell me, do you love me a little?

Bertha. I like you, Robert. I think you are good. [*Half rising.*] Are you satisfied?

Robert. [*Detaining her, kisses her hair.*] Do not go Bertha! There is time still. Do you love me too? I have waited a long time. Do you love us both—him and also me?

Do you, Bertha? The truth! Tell me. Tell me with your eyes. Or speak!

[*She does not answer. In the silence the rain is heard falling.*]

Act III

(*The drawing room of Richard Rowan's house at Merrion.... It is early in the morning of the next day....*)

[Brigid *comes in through the folding doors on the right with a feather broom and duster. She is about to cross but, seeing* Bertha, *she halts suddenly and blesses herself instinctively.*]

"Brigid. Merciful hour, ma'am. You put the heart across me. Why did you get up so early?

Bertha. What time is it?

Brigid. After seven, ma'am. Are you long up?

Bertha. Some time.

Brigid. [*Approaching her.*] Had you a bad dream that you woke?

Bertha. I didn't sleep all night. So I got up to see the sun rise."

Brigid tells her it is a "lovely morning now after all the rain we had. [*Turns round.*] But you must be dead tired, ma'am." Brigid calls out at Master Richard. Bertha tells her that he went out "an hour ago." Brigid suspects that Bertha is fretting about something—about Master Richard. She advises bertha: "Don't be. He was always like that, meandering off by himself somewhere. He is a curious bird, Master Richard, and always was. Sure there isn't a turn in him I don't know. Are you fretting now may be because he does be in there [*pointing to the study.*] half the night at his books? Leave him alone. He will come back to you again. Sure he thinks the sun shines out of your face, ma'am."

"Bertha. [*Sadly*.] That time is gone.

Brigid. [*Confidentially*.] And good cause I have to remember it—that time when he was paying his addresses to you.... Do you know that he used to tell me all about you and nothing to his mother, God rest her soul? Your letters and all.

Bertha. What? My letters to him?

Brigid. [*Delighted*.] Yes... [*Suddenly looks at Bertha*.] Is it crying you are now? Ah, sure, don't cry. There's good times coming still.

Bertha. No, Brigid, that time comes only once in a lifetime. The rest of life is good for nothing except to remember that time."

Brigid will bring her a cup of tea to revive her, but she will first go to wake Archie. A moment afterwards, Archie comes to Bertha, followed by Brigid.

"Archie. [*Comes to her and, putting up his face to be kissed, says*:] Buon giorno [good morning], mamma!

Bertha. [*Kissing him*.] Buon giorno, Archie! [*To Brigid*.] Did you put another vest on him under that one?

Brigid. He wouldn't let me, ma'am.

Archie. I'm not cold, mamma.

Bertha. I said you were to put it on, didn't I?

Archie. But where is the cold?

Bertha. [*Takes a comb from her head and combs his hair back at the side*.] And the sleep is in your eyes still.

Brigid. He went to bed immediately after you went out last night, ma'am.

Archie. You know he is going to let me drive, mamma.

Bertha. [*Replacing the comb in her hair, embraces him suddenly*.] O, what a big man to drive a horse!

Brigid. Well, he's daft on horses, anyhow.

Archie. [*Releasing himself*.] I'll make him go quick. You will see from the window, mamma. With the whip. [*He makes the gestures of cracking a whip, and shouts at the top of his voice.*] *Avanti*! [forward].

Brigid. Beat the poor horse, is it?"

Brigid about to lead Archie to the horse. Bertha cautions him: "Mind yourself, Archie, and don't be long or I won't let you go any more. Archie says good-bye to Bertha: "All right. Look out of the window and you'll see me. Good-bye." Bertha and Brigid look out the window to see Archie.

A knock is heard at the hall door. Bertha tells Brigid: "Say I have just got up." Beatrice Justice enters, with a newspaper.

"Beatrice. [*Advances rapidly.*] Mrs. Rowan, excuse me for coming at such an hour.

Bertha. [*Turns.*] Good morning, Miss Justice. [*She comes towards her.*] Is anything the matter?

Beatrice. [*Nervously.*] I don't know. That is why I wanted to ask you.

Bertha. [*Looks curiously at her.*] You are out of breath. Won't you sit down?

Beatrice. [*Sitting down.*] Thank you.

Bertha. [*Sits opposite her, pointing to her paper.*] Is there something in the paper?

Beatrice. [*Laughing nervously: opens the paper.*] Yes.

Bertha. About Dick?

Beatrice. Yes. Here it is. A long article, a leading article, by my cousin. All his life is here. Do you wish to see it?

Bertha. [*Takes the paper, and opens it.*] Where is it?

Beatrice. In the middle. It is headed: *A Distinguished Irishman.*

Bertha. Is it...for Dick or against him?

Beatrice. [*Warmly.*] O, for him! You can read what he says about Mr. Rowan. And I know that Robert stayed in town very late last night to write it."

Beatrice says Robert returned home in the night long after two. Bertha asks if she (Beatrice) was alarmed at that. Beatrice says in the yester-afternoon Robert told her that Richard had accepted the university position. So she was thinking naturally that Robert's writing would be about this acceptance. Therefore Beatrice was not alarmed about Robert's returning late (because his article would be long, perhaps). Beatrice says the cause of her being alarmed was something else.

> "Beatrice. Only the noise of his valise being pulled along the floor. Then I heard him walking about his room. Whistling softly. And then locking it and trapping it.
>
> Bertha. He is going away!
>
> Beatrice. That is what alarmed me. I feared he had had a quarrel with Mr. Rowan and that his article was an attack.
>
> Bertha. But why should they quarrel? Have you noticed anything between them?
>
> Beatrice. I thought I did. A coldness.
>
> Bertha. Lately?
>
> Beatrice. For some time past."

None of them knows the reason of the suspected quarrel, or coldness, between Robert and Richard. But Beatrice suggests that if there is really a quarrel, or a coldness, between them, then, as a first cousin of Robert Hand, she will suffer in her conscience because when Richard was away, it was she who urged Robert Hand to bring back Richard.

> "Bertha. [*Almost cheerfully.*] It looks as if it was you, Miss Justice, who brought my husband back to Ireland.
>
> Beatrice. I, Mrs. Rowan?
>
> Bertha. Yes, you. By your letters to him and then by speaking to your cousin as you said just now. Do you not think that you are the person who brought him back?
>
> Beatrice. [*Blushing suddenly.*] No. I could not think like that."

Bertha tells Beatrice that of late Richard is heavily engaged in writing, in his study, which he also sometimes uses as bedroom.

They both peep into the study and see his study. Bertha tells her: "it must be about something which has come to his life lately—since we came back to Ireland. Some change." She asks Beatrice if she knows about the change. Beatrice tells her: "If any change has come into his life since he came back you must know and feel it."

"Bertha. You could know it just as well. You are very intimate in this house.

Beatrice. I am not the only person who is intimate here. [*They both look at each other coldly in silence for some moments. Bertha lays aside the paper and sits down on a chair nearer to Beatrice.*]

Bertha. [*Placing her hand on Beatrice's knee.*] So you also hate me, Miss Justice?

Beatrice. Hate you? I?

Bertha. [*Insistently but softly.*] Yes. You know what it means to hate a person?

Beatrice. Why should I hate you? I have never hated anyone.

Bertha. Have you ever loved anyone? [*She puts her hand on Beatrice's wrist.*] Tell me. You have?

Beatrice. [*Also softly.*] Yes. In the past.

Bertha. Not now?

Beatrice. No.

Bertha. Can you say that to me—truly? Look at me.

Beatrice. [*Looks at her.*] Yes, I can. [*A short pause. Bertha withdraws her hand, and turns away her head in some embarrassment.*]

Bertha. You said just now that another person is intimate in this house. You meant your cousin.... Was it he?

Beatrice. Yes.

Bertha. Have you not forgotten him?

Beatrice. [*Quietly.*] I have tried to.

Bertha. [*Clasping her hand.*] You hate me. You think I am happy. If you only knew how wrong you are!

> Beatrice. [*Shakes her head.*] I do not.
>
> Bertha. Happy! When I do not understand anything that he writes, when I cannot help him in any way, when I don't even understand half of what he says to me sometimes! You could and you can. [*Excitedly.*] But I am afraid of him, afraid of both of them. [*She stands up suddenly and goes towards the davenport.*] He must not go away like that. [*She takes a writing pad from the drawer and writes a few lines in great haste.*] No, it is impossible! Is he mad to do such a thing? [*Turning to Beatrice.*] Is he still at home?
>
> Beatrice. [*Watching her in wonder.*] Yes. Have you written to him to ask him to come hear?
>
> Bertha. [*Rises.*] I have. I will send Brigid across with it. Brigid! [*She goes out by the door on the left rapidly.*]
>
> Beatrice. [*Gazing after her instinctively.*] It is true, then!
>
> Beatrice takes the paper from the table and reads. Richard enters from the garden.

Richard stands at the doorway, observing Beatrice for some moments. Then pronounced: "There are demons [*he points out towards the strand*] out there. I heard them jabbering since dawn."

> "Beatrice. [*Starts to her feet.*] Mr. Rowan!
>
> Richard. I assure you. The isle is full of voices. Yours also. *Otherwise I could not see you*, it said. And her voice. But I assure you, they are all demons. I made the sign of the cross upside down and that silenced them.
>
> Beatrice. [*Stammering.*] I came here, Mr. Rowan, so early because...to show you this... Robert wrote it... about you...last night."

Beatrice hands over the newspaper and Richard reads it: "*Death of the Very Reverend Canon Mulhall*. Is that it?" Bertha appears to listen.

> "Richard. [*Turns over a page.*] Yes, here we are! *A Distinguished Irishman.* [*He begins to read in a rather loud hard voice.*] Not the least vital of the problems

which confronts our country is the problem of her attitude towards those of her children who, having left her in her hour of need, have been called back to her now on the eve of her long awaited victory, to her whom in loneliness and exile they have at last learned to love. In exile, we have said, but here we must distinguish. There is an economic and there is a spiritual exile. There are those who left her to seek the bread by which men live and there are others, nay, her most favoured children, who left her to seek in other lands that food of the spirit by which a nation of human beings is sustained in life. Those who recall the intellectual life of Dublin of a decade since will have many memories of Mr. Rowan. Something of that fierce indignation which lacerated the heart....

[*He raises his eyes from the paper and sees Bertha standing in the doorway. Then he lays aside the paper and looks at her. A long silence.*]

Beatrice. [*With an effort.*] You see, Mr. Rowan, your day has dawned at last. Even here. And you see that you have a warm friend in Robert, a friend who understands you.

Richard. Did you notice the little phrase at the beginning: those who left her in her hour of need?

[*He looks searchingly at Bertha, turns and walks into his study, closing the door behind him.*]

Bertha. [*Speaking half to herself.*] I gave up everything for him, religion, family, my own peace. [*She sits down heavily in an armchair*. Beatrice *comes towards her*.]"

After a moment, Bertha divulges to Beatrice her secret sorrow—herself being ignored, belittled, forgotten by Richard, and that in the view of the public: "I am only a thing he got entangled with and my son is—the nice name they give those children. Do you think I am a stone? Do you think I don't see it in their eyes and in their manner when they meet me?" Beatrice asks her if she feels humbled by the people.

"Bertha. [*Haughtily.*] Humble me! I am very proud of myself, if you want to know. What have they ever done for him [Richard]? I made him a man. What are they all in his life? No more than the dirt under his boots! [*She stands up and walks excitedly to and fro.*] He can despise me, too, like the rest of them—now. And you despise me. But you will never humble me, any of you.

Beatrice. Why do you accuse me?

Bertha. [*Going to her impulsively.*] I am in such suffering. Excuse me if I was rude. I want us to be friends. [*She holds out her hands.*] Will you?

Beatrice. [*Taking her hands.*] Gladly.

Bertha. [*Looking at her.*] What lovely long eyelashes you have! And your eyes have such a sad expression!

Beatrice. [*Smiling.*] I see very little with them. They are very weak.

Bertha. But beautiful. [*She embraces her quietly and kisses her. Then withdraws from her a little shyly.* Brigid *comes in from the left.*]"

Brigid reports that she has handed over Bertha's letter ("it") to Robert Hand and that Robert has conveyed no message through her but has told her that he will come here (Richard's house) soon ("after me").

"Beatrice. I will go now, Mrs. Rowan, before he comes.

Bertha. [*Somewhat timidly.*] Then we are friends?

Beatrice. [*In the same tone.*] We will try to be. [*Turning.*] Do you allow me to go out through the garden? I don't want to meet my cousin now.

Bertha. Of course. [*She takes her hand.*] It is so strange that we spoke like this now. But I always wanted to. Did you?

Beatrice. I think I did, too.

Bertha. [*Smiling.*] Even in Rome. When I went out for a walk with Archie I used to think about you, what you were like, because I knew about you from Dick. I used to look at different persons, coming out of churches or going by in carriages, and think that perhaps they were like you. Because Dick told me you were dark.

Beatrice. [*Again nervously.*] Really?

Bertha. [*Pressing her hand.*] Goodbye then—for the present.

Beatrice [*Disengaging her hand.*] Good morning.

Bertha. I will see you to the gate."

Bertha accompanies her through the garden to the gate.

Richard emerges from the study and looks down the garden. Some moments afterwards, Bertha appears and views Richard.

"Bertha. Dick!

Richard. [*Stopping.*] Well?

Bertha. You have not spoken to me.

Richard. I have nothing to say. Have you?

Bertha. Do you not wish to know—about what happened last night?

Richard. That I will never know."

Bertha says that she will tell him the truth as she has done always. But before that she asks him why did he leave her (there in the house of Robert) last night.

"Richard. [*Bitterly.*] In your hour of need.

Bertha. [*Threateningly.*] You urged me to it. Not because you love me. If you loved me or if you knew what love was you would not have left me. For your own sake you urged me to it.

Richard. I did not make myself. I am what I am.

Bertha. To have it always to throw against me. To make me humble before you, as you always did. To be free yourself. [*Pointing towards the garden.*] With her! [Beatrice] And that is your love! Every word you say is false.

Richard. [*Controlling himself.*] It is useless to ask you to listen to me.

Bertha. Listen to you! She is the person for listening. Why would you waste your time with me? Talk to her.

Richard. [*Nods his head.*] I see. You have driven her away from me now, as you drove everyone else from my side—every friend I ever had, every human being that ever tried to approach me. You hate her [Beatrice].

Bertha. [*Warmly.*] No such thing! I think you have made her unhappy as you have made me and as you made your dead mother unhappy and killed her. Woman-killer! That is your name.

Richard. [*Turns to go.*] Arrivederci [goodly until we meet again]!

Bertha. [*Excitedly.*] She is a fine and high character. I like her. She is everything that I am not—in birth and education. You tried to ruin her but you could not. Because she is well able for you—what I am not. And you know it.

Richard. [*Almost shouting.*] What the devil are you talking about her for?

Bertha. [*Clasping her hands.*] O, how I wish I had never met you! How I curse that day!

Richard. [*Bitterly.*] I am in the way, is it? You would like to be free now. You have only to say the word.

Bertha. [*Proudly.*] Whenever you like I am ready.

Richard. So that you could meet your lover—freely?

Bertha. Yes.

Richard. Night after night?

Bertha. [*Gazing before her and speaking with intense passion.*] To meet my lover! [*Holding out her arms before her.*] My lover! Yes! My lover!

[*She bursts suddenly into tears and sinks down on a chair, covering her face with her hands. Richard approaches her slowly and touches on the shoulder.*]

Richard. Bertha! [*She does not answer.*] Bertha, you are free.

Bertha. [*Pushes his hand aside and starts to her feet.*] Don't touch me! You are a stranger to me. You do not understand anything in me—not one thing in my heart or soul. A stranger! I am living with a stranger!"

A knock is heard at the hall door. Bertha dries her eyes with handkerchief. Richard goes to the study. Robert Hand arrives. Robert tells Bertha: "You sent for me." Bertha says she did and questions him: "Are you mad to think of going away like that—without even coming here—without saying anything? Robert tells her that what he had to say he wrote on the paper last night. He means the newspaper that is lying on the table.

"Bertha. And you could write last night!

Robert. [*Shrugs his shoulders.*] I am a well-trained animal. [*He comes closer to her.*] I passed a long wandering night after...in my office, at the vice-chancellor's house, in a nightclub, in the streets, in my room. Your images was always before my eyes, your hand in my hand. Bertha, I will never forget last night. [*He lays his hat on the table and takes her hand.*] Why do you not look at me? May I not touch you?

Bertha. [*Pointing to the study.*] Dick is in there.

Robert. [*Dropping her hand.*] In that case children be good.

Bertha. Where are you going?

Robert. To foreign parts. That is to my cousin, Jack Justice, alias Doggy Justice, in Surrey. He has a nice country place there and the air is mild.

Bertha. Why are you going?"

Robert will not tell her the reason: rather he asks her whether Richard has enquired about what has come to pass. Bertha says that Richard will never be interested to know; and yet she insists on Robert to tell Richard the truth—everything. Robert declines: "I cannot tell him everything."

"Bertha. He [Richard] will believe that you are going away because you are afraid to face him after last night.

Robert. [*After a pause.*] Well, I am not a coward any more than he. I will see him.

Bertha. [*Rises.*] I will call him.

Robert. [*Catching her hands.*] Bertha! What happened last night? What is the truth that I am to tell? [*He gazes earnestly into her eyes.*] Were you mine in that sacred night of love? Or have I dreamed it?

Bertha. Remember your dream of me. You dreamed that I was yours last night.

Robert. And that is the truth—a dream? That is what I am to tell?

Bertha. Yes.

Robert. [*Kisses both her hands.*] Bertha! [*In a softer voice.*] In all my life only that dream is real. I forget the rest. [*He kisses her hands again.*] And now I can tell him the truth. Call him."

Bertha calls Richard and he at once comes from the study.

Richard. [*Calmly.*] I thank you for your kind article about me. Is it true that you have come to say goodbye?

Robert. There is nothing to thank me for, Richard. Now and always I am your friend. Now more than ever before. Do you believe me, Richard?"

There is a long silence. "*A Fisher woman is heard crying out as she posses along the road outside.*" She cries out: "Fresh herrings! Dublin bay herrings!"

"Robert. I failed, Richard. That is the truth. Do you believe me?

Richard. I am listening.

Robert. I failed. She is yours, as she was mine, when you met her first.

Richard. When we met her first, you mean.

Robert. Yes. [*He looks down for some moments.*] Shall I go on?

Richard. Yes.

Robert. She went away. I was left alone—for the second time. I went to the vice-chancellor's house and dined. (...I drank claret cup. I went to my office and wrote my article. Then....

Richard. Then?

Robert. Then I went to a certain nightclub. There were men there—and also women. At least, they looked like women. I danced with one of them. She asked me to see her home. Shall I go on?

Richard. Yes.

Robert. I saw her home in a cab. She lives near Donnybrook. In the cab took place what the subtle Duns Scotus calls a death of the spirit. Shall I go on?

Richard. Yes.

Robert. She wept. She told me she was the divorced wife of a barrister. I offered her a sovereign as she told me she was short of money. She would not take it and wept very much. Then she drank some melissa water from a little bottle which she had in her satchel. I saw her enter her house. Then I walked home. In my room I found that my coat was all stained with the melissa water. I had no luck even with my coats yesterday: that was the second one. The idea came to me then to change my suit and go away by the morning boat. I packed my valise and went to bed. I am going away by the next train to my cousin, Jack Justice, in surrey. Perhaps for a fortnight. Perhaps longer. Are you disgusted?

Richard. Why did you not go by the boat?

Robert. I slept it out.

Richard. You intended to go without saying goodbye—without coming here?"

Robert tells him that he has come because "Bertha sent me a message to come." Robert repeats what he told Richard a few seconds earlier: "I wish you to believe that I failed. That Bertha is yours, now as she was mine years ago, when you—when we—met her first."

> "Robert. Did you hear Bertha return?
>
> Richard. No. I wrote all the night. And thought. [*Pointing to the study.*] In there. Before dawn I went out and walked the strand from end to end.
>
> Robert. [*Shaking his head.*] Suffering. Torturing yourself.
>
> Richard. Hearing voices about me. The voices of those who say they love me.
>
> Robert. [*Points to the door on the right.*] [meaning Bertha] One. And mine?
>
> Richard. Another still.
>
> Robert. [*Smiles and touches his forehead with his forefinger.*] True. My interesting but somewhat melancholy cousin. And what did they tell you?
>
> Richard. They told me to despair.
>
> Robert. A queer way of showing their love, I must say! And you will despair?
>
> Richard. [*Rising.*] No."

A noise is heard at the window—Archie calling out: "Open the window!"

> "Robert. Perhaps, there, Richard, is the freedom we seek—you in one way, I in another. In him and not in us. Perhaps....
>
> Richard. Perhaps...?
>
> Robert. I said perhaps. I would say almost surely if....
>
> Richard. If what?
>
> Robert. [*With a faint smile.*] If he [Archie] were mine.

[*He goes to the window and opens it. Archie scrambles in.*]"

Archie enters and salutes Robert and goes to Richard.

> "Archie. Good morning, Mr. Hand. [*He turns to Richard and kisses him.*] Buon giorno, babbo [*Good morning father*].
>
> Richard. Buon giorno, Archie."

Archie tells Richard that he drove the horse to Booterstown and so he is very hungry. Robert says goodbye to Richard.

Richard takes his hand and says: "Goodbye." Bertha appears at the door on the right.

> "Robert. [*Catches sight of her: to Archie.*] Get your cap. Come on with me. I'll buy you a cake and I'll tell you a story.
>
> Archie. [*To* Bertha.] May I, mamma?
>
> Bertha. Yes.
>
> Archie. [*Takes his cap.*] I am ready.
>
> Robert. [*To* Richard *and* Bertha.] Goodbye to pappa and mamma. But not a big goodbye.
>
> Archie. Will you tell me a fairy story, Mr. Hand?
>
> Robert. A fairy story? Why not? I am your fairy godfather.

[*They go out together through the double doors and down the garden. When they have gone Bertha goes to Richard and puts her arm round his waist.*]

> Bertha. Dick, dear, do you believe now that I have been true to you? Last night and always?
>
> Richard. [*Sadly.*] Do not ask me, Bertha.
>
> Bertha. [*Pressing him more closely.*] I have been, dear. Surely you believe me. I gave you myself—all. I gave up all for you. You took me—and you left me.
>
> Richard. When did I leave you?
>
> Bertha. You left me: and I waited for you to come back to me. Dick. Dear, come here to me. Sit down. How tired you must be!"

[*She draws him toward the lounge. He sits down, almost reclining, resting on his arm. She sits on the mat before the lounge, holding his hand.*]

> "Bertha. Yes, dear. I waited for you. Heavens, what I suffered then—when we lived in Rome! Do you remember the terrace of our house?
>
> Richard. Yes.
>
> Bertha. I used to sit there, waiting, with the poor child with his toys, waiting till he got sleepy. I could see all

the roofs of the city and the river, the Tevere. What is its name?

Richard. The Tiber.

Bertha. [*Caressing her cheek with his hand.*] It was lovely, Dick, only I was so sad. I was alone, Dick, forgotten by you and all. I felt my life was ended.

Richard. It had not begun.

Bertha. And I used to look at the sky, so beautiful, without a cloud and the city you said was so old: and then I used to think of Ireland and about ourselves.

Richard. Ourselves?

Bertha. Yes. Ourselves. Not a day passed that I do not see ourselves, you and me, as we were when we met first. Every day of my life I see that. Was I not true to you all that time?

Richard. [*Sighs deeply.*] Yes Bertha. You were my bride in exile.

Bertha. Wherever you go, I will follow you. If you wish to go away now I will go with you.

Richard. I will remain. It is too soon yet to despair.

Bertha. [*Again caressing his hand.*] It is not true that I want to drive everyone from you. I wanted to bring you close together—you and him. Speak to me. Speak out all your heart to me. What you feel and what you suffer.

Richard. I am wounded, Bertha.

Bertha. How wounded, dear? Explain to me what you mean. I will try to understand everything you say. In what way are you wounded?

Richard. [*Releases his hand and, taking her head between his hands, bends it back and gazes long into her eyes.*] I have a deep wound of doubt in my soul.

Bertha. [*Motionless.*] Doubt of me?

Richard. Yes.

Bertha. I am yours. [*In a whisper.*] If I died this moment, I am yours.

Richard. [*Still gazing at her and speaking as if to an absent person.*] I have wounded my soul for you—a deep wound of doubt which can never be healed. I can never know, never in this world. I do not wish to know or believe. I do not care. It is not in the darkness of belief that I desire you. But in restless living wounding doubt. To hold you by no bonds, even of love, to be united with you in body and soul in utter nakedness—for this I longed. And now I am tired for a while, Bertha. My wound tires me.

[*He stretches himself out wearily along the lounge. Bertha holds his hand still, speaking very softly.*]

Bertha. Forget me, Dick. Forget me and love me again as you did for the first time. I want my lover. To meet him, to go to him, to give myself to him. You, Dick. O, my strange wild lover, come back to me again!

[*She closes her eyes.*]"

DISCUSSION

Like "The Dead" and *A Portrait*, *Exiles* also has autobiographical elements, in amount, perhaps, more than in the former two. Joyce's basic themes of betrayal, loneliness and exile run through these three, and also through *Ulysses*. Particularly the relation between Joyce and Nora, heavily complicated by some of Joyce's close friends is easily recognizable in *Exiles*, only if we keep in mind the equations: Richard Rowan is to Joyce, Bertha is to Nora, and Robert Hand is to the company of Joyce's four betraying friends—Prezioso, Gogarty, Cosgrave and Kettle. And if we think of the four on one hand and Joyce on the other and the tug of war between the two sides on the trophy that is Nora, Joyce's dubbing of *Exiles* as "cat and mouse three acts" play is genuine.

Prezioso was a journalist and intellectual—"the jaunty, dapper Venetian who had been one of Joyce's best friends in Trieste" (Ellmann, 316). Oliver St. John Gogarty adulated Joyce calling him "Dublin's Dante" but Joyce suspected Gogarty to betray him. It was Gogarty who asked Joyce to live in the Martello Tower (along with Nora) where he lived. Vincent

Cosgrave was Joyce's college friend. He tried hard to seduce Nora but failed. He was drowned in Tames. And Thomas Kettle, though a friend of Joyce, nursed a hostility towards him. He was killed in France. Richard Ellmann writes about these four friends of Joyce: "From his experiences with them Joyce drew the picture of friendship which appears in the play [*Exiles*]: a friend is someone who wants to posses your mind (since the possession of your body is forbidden by the society) and your wife's body, and longs to prove himself your disciple by betraying you" (Ellmann, 356). However, the three—Richard, Bertha and Archie—are analogues respectively of Joyce, Nora and George (their son). Like Joyce went into exile in the Continent (Italy and elsewhere), taking Nora with him, Richard eloped with Bertha and settled in Italy. And like George might be taken to be illegitimate (for Joyce officially married Nora in 1931 but George was born in 1905), Archie may be taken to be illegitimate because we do not hear of Richard marrying Bertha ceremonially in the play. And, lastly, Richard returns to Dublin after nine years and Joyce, the author of the play, imaginatively returns to his "dear, dirty Dublin" because the setting of *Exiles* is the city of Dublin.

Exiles is a domestic drama, like G.B. Shaw's *Candida* (1894) and Henrik Ibsen's *A Doll's House* (1879), being concerned with domestic problems, particularly the problem of relation between husband and wife. In *Candida*, Candida, the wife of a famous clergy, the Reverend James Mavor Morell, is disgusted with the dull chores and the unimaginative life of the household. She goes out on a brief sojourn with the young poet Eugene Marchbanks who proposes to bring her out of that depressing, cheerless atmosphere. Candida now swings in her affection between Morell and Marchbanks, but ultimately chooses to take side with Morell. So far, *Exiles* bears some similarity to *Candida*, but *Exiles* is more complicated because here Bertha is in tenterhooks between two jealous and inimical lovers—Richard and Robert—with both of whom she has been very intimate, emotionally and physically. Consequently her tension is more acute. *Exiles* is all the more complicated than *Candida* because here Richard suffers from the twisting pain of doubt about the "sacred night of love" between Robert and Bertha. However, some commentators have found the influence of *A Doll's House* on *Exiles*, but if there be any, it is superficial; they assume the influence, perhaps, because Joyce was a great votary of Ibsen's drama.

Is *Exiles* a modern or postmodern play? This a difficult question, for Joyce straddled between modernism and postmodernism. Modernism is generally thought to have flourished between the two World Wars, and postmodernism since the conclusion of the Second World War. Almost all the works of Joyce were done well before the beginning of the Second World War. But then if we say that all his works are modernist we will make a mistake, because his *Finnegans Wake* is definitely postmodernism. Modernism is "A general, non-specific and comprehensive term for a movement (or tendency) in literary productions prevalent roughly between two World Wars...featuring radical break with the traditional literary modes, style, concepts and subject-matters; a credo for experimentation in all the literary elements and forms; a doubt about the legitimacy of religion, morality and the prevailing social organization; a craze for *Avant-garde-ism* and the motto of 'make it new' (Ezra Pound); introduction into literary oeuvres the effects of drugs, dreams and automatic writing; inclusion of previously forbidden subject-matters; a sense of 'alienation'; and an unexampled rapidity of change. Modernism was influenced by Dadaism, imagism, vorticism, futurism, symbolism, impressionism, expressionism, existentialism and stream-of-consciousness technique. It was also influenced by such thinkers as Sigmund Freud, Karl Marx, Friedrich Nietzsche and James G. Frazer (*The Golden Bough*)" (Sarker, 108).

Postmodernism has retained all the above features of modernism and added to it more radical departures from the tradition. In modernism, the writer is the judge of truth and beauty; he looks within himself and what he sees there he expresses in his works; he is not much concerned with the world outside. The modernist writer's world is created by himself, it is his world, it is absolute, whatever be the real world out there. To the postmodernist, the modernist's world is solipsistic and therefore erroneous. The writer must stand face to face before the world and what he will see then he will produce in his works. The writer must have his conception of the true world which is not absolute but relative, as Einstein and Heisenberg said, and chaotic, and ever-changing, like Herclitus's river. So whatever we predicate about whatever, there must be doubt, and there must be mystery. With such a relative, chaotic and ever-changing *Weltanschauung* in his head the postmodernist writer must be queer and unpredictable and mysterious which Joyce, for one thing, certainly is.

And in *Exiles* such a fictional character is Richard Rowan. His sudden distancing himself from Beatrice and eloping with Bertha and then offering her to Robert, like Candaules, King of Lydia, offered his minister Gyges to view the naked beauty of his wife, and thus wounding his soul, are all features of a postmodernist drama—its jauntiness, quixoticality, profanity and antiethos. But the "doubt" and the "dream"—the doubt of Richard and the dream of Robert? Yes, these two are too parts of Joyce's postmodernism. Joyce had a fair general knowledge of contemporary scientific attainments, including Einstein's theory of relativity and Heisenberg's uncertainty principle. Joyce's philosophy of doubt was informed by his knowledge of the science of his day. Richard's doubt about the "sacred night of love" between Robert and Bertha and Robert's doubt about whether it was "the truth" or "a dream" (Act III) are components of the parameters of Joyce's postmodernism.

Exiles generated out of "The Dead", the ultimate story of *Dubliners* that replaced Joyce's earlier planned but abandoned short story "Ulysses" which long later on evolved as the great novel *Ulysses*. Interestingly, in all the three—"The Dead", *Exiles* and *Ulysses*—the theme is the same or similar: doubt of conjugal betrayal. In this sense, it is not very far from truth that Joyce wrote only one book, the first part of which is a short story, the second part a drama, and the third part a novel, and that in all the three the nuptial life of Joyce and Nora appears as a thin film through. D.S. Savage, in his *The Withered Branch*, shows the continuation of "The Dead" in *Exiles*: "*Exiles*, which, in the words of Harry Levin, 'is an attempt to externalize the situation of domestic estrangement in "The Dead"—a story in *Dubliners*'" (Savage, 186). The domestic estrangement in "The Dead" is between Gabriel Conroy and Gretta Conroy, in *Exiles* it is between Richard Rowan and Bertha, and in *Ulysses* it is between Leopold Bloom and Molly Bloom. Gabriel metamorphoses into Richard, and then into Leopold. Gretta turns out to be Bertha and then Molly. But everywhere the estrangement ultimately resolves into sorts of dubious reconciliation.

Another feature of *Exiles* should be mentioned: *Exiles* puzzles us with riddles—riddles which are a favourite creative tool of Joyce. Riddles are there in *Dubliners*, in *A Portrait* and in *Ulysses*, and *Finnegans Wake* is redolent of "riddle-me-re" or riddle my riddle—rigmarole. In *Exiles*, from the very beginning we begin to face riddles: why should Richard, lover of Beatrice, suddenly elope with Bertha? Why does Robert, lover of Beatrice, try to seduce Bertha, mother of 8-year-old Archie? Why does Bertha allow Robert to kiss her? Why, knowing everything, Richard does not tether in his wife? And so on so many riddles. And compounded with all these is the riddle of the proper names of the principal characters: Richard, beginning with 'R' and Robert, beginning with 'R'; and likewise, Bertha, beginning with 'B' and Beatrice, beginning with 'B'. Are Richard and Robert and Bertha and Beatrice mutually obverse and reverse, or are the two pairs two single souls, each torn into two—one part for flesh, the other for spirit?

And lastly, the riddle par excellence: like in his all other works, where intellectual and artistic women do not play a major role, in *Exiles* also both Bertha and Beatrice (though she is an intellectual) are mere marionettes at the hands of Richard and Robert, albeit Joyce personally knew some remarkable women, like Hannah Sheehy and Maud Gonne, and, astonishingly, though, "one of the primary reasons of his admiration of Henrik Ibsen was in fact the playwright's feminism" (Beja, 22).

EXILES: APPRECIATION

Whatever the critics said about it, Joyce himself was confident with *Exiles*: he "found merits [in it] that escaped less generous critics" (Tindall, 104). But there are now critics whom the merits of the play have not evaded: Francis Fergusson, for one, is such a critic. Fergusson, is effusive about the merits of *Exiles*. William York Tindall writes about Fergusson: "'The *Portrait*,' says Mr. Fergusson, 'shows us the process of construction; *Exiles* gives us the completed masterpiece'" (Tindall, 108). But though Tindall himself is not very happy with *Exiles*, yet he sees some saving graces in it; for one, says he, the play is "neat", and secondly, its subject matter is "familiar." Why "familiar"? Tindall explains: "Familiarity also promises meaning without discomfort; for commonly what we are accustomed to yields more of the same thing" (Tindall, 108).

Even admitting that *Exiles* has not been received well, A. Nicholas Fargnoli and Michael Patrick Gillespie write that the play incorporates "a vital principle in Joyce's aesthetics": "In fact, *Exiles* is rarely performed, and infrequently read and studied. Nonetheless, the play remains an important document for anyone interested in the evolution of Joyce's canon and the development of his art. As a dramatic work, it embodies, albeit imperfectly, a vital principle in Joyce's aesthetics, one that he formulated years earlier in his *Paris Notebook* (March 6, 1906). In Aristotlean style, Joyce characterized the differences among the lyrical, the epical and the dramatic forms of art, the dramatic being the least personal and thus the purest: 'that art is dramatic whereby the artist sets forth the image in immediate relation to others.' Particular concern for the dramatic mode can be found in Joyce's early essays as well as in the thoughts of Stephen Dedalus in A *Portrait of the Artist as a Young Man*" (Fargnoli and Gillespie, 86). But Joyce's full-blown dramatic work is *Exiles* where, whatever aesthetic value it may harbour, Joyce is like a god, paring finger nails.

Some critics have raised the charge against *Exiles* that it is not successful on the stage. This charge was first broached by none other than the master critic Ezra Pound: "'When you are a recognized classic', Ezra Pound wrote to James Joyce on first reading 'that damn play' *Exiles*, 'people will read it because you wrote it and be duly interested and duly instructed...but until then I'm hang'd if I see what's to be done with it'" (quoted by Kirsten Shepherd-Barr in essay "Reconsidering Joyce's *Exiles* in the Theatrical Context"). Now, why did Pound expect *Exiles* to be a flop on the stage? Theatre is a space where both intellectuals and commoners congregate—the commoners all the more. So a play must be commonly understandable (like, say, the plays of Shakespeare). But *Exiles* is a difficult play, indeed. Secondly, the success of a play on the stage in a great measure depends on the quality of its performance. The cold reception of the performances of *Exiles* before Harold Pinter's encomiumistic 1970 and 1971 productions may be attributed to the rather poor quality of the previous performances.

Before we evaluate *Exiles*, we should keep in mind that it is a postmodernist drama with modernist hang-over (for instance, Richard in Act II: "Because in the very core of my ignoble heart I longed to be betrayed...., to be...") and its stream-of-consciousness (for instance, Robert in Act III: "Were you mine in that sacred night of love? Or have I dreamed of it?") are lineaments of postmodernism. And the core "doubt" and the frank sexuality and the stupefying puzzles in *Exiles* are star marks of postmodernism. Any evaluation of *Exiles*, therefore, must be done from the perspective of postmodernism. And if so done, so good it is.

Ezra Pound, in 1916 re-read the play "at a sitting with intense interest" and called it commendable: "It is distinctly a play. It has the form of a play—I do not mean that it is written in dialogue with the names of the speakers put in front of their speeches. I mean that it has inner form; that the acts and speeches of one person work into the act and speeches of another and make the play into an indivisible whole. The action takes place in less than twenty-four hours, in two rooms, both near Dublin, so that even the classical unities are uninjured. The characters are drawn with that hardness of outline which we might compare to that of Durer's painting if we are permitted a comparison with effects of an art so different. There are only four main characters, and a fishwoman who passes a window, so that the whole mechanics of the play have required great closeness of skill. I see no way in which the play could be improved by redoing it as a novel. It could not, in fact, be anything but a play" (Deming, 134). We have quoted Ezra Pound at such a length only to show that he was effusive in praising the play. And yet, we know, he said that it was unstageable, because the play was away from the moral tune of the time. But that is a different thing altogether.

EXILES: CRITICISM

Joyce had to overcome hurdles finally to get *Exiles* published as he had to face rejections from producers for different reasons—obscurity, dullness, and sensuality—but principally for its aberrant sexuality. When, for instance, Joyce submitted the play to the Stage Society of London for production, one person of the society called the play "Filth and Disease" and Barnard Shaw "found it obscene" (Ellmann, 415). Robert's kissing of submissive Bertha, more than once, and Richard's king Candaules-like pandering of her to Robert are proofs of the play's moral depravity.

The great American Joyce scholar, William York Tindall says that "*Exiles seems a drama*" (*emphases added*) (Tindall, 106), and is not a drama. According to him, Joyce's fictional character Stephen Dedalus is his theorist of dramatic art. Tindall says that in spite of having enough *métier* in dramatic art Joyce has not been successful in satisfying his Stephen Dedalus with the dramatic art that is there in *Exiles*. Tindall writes: "[Yet] Joyce, dramatic enough to please Stephen in *Chamber Music*, *Dubliners*, and *A Portrait*, longed for dramatic drama [in *Exiles*].... The pity is that Joyce's drama is less 'dramatic' in Stephen's sense, than Joyce's stories, verses, and novels. Sufficiently impersonal to distinguish Richard from Joyce, *Exiles* is not objective enough to be a play. Inclining toward what Stephen would call 'lyric' art, *Exiles* fails to play in a stage.... The reader, to whom this play is now committed, is equally at a loss. Joyce liked riddles and created many; but what he fooled with here seems less riddle than confusion" (Tindall, 106-07).

Tindall, next, charges Joyce with Joyce's one favourite trick—enigma (or puzzle or mysticism). What exactly is the problem in the play we do not know and so *Exiles* does not bestow upon us any satisfaction. Tindall writes: "That enigma can be successful on the stage is proved by *Hamlet* and *Waiting for Godot*; but enigma, as they are, must be embodied—massively. Here, although Richard is central, he lacks body to carry and offer what Joyce burdens him with.... What matters is that the conflicts centered in Richard and caused by him remain unsettled for those on stage or off it alike. Whether the play is tragic or comic as Joyce insisted (*Letters*, 78) no satisfaction is forth-coming. All is lost, unhappily scattered—though that, of course, could be Joyce's point" (Tindall, 107). What is the problem of Richard, let us ask again? He panders his wife to his close friend and suffers from doubt. Is he a mesochistic neurotic? No answer. We are puzzled. *Exiles* is no enigma: is it an intended puzzle, merely?

From the beginning to the end, *Exiles* is full of crisp, monotonous, stichomythic dialogues, unpunctuated by any noticeable action. In this regard, the play may be compared with *Waiting for Godot*. But Beckett's play, from the very beginning grabs our attention with an assurance (though futile) of something coming, while no such thing is there in *Exiles* to hold sway over our head.

In *Exiles*, Joyce has employed many "symbols" or "attendant images"—stone, roses, cows, water, wind and light—but none of them produce potential meaning, save the roses. The roses signify Robert's love of Bertha, and when Richard says that they are "overblown" we understand that he means that Robert's show of love to Bertha is exaggerated. But stone refers to nothing definite. The stone was fetched by Bertha from the beach where Richard does his constitutional. It is round and beautiful and when Robert fondles it, it refers to Bertha. But when Bertha says that Robert swims "like a stone", the earlier meaning of stone is nullified. So, Tindall is right when he writes that "Associated with too many people, the stone corresponds to none. Richard, with whom it is associated least, seems stonier than the others.... Bertha and the stone have nothing in common but roundness and beauty. Obviously important, this stone lacks definite import" (Tindall, 117-18).

And Tindall's last two objections to *Exiles* are not less important: "not much of a world, *Exiles* lacks the roundness and harmony of Joyce's great creations. It also lacks his customary attitudes toward his creation and its observers, embodied attitudes that I.A. Richards calls feeling and tone. There is little here of Joyce's irony and little of the gaiety that was to return in *Ulysses* and *Finnegans Wake*" (Tindall, 116).

However, ironically, though, the title of the play is, perhaps, justified, for in spite of Joyce's attempt, at the end of it, at some kind of ramshackle reconciliations, there are multiple "exiles" rather than only of Richard and Bertha. Psychologically, Richard is exiled from Bertha, as she is from him; Richard is exiled from Beatrice, as she is from him; Robert is exiled from Bertha, as she is from him; and Richard and Robert are exiled from each other. Or, may we say, each one of them is exiled from all others, so that each one is as alone as Richard (or Gabriel, or Stephen, or Leopold Bloom, or Joyce himself)—"Alone, alone, all, all alone,/ Alone on a wide, wide sea!/ And never a saint took pity on,/ My soul in agony."

5
Conclusion

Now, we have had some knowledge of Joyce and his three important books of three different genres: *Dubliners* (short story), *A Portrait of the Artist as a Young Man* (novel) and *Exiles* (drama). Now then we can make an evaluation of Joyce on the basis of these three books. But before that we should situate him in a particular literary age or aesthetic movement against which his creations are to be judged. But here is the "rub"; it is very difficult to fix Joyce in a particular age or period of certain aesthetic movement. However, Joyce may be called a modernist verging on postmodernism or may we call him a pre-post-modernist.

Modernism is "a general term applied retrospectively to the wide range of experimental and *avant-garde* trends in the literature of the 20th century" (Baldick, 159). Modernist features of literature comprise "impressionism and subjectivity"; "a movement away from the apparent objectivity"; "an emphasis on fragmented forms, discontinuous narratives and random-seeming collages of different materials"; "a tendency toward reflexivity, or self-consciousness about the production of the work of art"; "a rejection of elaborate formal aesthetics in favour of minimalist designs (...) and a rejection, in large part, of formal aesthetic theories, in favour of spontaneity and discovery in creation"; and "a rejection of the distinction between 'high' and 'low' or popular culture, both in choice of materials used to produce art and in methods of displaying, distributing, and consuming art" (Klages, 165).

A close look at the three books of Joyce—*Dubliners, A Portrait,* and *Exiles*—will show that many of the features of modernism are present in them. Let us take up the first book first, *Dubliners,* where the stories are impressionistic and subjective, fragmented in forms, and minimalist. "Sisters", for instance, is the story of the narrator boy's subjective experience as "Araby" is that of the romantic boy's, and "The Dead" is Gabriel's flabbergasting experience. And all the three stories are fragmented or non-liner and minimalist. The novel *A Portrait* is but an "emotional curve" of Stephen Dedalus stochastically conveyed, and the drama of *Exiles* is Richard Rowan's experiment of a queer love shown in three short acts.

Joyce was not only a modern writer but he went beyond the bourn of modernism and, in his later works, *Ulysses* and *Finnegans Wake,* he has betrayed some features of postmodernism, such as "pastiche, parody, bricolage, irony and playfulness" (Klages, 1650). Nevertheless, predicating to Joyce's works the terms modernism or postmodernism or both at the same time, as some scholars do, will also not do justice to Joyce's creations, because his literary productions are unique, "Joycean", if we may say so. Joyce was never an imitator; he held his spirit of independence not only in the fields of religion and politics but also in his most valued province of literary creations. He was against any theory of literature. He had shown evidences of this at an early age in his semi-autographical novel *A Portrait of the Artist as a Young Man* wherein he used a verse from Ovid's *Metamorphoses* (VIII, 18) as the book's epigraph:

> *Et ignotas animum dimittit in artes*
> ("And he turned his mind to unknown arts.")

2

Since the beginning of his creative life, to cross the boundary of the existing domain of literature was Joyce's avowed promise. And to that end throughout his literary life he conducted experiments in his creative works, and that ever most successfully.

It is impossible to put Joyce's art into any orthodox literary tradition or movement. For instance, he is both a realist and not a realist. He is a realist when, for instance, he draws a map of

Dublin's roads and lanes, nooks and corners, bars and beaches in his fictions and thus make a veritable map of Dublin. But he is not a realist when he introduces epiphanies in them, especially in his *Dubliners*. In fact *Dubliners* stories, each one of them, is an illustration of epiphany. In *A Portrait*, there are a few epiphanies, among them is the noted epiphany of Stephen: the epiphany of the "seabird" (the girl-bird) in Chapter IV, Section iii. And in *Exiles* Richard experiences an epiphany at the close of the play when Bertha innocently implores to him: "Forget me, Dick. Forget me and love me again as you did for the first time. I want my lover. To meet him, to give myself to him. You, Dick, O my strange wild lover, come back to me again!" Or, when Richard Rowan realized that in the previous night Bertha and Robert Hand were not alone in Hand's house.

Now, let us look at some of the characteristic features of Joyce's fictions that we have not so far mentioned.

1. The basic themes of the stories of *Dubliners*, and of *A Portrait* and *Exiles* (and also of *Ulysses*) are relations among family members. In "Eveline", Eveline is on tenterhooks between her romance and her mother's "categorical imperative" and between her exacting father and her love of home; in "A Little Cloud", Little Chandler's relations with his insouciant wife and his baggage-like innocent little son; and in "The Dead" the relation between Gabriel and his wife Gretta after the memory of Michael disrupts Gabriel's peace of mind, to take only three clearer instances. In *A Portrait*, Stephen's unsympathetic father and his dogmatic mother contributed not a little to his feeling of being betrayed and his consequent flight. And, lastly, *Exiles* is a drama of complex suspicious relations among four characters—Richard Rowan, Robert Hand, Bertha and Beatrice.

2. Joyce was wont to model his characters on known persons and acquaintances and there are many such characters in the three books we are discussing here as well as in *Ulysses*. Some instances:

A. *Dubliners*

(i) In "Clay", the two brothers, Alphy and Joe are modelled on Joyce's uncles.

(ii) In "A Painful Case", James Duffy is modelled on Joyce's brother Stanislaus Joyce.

(iii) In "The Dead", Michael Furey is modeled on Michael Bodkin, Nora's friend in Galway.

B. *A Portrait of the Artist as a Young Man*

Lynch modelled on Vincent Cosgrave, Joyce's college friend.

C. *Exiles*

Robert Hand is modelled on Robert Prezioso who actually tried to seduce Nora.

D. *Ulysses*

(i) Buck Mulligan is modelled on St. John Oliver Gogarty whom Joyce expected to be betrayed by on the cause of Nora.

(ii) Molly Bloom is modeled on Nora and Mrs. Charles Chance, a Dublin singer.

3. All of Joyce's major fictions, barring *Exiles* and *Finnegans Wake*, were most probably written as per a projected sequence of Joyce from *Dubliners* through *Stephen Hero* and *A Portrait* to *Ulysses*. We say this because we see many characters of the first three books from *Dubliners* to *A Portrait* reappear in *Ulysses* as shown below.

A. *Dubliners* (characters that reappear in *Ulysses*)

(i) "Two Gallants": Corley and Lenehan.

(ii) "Grace": Cunningham, Flynn, Kernan and Power.

(iii) "The Boarding House": Bob Doran and Polly Mooney.

(iv) "Ivy Day in the Committee Room": Joe Hynes and Lyons.

(v) "A Painful Case": M'Ontosh.

B. *Stephen Hero* (characters that reappear in *Ulysses*): Mrs. Dedalus and Uncle John.

C. *A Portrait of the Artist as a Young Man* (characters that reappear in *Ulysses*): Katey Dedalus, Simon Dedalus, Stephen Dedalus, Vincent Lynch, Mac Cann and William Madden.

4. Joyce's concept of hero or protagonist is uncommon, unique, in the sense that his concept of the hero deviates from

the classical or Aristotelian concept of the (tragic) hero, where the hero is never a common personage but is a person between the upper and the middle classes whereas Joyce's hero is always a commoner in every aspect of a commoner. Further, Aristotle's hero must be powerful ("heroic") and of sublime character. Joyce, on the contrary, brought Aristotle's hero or classical hero from his high pedestal down to the commoners. Thus in *Ulysses* he has metamorphosed Homer's Odysseus into Leopold Bloom, a hen-pecked ordinary advertising agent. The protagonists of *A Portrait*, *Stephen Hero* and *Exiles* are not born great nor do they achieve greatness, and so are all the protagonists in the stories of *Dubliners*. Joyce's contrarieity is deliberate; he did it according to his declared motto—"scrupulous meanness." It was his challenge to classicism, perhaps, or it was a part of his "*ignatas...artes*"—"unknown art."

5. Joyce is a very well-read artist and as such far exceeds the range of S.T. Coleridge or T.S. Eliot. He graduated in modern languages and is said to have smacking knowledge of dozens of languages, some archaic, some somewhat archaic (like Sanskrit, Hibernian, etc.) and some modern, and with this wide range of languages he could gather a vast knowledge of varieties of myths, mysticisms, philosophies and cultures. And he had woven all these into the fabric of his works. And this has made his books difficult to read.

Besides his linguistic proficiency, Joyce's mastery over other writers' works is also enormous. He was versed in Aeschylus, Seneca, Homer, Virgil, Dante, Shakespeare and other noted Elizabethan dramatists, Tolstoy, Dostoevsky, Chekhov, Henrik Ibsen, Maurice Maeterlinck, Victor Hugo, Alexander Dumas, Honore de Balzac, Emile Zola, Gustav Flaubert, Marcel Proust, Emile Zola *et cetera*, and also good knowledge of the Bible and working knowledge of Hinduism, Islam and Buddhism. He had comfortable knowledge of Western philosophy, ancient, medieval and modern, especially of the philosophies of Aristotle, St. Thomas Aquinas, Giordano Bruno and Giambatista Vico. He read *Kabbalah* and *The Egyptian Book of the Dead*. And he has concealed his knowledge of all these very cunningly in his works (mostly in *Ulysses*) making them more difficult to comprehend adequately. Besides, from the very first story of *Dubliners* to the last pages of *Finnegans Wake*, Joyce's works are heavily stuffed with references to innumerable sources.

6. Joyce's paronomasia or play on words is well known; he is perhaps second only to Shakespeare in juggling with words. He is certainly greater than Shakespeare in the field of neologism: he has made new words, thousands of them, by combining multiple words from different languages into new terms. Such words may not have found spaces in the vocabularies but they well serve Joyce's special purpose in his two books *Ulysses* and *Finnegans Wake*. Interestingly, one queer neologism of Joyce, the logodeedalus, has been honoured by the scientific community—the neologism "quark" which now denotes the most basic unit of proton.

7. Joyce's themes are as heavy or lugubrious as his handling of them is trifling, trivial. Humour and satire are the mainstay of Joyce's compositions. Add to these his use of four-letter words and obscene and emetic terms. Charges have been hurled at him for all these his indecencies, but to no avail, for he wrote only the truths, uneasy truths of quotidian life that we always keep hidden under the purple velvet of proud civilization.

8. Joyce is one of the pioneers of employing the free indirect style in fiction, after Gustav Flaubert first used this technique in *Madame Bovary* (1857). This technique has given much freedom from the iron rules of grammar to writers. Free indirect style or discourse is "a manner of presenting the thoughts or utterances of a fictional character as if from that character's point of view by combining grammatical and other features of the character's 'direct speech' with features of the narrator's 'indirect' report. Direct discourse is used in the sentence *She thought, 'I will stay here tomorrow'*, while the equivalent in indirect discourse would be *She thought that she would stay there the next day.* Free indirect style, however, combines the person and tense of indirect discourse ('She would stay') with the indirection of time and place appropriate to direct discourse ('here tomorrow'), to form a different kind of sentence: *She would stay here tomorrow*" (Baldick, 102). Just two instances of Joyce's use of free indirect style:

1. At the very close of "Eveline", when Frank insistently shouts at Eveline "Come!", she, now free from her hesitation and indecision and determined, responds (through the mouth of Joyce, so to say): "No! No! No!" Like Frank's "Come", The triple negatives "No! No! No!" do not come from Eveline's tongue; they are put by Joyce into her mouth (notice the dual quotation marks of Frank's "Come" and the single quotation mark of Eveline's "No! No! No!").
2. At the close of "The Dead", Joyce uses the free indirect style (or technique): "Yes, the newspapers were right: snow was general all over Ireland. It was falling on every part of the dark central plain, on the treeless hills, falling softly upon the Bog of Allen and, farther westward, softly falling into the dark mutinous Shannon waves. It was falling, too, upon every part of the lonely churchyard on the hill where Michael Furey lay buried. It lay thickly drifted on the crooked crosses and headstones, on the spears of the little gate, on the barren thorns." These words are not the narrator's; they belong to Gabriel—they are Gabriel's mute monologue. The narrator resumes his narration only after the last word in the quotation: "*His soul swooned*...upon all the living and the dead" (*emphasis added*). Gabriel's words, here, are written in the free indirect style.

Joyce is also an early practitioner of the newfangled technique of stream of consciousness narrative, following Edouard Dujardin (who first used this technique in *The Laurels are Cut*) and along with Dorothy Richardson, Virginia Woolf and William Faulkner. Stream of consciousness device or style may be called "a special style of interior monologue." In the stream of consciousness device of narrative, a fictional character's "continuous flow of sense-perceptions, thoughts, feelings, and memories" are recorded. By this method of narrative the writer can give the reader an "authentic" picture of the character's inner or mental horizon so that he can understand the character better. Two instances of Joyce's employment of this technique are being given below.

1. *A Portrait of the Artist as a Young Man* (Chapter 5, Part 2): The previous day when it was raining Stephen and Lynch were under the arcade of the library and there discussed about Aquinas' theory of beauty. There were also a group of girls. Lynch whispered to Stephen: "...Your beloved is here." As Stephen saw her, his mind was "emptied of theory" and he "lapsed back into a listless peace." Next day he woke up from sleep early and had a stream of consciousness....

   "Towards dawn he awoke. O what sweet music! His soul was all dewy wet. Over his limbs in sleep pale cool waves of light had passed. He lay still, as if his soul lay amid cool waters, conscious of faint sweet music. His mind was waking slowly to a tremulous morning knowledge, a morning inspiration. A spirit filled him, pure as the purest water, sweet as dew, moving as music. But how faintly it was inbreathed, how passionlessly, as if the seraphim themselves were breathing on him! His soul was waking slowly, fearing to wake wholly. It was the windless hour of dawn when madness wakes and strange plants open to the light and the moth flies forth silently. An enchantment of the heart! The night had been enchanted. In a dream or vision he had known the ecstasy of seraphic life. Was it an instant of enchantment only or long hour and years and ages?"

   In the above quotation, Joyce is just narrating the stream of consciousness of Stephen, not of his own.

2. Joyce's most famous passage of stream of consciousness is that of Molly Bloom, which is her 51-page-long semi-conscious interior monologue that closes *Ulysses*. The interior monologue consists of just two sentences (eight parts) none of them have any punctuation marks but only one full stop after the fourth part and one at the end. Below we are quoting only a small

> portion from the concluding part of the total interior monologue or soliloquy of Molly in her hypnagogic state. "....and Gibralter as a girl where I was a Flower of the mountain yes when I put the rose in my hair like the Andalusian girls used or shall I wear a red yes and how he kissed me under the Moorish wall and I thought well as well him as another and then I asked him with my eyes to ask again yes and then he asked me would I yes to say yes my mountain flower and first I put my arms around him yes and drew him down to me so he could feel my breaths all perfume yes and his heart was going like mad and yes I said yes I will yes."

The above passage (in fact, the total 51 pages of Chapter 18 of *Ulysses*) of Molly's monologue may seem eerie, quarky, but, according to William James (see his *The Principles of Psychology*), so is the stream of consciousness "which flows continuously through our waking minds by day and intermittently through our sleeping brains by night in the strange, uncertainty of dreams" (Potter, 162). And Molly was exactly dreaming.

9. Joyce used varieties of narrative techniques and frequently changed one for the other. Besides, the techniques we have discussed above there are the techniques of anacoluthon, aposiopesis, punning, double entendre, fragmentary sentence, open-endedness, *in media res*, etc. Besides, his works are studded with innumerable references to other writers and quotations from their works, principally in English and Latin. All these are no decorations of his narratives but are organically integrated to them; and these facilitate our understanding of his works, if only we understand them, but if we do not, they puzzle us.

10. Joyce's books may be said to be palimpsestic, in the sense that they are layered; at one level we may understand what he means to say but below that level he may have something more as well. One simple instance. Below the story line of *Ulysses* (and of *Finnegans Wake*) and also of some of the stories of *Dubliners* one may discover Giambatista Vico's theory of *ricorso* (the return to the beginning). At another level the same books bear a Baedeker (a guiding map) of Dublin. In 1918,

Joyce, when he was composing *Ulysses*, said to Frank Budgen, the English painter, in Zurich about the book: "I want to give [in *Ulysses*] a picture of Dublin so complete that if the city suddenly disappeared from the earth it could be reconstructed out of my book." In *A Portrait* and in *Finnegans Wake* as well one may find a cadastral survey of Dublin.

At yet another level, a shadow of Joyce's life is to be found in Joyce's books, beginning with *Dubliners*, through *A Portrait*, (which he connoted as his "curve of emotion") to *Ulysses* (wherein his somewhat troubled married life is woven) or even to *Finnegans Wake*. *Exiles* is a drama, the most objective genre, but here also Joyce is not absolutely absent. In this drama, the husband queerly pushes his wife to his male friend to suffer the pains of betrayal by both of them. Was Joyce another Sacher-Masoch? Let us hear what Jeffrey Meyers has to say on this point: "...Nora tearfully confessed to the English painter, Frank Budgen, that Jim [James Joyce] wanted her to 'go with the other men so that he would have something to write about'" (Meyers, 83). Meyers continues: "Joyce frequently portrayed the relation of desire and doubt, and the heroes of *Exiles*, 'The Dead' and *Ulysses* are all obsessed by their jealousy and fear of betrayal" (*ibid.*). We may say that Joyce's relation with Nora is thinly reflected in some of his works. And, nevertheless, we may asseverate that Joyce, the artist is absolutely objective in his fictions, absolutely non-attached to his creations, absolutely committed to his own injunction: "The artist, like the God of creation, remains within or beyond or above his handiwork, invisible, refined out of existence, indifferent, paring his fingernails" (*A Portrait of the Artist as a Young Man*, Chapter 5, Part 1).

11. Joyce's fictions may claim a special distinction on the score of their having inordinately large number of songs in them. Joyce was very interested in songs and himself was a good soprano singer and once even participated in a music competition. The songs and references to songs in Joyce's fictions function as illustrators of his narratives or as sharpeners of emotions already created by the narratives. Joyce has employed songs and references to songs in some stories of *Dubliners*,

throughout *A Portrait of the Artist as a Young Man*, throughout Ulysses and even in the oneiric novel *Finnegans Wake*. Some of the songs from Joyce's fictions are being given below.

A. *Dubliners*

(i) "Two Gallants": "Silent, O Moyle"

(ii) "The Boarding House": "I'm a naughty girl"

(iii) "Clay": "I dreamt that I dwelt in marble hall"

(iv) "The Dead":

(a) "Arranged for the Bridal"

(b) "Let me like a Soldier fall"

(c) "The Lass of Aughrim"

(d) "O, the rain falls on my heavy locks"

B. *A Portrait of the Artist as a Young Man*

(i) "O, the wild rose blossoms" (ch. 1, pt. 1)

(ii) "Tralala lala" (ch. 1, pt. 1)

(iii) "Dingdong! The Castle bell!" (ch. 1, pt. 2)

(iv) "O, come all you Roman Catholics" (ch. 1, pt. 3)

(v) "Tis youth and folly" (ch. 5, pt. 1)

C. *Ulysses* (select songs)

(i) "Silent, O Moyle" (episode: "Scylla and Charybdis")

(ii) "Love's Old Sweet Song": This song is most frequently referred to throughout *Ulysses*.

(iii) "Blumenlied": It is also known as "The Flower Song" and is referred to throughout *Ulysses*.

(iv) "Seaside Girls": It is perhaps the most frequently mentioned song in *Ulysses*.

(v) "My Girl's a Yorkshire Girl" (episode: "Wandering Rocks")

(vi) "The Holy City" (episode: "Circe")

(vii) "M'appari (or Martha)" (episode: "Sirens")

(viii) "The Bloom is on the Rye" (episode: "Sirens")

(ix) "The Low-back'd Car" (episode: "Eumaeus")

(x) "The Croppy Boy" (episode: "Circe")

12. Like William Wordsworth perceived the world with his eyes, even though he had a normal pair of ears, Joyce perceived the world through his ears, for not having a pair of normal eyes. It is for this reason that we delight in the colours and waves in Wordsworth's poetry, where no bees buzz about:

> ...Once again
> Do I behold these steep and lofty cliffs,
> That on a wild secluded scene impress
> Thoughts of more deep seclusion; and connect
> The landscape with the quiet of the sky.
>
> ("Tintern Abbey")

or

> The Rainbow comes and goes,
> And lovely is the Rose,
> The Moon doth with delight
> Look round her when the heavens are bare,
> Waters on a stary night
> Are beautiful and fair;
> The Sunshine is a glorious birth;
> But yet I know, where'er I go,
> That there hath past away a glory from the earth.
>
> ("Ode: Intimations of Immortality from Recollections of Early Childhood")

On the other hand, as Joyce's fictions display no colours, we become enchanted by the rhythms of his musical words: "His soul swooned slowly as he heard the snow falling faintly through the universe and faintly falling, like the descent of their last end, upon all the living and the dead."

("The Dead", *Dubliners*)

or

> "...A day of dappled seaborne clouds."
>
> (*A Portrait*, ch. 4, pt. 3)

Once, around 1930s, the number of Joyce's admirers was less than that of his detractors, but since then the number of his admirers is fast increasing and that of his detractors is sharply decreasing. Once, around 1920s, his manuscripts were rejected by whoever was a publisher, if you like, and anti-Joyce sentiment for his free-wheeling treatment of libidinal matters led some people to make bonfire of his books. Now the weather has cleared—those who burnt his books are now buying them; readers of Joyce are increasing in number by the day; his works are being translated in dozens of tongues; films are being made on his fictions; and his fictions are being dramatized (perhaps only manga versions of Joyce's fictions are yet to come out).

Writers are now increasingly being drawn to Joyce's Zeuxian style of composition as well as to his postmodern *Weltanschauung* or vision of life and the world. We are here citing at random the names of certain writers who have been influenced by Joyce's notion of literary creations and artistry: Vladimir Nabokov, John Dos Passes, Jorge Luis Borges, Nathanael West, Katherine Mansfield, Thomas Pynchon, Kate O'Brien, Flann O'Brien, Sally Rooney, Zadie Smith, Don Delillo, Roni Morrison, Nadim Aslam, Joyce Carol Oates, George Orwell, Eimear McBride, Salman Rushdie and Jacques Derrida.

Now, two or three encomiums for Joyce from noted writers:

1. Kate O'Brien said that Joyce was "the greatest Artist—there will never be another" (Vincente, 8).

2. In their Introduction to *Joyce's Heirs* (edited by Olga Fernandez Vincente), Richard Jorge Fernandez and Olga Fernandez Vincente wrote about Joyce: "The figure of James Joyce is intangible, an almost all-encompassing figure whose height and breadth bypass countries and even time constraints and limitations. Many writers have confessed to their being indebted to his works and readings, as have many scholars over the years. Declan Kiberd in his famed *Inventing Ireland: The Literature of the Modern Nation* (1995) writes that Joyce's *Ulysses* is 'one of the first major literary utterances in the modern period by an artist who spoke for a newly liberated period'" (Vincente, 5). Vincente further writes in the same page: "... Joyce's figure is larger than life.... Joyce can be pronounced a figure of almost Biblical proportions."

3. Jacques Derrida was not a person directly linked with literature; he was a semiotic analyst or a deconstructionist. But, "When Derrida was invited to deliver the opening address at

the Ninth International James Joyce Symposium in Frankfurt in 1984, he had already on a number of occasions made clear the importance of Joyce's writing to his own work, and in the one essay on Joyce he had published at that time, 'Two Words for Joyce' (which devotes most attention to *Finnegans Wake*), he had given some account at this continuing importance" (Attridge, 253).

Today Joyce's importance and influence is impossible to ignore. Joyce has reformed the institution of the novel lock, stock, and barrel—its form, its language, its style, everything. He has influenced not only writers of fictions or word-artists but visual artists or painters as well. Painters have found in his fictions ekphrastic passages and are trying to give them visual expressions, i.e., they are striving to explore the visuality of Joyce's prose. What benefit will we be able to derive from this? Joyce's thoughts and imaginings are bottomless, hard to realise. Should visual artists bring before us through form and colours what Joyce has given us through the sounds of words, he would be clearer to us. We will not dwell on this point any more. Readers interested about Joyce's Zeuxian word-painting may go through Christa-Maria Lerm Hayes' *Joyce in Art: Visual Art Inspired by James Joyce* for an elaborate discussion on this matter. But we only say that Joyce had interest not only in music, as we have said, but also in visual art and that from early on. Evidences of this was evinced when he wrote an essay in 1899 (when he was only 17) on visual art: "James Joyce's first essay on visual art from 1899, written when he was an undergraduate, concerns a painting exhibited at the Royal Hibernian Academy" (Hayes, ix).

Now, perhaps, we may cease. In this book we were striving to understand Joyce's three important books—*Dubliners, A Portrait* and *Exiles*—and with our knowledge of them to understand Joyce as a great writer. But only these three books cannot help us comprehend Joyce's art completely without going through intelligently and diligently his two epical masterpieces—*Ulysses* and *Finnegans Wake*. With an eye to them in future here we end.

Bibliography

Attridge, Derek (ed.), *Jacques Derrida: Acts of Literature*, 1992, Routledge, New York and London.

Beja, Morris, *James Joyce: A Literary Life*, 1992, Ohio State University Press, Columbus.

Barry, Kelvin, *James Joyce: Occasional, Critical, Political Writing*, 2000, Oxford University Press.

Burgess, Anthony, *Joysprick: Introduction to the Language of James Joyce*, 1975, Harcourt Brace Jovanovich, New York, London.

Bulson, Eric, *The Cambridge Introduction to James Joyce*, 2006, Cambridge University Press.

Baldick, Chris, *The Concise Oxford Dictionary of Literary Terms*, 2001, Oxford University Press, New York.

Bosinelli, Rosa M. Bollettieri and Mosher, Harold F. (eds.), *Re-Joycing: New Reading of Dubliners*, 1998, The University Press of Kentucky.

Budgen, Frank, *James Joyce and the Making of Ulysses*, 1972, Oxford University Press, London, Oxford, Melbourne.

Bloom, Harold (ed.), James Joyce, 2009, *Bloom's Literary Criticism*, an imprint of Infobase Publishing.

Cuddon, J.A., *The Penguin Dictionary of Literary Terms and Literary Theory*, 1999, Penguin Books, England, U.S.A., etc.

Deming, Robert H. (ed.), *James Joyce: The Critical Heritage*, Vol. I (1902-27), 1970, Vikas Publications, Delhi, London, etc.

Daiches, David, *The Novel and the World*, 1984, Midway Reprint, University of Chicago, U.S.A.

Ellmann, Richard, *James Joyce*, 1982, Oxford University Press, New York, etc.

Fargnoli, A. Nicholas and Gillespie, Michael Patrick, *Critical Companion to James Joyce: A Literary Reference to His Life and Work* (previously, James Joyce A to Z, 1995), 2006, Fact On File (www).

Gorman, Herbert, *James Joyce: A Definitive Biography*, 1949, John Lane the Bodley Head, London.

Gabler, Hans Walter, *Genetic Criticisms in Modern Literature*, 2008, Open Book Publishers, Cambridge, U.K.

Gifford, Don and Seidman, Robert J., *Ulysses Annotated*, 1989, The Regents of the University of California.

Hayes, Christa-Maria-Lerm, *Joyce in Art,* 2004, Lilliput Press, Dublin.

Joyce, James, *Dubliners*, 1996, Penguin Popular Classics (Penguin Books).

———, *A Portrait of the Artist as a Young Man*, 1996, Penguin Popular Classics (Penguin Books).

———, *Exiles: A Play in Three Acts*, 1918, B.W. Huebsch, New York.

———, *Ulysses*, 2020, Finger Print Classics (an imprint of Prakash Books India).

———, *Finnegans Wake*, 1939, The Viking Press, New York.

Klages, Mary, *Literary Theory: A Guide for the Perplexed*, 2011, Continuum International Publishing group, New York.

Kock, Stephen, *A Guide to the Craft of Fiction*, 2003, Modern Library Paperbacks.

Kenner, Hugh, *Dublin's Joyce*, 1955, Chatto and Windus.

Levin, Harry, *James Joyce: A Critical Introduction*, 1960, Faber and Faber, London, 28.

McCourt, John (ed.), *Joyce, Yeats, and the Revival* (Joyce studies in Italy, December 2015), James Joyce Italian Foundation, Italy.

——— (ed.) *Shakesperean Joyce, Joycean Shakespeare*, 2016, James Joyce Italian Foundation, Rome.

Mahon, Peter, *Joyce: A Guide for the Perplexed*, 2009, Continuum International Publishing Group, London, New York.

MacDuff, Sangam, *Panepiphenal World: James Joyce's Epiphenies*, 2020, The Floda James Joyce Series, University of Florida.

McNeille, Andrew (ed.), *The Essays of Virginia Woolf*, Vol. 4 (1925-28), 1984, The Hogarth Press, London.

Moretti, Franco, *The Way of the World: The Bildungsroman in European Culture* (2nd edn.), 2000, Verso, London.

Meyers, Jeffrey, *Married to Genius*, 1979, Rupa & Co., Calcutta, Bombay and New Delhi (by arrangement with London Magazine Edition, 1979).

O'Rourke, "Joyce's Early Aesthetics" in *Journal of Modern Literature*, Vol. 34, No. 2, January 2011, University College Dublin.

Ousby, Ian (ed.), *The Wordsworth Companion to Literature in English*, 1994, Wordsworth Editions, Cumberland House, Hertfordshire, England.

Parsons, Deborah, *Theorists of the Modern Novel: James Joyce Dorothy Richardson, Virginia Woolf*, 2007, Routledge, London.

Potter, Simeon, *Language in the Modern World*, 1966, Penguin Books, England, USA, and Australia.

Scholes, Robert and Litz, A. Walton, *Dubliners: James Joyce,* 1996, Penguin Books, USA.

Scholes, Robert and Richard M. Kain (collected and edited), *The Workshop of Daedalus*, 1965, Northwestern University Press.

Sarker, Sunil Kumar, *A Dictionary of Novel*, 2010, Atlantic Publishers, New Delhi.

Slingsby, G.V.L. and Dixon, Vladimir, *Our Exgamination round His Factification for Incamination of Work in Progress, 1929*, 1961, Faber and Faber, London.

Savage, D.S., *The Withered Branch: Six Studies in the Modern Novel,* Eyre & Spottiswoode, 1950, London.

Sherry, Vincent B., *James Joyce: Ulysses*, 2004, Cambridge University Press, U.K.

Skeat, Walter W., *The Concise Dictionary of English Etymology*, 1993, Wordsworth Editions Ltd., Hertfordshire, England.

Spencer, Theodore (ed.), *Stephen Hero by James Joyce*, 1955, A New Direction Book, New York.

Symons, Arthur, *The Symbolist Movement in Literature*, 1899, William Heinmann, London.

Smith, Sir William, *A Smaller Dictionary of the Bible*, 1927, John Murray, Albemarle, W. London.

Tindall, William York, *A Reader's Guide to James Joyce*, 1959, The Noonday Press, Inc., New York.

Vichnar, David, *Joyce Against Theory*, 2008, [*Diplomova Prace*] Univerzita Karlova V Praze.

Vincent, Olga Fernandez (ed.), *Joyce's Heirs: Imprint on Recent Global Literatures*, 2019, Universidad del Pais Vasco, Spain.

Wilson, Edmund, *Axel's Castle: A Study in the Imaginative Literature of 1870-1931*, 1959, Charles Scribner's Sons, New York.

Index